SCEPTICISM AND BELIEF IN ENGLISH WITCHCRAFT
DRAMA, 1538–1681

Scepticism and belief in English witchcraft drama, 1538–1681

ERIC PUDNEY

Lund University Press

Copyright © Eric Pudney 2019

The right of Eric Pudney to be identified as the author of this work has been asserted by him in accordance with the Copyright, Designs and Patents Act 1988.

Lund University Press

The Joint Faculties of Humanities and Theology

**LUND
UNIVERSITY
PRESS**

P.O. Box 117
SE-221 00 LUND
Sweden
http://lunduniversitypress.lu.se

Lund University Press books are published in collaboration with Manchester University Press.

British Library Cataloguing-in-Publication Data
A catalogue record for this book is available from the British Library

ISBN 978 9 1983 7686 9   hardback
ISBN 978 9 1983 7687 6   open access

First published 2019

An electronic version of this book is also available under a Creative Commons (CC-BY-NC-ND) licence, thanks to the support of Lund University, which permits non-commercial use, distribution and reproduction provided the author(s) and Lund University Press are fully cited and no modifications or adaptations are made. Details of the licence can be viewed at https://creativecommons.org/licenses/by-nc-nd/4.0/

The publisher has no responsibility for the persistence or accuracy of URLs for any external or third-party internet websites referred to in this book, and does not guarantee that any content on such websites is, or will remain, accurate or appropriate.

Lund University Press gratefully acknowledges publication assistance from the Thora Ohlsson Foundation (*Thora Ohlssons Stiftelse*)

Typeset by Toppan Best-set Premedia Limited
Printed in Great Britain by TJ International Ltd, Padstow

Contents

Acknowledgements	page vii
A note on references and abbreviations	ix
Introduction	1
1 Scepticism in the Renaissance	**10**
Sceptics and believers	14
Evidence, authority, and ridicule	19
Histories and stories: facts, fictions, and lies	27
Rhetorical scepticism	33
Submerged scepticism	40
Protestant scepticism and the origins of witchcraft drama	45
2 Witchcraft in Elizabethan drama	**58**
Gender, scepticism, and magic in Elizabethan England	61
Fedele and Fortunio: the female witch as male magician	77
Classical witches and Elizabethan prophecy	81
The Golden Asse and early modern witchcraft	89
A Midsummer Night's Dream: witchcraft without witches	97
Joan of Arc, Margery Jourdain, and the historical witch	103
Magic and demonology in *Dr Faustus* and its competitors	110
3 Witchcraft in Jacobean drama	**130**
Sophonisba	132
Macbeth	137
The Masque of Queens	155
Frances Howard, court scandal, and *The Witch*	160

4	*The Witch of Edmonton*	182
	Scepticism in *The Witch of Edmonton*	184
	The devil and sin in *The Witch of Edmonton*	192
	The social and the demonic	200
	Evidence and authority in *The Witch of Edmonton*	206
5	*The Late Lancashire Witches*	209
	Witchcraft in the 1630s	210
	Thomas Heywood and witchcraft	217
	The play and the case	220
	Debating witchcraft in *The Late Lancashire Witches*	226
	Two types of witchcraft	238
6	Witchcraft in the Restoration	244
	The nature of spirit and body	247
	Witchcraft in the theatre	260
7	*The Lancashire Witches*	278
	Scepticism in *The Lancashire Witches*	279
	Good and bad witchcraft	287
	The play and the plot	291

Conclusion	306
Bibliography	320
Index	336

Acknowledgements

No project of this length can be completed without a great deal of help, and I wish to express my heartfelt gratitude to the many people who have provided advice, support and feedback. The book was written while I was at Lund University, where the higher seminar in English Literature provided a great deal of support, guidance and encouragement, and played a major part in shaping the book. Thanks to all those members of the seminar, past and present, who have commented on my work: Professor Marianne Thormählen, Professor Cian Duffy, Dr Birgitta Berglund, Dr Kiki Lindell, Dr Sara Håkansson, Dr Cecilia Wadsö Lecaros, Dr Ellen Turner, Dr Annika J. Lindskog, Dr Claes Lindskog, Dr Anna Lindhé, Dr Mette Hildeman Sjölin, Associate Professor Alexander Bareis, Professor Jane Mattisson Ekstam, Dr Sanna Melin Schyllert, Katie Anderson Ahlstedt, Charlotte Hansson Webb, and Lisa-Marie Teubler.

Outside of Lund, this book owes a great deal to a number of scholars with particular expertise on witchcraft who have contributed to it in a variety of ways. Special mention must be made of Dr Roy Booth of Royal Holloway for his advice on the project: he provided expert knowledge, a critical eye, and an endless supply of good humour. I had the privilege of discussing a draft version of the book at some length with Professor Marion Gibson of the University of Exeter, and I am immensely grateful to her for everything I learned in the course of our conversation. Thanks are also due to both of the peer-reviewers engaged by Lund University Press for their generous and very helpful comments, which improved the book considerably.

Several institutions have also been generous in supporting my work. Olof Sagers stipendiefond made it possible for me to spend half a year in London, with access to the British Library's resources. This time made a major contribution to the book and was spent very happily, as well as very productively. A grant from Stiftelsen Fil. Dr Uno Otterstedts fond allowed me to attend a conference on Demonology at UiT in Tromsö, which was extremely helpful to me, and I would also like to thank the organisers, Professors Liv Helene Willumsen and Rita Voltmer, and all of the participants. In addition, I am particularly grateful to the Royal Swedish Academy of Letters, History and Antiquities for honouring this book with the 2019 Warburg Prize for an outstanding work of literary history published in Sweden.

Last but certainly not least, I would like to thank my family for keeping my feet on the ground and for dragging me out of the early modern period and into the present from time to time. Thanks to my parents, Steve and Linda, and my parents-in-law, Chris and Björn, for all the support, free babysitting, and practical help. Most thanks of all to Charlotte, my wonderful wife and most steadfast supporter; and to Jake and Gabriel, the best sons in the world, for drawing me all those pictures and being so interested in everything.

A note on references and abbreviations

All references to the Bible are to the King James Version unless otherwise stated.

References to all books printed during the early modern period are to electronic copies accessed via the *Early English Books Online* database.

All references to laws (appearing in the format v Elizabeth c. 13) are from *The Statutes of the Realm*.

The following abbreviations have been used:

CSPD	Calendar of State Papers (Domestic series)
ODNB	Oxford Dictionary of National Biography
OED	Oxford English Dictionary
SP	State Paper

Introduction

Witchcraft is often thought of, wrongly, as a thing of the past. In fact, it continues to be taken seriously by people all over the world. But because the subject of this study is, specifically, early modern witchcraft and its dramatic representation, it will be necessary to clarify what the term 'witch' meant within this specific context. As several early modern authors on witchcraft argued, the meaning of the word has changed over time. The senses in which ancient Latin or Greek authors used the terms that are typically translated as 'witch' are distinct from the senses in which sixteenth- and seventeenth-century English people used those terms, as well as from the senses in which the word might be understood in the present. The situation is further complicated by the variety of different understandings of what defined witchcraft in early modern England. Accusations of witchcraft tended to focus on the issue of *maleficium* – the harm it caused – while theoretical writings on witchcraft were usually more interested in the witches' supposed pact with the devil. Magical power might be conceived of as inherent in the witch herself, in the objects or words she used, in the spirit with which she bargained, or as merely illusory. Disagreement over these and other issues continued throughout the period during which witchcraft was a criminal offence.[1]

One assumption of this study – widely but not universally shared today – is that magic operating outside the laws of nature and bargains with the devil are not and never were possible, and that people, both past and present, who believed these things to be possible were, and are, mistaken. Consequently, there can be no definitive

---

1 Jonathan Barry, *Witchcraft and Demonology in South-West England, 1640–1789* (Basingstoke: Palgrave Macmillan, 2012) summarises the key issues (p. 5).

description of what a witch was, only a description of what a given person or group of people imagined a witch to be. Assuming that witches did not exist in the sense that they were often believed to, it is hardly surprising that early modern society did not reach a consensus on what witchcraft was; the subject was debated for centuries and eventually faded from public discourse without ever having been resolved. No work on early modern witchcraft, therefore, can ignore the fact that there was a wide range of opinion on the matter. Furthermore, it would be misleading simply to rely on an exhaustive list of the various opinions (even assuming all of these were documented). Many early modern people appear to have been quite flexible in what they were prepared to believe, and ideas about witchcraft were often fluid rather than fixed points of reference against which real-life situations might be judged. Many people were open to persuasion and argument, evidence was often open to interpretation, and whether a given proposition about an alleged witch was accepted or not might depend on a variety of local factors.

Nonetheless, some broad generalisations are possible. One important point is that the late medieval and early modern period in Europe saw the emergence of a specifically Christian conception of witchcraft. Witchcraft belief, and laws against witchcraft, had existed long before this. But from the fifteenth century onwards, important people within the late medieval Church began to accept the idea that witches were evil and genuinely powerful servants of the devil, and could therefore be punished as a species of heretic. Perhaps the most important texts here are the *Malleus Maleficarum* (1486) of Institoris and Sprenger and the decree made by Innocent VIII, which lent papal authority to the subsequent witch-hunts in Germany.[2] Always controversial, always contested, this idea nevertheless spread through Europe and led to a period of intense witchcraft persecution, peaking in the late sixteenth century. This conception of witchcraft is described in a variety of theological, medical, and philosophical writings and constitutes an important part of the body of work known as demonology. Demonological views of witchcraft frequently form the intellectual context of this study.

A second important point to make about witchcraft belief is that it was to a considerable extent based on fiction, and not merely in the sense that stories about witches were not true. These stories were

---

2 As Diarmaid MacCulloch points out, the *Malleus* was taken seriously by Protestants as well as Catholics throughout Europe: *A History of Christianity* (London: Penguin, 2010), p. 686.

also frequently drawn from literary sources. Characters who could be described as witches feature in some of the best-known works of classical literature, including the *Odyssey*, the *Metamorphoses* of Apuleius and Ovid and Lucan's *Pharsalia*. Stories derived from classical sources found their way into demonological literature, which routinely refers to Circe, for example, as if she had been a historical person. Other stories told about witches had less exalted origins. One frequently recurring story, which appears in several slightly different versions, concerns the witch's transformation into the shape of an animal. The witch is injured while in animal form, and can be identified and captured because she displays the same injuries when she has turned back into human form. This type of story, according to George Lyman Kittredge, can be found in English sources of the twelfth and thirteenth centuries, and is probably of folkloric origin.[3] A particular version of it is incorporated into the *Malleus*, a text whose authors seem to have been willing, as Walter Stephens points out, to use virtually anything to back up their argument.[4] Probably taken from this purportedly factual source, it made its way into a play in the seventeenth century, *The Late Lancashire Witches* (1634).[5]

At a later date, another version of the story turns up as evidence provided by eyewitnesses in a criminal trial presided over by Sir Matthew Hale in the 1660s.[6] Even more striking is the case of the 1592 witchcraft pamphlet mentioned by Marion Gibson, which 'plagiarized a long extract from a play, Robert Greene's *Friar Bacon and Friar Bungay*, inserting incidents from it into the story of a Middlesex farmhand'.[7] Stories about witchcraft move easily between

---

3 George Lyman Kittredge, *Witchcraft in Old and New England* (Cambridge, MA: Harvard University Press, 1929), p. 41.

4 Walter Stephens, *Demon Lovers* (Chicago: University of Chicago Press, 2002), p. 304.

5 Another possible source of this incident is discussed in Brett D. Hirsch, 'Werewolves and Severed Hands: Webster's *The Duchess of Malfi* and Heywood and Brome's *The Witches of Lancashire*', *Notes and Queries* 53:1 (March 2006), 92–94; see also Chapter 5 on *The Late Lancashire Witches*.

6 Anon., *A Tryal of Witches Held at the Assizes at Bury St. Edmonds* (London, 1682), pp. 6–7. See also John Stearne, *A Confirmation and Discovery of Witchcraft* (London, 1648), p. 19 (these and other examples are briefly discussed in Kittredge, pp. 176–79).

7 Marion Gibson, 'Understanding Witchcraft? Accusers' Stories in Print in Early Modern England', in *Languages of Witchcraft*, edited by Stuart Clark (Basingstoke: Macmillan, 2001), pp. 41–54 (p. 43). For more detail, see Gibson, *Reading Witchcraft* (London: Routledge, 1999), pp. 153–56.

fiction and reality at this time, and in some cases the status of a given text (as either fictional or purportedly true) is unclear.

Historians have recognised that the pamphlets which constitute the richest source of information about contemporary beliefs about, and attitudes towards, witchcraft are not only frequently unreliable as factual records of events; they are also very often literary, or at least rhetorical, in character. Pamphlets, which only exist for a small and probably unrepresentative minority of cases of alleged witchcraft, tended to be published at least partly in order to justify the condemned witch's conviction and punishment. They both depended on and perpetuated what Gibson has described as 'a narrational stereotype' of the witch: an old, impoverished, and vindictive woman – usually a widow – seeking revenge on her neighbours.[8] There is at least one individual case in which this stereotype, used in a pamphlet account to describe a convicted witch, sits uncomfortably with independent evidence of the accused witch's character.[9] Any relationship that the pamphlets bear to historical reality is tenuous at best, and caution should be exercised before accepting anything in them – including elements that are, on the face of it, entirely plausible – as historically accurate.

These considerations point to witchcraft as a historical phenomenon especially open to literary analysis, and one in which, as Gareth Roberts pointed out, some of the theoretical premises of New Historicism acquire concrete support.[10] This is a field in which it can be difficult to distinguish between text and history, fiction and reality, literary work and historical document. The history of witchcraft is one in which literary and quasi-literary texts, from ancient myth to cheap news pamphlet, influenced real events just as much as events influenced the texts. Literature – not least in the form of the supposedly factual witchcraft pamphlets' formulaic plots and characters – was employed in an attempt to influence opinion, while real events – or the literary representation of those events – were

---

8 Gibson, 'Understanding Witchcraft?', p. 46.
9 The case in question is that of Joan Cariden of Faversham in Kent, discussed by Malcolm Gaskill, 'Witchcraft in Early Modern Kent: Stereotypes and the Background to Accusations', in *New Perspectives on Witchcraft, Magic, and Demonology*, vol. 3, edited by Brian Levack (New York: Routledge, 2001), pp. 173–203 (pp. 182–85).
10 Gareth Roberts, 'The Descendants of Circe: Witches and Renaissance Fictions', in *Witchcraft in Early Modern Europe: Studies in Culture and Belief*, edited by Jonathan Barry, Marianne Hester, and Gareth Roberts (Cambridge: Cambridge University Press, 1996), pp. 183–206 (p. 186).

used to inspire new, and more explicitly fictional, works of literature. Literature or, more broadly, the literary impulse – the urge to tell stories – is therefore far from innocent in the history of witchcraft.

Theatre and witchcraft have a good deal in common, as a number of eminent literary critics have observed.[11] The stress laid on the deceptive nature of witchcraft and the frequent use of magic as a metaphor for stagecraft in early modern drama suggest a degree of sympathy for witchcraft (if not for actual witches) on the part of the theatre. Several scholars of witchcraft drama have suggested that seeing witches on stage may have helped to produce scepticism about witchcraft. These suggestions have sometimes been made in relation to specific plays.[12] While the storytelling impulse was certainly implicated in perpetuating and spreading witchcraft belief, the stage representation of witchcraft, according to many critics, may have undermined that belief by its very artificiality.

The phenomenon of witchcraft therefore highlights both the need to believe in stories and the capacity to see through them. This study explores the role played by the theatre in both reflecting and generating belief and scepticism about witchcraft, but it will also reveal that scepticism and credulity are ideas inseparable from the idea of witchcraft, and the idea of a witch, in early modern Europe. The first step in understanding the role played by these opposing impulses is to look at the developing notion of scepticism itself in the Renaissance. Scepticism re-emerged at this time as a powerful driver of intellectual and cultural change, and the debate about witchcraft needs to be set in this broader context. Doing so leads to an understanding that the categories of scepticism and belief are a good deal more complex than might at first be assumed, and that these attitudes are not static and inflexible positions, but are amenable to being utilised for various argumentative purposes. Controlled

---

11 See, for example, Stephen Greenblatt, 'Shakespeare Bewitched' in *New Historical Literary Study*, edited by Jeffrey N. Cox and Larry J. Reynolds (Princeton: Princeton University Press, 1993), p. 127; Diane Purkiss, *The Witch in History* (London: Routledge, 1996), pp. 182–83.

12 Diane Purkiss writes that the stage 'certainly contributes to the growth of the kind of scepticism that eventually ensures the end of the successful prosecution of the witch' (*The Witch in History*, p. 283). Frances Dolan, *Dangerous Familiars* (Ithaca: Cornell University Press, 1994), suggests that plays 'might ultimately have helped to spare women's lives' (p. 217). Lisa Hopkins, *The Female Hero in English Renaissance Tragedy* (Basingstoke: Palgrave Macmillan, 2002), makes the case for *The Witch of Edmonton* specifically (p. 98), while Greenblatt makes similar claims for *Macbeth*.

scepticism can be used to generate belief, while even the most radical scepticism tends to conceal an underlying and unquestioned set of beliefs. Within the debate that took place during the sixteenth and seventeenth centuries about the nature of witchcraft, belief, and scepticism were employed by all writers on the subject. They also found their way into dramatic representations of the subject to an increasing degree as the seventeenth century progressed.

In view of the centrality and complexity of the issue of scepticism and credulity, the first chapter is devoted to examining Renaissance scepticism, both in general and in relation to witchcraft specifically, and to the earliest plays to feature witches, which date back to before the Elizabethan criminalisation of witchcraft. Chapters 2 and 3 deal with the Elizabethan and the Jacobean representation of witches on stage. The conventional division of the period according to the reigning monarch is appropriate in this case, as the witch dramas are noticeably different after 1603, and the identity of the monarch is a relevant factor in explaining this difference. Chapters 4 and 5 are devoted to a play each: *The Witch of Edmonton* and *The Late Lancashire Witches*. These plays have been given a prominent place in the study owing to their close connection to the historical cases of witchcraft which inspired them.

Chapter 6 moves past the Civil War and Interregnum period, during which the theatres were closed, dealing instead with the Restoration witchcraft debate and its connection to the theatre of the time. This period has often been neglected by scholars of witchcraft theatre, which is unfortunate since witches and witchcraft, along with other supernatural phenomena, are particularly well represented in the theatre of the second half of the seventeenth century. The final chapter focuses on Thomas Shadwell's play *The Lancashire Witches* in detail. While this play is not based on a recent case of witchcraft, as were *The Witch of Edmonton* and *The Late Lancashire Witches*, it is certainly a play with great topical relevance. It is also a play which engages with witch-hunting in the broader sense, as well as with witchcraft.

Previous book-length studies of witchcraft in English drama have often touched on the question of scepticism towards the phenomenon. The folklorist Katherine Briggs's ground-breaking study, *Pale Hecate's Team* (1962), frequently draws inferences about popular belief, using dramatic literature partly as evidence of it. Briggs's very wide scope and range of interests limits the depth of her study somewhat, although the extensive reading behind it makes it very useful. In a fairly similar vein is Anthony Harris's *Night's Black Agents* (1980), although his book is focused specifically on drama. Harris discusses many of the plays he covers in terms of their belief in or scepticism towards the phenomenon of witchcraft, but again this is largely on the level of drawing inferences about whether the plays encourage or discourage belief in witchcraft. Harris tends to regard the earlier plays, in particular, as credulously reinforcing witchcraft belief.

Feminist and gender-related perspectives have, for obvious reasons, been important in studies of the literature of witchcraft. Diane Purkiss's *The Witch in History* (1996) seeks to recapture women's perspectives on witchcraft and, in the process, produces a more nuanced argument than that of Harris. Purkiss recognises the close and complex relationship between literature and reality in the case of witchcraft and poses both historical and literary questions. In terms of drama, she tends to regard the effect of the plays, and perhaps of the institution of the theatre itself, as increasing the scepticism of the watching audience and of society in general. Deborah Willis's *Malevolent Nurture* (1995), another cross-disciplinary work, also pays close attention to the gendered aspects of witchcraft, exploring the idea of witches as perverted 'mothers' to their spirit familiars. Like Purkiss, Willis tries to approach the concerns of ordinary women at the level of village accusations of witchcraft, and she also utilises theatre as part of her argument. Willis suggests that comic representations of witches may have generated scepticism about witchcraft, but avoids drawing more general conclusions in favour of focusing exclusively on Shakespeare's plays. Willis's interpretations of Shakespearean witchcraft draw on psychoanalytic concepts and highlight the witch characters' disruption of accepted gender norms.

Heidi Breuer's *Crafting the Witch* (2009) is another gender-focused study covering a longer time period, moving from the early Arthurian literature of the twelfth and thirteenth centuries, where Breuer finds witches to be peripheral figures, through to later medieval romances and the sixteenth-century continuation of the romance tradition in Malory and Spenser. Breuer goes on to consider Shakespeare's dramatic representations of magic and witchcraft, before looking at the persistence of witchcraft imagery in present-day culture. Like Willis, Breuer regards witches as being 'anti-mothers',[13] although she also finds more sympathetic representations of witchcraft emerging in recent years. Frances Dolan's *Dangerous Familiars* (1994), a study covering a range of 'domestic' crimes including witchcraft,

---

13 Heidi Breuer, *Crafting the Witch* (New York: Routledge, 2009), p. 11.

finds an inverse relation between the centrality of witch characters in plays and the seriousness with which they are taken: in other words, witches that are genuinely powerful are kept in the margins of the action, while witches that are present throughout a play are trivialised. As noted above, Dolan also finds that the theatre 'participated in the cultural process that gradually marginalised and discredited belief in witchcraft'.[14]

Scepticism plays a more prominent role in Ryan Curtis Friesen's study of *Supernatural Fiction in Early Modern Drama and Culture*.[15] This monograph, as the title suggests, covers more than just witchcraft, and sets out to deal with writings not normally considered fictional – such as the occult writings of Giordano Bruno, Heinrich Agrippa, and John Dee – alongside the theatre of Marlowe, Shakespeare, Jonson, and Middleton. Friesen studies a range of such texts for evidence of scepticism or duplicity on the parts of the authors, but while his readings of the dramatic texts are focused on magic and witchcraft, they do not specifically address the questions of scepticism and belief. A shorter work which is also concerned with scepticism and belief, and the theatre's role in it, is Stephen Greenblatt's important essay on *Macbeth*, 'Shakespeare Bewitched'. Greenblatt points to the imaginative sympathy between witchcraft and the theatre, both of which are concerned with illusion, as well as recognising that narrative strategies were employed by those who sought to encourage or perpetuate witchcraft belief. Like many other critics, Greenblatt finds Shakespeare not guilty of collusion in the persecution of witches.

While the question of scepticism and belief in relation to witchcraft always surfaces at some point in discussions of literary witchcraft, none of the studies described above has made this question its organising principle, nor have many of them focused on the issues of scepticism and belief as they are presented within the plays themselves. In much of the work described here, there has been a tendency to treat drama as a type of historical evidence which casts light on the sceptical or credulous attitudes of playwrights or audiences. This is one important aspect of the issue, and one which this study does not neglect; but it is also important to recognise that scepticism and belief are often of central concern within the plays themselves, albeit in widely differing ways. This book traces the development

---

14 Dolan, p. 217.
15 Ryan Curtis Friesen, *Supernatural Fiction in Early Modern Drama and Culture* (Brighton: Sussex Academic, 2010).

of the stage representation of witchcraft and its connections with the society and the theoretical writings about witchcraft of the time. The relationship between the two is complex, but the issues of scepticism and belief are central to both the theatre and culture more generally, not only in relation to witchcraft but also in relation to wider questions of an epistemological and theological nature. In witchcraft drama, scepticism and belief are constantly recurring, constantly conjoined, and constantly shifting themes; they are never absent, but their significance is rarely as straightforward as it seems.

1
Scepticism in the Renaissance

Scepticism has long been acknowledged to be a vital feature of Renaissance thought, and one which has been said to distinguish the period from the Middle Ages. Conventionally, Renaissance scepticism has been seen as part of what puts the 'modern' into 'early modern': the questioning of old certainties which ultimately helped to usher in the Enlightenment. This view understates the importance of sceptical attitudes within the medieval period; as early as the fifth or sixth century, Pseudo-Dionysius was emphasising the unknowability of God and the severe limitations of human reason, a sceptical tradition brought into Western Europe in the ninth century by John Scottus Eriugena.[1] William of Ockham and other nominalist thinkers provide further evidence of sceptical thought within medieval theology.[2] Nonetheless, the rediscovery of a wide range of ancient thought during the Renaissance, including the sceptical writings of Cicero but especially those of the Greek Pyrrhonist Sextus Empiricus, was part of what brought about the 'sceptical crisis' of the period.[3] Philosophical scepticism played a significant role in undermining the certainties offered by the philosophy of the later medieval period, which was dominated by Aristotelian scholasticism (Aristotle's dominance was such that he was frequently known simply as 'the philosopher'). In doing so, scepticism left a mark on the work of many of the period's most famous thinkers, eventually making a significant contribution to the development of scientific method, as Richard Popkin's history of the phenomenon shows. Even those who did not embrace scepticism were forced to take account of these ideas.

---

1 Jeffrey Burton Russell, *Lucifer: The Devil in the Middle Ages* (Ithaca: Cornell University Press, 1984), pp. 30, 114–15.
2 Russell, p. 276.
3 Richard Popkin, *The History of Scepticism*, 3rd edn (Oxford: Oxford University Press, 2003, first published in 1960), p. xx.

The most obvious role for this newly sceptical mentality in relation to witchcraft would seemingly be to encourage people to deny the possibility of such a thing. Modern assumptions about witchcraft tend to treat it as the product of blind credulity, so a modicum of scepticism would seem to be fatal to witchcraft belief – and this appears to have been the dominant view of most historians of witchcraft in the early twentieth century. Support for such a view is not entirely lacking: the Aristotelian natural philosophy that was gradually eroded by sceptical thought has frequently been linked to witchcraft belief,[4] and Thomas Aquinas was a vital authority for later witchcraft theorists.[5] Furthermore, some writers on witchcraft explicitly rejected epistemological scepticism as part of their argument in favour of witchcraft persecution, among them Jean Bodin and John Cotta.[6] But despite its intuitive appeal and some superficial support, a straightforward correlation between philosophical scepticism and scepticism about witchcraft does not hold up.

The most obvious problem is one of chronology. During the blindly credulous medieval period of popular caricature, witches were not persecuted in great numbers. Orthodox opinion, as represented in the ecclesiastical law recorded in the Canon *Episcopi*, held that the stories told by self-proclaimed witches were delusions, and that believing them to be true was heretical.[7] Meanwhile, in the sceptical and questioning Renaissance, witchcraft was widely proclaimed to be real, and executions for it reached levels never seen before, or since, anywhere in the world. The rise of witchcraft belief, therefore, seems to have coincided with the rise of scepticism, rather than being ended by it. Nor does this appear to be a coincidence. As Stephens points out, one of the earliest sceptics was also a persecutor of witches:

> Gianfrancesco Pico della Mirandola (d. 1533) was the first modern philosopher to quote the arguments of the ancient Pyrrhonian sceptic Sextus Empiricus (d. CE 210) extensively. At the same time, Pico was

---

4 See, for example, Russell, p. 296; Stuart Clark, *Thinking with Demons* (Oxford: Oxford University Press, 1997), p. 153; Stephens, *Demon Lovers*, pp. 30–31.
5 Stephens, *Demon Lovers*, pp. 61–62.
6 On Bodin, see Popkin, p. 77; John Cotta, *The Triall of Witch-craft* (London, 1616), pp. 2–3, 41–42.
7 Stephens, *Demon Lovers*, pp. 127–28. The Canon *Episcopi* held that the stories of witches were delusions in the sense that they did not happen *physically*. The stories were not, however, unreal – they could be said to take place in spirit.

a major theorist of witchcraft, and vehemently defended the prosecution of witches. This apparent paradox, the exploitation of radically sceptical arguments in order to *defend* the reality of witchcraft rather than to attack it, is essential to understanding the context and complexities of scepticism about witchcraft.[8]

Clearly, the impact of scepticism was not a straightforward matter. Part of the reason for this was that scepticism in early modern argument was frequently used not for its own sake but in a rhetorical manner. In other words, scepticism was frequently used in order to argue not for the suspension of judgement, but in support of a particular conclusion.

To illustrate this point, it is worth briefly considering the role played by scepticism in related areas of early modern intellectual life – perhaps the most fundamental being that of religious controversy. One of the reasons identified by Popkin for the rise in importance of sceptical ideas during this period was the Protestant Reformation. Scepticism was used by both sides in the debates between Catholics and Protestants. The Protestant reformers challenged the authority of popes and councils, which the Catholic Church insisted was beyond question. Catholic writers responded by pointing out that reliance on personal revelation or an individual interpretation of scripture required relying on one's own, necessarily fallible, reasoning and intuition. Any such reliance on individual conscience, it was argued, led inevitably to relativism and, therefore, complete uncertainty. As a result, 'it became a stock claim of the Counter-Reformers to assert that the Reformers were just sceptics in disguise'.[9] But while they depicted Protestants (unflatteringly) as sceptics, these anti-Protestant arguments themselves incorporated scepticism, as they were founded upon an insistence on human fallibility. If, in the absence of certain knowledge, one should rely on faith and trust in the established church rather than trying to reach a truth that is inaccessible to human beings, then that faith is based on highly sceptical intellectual premises.

A sceptical argument can therefore be used to provide certainty, or at least a semblance of certainty. The most illustrious example of the philosophical use of scepticism is found in the work of René

---

8 Walter Stephens, 'The Sceptical Tradition', in *The Oxford Handbook of Witchcraft in Early Modern Europe and Colonial America*, edited by Brian Levack (Oxford: Oxford University Press, 2013), pp. 101–21 (p. 105).
9 Popkin, p. 10.

Descartes. In his *Meditations on First Philosophy* (1641), Descartes doubted all the evidence of his senses, stripping away all knowledge that could conceivably be doubted in an attempt to arrive at indubitable knowledge.[10] This project resulted in the famous proposition *cogito ergo sum*: I think, therefore I am. Descartes' use of scepticism does not treat it as an end point; instead, Descartes is actually in quest of certainty. *Cogito ergo sum* is the first step in that it establishes the outer limit of doubt, but by itself it is not very helpful, since nothing else directly follows from it. Descartes could only move beyond the cogito by proving the existence of God, which he proceeded to do in more or less the same way as Thomas Aquinas had before him. Descartes is not a doubter but a striver after certainty, much like the scholastic philosophers with whom he is usually contrasted. His use of scepticism is never more than a thought experiment; his doubts are put forward in order that they can be defeated. The cases of Cartesian method and the arguments of the Reformation show that scepticism is in practice more flexible than a 'pure' sceptic might wish it to be. The apparent paradox of scepticism used to reinforce belief in witchcraft dissolves when it becomes clear that scepticism is frequently used in this way.

The notion that scepticism, rather than merely opposing belief, could actually support and even form an important part of it, has as its corollary the idea that excessive credulity ultimately undermines belief. The alleged tendency of 'simple people' to believe virtually anything about witches could lead to dangerous incredulity in others, according to the seventeenth-century scholar Meric Casaubon.[11] And while credulity could lead to incredulity, Casaubon held that the reverse was also true. Part of what made the divine mystery so powerful and compelling was precisely the fact that it was difficult to believe:

> the more we are apprehensive of Gods Greatness and Omnipotency, which makes other miracles, probable; doth make this, or seem to

---

10 Descartes does not mention witches in the *Meditations*; but as Stuart Clark has pointed out, his strongest statement of sceptical doubt is the so-called demon hypothesis: the idea that all sensory perception is the product of an all-powerful and deceitful demon. See Clark, *Thinking with Demons*, pp. 174–75 and René Descartes, *Meditations on First Philosophy*, translated by John Cottingham (Cambridge: Cambridge University Press, 1986), I.22–23, p. 15.

11 Meric Casaubon, *Of Credulity and Incredulity in Things Divine & Spiritual* (London, 1670), p. 176 (incorrectly marked 172).

make it, the more improbable, and incredible. To say therefore the more credible, because incredible; and that such things become God best; that may seem most incredible to men.[12]

Casaubon claims that God's existence is the greatest of miracles, and its incredible nature makes other miracles (which include everything in nature, he argues, since everything proceeds from God) seem probable by comparison. But, he continues, God's existence is credible precisely because it is so incredible, so remarkable: the sheer vastness of the idea is what convinces people of the existence of a vast creator.[13] A properly controlled sense of incredulity – one that only makes itself felt occasionally, and without seriously threatening Christian faith – is in fact an essential part of that faith, and Casaubon writes that he 'shall not much applaud' the faith of those who do not have moments of incredulity, or doubt.[14] With the complexity of the relationship between scepticism and belief in mind, I now turn back to the importance of these concepts within the debate on witchcraft.

Sceptics and believers

[I]f I heard any body speake, either of ghosts walking, of foretelling future things, of enchantments, of witchcrafts, or any other thing reported, which I could not well conceive, or that was beyond my reach ... I could not but feele a kinde of compassion to see the poore and seely people abused with such follies. And now I perceive, that I was as much to be moaned myselfe: Not that experience has since made me to dicerne any thing beyond my former opinions ... but reason hath taught me, that so resolutely to condemn a thing for false, and impossible, is to assume unto himselfe the advantage, to have the bounds and limits of Gods will, and of the power of our common mother Nature tied to his sleeve ... Let us consider through what clouds, and how blinde-fold we are led to the knowledge of most things, that passe our hands: verily we shall finde, it is rather custome, than science that removeth the strangenesse of them from us.[15]

---

12 Casaubon, *Of Credulity and Incredulity*, p. 123 (marked 119).
13 In making this argument, Casaubon forms part of a theological tradition based on the idea that *credo quia absurdum est* – I believe because it is absurd – a phrase often erroneously attributed to Tertullian.
14 Casaubon, *Of Credulity and Incredulity*, p. 207 (marked 203).
15 Michel de Montaigne, *Essays*, vol. 1, translated by John Florio (London: Folio, 2006, first published 1603), pp. 176–77.

In this passage Michel de Montaigne, dubbed by Popkin the most important sceptical thinker of the sixteenth century,[16] describes his transition from an impious incredulity to a humble and Christian scepticism. Having reached what he later perceives to be an overconfident and unjustified conclusion, Montaigne realises his mistake and suspends his judgement entirely. True scepticism, in this case, precludes scepticism about witchcraft in the sense of the word which is ordinarily used. The young Montaigne is, properly speaking, a witchcraft denier (the negative connotations of this word notwithstanding), while the older is a witchcraft sceptic.

However, the word 'sceptic' is much more commonly used to denote a denier, certainly in relation to witchcraft. Histories of English witchcraft written in the early twentieth century tended to categorise authors on witchcraft as either sceptics or believers, celebrating the former, in particular Reginald Scot, while condemning or apologising for the latter.[17] More recently, however, the validity of a clear distinction between authors in terms of scepticism and belief has been called into question by historians of witchcraft, notably Peter Elmer and Stuart Clark.[18] Using the examples of Henry Boguet and Johannes Weyer, Clark makes the important point that texts written by authors traditionally characterised as 'believers' often contain much that is sceptical, while authors regarded as sceptical often concede a great deal to the believers.[19]

Nonetheless, it is important to recognise a fundamental dividing line in the motivations of different authors in the period up until the Restoration: some write in order to encourage witchcraft persecution, while others write in order to discourage it. (In the second half of the seventeenth century, as prosecutions became much rarer, what was at stake in the debate on witchcraft changed considerably, as discussed in Chapter 6.) The views of 'sceptics' and 'believers' about what is and is not possible can be much closer than is sometimes

---

16 Popkin, p. 44.
17 Wallace Notestein, *A History of Witchcraft in England from 1558 to 1718* (Washington: American Historical Society, 1911), for example, portrays Scot as heroically 'battling with the single purpose to stop a detestable and wicked practice' (p. 58), while Matthew Hopkins is said to be 'a figure in the annals of English roguery' (p. 164).
18 Peter Elmer, 'Towards a Politics of Witchcraft in Early Modern England', in *Languages of Witchcraft*, edited by Stuart Clark (Basingstoke: Macmillan, 2001), pp. 101–18 (p. 105).
19 Clark, *Thinking with Demons*, p. 203.

recognised, but the more practical question of what they wish to recommend does separate them. To take two examples from England, George Gifford and William Perkins are very close indeed in terms of their theoretical and theological positions, but they are almost diametrically opposed in terms of their tone and recommendations. Gifford writes in order to discourage witchcraft persecution in the strongest possible terms, while Perkins advocates increased zeal in hunting witches. The demonological beliefs of the two authors are similar, but their prescriptions as to what evidence should be required for the conviction of a witch are very different: Gifford's demands would have made it almost impossible for any witch to be convicted.[20] It is hard to read Gifford's works without coming to the conclusion that he would, in spite of his declared beliefs, have been very much opposed to any accusation of maleficent witchcraft.

Why should this difference exist between two Protestant clergymen with much in common in other respects? One way to answer this question is to consider the specific circumstances under which individual authors wrote. Gifford had personal experience of witchcraft accusations as minister for the parish of Maldon in Essex, a county which underwent a much higher level of witchcraft persecution than the rest of the Home Counties, and his works suggest that he was horrified by what he saw.[21] Perkins's book on witchcraft was published posthumously in 1608, at a time when witchcraft prosecutions seem to have begun to decline. There is no suggestion of any personal involvement in witchcraft accusations or trials in Perkins's treatise on the subject, although he was rumoured to have been involved in astrology as a student, which, it has been suggested, might account for a later hostility towards magic.[22]

---

20 George Gifford's mouthpiece in his *Dialogue concerning Witches and Witchcraftes* (London, 1593), Daniel, seems to argue that two witnesses to the actual pact between witch and devil should be required for a witchcraft conviction (sig. H2ʳ). I am not aware of any case in which witnesses swore to having seen the pact between witch and spirit take place.

21 On Gifford see Peter Elmer, *Witchcraft, Witch-Hunting, and Politics in Early Modern England* (Oxford: Oxford University Press, 2016), pp. 42–43 and Alan Macfarlane, 'A Tudor Anthropologist: George Gifford's *Discourse* and *Dialogue*', in *The Damned Art*, edited by Sidney Anglo (London: Routledge & Kegan Paul, 1977), pp. 140–55 (p. 144).

22 *ODNB*, 'William Perkins'. A later Puritan writer on witchcraft, Thomas Cooper, also claims to have dabbled in magic; *The Mystery of Witchcraft* (London, 1617), pp. 11–13. While there is no evidential basis for doubting these claims, both writers follow in the illustrious footsteps of St Augustine,

Paying attention to the immediate context in which writers operated, as well as the broader intellectual context, is important because it helps to provide some indication of what shaped their thinking, and what the concerns might have been that drove them to write. The rhetorical purpose of the author, where this is possible to infer, is particularly important in the case of witchcraft because a variety of aims and objectives are consistent with broadly similar theoretical positions. Classifying an author like Gifford as a 'believer' in witchcraft, while basically accurate in terms of his declared beliefs, fails to acknowledge his self-evident commitment to arguing against the persecution of actual witches. Richard Bernard, likewise, would normally be classified as a 'believer'; but by his own admission, he wrote in order to counter potentially damaging accusations of scepticism about witchcraft.[23] Furthermore, despite his stated purpose of proving his belief in witchcraft, Bernard devotes the entirety of the first section of his book to discouraging witchcraft accusations on grounds very similar to those of Gifford. Bernard even cites Scot, from whose views he distances himself in his preface, as an authority. Belief in witchcraft and support for the persecution of witches are entirely distinct in principle, and often also in practice: as well as 'sceptical believers' like Gifford and Bernard, there are cases of witchcraft sceptics who nonetheless supported the continued existence and enforcement of the laws against witchcraft.[24]

While the dividing line between believer and sceptic cannot be drawn in a simplistic manner, there is good reason to retain the ideas of scepticism and credulity themselves, since these ideas appear so often in early modern writings on witchcraft. Believers in witchcraft often present themselves as sceptical, and accuse their opponents

---

who describes a similar involvement in astrology, and later repented: St Augustine, *Confessions*, translated by E. B. Pusey (London: J. M. Dent, 1962), vii.8–9, pp. 125–27. The narrative of sin and repentance – whether based on actual experience or not – may be a means of emphasising the moral authority of the authors.

23 Richard Bernard, *A Gvide to Grand-Ivry Men* (London, 1627), sigs A3^v–A4^r.

24 John Selden, in *Table Talk* (London, 1689), writes that 'The Law against Witches does not prove there be any; but it punishes the Malice of those people, that use such means, to take away mens Lives. If one should profess that by turning his Hat thrice, and crying Buz; he could take away a man's life (though in truth he could do no such thing) yet this were a just Law made by the State, that whosoever should turn his Hat thrice, and cry Buz; with an intention to take away a man's life, shall be put to death' (p. 59).

of credulity. Gifford, for example, arguing against Scot, writes 'Alacke, alacke, I see that those which take upon them to be wiser than all men, are soonest deceived by the divell.'[25] Scot's scepticism, according to Gifford, is in fact credulity; he reveals himself to have been duped. Early modern writers, like early twentieth-century historians, frequently prize scepticism and pour scorn on credulity. Scepticism was the mark of a discerning judgement, while credulity was frequently ascribed by learned authors to the ignorant masses.

At the same time, however, incredulity was also frequently presented as reprehensible – the error of the fool of Psalm 14 who 'hath said in his heart, There is no God'.[26] Meric Casaubon's book on the subject certainly treats incredulity as more problematic than credulity. Writing about incredulity in relation to witchcraft, Casaubon almost identifies it with witchcraft itself, and states in no uncertain terms that disbelief in witchcraft, while not necessarily equivalent to witchcraft itself, certainly derives from 'the same cause, or agent, as ordinary witchcraft doth'. The word 'agent', in this context, leaves the reader in little doubt that Casaubon thinks incredulity is inspired by the devil.[27] James I, in his work on witchcraft, is even more forthright, accusing Johannes Weyer of witchcraft simply for having written a sceptical book on the subject.[28]

For most early modern Christians, the importance of pure belief, humility, and trust in God rather than in one's own corrupt and earthly wisdom could hardly be overstated. From this point of view, scepticism could be presented as false wisdom, and a sceptic who, like Scot, mocked belief in witchcraft or other supernatural phenomena might resemble the 'natural man' of I Corinthians 2:14, who 'receiveth not the things of the Spirit of God: for they are foolishness unto him'. For obvious reasons, it was easier for those authors writing to persuade others of the real existence of witches to accuse their opponents of lacking faith. However, sceptics about witchcraft were also able to employ the charge of incredulity in the related sense of infidelity to God. Reginald Scot, for example, argues

---

25 George Gifford, *A Discourse of the Subtill Practises of Deuilles by Witches and Sorcerers* (London, 1587), sig. E3^v.
26 A complex attitude towards scepticism and credulity is likewise evident in the Bible itself. While sceptical doubt is repeatedly condemned (see, for example, Romans 14:23), an attitude not dissimilar to philosophical scepticism is also expressed quite often, most famously when it is said that 'we see through a glass, darkly' (I Corinthians 13:12).
27 Casaubon, *Of Credulity and Incredulity*, p. 113 (marked 109).
28 James I, *Daemonologie* (Edinburgh, 1597), preface to the reader, p. 2^v.

that those who credit witches with the power to raise storms are, in effect, denying that power to God, and are therefore guilty of the sin of idolatry.[29] Scot also accuses the believers of secret scepticism, arguing that 'some of these crimes ... are so absurd, supernaturall, and impossible, that they are derided almost of all men, and as false, fond, and fabulous reports condemned: insomuch as the very witchmoongers themselves are ashamed to heare of them'.[30] He even presents himself, implausibly, as a believer when he claims in his epistle to the reader that he does not deny the existence of witches – only impious opinion concerning them. Belief and scepticism, when closely examined, are best understood not as fixed positions within the witchcraft debate, but as rhetorical tools used by all of the contributors to that debate. Every author on witchcraft needed to find a way to utilise both belief and scepticism, and to strike a balance between them, whatever the exact nature of the argument.

Evidence, authority, and ridicule

> [T]he sheer fact that something is written down gives it special authority. It is not altogether easy to realize that what is written down can be untrue.[31]

One of the effects of the sceptical crisis described by Popkin was a gradual shift in the kinds of evidence that were required to support claims to truth. The general picture here is again well established. The Renaissance saw a gradual shift in attitudes, based in part on the recovery of sceptical thought and newly sceptical attitudes, which slowly led from a reliance on authority to a new emphasis on empirical evidence and independent investigation.[32] Many Renaissance authors started to display a more critical attitude towards their sources.[33] This development is particularly evident in historical

---

29 Reginald Scot, *The Discoverie of Witchcraft* (London, 1584), I.5, p. 12.
30 Scot, II.10, p. 34.
31 Hans-Georg Gadamer, *Truth and Method*, translated by Joel Weinsheimer and Donald G. Marshall (New York: Continuum, 1998, first published in 1960 as *Wahrheit und Methode*), p. 272.
32 John Selden made an explicit connection between sceptical philosophy and a sceptical attitude towards historical sources; see Peter Burke, *The Renaissance Sense of the Past* (London: Edward Arnold, 1969), p. 69.
33 Lorenzo Valla's exposure of the forged Donation of Constantine in 1439 is a celebrated example (Burke, pp. 55–58).

writing. In England, for example, stories about the founding of London by the Trojan Brutus were dismissed by the early Tudor historian Polydore Vergil. Most historians after Vergil continued to include these old stories in their chronicles, but during the seventeenth century scepticism about their historical foundation became much more open and widespread.

In connection with witchcraft, the view of early twentieth-century historians was in line with what common-sense assumptions might suggest: that questioning authority and turning to empirical evidence helped to undermine witchcraft belief. Again, this is not an indefensible position; Sidney Anglo's view of Reginald Scot as a rational empiricist who was simply ahead of his time was supported by Scot's claims to have investigated the mechanics of magic thoroughly.[34] Frequent references to the ultimate written authority – the Bible – in the texts of those supporting continued persecution of witches suggest a basis in faith rather than fact. The *Malleus Maleficarum*, a foundational witchcraft text, also provides a very good example of typically medieval attitudes towards written sources: virtually anything that supports the argument of the authors is thrown in, including crude anti-clerical jokes.[35]

However, just as philosophical scepticism and scepticism about witchcraft are not linked in the way that might be expected, so the association of an empirical approach with scepticism and reliance on authority with belief in witchcraft is not tenable. All early modern authors (and, for that matter, all present-day academic researchers) make use of authority. Even Reginald Scot, for all his claims to have subjected the practices of various tricksters to empirical investigation, relies heavily on authority of various kinds. In recent years, scholars have increasingly pointed to the theological elements of Scot's argument, and scriptural authority is of particular importance to him, as are the opinions of Calvin or St Augustine. Other sceptics, in contrast to Scot, rely almost entirely on authority rather than on empirical evidence, notably Thomas Ady, who proclaims in his preface that he does not wish to make any reference to the kind of anecdotal evidence used by proponents of witchcraft, but will rest

---

34 Sidney Anglo, 'Reginald Scot's *Discoverie of Witchcraft*: Scepticism and Sadduceeism', in *The Damned Art*, edited by Sidney Anglo (London: Routledge & Kegan Paul, 1977), pp. 106–39. Scot stresses that he writes on the basis of 'due proofe and triall'; III.6, p. 48.

35 Stephens, *Demon Lovers*, pp. 303–4.

his argument entirely on scriptural authority.[36] The witch-finder Matthew Hopkins, on the other hand, writes that his skill in detecting witches depends not on any great learning but upon 'experience, which though it be meanly esteemed of, yet [is] the surest and safest way to judge by'.[37] Other believers, too, including James I and Bodin, make reference to everyday experience as sufficient proof of the existence of witchcraft. Perhaps the biggest problem for linking an empiricist outlook to scepticism about witchcraft is the case of Joseph Glanvill, a proponent of both witchcraft belief and the developing scientific method in the later seventeenth century. In historical cases of witchcraft, too, empirical evidence was often vital to the prosecution case; the discovery of teats or witches' marks was an important source of evidence in trials, and the infamous 'swimming test' could even be presented as a scientific experiment, with an innocent person used as a control.[38]

Empirical evidence and authority, like scepticism and belief, cannot be understood as two mutually exclusive and antagonistic categories which are straightforwardly associated with particular attitudes towards witchcraft. Rather, empirical evidence and written authority are the two most important means of supporting any argument, and they are invoked to varying degrees by all writers, whatever their particular position on the question of witchcraft. But again, this does not mean that the increasing importance of empirical reasoning is irrelevant to the topic of witchcraft. The essence of Walter Stephens's argument is that the witch hunts began precisely in order that empirical evidence could be found for propositions that had previously been accepted on the basis of authority: propositions concerning the existence of spirits, the devil and, ultimately, God himself. Witches, as a point of contact between the human world and the spirit world, proved the existence of the latter. This, Stephens argues, is why it was necessary to *find* witches: the existence of witchcraft was itself a form of empirical evidence, or evidence posing as empirical, used to reinforce the dictates of medieval authorities that no longer seemed sufficiently authoritative.

---

36 Thomas Ady, *A Candle in the Dark* (London, 1655), p. 5.
37 Matthew Hopkins, *The Discovery of Witches* (London, 1647), p. 1.
38 Orna Alyagon Darr, *Marks of an Absolute Witch* (Farnham: Ashgate, 2011), pp. 167, 183; Darr notes that the swimming test was widely used in England, despite its illegality (pp. 44–45). On the 'witch's mark' see Darr, pp. 111–40.

Some caution is needed in making any distinction between evidence and authority. It is especially important to recognise that, while such a distinction could be made in early modern Europe as well as today, it might be understood in rather different ways. Meric Casaubon, for example, accepts a distinction between authority and reason and places greater value on reason; but he nonetheless maintains that '*Divine Authority* is equivalent to Sense and Reason'.[39] Furthermore, while claiming to argue on the basis of what he calls reason, rather than authority, Casaubon cites a huge number of authors in support of his claims, often simply praising them as learned and wise rather than presenting arguments to show that they are right. What Casaubon means by the terms 'reason' and 'authority' is, in practice, not always clear, but it does seem safe to conclude that the two cannot be neatly separated in early modern usage.

In fact, the distinction between authority on the one hand and evidence on the other breaks down altogether in view of some of the 'empirical evidence' offered by witchcraft theorists. For obvious reasons, finding what would now be regarded as empirical evidence of witchcraft was difficult, so it was necessary to manufacture it.[40] Often, especially within the pages of the *Malleus Maleficarum*, evidence offered as empirical – the testimony of eyewitnesses – could equally be described as authority, since it is ultimately written material of various kinds, presented as if it were a record of true events. In the *Malleus* the effect can be grimly comical, as patently absurd stories are solemnly presented as factual. Jean Bodin, too, invites derision on occasion, such as when he claims that one witch 'caused her neighbour's chin to turn upside down, a hideous thing to see'.[41]

---

39 Casaubon, *Of Credulity and Incredulity*, p. 7. From a modern point of view, Casaubon relies almost entirely on authority throughout the book.

40 In this sense, witchcraft theorists followed in a long tradition of manufacturing evidence in support of the faith, which was a notable feature of early and medieval Christianity. Particularly interesting in relation to the demand for the credible eyewitness testimony that was so important to the witchcraft phenomenon is the 'gynaecological examination performed on Mary after the nativity by two sceptical and reputable midwives', described in an apocryphal gospel attributed to Matthew (William Nelson, *Fact or Fiction: The Dilemma of the Renaissance Storyteller* (Cambridge, MA: Harvard University Press, 1973), p. 20). On the use of panels of 'honest matrons' or midwives in witchcraft trials, see Darr, pp. 117, 121–23. See also Chapter 3 on the examination of Frances Howard.

41 Jean Bodin, *On the Demon-Mania of Witches*, translated by Randy A. Scott (Toronto: Centre for Reformation and Renaissance Studies, 1995, first published as *De la Demonomanie des Sorciers* in Paris in 1580), p. 140.

Despite the differences between modern and early modern perceptions about the validity of different types of evidence, it is important to emphasise that Bodin's claim is not only ridiculous from the anachronistic perspective of a present-day reader. Witchcraft sceptics in England frequently, if not invariably, described the evidence offered by sources like the *Malleus* as absurd.

Reginald Scot, in particular, makes use of this tactic. Scot attacks evidence that is offered as empirical by simply asking the reader to judge its plausibility, with a heavy dose of irony. While Scot has been characterised as an ultra-empiricist by Anglo and earlier historians, and more recently as a writer with serious theological concerns,[42] few historians have placed much emphasis on his extensive use of mockery. This is odd, since ridicule is probably the single most distinctive feature of Scot's text. The rhetorical strategy of much of the *Discoverie* is simply to repeat what witchcraft believers have said to justify their beliefs, occasionally pausing to highlight contradictions or make sarcastic comments.[43] It is striking how infrequently Scot feels the need to actually argue against witchcraft beliefs. Scot even says, in relation to the legal treatment of witches, that 'I neede not staie to confute such parciall and horrible dealings, being so apparentlie impious and full of tyrannie ... I will passe over the same; supposing that the citing of such absurdities may stand for a sufficient confutation thereof.'[44] Scot almost defies the reader to disagree; claims not worth disproving, he implies, could only be taken seriously by a fool.

Scot's representation of the witchmongers' claims is often quite skewed, but even more important than this is his consistently mocking tone. Scot's contemptuous authorial persona is designed to undermine witchcraft belief in the reader, based on the assumption that the reader does not wish to feel like a fool. Discussing animal transformation, Scot mocks his favourite antagonist by writing that '*Bodin* saith, that this was a man in the likenesse of an asse: but I maie rather thinke that he is an asse in the likenesse of a man'.[45] Telling

---

42 See, for example, Clark, pp. 211–12; Philip Almond, *England's First Demonologist* (London: I. B. Tauris, 2011), pp. 183–92; and David Wootton, 'Reginald Scot/Abraham Fleming/The Family of Love', in *Languages of Witchcraft*, edited by Stuart Clark (Basingstoke: Macmillan, 2001), pp. 119–38.
43 Almond, p. 106.
44 Scot, II.6, pp. 27–28.
45 Scot, XII.15, pp. 253–54.

the story of an archer punished because he was so skilful that a judge assumed he must have magical help, Scot comments with heavy irony that 'the archer was severelie punished, to the great encouragement of archers, and to the wise example of justice'. Scot's sarcasm is on display again when he tells the story of an evil spirit which

> came to a ladies bed side, and made hot loove unto hir: whereat she … cried out so lowd, that companie came and found him under hir bed in the likenesse of the holie Bishop Sylvanus, which holie man was much defamed thereby, until at length this infamie was purged by the confession of a divell made at S. Jeroms toombe. Oh excellent peece of witchcraft or cousening wrought by Sylvanus![46]

Scot's implied question to the reader, posed every time he tells one of these tall stories, is 'what kind of idiot would believe this'? As important as Scot's sarcastic commentary is the language in which these stories are told. When discussing sex, for example, witchcraft theorists tend to use formal terms like 'carnal copulation'. Scot refers instead to the incubus making 'hot loove' to the lady, an unusual phrase more reminiscent of the 1970s than the 1580s. Scot also recounts one of the stories told in the *Malleus*, about a penis-stealing witch. According to the *Malleus*, the victim of this theft is restored when he threatens the witch with violence, saying somewhat primly: 'Unless you restore my health to me, you shall die at my hands.' In Scot's telling, the young man says to the witch: 'Restore me my toole, or thou shalt die for it.'[47] Scot's use of the informal term 'toole' – in contrast to the *Malleus's* vague reference to 'health' – seems to be designed to provoke amusement and heighten the reader's sense of the story's absurdity. When Scot describes a lustful abbot who was visited by an angel, and 'after that (forsooth) was as chaste as though he had had never a stone in his breech', Scot's derisive, bracketed 'forsooth' and clever punning ridicule the story simply by telling it.[48] Proponents of witchcraft, in their texts, prefer to keep things as serious as possible. Scot, while making disingenuous apologies for the filthiness of the stories he is sadly

---

46 Scot, IV.5, p. 79.
47 Scot, IV.4, pp. 77–78; Heinrich Institoris and Jakob Sprenger, *The Hammer of Witches*, translated by Christopher S. Mackay (Cambridge: Cambridge University Press, 2009); II.7.115C, p. 323.
48 Scot, IV.7, p. 81.

forced to relate, clearly aims to make his readers laugh, both at his jokes and at the claims of witchcraft theorists.

Scot does also provide some logical argument against the reality of witchcraft, devoting much space to discussions of the signification of words in the Hebrew Bible and discussing the nature of spirit in the final book of the *Discoverie*, a section which has attracted much attention from recent historians. But Scot's actual arguments against witchcraft are not the strong point of his book; if anything, they are its weakness. To engage in argument with belief in witchcraft is to take it seriously, and Scot's book is most effective when it refuses to do this. Responding to a story in the *Malleus Maleficarum* concerning a witch who could not be burned until a charm had been removed from her possession, Scot simply dismisses it, saying that 'This is so gravelie and faithfullie set downe by the inquisitors themselves, that one may believe it if he list, though indeed it be a verie lie.'[49] Scot boldly accuses his opponents of lying – a charge he repeats regularly – but he also mocks their gravity, refusing to adopt an equally serious attitude himself. When Scot does make a logical objection to the arguments of believers in witchcraft, it is not always clear that logic is the point. Scot proudly recounts that, 'I have put twentie of these witchmongers to silence with this one question; to wit, Whether a witch that can turne a woman into a cat, &c: can also turne a cat into a woman?'[50] This question ought, in principle, to be answerable, but it reduces witchmongers to silence because it is not really a question: it is mockery dressed as a question. The suggestion that cats could be turned into humans – an idea that was not part of the folkloric tradition – was so unfamiliar that its absurdity was immediately obvious.

From a literary and rhetorical point of view, it is the destructive aspects of the *Discoverie*, the parts which reject and ridicule the claims of witchmongers, which are the most memorable, and the most extensive, parts of the book. Mockery is present from the first page and continues throughout the book, while Scot's thoughts on the nature of spirits are appended to the main text in a separate book, not appearing until page 489 of the 1584 edition. Scot's intellectually sophisticated attempt to build an alternative understanding of spirit is indeed fascinating, but most early modern opponents of Scot paid little attention to these ideas; James I's offhand claim

---

49 Scot, II.8, p. 30.
50 Scot, v.1, p. 92.

that Scot fell into 'the old error of the Sadducees' misrepresents Scot completely, knowingly or not.[51] Most authors hostile to Scot simply condemn him and move quickly on to their own positions on witchcraft, often rejecting his arguments without referring to him by name.[52] But there are some detailed and explicit criticisms of Scot's arguments in manuscript sources which, as far as I know, have yet to be discussed by historians of witchcraft. One such manuscript is by George Wyatt, a grandson of the poet Thomas Wyatt and biographer of Anne Boleyn. Wyatt displays great concern with what he regards as Scot's distortion of Calvin's commentary on Job:

> Trewly a ma[n] would hardly thinke yt a Gentelma[n] yt in al things proffesseth faithfulnes and spetialy a kentisma[n] where ther are so many able to deserne what is right shuld so far corrupt his pen to take so many sente[n]sese scattered so diversly in so few sermo[n]s of Job and yet to be carried w[ith] so co[n]trarie an opinio[n] to ye plaine words of ye Authour.[53]

Wyatt has read Calvin on Job, and is scandalised by what he sees, with justification, as Scot's use of selective quotation and the abuse of Calvin's authority, but he makes no mention of Scot's views on the nature of spirit.[54] Another manuscript source is a lengthy (albeit incomplete) point-by-point rebuttal of Scot's arguments in the Harley collection at the British Library. The only published mention of this document that I have been able to discover is in a footnote in Wallace Notestein's *History of Witchcraft in England*, which is more than a century old; Notestein credits 'Professor Burr' with informing him of the manuscript's existence but did not read it himself.[55] The anonymous author of the Harley MS also rejects

---

51 James I, p. 2ᵛ. The Sadducees were a Jewish sect, treated with hostility in the New Testament, which denied both the existence of spirits and the immortality of the soul. One author who does seem to be aware of Scot's views on spirit is Thomas Nashe, who refers to them twice; *Works of Thomas Nashe*, vol. 1, edited by R. B. McKerrow (London: A. H. Bullen, 1904), pp. 309, 351. However, Nashe is sympathetic to Scot and cites him as an authority on this question.
52 Henry Holland's *Treatise Against Witchcraft* (Cambridge, 1590) is an exception, as it contains responses to Scot's book, complete with page references in the margins.
53 London, British Library, Add. MS 62135, fols 416–423 (fols 421ʳ–421ᵛ).
54 Holland also takes issue with Scot's interpretation of Calvin: sig. E4ʳ; cf. Scot, v.7, pp. 104–5.
55 Notestein, p. 69. George Lincoln Burr (1857–1938) was professor of history and librarian at Cornell University.

Scot's interpretation of Calvin, writing that: 'I can not p[er]use Mr Calvins words uppon yt place because I have not his homelies uppon the book of Job. but at adventur I dare wager w[ith] yow the price of that booke yt y[ou] are deceaved in his opynion.'[56] The author of this work also expresses disapproval of Scot's irreverent attitude.

The idea that the kind of mockery at which Scot excels could be a threat to belief in witches, on the other hand, is tacitly acknowledged by Bodin. Claiming that judges who are too lenient may themselves be witches, Bodin writes that 'the first presumption against the magistrate who is a witch is when he makes a joke of such witchcraft. For under the pretence of laughter he brews his fatal poison.'[57] Bodin accepts, in the early part of his book, that people may find witchcraft hard to believe. If people are prepared to take the discussion seriously, he is, it seems, comfortable with the debate to which his book is a contribution; logical objections can be met with argument, and such a discussion presupposes that the possibility of witchcraft *might* be accepted. But ridicule is a threat which cannot be tolerated, because it puts the credibility of witchcraft, and Bodin himself, at stake. Bodin therefore needs to make what is, under the circumstances, an ominous and threatening statement against such mockery, to make sure that nobody begins to laugh. If Bodin, or any other witchcraft theorist, is made the subject of ridicule, he looks like a fool – a naked emperor who cannot distinguish between fact and fiction.

Histories and stories: facts, fictions, and lies

> DOUBT. When I hear a very strange story, I always think 'tis more likely he should lye that tells it me, than that [it] should be true.
> SIR EDW. 'Tis a good rule for our belief.[58]

While Scot amuses himself and his readers at the expense of the witchcraft theorists, and while he does seem to have been an important figure within the English witchcraft debate, *The Discoverie*

---

56 London, British Library, Harley MS 2302, fol. 77ʳ. The author also criticises Scot's readings of other theologians, such as Chrysostom (fol. 80ʳ), but returns most frequently to Calvin (e.g. fols 84ʳ–84ᵛ).
57 Bodin, p. 216.
58 Thomas Shadwell, *The Lancashire Witches*, edited by Judith Bailey Slagle (New York: Garland, 1991), II.415–17.

of *Witchcraft* did not end that debate.⁵⁹ Clearly, it was possible for some early modern people to dismiss stories like Bodin's as absurd, just as it is for people today. The difference between then and now is that it was not then, as it is now, more or less impossible to take such stories seriously while maintaining any kind of credibility. Part of the reason for this difference can be found in the confused epistemic status of stories in the Renaissance.

It has already been noted that a critical attitude towards the past, and towards texts that purported to record it, had begun to emerge during the sixteenth century. It was in the Renaissance that the methods of what would now be called archival research began to be applied to the study of the past.⁶⁰ But while histories began to have a greater factual basis during the Renaissance, the period also saw an increased emphasis on the literary nature of historical writing, in contrast to the list-like nature of some early chronicles. Renaissance historians considered history to be closely allied to rhetoric and poetry, and they modelled themselves on ancient examples. This included mimicking ancient devices, like the lengthy speeches most Renaissance historians put into the mouths of historical personages.⁶¹ This kind of embellishment of the bare facts was usually left unacknowledged and may, by some readers at least, have been accepted as factual.

Fiction, meanwhile, was not always accepted as a category at all. There was prose writing in the sixteenth century that advertised its self-consciously fictional nature – Thomas More's *Utopia* (1516) would be one example – but the difference between fiction and lie was, for many people, hazy at best. In fact, More's Protestant opponents attacked him on the basis that he had written *Utopia* and was therefore a liar.⁶² His critics may well have been disingenuous, but the fact that they advanced the argument at all reveals that they expected readers to feel unease, at the very least, with invented stories. While it seems to have been accepted that a person telling

---

59 On Scot's influence see Almond, pp. 2–4, and S. F. Davies, 'The Reception of Reginald Scot's Discovery of Witchcraft: Witchcraft, Magic, and Radical Religion', *Journal of the History of Ideas* 74:3 (July 2013), 381–401. Davies writes of the *Discoverie* that 'No other English witchcraft treatise was as widely cited' (p. 389).
60 John Burrow, *A History of Histories* (London: Penguin, 2009), p. 299.
61 Geoffrey of Monmouth was an early adopter of these more literary techniques; see Burrow, p. 237.
62 Alan H. Nelson, *Monstrous Adversary: The Life of Edward de Vere, 17th Earl of Oxford* (Liverpool: Liverpool University Press, 2003), p. 7.

a true story had licence to embellish and invent, embellishment and invention for their own sake were less excusable.

The most famous defence of fiction from the period is Sir Philip Sidney's. Tackling the accusation that fiction is equivalent to lying, Sidney dismisses it as absurd with reference to the example of Aesop's fables: 'who thinketh that Aesop wrote it for actually true, were well worthy to have his name chronicled among the beasts he writeth of'.[63] This is a telling example to use. Long before Sidney wrote, St Augustine and other theologians had defended those fictions which were so implausible that their fictitiousness was obvious; since nobody would accept them as true, such stories need not be considered lies.[64] Sidney's discussion skirts around the question of those morally dubious stories that are a little more plausible than beast fables. Conditioned as we are by a few centuries of the realist novel, this may appear less troubling to modern people than it did to Sidney's contemporaries, many of whom may have felt that the area between obvious fiction and obvious truth was worryingly crowded. Nelson points out a striking example of an educated person getting it wrong: 'Although *Amadis* was usually thought of as a delightful fiction, an English translator saw fit to introduce it with reference to Cicero's praise of histories and to dilate on the advantage of learning from the lessons of the past.'[65] It might be difficult to see how *Amadis de Gaule*, with its giants and wizards, could be accepted as history by anyone, but the translator's mistake is perhaps understandable given that even 'true' histories contained so much fabrication.

The distinction between 'history' and 'story' that exists today was uncertain in early modern England. The term 'history' is used indiscriminately in sixteenth-century English texts to describe both fiction and historical writing; the adjective 'tragical' – with its theatrical associations – is used to describe historical events as well as stage plays. The embellishments of historical writers were not normally regarded as problematic because the aim of history was not to recreate past events as accurately as possible, but to provide exemplary moral lessons from the past. This didactic purpose – or at least the pretence of it – was one that historians shared with

---

63 Philip Sidney, *An Apology for Poetry* (Manchester: Manchester University Press, 2002, first published in 1595), p. 103.
64 Nelson, pp. 14–15.
65 Nelson, p. 39. The translator is A. M., in his epistle to the *Third Booke of Amadis de Gaule* (London, 1618).

poets and writers of fiction: it is central to Sidney's defence. This convention also allows both fictional and historical sources to be cited in support of particular arguments without addressing the question of whether or not the events described actually took place: this question is ultimately unimportant, because all stories should contain a deeper moral truth. This is not to say that early modern people were incapable of distinguishing between factual relation and fictional representation. Scot, for one, was able to do so:

> I doo not thinke that there will be found among all the heathens superstitious fables, or among the witches, conjurors, couseners, poets, knaves, fooles, &c: that ever wrote, so impudent and impious a lie or charme as is read in Barnardine de bustis; where, to cure a sicke man, Christs bodie, to wit: a wafer cake, was outwardlie applied to his side, and entred into his heart, in the sight of all the standers by. Now, if grave authors report such lies, what credit in these cases shall we attribute unto the old wives tales, that Sprenger, Institor, Bodine, and others write? Even as much as to Ovids *Metamorphosis*, Aesops *fables*, Moores *Utopia*, and diverse other fansies; which have as much truth in them, as a blind man hath sight in his eie.[66]

While Scot lumps falsity and fiction (and knaves and poets) together in this passage, he does seem to be aware of them as distinct. The tales of Catholic authors and witchmongers are described as 'lies' while the fictional works of Ovid and More are termed 'fansies' (although Scot also writes that he is unsure whether the ancient poets were serious or joking).[67] Nevertheless, even with these fictional works, Scot does feel the need to repeatedly state that they are untrue. He cannot take for granted that his readers will automatically accept this to be the case – although he thinks most of them will[68] – and in fact the authors he disagrees with seem not to. The respect given to all stories, and the understanding that even a fabrication can convey a higher truth of practical value, allows fiction to be used as a means of argument. While fiction is typically more useful to the persecutors of witches than it is to writers like Scot, who dismisses the stories told by ancient poets, it is also worth noting that Scot is happy to use some of Ovid's more obscure writings as evidence that love magic does not work, as Cora Fox has pointed out.[69]

---

66 Scot, XII.14, p. 248.
67 Scot, XII.8, p. 229.
68 Scot, XII.8, p. 229.
69 Cora Fox, *Ovid and the Politics of Emotion in Elizabethan England* (Basingstoke: Palgrave Macmillan, 2009), p. 135; Scot, VI.6, pp. 121–23.

Scot himself quotes the more sceptical (and comical) poet Chaucer, repeatedly and approvingly.[70]

There were other, perhaps more pressing, reasons to take the stories of ancient poets seriously. Casaubon illustrates these succinctly when he explains that

> in reading ancientist Authors, Poets, and others; but Homer especially, I have received such satisfaction, as that, had I no other ground to induce me to believe the antiquity of the Scriptures, which they pretend unto ... this very consideration would have been a great motive unto me: so many things do I find of that nature from the beginning to the end, which, to me, seem in a manner indubitable.[71]

In other parts of his book, Casaubon provides concrete examples of why ancient poets support the truth of Christianity. Ovid, for example, describes a 'deluge' that Casaubon identifies with the story of Noah.[72] Later, the myth of Prometheus is taken to be a corrupted version of the true story of Adam's fall from grace.[73] Many authors on witchcraft found evidence of the interactions of evil spirits and human beings in Greek and Roman myth, on the basis that the pagan gods could only have been devils in disguise.[74] The apparent support for the Christian story of creation and God offered by pagan stories of creation and the gods was too valuable to be abandoned, so despite the obvious implausibility of much ancient poetry, it had to be taken seriously.

The confusion of story and history, or fiction and reality, played a prominent role in the witchcraft debate; but quite apart from the arguments that took place about which sources could legitimately be used as evidence, questions of deception and falsehood were central to the early modern demonological discourse of witchcraft. Witches themselves were said to be both deceivers and deceived;

---

70 Scot dismisses accounts of witchcraft in Ovid, Horace, and Virgil, who are sarcastically referred to as 'grave authors'; I.4, p. 10, XII.7, pp. 224–29. He quotes Chaucer's *Canterbury Tales* in support of his sceptical arguments: IV.12, p. 88; XIV.1–3, pp. 353, 355–56.
71 Casaubon, *Of Credulity and Incredulity*, p. 60 (marked 56).
72 Casaubon, p. 30 (marked 26).
73 Casaubon, p. 36 (marked 32).
74 See, for example, Cotta, pp. 30–31: 'Who almost that readeth any ancient classical Author, can auoide the common mention of fained gods ... offering themselues vnto men and people, sometimes in one shape, sometimes in another; requiring worship, ceremonies and rites ... doing strange and admired workes oft-times.' All such 'fained gods' could be recognised by Christians as devils.

they were credulous tricksters. Their magic was often described as primarily a matter of deceiving the senses of their victims. If witches were able to transform human beings into animal form, as some maintained, this transformation was usually said to be a mere deception affecting form rather than substance (albeit indistinguishable to human senses from a genuine transformation).[75] A more common view, in England at least, was that the witches' magic lacked even this much reality, and it was frequently asserted that witches were deluded about the extent of their power, even by writers not normally regarded as sceptics. Any magical powers witches seemed to have, it was often argued, were in fact provided by the devil – or perhaps the devil did nothing more than predict events that would have taken place anyway, before tricking the witches into believing that they had brought these things about by magic.

The witches themselves, then, were even more deluded than those victims whose senses they deceived: they mistook the devil's lies for truth. Like their master, the devil, witches delighted in tricking others because they had themselves been deceived.[76] Witches were often regarded as the greatest victims of their own witchcraft (although this did not always generate much sympathy for them) since, by allowing themselves to be seduced by the devil, they had condemned themselves to eternal damnation, often without getting anything in return. The foolish credulity of the witches and their defenders – who were also foolish enough to believe the devil's lies – was frequently noted by demonologists, in what a Freudian might call an example of projection. Others, like Reginald Scot, who scornfully noted the credulity of those who believed that witches could perform genuine feats of magic, also accounted for the existence of self-proclaimed witches in terms of delusion induced by melancholy. Distinguishing truth from lies and fictions was thus at the heart of early modern thought about witchcraft.

---

75 An exception is Jean Bodin, who maintained the reality of lycanthropy; see Bodin, pp. 122–29 and note 73. The *Malleus* maintains that such transformations do occur but are illusory; 1.10.59C–62D (pp. 201–09).

76 A point made, for example, by Robert Burton in *The Anatomy of Melancholy* (London: J. M. Dent, 1972, first published in 1621), 1.2.1.2, p. 196, on the authority of St Augustine. As Russell points out, Dante established a strong literary precedent for the idea that '[d]eception and self-deception ... are the key to all sin' by placing traitors in the lowest circle of hell (p. 227).

Avoiding accusations of credulity was more important for those authors arguing in favour of witchcraft persecution than for those who argued against it, for obvious reasons. (Thomas Ady's claim to rely entirely on scripture may reveal an equivalent desire to avoid accusations of incredulity: Ady was a physician, not a clergyman.) One strategy employed by witchcraft theorists bears a resemblance, albeit on a much more modest scale, to the methodology of Descartes: using scepticism, or the pretence of scepticism, as an argumentative and narrative tactic to persuade others that all reasonable sceptical doubts have been overcome. This type of scepticism is referred to in this study as rhetorical scepticism, since it is used with a persuasive purpose. The following section discusses the features of such rhetorical scepticism with reference to specific examples.

Rhetorical scepticism

The rhetorical use of scepticism is in evidence in a wide range of purportedly factual texts, including pamphlets describing specific trials or cases, as well as more theoretical and learned works. At the more popular end of the spectrum, the author of a pamphlet describing the career of Stubbe Peeter, a German sorcerer, produces evidence of the veracity of his account towards the end of the text:

> And that this thing is true, Maister Tice Artine a Brewer dwelling at Puddlewharfe, in London, beeing a man of that Country borne, and one of good reputation and account, is able to iustifie, who is neere kinsman to this Childe, and hath from thence twice receiued Letters conserning the same, and for that the firste Letter did rather drive him into wondering at the act then yielding credit thereunto, he had shortlye after at request of his writing another letter sent him, whereby he was more fully satisfied, and divers other persons of great credit in London hath in like sorte received letters from their friends to the like effect.[77]

The standard tactic used in this passage is to emphasise the reliability of the person who is prepared to vouch for the truth of the story. Only one of the 'persons of great credit' is actually named, and his social standing as a brewer might not have impressed all contemporary readers. However, Master Artine's reliability is emphasised by the apparently trivial detail that he does not immediately believe the story. Instead of accepting the version of events as related in

---

77 Anon., *A Most True Discourse, declaring the life and death of one Stubbe Peeter, being a most wicked Sorcerer* (London, 1590), p. 14.

the first letter, he demands further evidence, and is only satisfied when he receives it, again in the form of a letter. The content of the two letters is left unspecified, but it is difficult to imagine what further details Master Artine's correspondent – if a correspondent ever existed – could possibly have supplied that would have convinced him of the existence of a magic belt that turned Stubbe Peeter into 'a greedy devouring Woolf'.[78]

Artine's supposedly sceptical attitude in this passage is being used, in a rather transparent way, to enhance his credibility as a witness, and this technique is frequently used in witchcraft writings. Typically, such rhetorical scepticism involves the author, usually early on in the text, claiming to have been sceptical about the allegation of witchcraft at first, only to be convinced by overwhelming evidence. Sometimes this claim is no more than a straightforward assertion. One anonymous pamphleteer writes that: 'It had been very difficult to convince me of that which I find to be true, concerning the wiles of that old Serpent the Divel.'[79] In this case, the author's supposed scepticism is not on display in any other part of the text: the reader is told in a matter-of-fact way about the existence of an English college of witches and a man transforming himself into a toad, among other things. Other texts build rhetorical scepticism into the narrative much more subtly and effectively. Edward Fairfax's lengthy tract describing his daughter's possession provides a good example. Fairfax spends a long time detailing his daughter's symptoms, which include falling into a trance, what would now be called hallucinations, and conversations with an invisible interlocutor (named by her as Satan), in which she defies the devil. Fairfax then tells a story about a penny left at his house by a woman reputed to be a witch. The penny has 'by the woman's confession ... been put to evil use',[80] and Fairfax attempts to destroy it, which is only achieved with great difficulty. He then claims that

> [u]ntil this time we had no suspicion that this should be Witchcraft; but the matter of the penny, and the fame of the woman who did bring it to the house, gave cause unto us to surmise that perhaps this might be the action of some Witch, many about being evil reputed of in that kind. Yet were we slow to believe.[81]

---

78 *A Most True Discourse*, p. 4.
79 Anon.,*The Divels Delusions* (London, 1649), sig. A2ʳ.
80 Edward Fairfax, 'A Discourse of Witchcraft', in *Miscellanies of the Philobiblon Society*, vol. 5 (London, 1859), p. 57.
81 Fairfax, p. 63.

Fairfax claims he was 'slow to believe', and it is indeed the case that he has not mentioned witchcraft until this point in the text. However, given the public interest generated by cases of demonic possession, and the fairly standard symptoms displayed by victims of it (which his daughter shares), it would be unwise to accept this claim at face value. The details provided to the reader all point to demonic possession induced by witchcraft, and any contemporary reader would probably have noticed this. In making these statements, Fairfax emphasises his own fair-mindedness to the reader, demonstrating that he is not a credulous or hasty person who will jump to unwarranted conclusions. He presents himself as a sceptic, a person who requires conclusive evidence before he will diagnose witchcraft. But persuading the reader to accept this diagnosis is his purpose for writing in the first place, as he makes clear in his preface.

In telling the story about the penny, Fairfax has clear ideas about what will count as empirical evidence of witchcraft. These ideas are presented as having been formulated and agreed upon prior to the situation which puts them to the test. Fairfax explains to his wife – who also shows her scepticism in that she 'gave no great respect' to the significance of the penny – that 'if Wait's wife were indeed a Witch (as she was reputed) then ... the penny would be gone' from the place where it had been left.[82] Of course, the penny had disappeared as predicted, at which Fairfax claims he and his wife were 'amazed'. A hypothesis is outlined in advance, an experiment is conducted, and the results point clearly to the outcome that the experimenter had least expected: the hypothesis is verified, and this really is a case of witchcraft. Exactly why the disappearance of the penny proves that a particular person – the owner of the penny – is guilty of a particular bewitchment is an issue that the author avoids. The important point, it seems, is that Fairfax decided *in advance* what would count as evidence, so the result cannot be said to be unfair or arbitrary.

Rhetorical scepticism was also used to pre-emptively answer possible objections that could be raised against an accusation. In a case of witchcraft tried at Bury St Edmunds, the prosecution claimed that Rose Cullender and Amy Duny had bewitched a number of children. The children displayed the classic signs of demonic possession, going into fits and coughing up pins. Margaret Arnold,

---

82 Fairfax, pp. 57–58.

aunt to two of the supposedly bewitched children, was called as a witness, and testified as follows:

> This Deponent said, that she gave no credit to that which was related to her, conceiving possibly the Children might use some deceit in putting Pins in their mouths themselves. Wherefore this Deponent unpinned all their Cloathes, and left not so much as one Pin upon them, but sewed all the Clothes they wore, instead of pinning of them. But this Deponent saith, that notwithstanding all this care and circumspection of hers, the Children afterwards raised at several times at least Thirty Pins in her presence.[83]

The most obvious sceptical counter-argument is anticipated and neutralised by this witness. The children cannot have been concealing pins in their mouths because all pins were removed from them. This trial took place in 1664, a time when there seem to have been very few convictions for witchcraft, at least on the Home Circuit, and cases of demonic possession always provoked greater scepticism than did 'ordinary' witchcraft cases. There are several recorded cases which were eventually exposed as fraudulent, many of them as a result of the involvement of James I.[84] The strength of the evidence required in this case was therefore high; the witnesses came prepared, and succeeded in securing the witches' execution.

Rhetorical scepticism seeks to demonstrate that a given accusation of witchcraft is not frivolous but has been carefully investigated. Typically the technique implies (as in the Stubbe Peeter pamphlet) or explicitly asserts (as in Fairfax's text) the existence of vital details which need to be checked, and can only then act as a guarantee of the veracity of the accusation. The fact that the stories are always difficult to believe – not just now but then too – is dealt with by focusing on particular details within the story. By stressing that witchcraft is a credible explanation if and only if certain evidential conditions are met, the authors of these accounts evade the larger and much more difficult problem of demonstrating that witchcraft is possible at all.

This reluctance to deal with the larger issues of the possibility, or otherwise, of witchcraft is especially evident in Henry Goodcole's pamphlet on Elizabeth Sawyer, the witch of Edmonton, a source for the play of the same name. Goodcole stresses his reluctance to

---

83 Anon., *A Tryal of Witches*, p. 25.
84 A detailed study of one such case is James Sharpe's *The Bewitching of Anne Gunter* (London: Profile, 1999).

write the pamphlet in the first place. He is so far from enthusiastically proclaiming the existence of witches that he refuses to take any general stance on witches and witchcraft, an issue which he acknowledges to be controversial. He complains that he has been pushed into writing against his will, and does so to get some peace from those who are demanding his version of events (who these people are, and why they want to know, is left tantalisingly vague). His reason for writing, he says, is to

> defend the truth of the cause, which in some measure, hath receiued a wound already, by most base and false Ballets, which were sung at the time of our returning from the Witches execution. In them I was ashamed to see and heare such ridiculous fictions of her bewitching Corne on the ground, of a Ferret and an Owle dayly sporting before her, of the bewitched woman brayning her selfe, of the Spirits attending in the Prison: all which I knew to be fitter for an Ale-bench then for a relation of proceeding in Court of Iustice.[85]

The pamphlet, according to its author, sets out to defend the truth from the wild exaggerations of uninformed and uneducated people. In contrast to these people, Goodcole himself, as the title page of his pamphlet says, had access to Elizabeth Sawyer during her trial and imprisonment. Goodcole's pamphlet stresses his position of authority, by virtue of his privileged knowledge of the Sawyer case. (Goodcole even admits that he 'with great labour ... extorted'[86] a confession from her, *after* her conviction.) The pamphlet is carefully positioned in opposition to the kind of 'base' and scurrilous entertainment which threatens the dignity of the criminal justice system. Goodcole's attitude, then, is in some respects sceptical about witchcraft beliefs. But this scepticism bears further examination.

The stories told by the (sadly lost) ballads about Elizabeth Sawyer are a threat to the official version of events represented by the verdict of the court against Sawyer, not because they are sceptical but because they are credulous. How seriously the ballads were taken by the people who listened to them, and what spirit they were composed in, is now impossible to say. But it is clear from Goodcole's account that he at least does not consider them credible or helpful to his 'cause'. Goodcole has less fanciful criteria in mind

---

85 Henry Goodcole, *The Wonderfull Discouerie of Elizabeth Sawyer, a Witch* (London, 1621), sig. A3^v.
86 Goodcole, sig. B4^r.

about what constitutes evidence of Sawyer's witchcraft, and even provides a list:

1 Her face was most pale & ghoast-like without any bloud at all, and her countenance was still deiected to the ground.
2 Her body was crooked and deformed, euen beinding together, which so happened but a little before her apprehension.
3 That tongue which by cursing, swearing, blaspheming, and imprecating, as afterward she confessed, was the occasioning cause, of the Divels accesse vnto her.[87]

No mention is made in this list of the supposed circumstance that the devil appeared to Sawyer in the form of a large black dog. Goodcole presents a list of characteristics which are easily verifiable, setting the burden of proof for witchcraft extremely low. If this is all that is required to prove witchcraft, then witchcraft is easy to prove; the pamphlet claims that the factor which was most important in determining the jury's guilty verdict was Elizabeth Sawyer's 'swearing and cursing'.[88] This kind of behaviour is not difficult to believe at all, while stories about owls and ferrets 'sporting' are not, on the face of it, either plausible or serious. As Anthony Harris points out, the play is less coy than Goodcole about endorsing some of these 'ridiculous fictions',[89] and this is probably because it is designed to entertain. Entertainment presents a threat to Goodcole's serious, 'true' version of events, in part because of the risk that it might provoke laughter, and laughter might then provoke disbelief.

Goodcole mentions in his '[a]pologie to the Christian readers' that the ballads have already caused a 'wound' to the truth which he presents. This is not the only sign that sceptical attitudes towards the Sawyer case may have been widespread. Immediately before the dialogue in which Goodcole represents Sawyer's confession, he mentions his desire to 'stop all contradictions of so palpable a verity',[90] and appeals to the authority of the men who he claims witnessed Sawyer's confession. While the pamphlet is in one sense responding with scepticism to the ballads it mentions, genuinely sceptical denials of Sawyer's status as a witch – which pass largely unmentioned – are what Goodcole is really concerned about.

---

87 Goodcole, sigs A4^v–B1^r.
88 Goodcole, sig. B1^r.
89 Anthony Harris, *Night's Black Agents* (Manchester: Manchester University Press, 1980), p. 92.
90 Goodcole, sig. B4^r.

Specific parts of his account lend further weight to this suspicion, as when Goodcole claims to have asked Sawyer, 'Did you ever handle the Divell when he came unto you?' Goodcole explains in a marginal note that, 'I asked of her this question because some might thinke this was a visible delusion of her sight only.'[91] Fortunately for Goodcole, Sawyer's answer confirms the tangible presence of the devil, which provides an answer to anyone who might otherwise have claimed that Sawyer's confession was the product of delusion. For Goodcole to have asked the question because he himself was concerned that the devil's appearance was a hallucination would have been understandable, but he ascribes this doubt not to himself but to 'some' people. Either Goodcole had the foresight to realise his actions would be questioned, or (as seems much more likely) he simply made up both question and answer after the event in order to strengthen his case. What really went on in Sawyer's prison cell can never be known for certain, but the partiality and defensiveness of Goodcole's account are undeniable.

By presenting themselves as having been gradually won over by compelling evidence, writers making use of rhetorical scepticism seek to provide compelling evidence for the reader as well. The pamphlet *Newes From Scotland* incorporates James VI's (later James I) initial scepticism and eventual belief about witchcraft into its story of the interrogation of the North Berwick witches.[92] Laura Kolb observes that 'as a character in the story, the king himself offers a model for the reader's response. He undergoes a passage from doubt to belief'.[93] A number of witchcraft treatises were written in the form of dialogues, including James's own contribution, *Daemonologie*, and the earlier works of Nider, Molitor, Pico, and others. The dialogue form allows a similar transition from scepticism to belief, with the reader identifying with the sceptical voice that is gradually persuaded as the evidence and argument accumulates.[94] In their use of narrative, character development, and dialogue, witchcraft texts demonstrate that they are not (or not only) lies, but (also) fictions.

---

91 Goodcole, sig. D1ʳ.
92 See also the discussion of *Macbeth* in Chapter 3.
93 Laura Kolb, 'Playing with Demons: Interrogating the Supernatural in Jacobean Drama', *Forum for Modern Language Studies* 43:4 (2007), 337–50 (p. 342).
94 On the progression from scepticism to belief in *Daemonologie* see Kolb, 344–45; on the dialogue form in witchcraft theory generally and Pico in particular see Stephens, *Demon Lovers*, pp. 92–99.

Submerged scepticism

> But what contempt, what dishonour, what more despicable villainy can one imagine than what witches suffer when they are forced to worship Satan in the guise of a stinking billy goat, and to kiss it on the part one does not dare write or frankly say? This would seem completely incredible to me if I had not read it in the confessions and convictions of innumerable witches.[95]

While rhetorical scepticism is clearly a tool of persuasion, one of the most provocative claims made by Walter Stephens is the argument that writers on witchcraft wrote to conquer their own scepticism, as much as that of others. As Stephens puts it, 'actual belief did not provoke the speculations of witchcraft theorists: belief is what they were *seeking*'.[96] Difficult though this claim might be to substantiate, it is one that must be taken seriously. While it may seem safer to take the claims of witchcraft theorists at face value – which is, in effect, to assume their sincerity – this is surely even more risky than trying to read between the lines in the case of documents that are so self-evidently inaccurate in their claims. It is worth noting, too, that all of the major early modern texts on witchcraft include arguments devoted to demonstrating that witches do, in fact, exist. The concern with proving the existence of witchcraft is maintained from the very start to the very end of the period in which witchcraft was a crime, suggesting that the degree of scepticism about the very possibility of witchcraft in early modern Europe was considerable, was never overcome, and may well be both understated and tacitly revealed by the surviving textual evidence.

The submerged scepticism that Stephens detects in some early Renaissance demonologists is displayed even more clearly in some of the later authors, perhaps most of all in the work of Jean Bodin. On the face of it, Bodin writes to overcome the scepticism of others, stating as much in the preface to his book *On the Demon-Mania of Witches* (1580).[97] But while Bodin acknowledges scepticism about witchcraft, the evidence for the existence of witchcraft is repeatedly described as overwhelming. Bodin calls sceptics 'fools or madmen' who 'do not want to believe'.[98] Similarly, James I declares the existence of witches to be a 'certainty' proved by the 'daily experience of the

---

95 Bodin, pp. 156–57.
96 Stephens, *Demon Lovers*, p. 179.
97 Bodin, p. 37.
98 Bodin, p. 38.

harmes that they do'.[99] The existence of scepticism about witchcraft is acknowledged (and its prevalence is deplored), but readers might be forgiven for wondering how scepticism can exist given the seeming confidence of authors like James and Bodin.

But while Bodin claims that the existence of witches is obvious and plainly proved by an abundance of evidence – by which he means stories that he has read or heard and confessions extracted under torture – it is impossible to miss a defensive quality to his arguments. St Augustine, according to Bodin, '[s]ays that one must not doubt in any way and that one would be very impudent to try to deny that demons and evil spirits have carnal relations with women'.[100] Bodin orders the reader not to doubt, but does not address the question of whether demonic copulation is actually possible. When assuring the reader of the existence of spirits, Bodin points out that 'to call it into doubt ... would be to deny the principles of all metaphysics, and the existence of God'.[101] Again, Bodin does not say that calling the existence of spirits into doubt is mistaken. He states that he is not prepared to contemplate doing so because the intellectual and theological consequences, in his view, are too dire. His reference to the existence, or otherwise, of God is revealing, as this is precisely what is at stake in these debates.[102] Bodin is writing to defend his belief in God, but this is also his ultimate argument for the reality of witchcraft. Witches' confessions are true even when they involve impossibilities, Bodin argues (against Johannes Weyer):

> [W]hen one asserts that a confession to be believable must report something which is possible and true; and that it cannot be true unless it is possible; and nothing is possible in law except what is possible by nature: it is a sophistic and specious argument – and nevertheless its assumption is false. For the great works and marvels of God are impossible by nature, and nonetheless true.[103]

The unstated logic is, of course, circular: God's existence is invoked in this passage in order to guarantee the existence of witches, and the existence of witches is primarily important because it proves the existence of God.

---

99 James I, p. 31.
100 Bodin, p. 41.
101 Bodin, p. 46.
102 See Stephens, *Demon Lovers*, esp. pp. 365–67.
103 Bodin, p. 193.

Bodin is not alone in connecting witchcraft belief to religious faith. The anonymous author of the Harley manuscript does so even more explicitly when he refuses to accept that the devil cannot appear in physical form on the following grounds:

> I wrytt not as confessing w[i]th y[ou] that he never appeareth to honest & credyble p[er]sons in some grosse or corporall forme. for yf I shuld confess yt I must denye & condemme as false & fabulous the hystories & testymonies of most credyble hystoryographers & wrytters yea the scriptures them sealves for I am of opynion that the dyvell appeared to Christ him sealfe in a corporall shape when he tempted him.[104]

As with Bodin, this author rejects Scot's claims not because they are implausible but because their consequences are unacceptable.

That Bodin's arguments are advanced in order to counter his own doubts, as well as those of others, becomes evident on the occasions when he is no longer able to suppress his own scepticism. In describing common magical techniques, or rather refusing to describe them so as not to encourage their use, Bodin in passing calls these techniques 'inept and ridiculous'.[105] This brief, throwaway comment sits so uneasily with what the treatise is actually arguing for that it is difficult to understand why Bodin wrote it at all. On other occasions, too, Bodin gives his opponents ammunition. Commenting on one phenomenon widely attributed to witches, he writes that

> There is no village peasant who does not know that by means of a verse from the Psalms, which I shall not write down, being pronounced while one churns butter, it becomes impossible to make any ... However, if one were to put a very small amount of sugar in it, it is quite confirmed by experience that the butter cannot coagulate.[106]

Bodin's refusal to spread magical knowledge is rendered rather pointless by his claim that the trick is already known to every peasant, but even more serious for the credibility of his argument is that he offers an entirely naturalistic and non-magical explanation for the failure to churn butter in the same paragraph as his stories about village-level witchcraft. It is natural enough to find Reginald

---

104 MS Harley 2302, fols 61ᵛ–62ʳ; cf. Scot, I.6, p. 13, where the phrases 'honest and credible persons' and 'grosse and corporall forme' are also used.
105 Bodin, p. 92.
106 Bodin, p. 97, cf. Scot, I.4, p. 11.

Scot making the point about sugar preventing butter from churning, but why does Bodin share this information? It is as if he wants both to believe and disbelieve at the same time – to believe, because of the theological imperative to do so, which he frequently stresses; and not to believe, because believing is not only difficult, as Bodin himself points out, but also rather foolish, as his comment about 'inept and ridiculous' magical techniques indicates. It is probably not coincidental that Bodin has often been seen as an exceptionally credulous witchcraft theorist, willing to believe even in genuine lycanthropy: his credulity – his need to believe – is in proportion to his own scepticism.

While theological concerns are often paramount, more human motivations also compel belief in witchcraft for some writers. Bodin, having had some personal involvement in a witchcraft trial, might have had reason to want to believe his own claim that burning people alive is not really cruel, but an act of mercy.[107] Edward Fairfax displays a similar anxiety even more clearly. He cannot disbelieve in witchcraft because it would be terrible if all the people executed for it had not been guilty. He condemns sceptics on the grounds that 'I cannot without horror think with what ungracious impudency these impure mouths do condemn so zealous a King, so religious magistrates, and so Christian a state as ours is, to be guilty of so much innocent blood, as in these last 20 years hath been shed for this one offence.'[108] Fairfax's inability to consider this prospect 'without horror' does not, of course, change the reality of the situation; but many people – past and present – have been unable to accept states of affairs which they consider to be ideologically unpalatable. Both Bodin and Fairfax suggest that certain thoughts, on certain topics, ought to be avoided altogether.

Another example of an author who appears to be struggling with his (or perhaps, though it seems unlikely, her) own disbelief can be seen in *The Wonderfvll Discouerie of the Witch-crafts of Margaret and Philip Flower* (1619), a document that is fascinating mainly because of the anxious and inconsistent nature of its argument.[109] The anonymous author begins, in similar vein to Goodcole, by refusing to take a position on witchcraft, claiming it is unnecessary

---

107 Bodin, p. 173.
108 Fairfax, p. 26.
109 For another discussion of the pamphlet see Gibson, *Reading Witchcraft*, pp. 177–81.

because of the authority of scripture, the King, and 'many worthy Writers', all of which agree

> that divers impious and facinorous mischefes haue beene effectuated through the instruments of the Deuill, by permission of God, so that the Actors of the same haue carried away the opinion of the world, to doe that which they did by Witch-craft; or at least to be esteemed Witches, for bringing such and such things to passe.[110]

This shambolic piece of prose is remarkable for its ambivalence and vagueness. At first, mischiefs are brought about by the instruments of the devil – a standard description of witches – and this seems quite clear. But the actual nature of these mischiefs is not specified. Not only that, but it seems uncertain whether actual witchcraft has been used – the author will only go so far as to say that this is so in 'the opinion of the world'. Everybody else believes in witchcraft, it seems, but the author remains non-committal. Even this statement is qualified further when it is added that, even if the murky deeds the agents of the devil have committed are *not* brought about by witchcraft, the deeds themselves are sufficient grounds for those responsible to be 'esteemed' witches. The author of the pamphlet is much more to the point when expressing scepticism than when attempting to express belief. Wise men and women who offer magical services, such as the finding of lost or stolen items, are summarily dismissed as

> meerely coseners and deceivers ... if they make you beleeve, that by their meanes you shall heare of things lost or stolne, it is either done by Confederacie, or put off by protraction, to deceive you of your money.[111]

At this point the author sounds every bit as sceptical as Reginald Scot. While wise women and men were often regarded as distinct from witches, the contrast between the direct statement above and the tortuous formulations which preceded it betrays a good deal of scepticism about maleficent witchcraft as well.

The author also resembles Scot – and Johannes Weyer – in describing witches as 'men and women grown in yeeres, and overgrowne with melancholie and Atheism'. But while Scot and Weyer regard this as a reason to spare witches from execution, the author

---

110 Anon., *The Wonderfvll Discouerie of the Witch-crafts of Margaret and Philip Flower* (London, 1619), sig. B1ʳ.
111 *The Wonderfvll Discouerie*, sig. B1ᵛ.

Scepticism in the Renaissance 45

of this pamphlet does not consider melancholy and delusion to imply innocence. Instead, the sceptical argument is appropriated and turned on its head: melancholy is what draws witches into the study of 'mischiefe and exoticke practises of loathsome Arts and Sciences'. Whether their studies actually provide them with any magical powers, again, is not entirely clear. On the one hand, the author speaks sceptically of witches 'making you beleeve with *Medea*, that they can raise tempests'.[112] At the same time, however, 'we know too well, what monstrous effects haue beene produced ... by such kinde of people'.[113] As always, the author declines to specify what it is that we already know so well, and is similarly non-committal about the promises made by the devil to his servants, which may or may not be deceptions. In the end, the author concludes uneasily, it does not actually matter whether witches have any power or not. The pamphlet lists ten lessons to be drawn from the case, and the tenth and final lesson is that

> private opinion cannot prevaile against publike censures ... Therefore though it were so, that neither Witch nor Devill could doe these things, yet Let not a Witch liue, saith God, and Let them dye (saith the law of England).[114]

The pamphlet bears clear traces of the author's doubts about the statements made in it. The question 'what is a witch?' – never asked or answered – nevertheless haunts the text. In the end, the answer implicit in the pamphlet is that a witch is simply a person who is considered to be a witch, because that is the only definition of a witch that all readers – and, it would seem, the author – can take seriously. The difficulty in taking witchcraft seriously is also evident in the earliest English plays to feature witches as characters, which are discussed in the following section.

Protestant scepticism and the origins of witchcraft drama

> [T]he witchmongers ... publish so palpable absurdities concerning such reall actions betwixt the diuell and man, as a wise man would be ashamed to read, but much more to credit: as that S. Dunstan lead the diuell about the house by the nose with a paire of pinsors or tongs, and made him rore so lowd, as the place roong thereof,

---

112 *The Wonderfvll Discoverie*, sig. B1ᵛ.
113 *The Wonderfvll Discoverie*, sig. B2ʳ.
114 *The Wonderfvll Discoverie*, sig. D3ʳ.

&c: with a thousand the like fables, without which neither the art of poperie nor of witchcraft could stand.[115]

The development of the professional theatre in sixteenth-century England was, like much else at the time, marked by the Protestant Reformation. Witchcraft first appeared in the theatre in connection with Catholicism, and this link remained intact throughout the period covered in this study, both inside and outside the theatre. The relationship between Catholicism and witchcraft is discussed by virtually all English writers of longer works on witchcraft, and in several pamphlets as well. The connection is made irrespective of the author's substantive position on witchcraft, and anti-Catholic rhetoric is a common feature of several texts on the subject.

Protestant zeal in early modern England, so-called 'puritanism', has traditionally been regarded as hostile to the theatre as well as to Catholicism. While this picture has been vigorously challenged, notably by Margot Heinemann and Paul Whitfield White,[116] it remains undeniable that many reform-minded clergymen, together with the City authorities, attacked the institution of the Elizabethan commercial theatre in no uncertain terms. Earlier in the sixteenth century, however, before the advent of permanent purpose-built theatres, things were quite different. Protestant reformers in the reign of Henry VIII, for instance, urged the King to use theatrical performance as a means of attacking the Catholic Church and establishing the authority of the Crown over church matters more firmly. Sir Richard Morrison wrote to the King in around 1535, pointing out that

> In summer, commonly upon the Holy Days in most places of your Realm, there be plays of Robin Hood, Maid Marion, Friar Tuck ... How much better is it that those plays should be forbidden and deleted and others devised to set forth and declare lively before the people's eyes the abomination and wickedness of the Bishop of Rome, monks, friars, nuns and such like, and to declare and open to them the obedience that your subjects, by God's and man's laws, owe unto your Majesty.[117]

---

115 Scot, v.8, p. 108.
116 Margot Heinemann, *Puritanism and Theatre: Thomas Middleton and Opposition Drama under the Early Stuarts* (Cambridge: Cambridge University Press, 1980); Paul Whitfield White, *Theatre and Reformation: Protestantism, Patronage and Playing in Tudor England* (Cambridge: Cambridge University Press, 1992).
117 Quoted in Glynne Wickham, Herbert Berry and William Ingram, *English Professional Theatre, 1530–1660* (Cambridge: Cambridge University Press, 2000), p. 20.

Morrison attacks secular plays on frivolous subjects; but the medieval cycle plays, originally designed as Church propaganda, were the real competition for Protestant reformers. According to Peter Happé, these plays were 'at their most vigorous' during the early sixteenth century, perhaps precisely because the old faith was felt to be under threat at this time.[118] Soon after Morrison's letter was written, the former Carmelite friar John Bale began writing his plays, as a dramatic response to, and a Protestant version of, the mystery and morality plays.[119] The enthusiasm with which the reformers embraced the theatre, at least in the first half of the sixteenth century, is suggested by the fact that so many extant plays from this period are written from an obviously Protestant perspective.

A major part of the Protestant attack on Catholic 'abomination and wickedness' was an attack on magic. Keith Thomas points out that the difference between religion and magic was both 'blurred by the medieval Church' and 'strongly reasserted by the propagandists of the Protestant Reformation'.[120] More recently, Eamon Duffy has argued that Thomas, if anything, understated the close relationship between Catholic ritual and magical ceremony. Magic, rather than being a popular corruption of Church practices or a survival of pre-Christian beliefs, is described by Duffy as a natural extension of the teachings of the Church. Discussing the use of charms against thunder and storms, for example, he argues that

> the rhetoric and rationale at work in such incantations cannot sensibly be called pagan. Instead, they represent the appropriation and adaptation to lay needs and anxieties of a range of sacred gestures and prayers, along lines essentially faithful to the pattern established within the liturgy itself. This is not paganism, but lay Christianity.[121]

Duffy emphasises the centrality of magic – the achievement of supernatural effects in the physical world through ritual – to Catholic teaching and practice in the late medieval period. It is this centrality which allowed Protestant polemicists to caricature

---

118 Peter Happé, *English Drama Before Shakespeare* (London: Longman, 1999), p. 93.
119 Happé, p. 125.
120 Keith Thomas, *Religion and the Decline of Magic* (Harmondsworth: Penguin Books, 1991, first published in 1971), p. 58.
121 Eamon Duffy, *The Stripping of the Altars* (New Haven: Yale University Press, 1992), p. 283.

the old faith as witchcraft, regardless of their attitude towards magic – Reginald Scot, for example, condemns the practice of exorcism on the grounds that it is a 'conjuration', appealing to the very hostility to magic that he seeks, in the case of witchcraft, to mitigate.[122] The association of Catholicism and witchcraft can only have been strengthened by the fact that Catholic authors admitted that a variety of religious props were used by witches for magical purposes. Bodin, for example, writes that 'the invocation of devils (which the most despicable witches do now) is full of prayers, fastings, crosses and consecrated hosts which witches use in this'.[123] These associations are exploited by the earliest witchcraft plays in England.

Perhaps the earliest English play to feature a witch is Bale's *Three Laws* (1538?), an allegorical anti-Catholic polemic which shows the three laws ordained by God – the laws of nature (Naturae Lex), Moses (Moseh Lex), and Christ (Christi Lex) – corrupted by various personified vices acting under the direction of Infidelitas. The Catholic Church, according to the logic of the play, has corrupted the law of Christ by hypocrisy (Hypocrisis) and false doctrine (Pseudodoctrina), while the laws of Moses – which within the play represent the laws of secular authority – have been corrupted by avarice (Avaricia) and ambition (Ambitio). Even the law of nature – in some ways the most fundamental of the three laws, as it has been humanity's only guide from the fall of Adam until the time of Moses – has been corrupted by idolatry (Idolatria) and sodomy (Sodomismus). Idolatria appears on stage in the form of a witch.

Decades before legally sanctioned witchcraft persecution had begun, almost all the characteristics of a witch that would be recorded by later writers like Reginald Scot are already present in Idolatria. She is able to interfere with the brewing of beer, she can find lost goods or buried treasure, she can cure various ailments, tell fortunes and even 'fatche the devyll from hell'.[124] There is a hint, too, that these activities are becoming increasingly associated with women rather than men: Idolatria is said to have been a man once, but is

---

122 Scot, xv.28, p. 446. Calvin himself compares the Catholic mass to 'a magic incantation': *Institutes of the Christian Religion*, edited by John T. McNeil, translated by Ford Lewis Battles (Philadelphia: Westminster Press, 1960), IV.14, p. 1279.
123 Bodin, p. 66.
124 John Bale, 'Three Laws', in *The Complete Plays of John Bale*, edited by Peter Happé (Cambridge: D. S. Brewer, 1986), l. 416. Subsequent references, in parentheses, are to this edition.

now female (425–26); she is also described as being 'sumwhat olde' (477). Finally, she demonstrates her specifically Catholic piety in a lengthy speech listing her magical practices, which involve the use of both saints' relics and more profane ingredients, establishing a link between witchcraft and Catholicism that would later be repeated by Scot, who identified both those accused of witchcraft and those who persecuted witches as papists. Infidelitas, too, connects Catholic liturgy to illicit magic, saying to Naturae Lex: 'I wolde have brought ye the paxe, / Or els an ymage of waxe, / If I had knowne ye heare' (184–86). Infidelitas's speech treats the pax – a tablet to be kissed during Mass – as interchangeable with the kind of wax effigy that was used in image magic.

Idolatria's identification with witchcraft is not fortuitous. The sin of idolatry is forbidden by the first commandment:

> Thou shalt have no other gods before me. Thou shalt not make unto thee any graven image, or any likeness of any thing that is in heaven above, or that is in the earth beneath, or that is in the water under the earth. Thou shalt not bow down thyself to them, nor serve them.[125]

The reference in the first commandment to 'other gods' required interpretation in an early modern Europe that only recognised the existence of one god. Stuart Clark has shown that the sin of idolatry was frequently linked to the practice of witchcraft.[126] The practice of magic could be interpreted as a form of idolatry because it appealed to spiritual forces other than God. Worse still, these 'other gods' could only be evil spirits in the service of the devil.

While many theologians, both Catholic and Protestant, would have accepted the characterisation of witchcraft as a form of idolatry, Bale's play uses witchcraft or idolatry as a stick with which to beat the papists. Idolatria's lengthy list of ingredients and magical charms identifies witchcraft with Catholic ritual by specifying which saints provide remedies for various ailments. As Infidelitas comments,

> It is a spoart I trowe
> To heare how she out blowe
> Her witche craftes on a rowe;
> By the Masse I must nedes smyle. (547–50)

Both the anti-Catholicism and the long list of magical ingredients and spells are recurring elements of witchcraft drama, still appearing

---

125 Exodus 20:3–5.
126 Clark, pp. 489–93.

in the late seventeenth century. Even more fundamental to the theatrical representation of witchcraft is the entertainment value to which Infidelitas refers. Witches on stage seem to have generated smiles, and perhaps laughter too, from the very start. The Tudor interlude *Thersites* (c.1562?) contains a similar scene which is even more obviously comical. The eponymous character's mother, a witch, recites a long and absurd list of charms in the course of an attempt to cure Ulysses' son Telemachus of worms.[127]

It has been suggested that laughter at the absurdity of witchcraft undermines belief in it more powerfully than any logical argument. But Bale presents moments that might induce scepticism closely juxtaposed with a more serious treatment of witchcraft. *Three Laws* refers to one of the earliest examples of a papal witch, Sylvester II:

> Sylvester the Seconde to the devyll hymself ones gave
> For that hygh offyce that he myght dampne and save.
> He offered also hys stones to Sathan they saye
> For prestes chastyte, and so went their marryage awaye. (1603–06)

Bale is presumably not joking in the first two lines about Sylvester II's pact with the devil. Sylvester, the scholar-pope whose achievements included reintroducing the abacus, the rediscovery of Aristotle and perhaps also the introduction of Arabic numerals into Europe, was for his pains depicted after his death as having sold his soul to the devil in return for forbidden knowledge, making him one of the earliest models for the Faust myth.[128] Like many other Protestant polemicists, Bale seizes on this centuries-old propaganda in order to attack Catholicism. But he follows this serious point with a crude joke; this pattern of serious theological and political discourse being suddenly deflated by bawdy humour is another enduring feature of witchcraft plays.

One reason for this combination of humour and gravity is that the anti-Catholicism of the play requires it. The status of Catholic magic is, in *Three Laws*, quite uncertain. Idolatria's charms are

---

127 'Thersites', in Marie Axton (ed.), *Three Tudor Classical Interludes* (Cambridge: D. S. Brewer, 1982), ll. 697–754.
128 A concise account of Sylvester's life and later reputation can be found in E. R. Truitt, 'Celestial Divination and Arabic Science in Twelfth-Century England: The History of Gerbert of Aurillac's Talking Head', *Journal of the History of Ideas* 73:2 (April 2012), 201–22. The fabled talking head apparently inspired the prop used in Robert Greene's plays *Friar Bacon and Friar Bungay* and *Alphonsus King of Aragon* (see Chapter 3).

ridiculous; even Infidelitas has to smile at them. Nonetheless, they do constitute witchcraft, and the possibility of giving oneself to the devil seems entirely real in the play. The kind of Catholic witchcraft represented by Idolatria must be both dismissed *and* taken seriously. Catholic magic must be shown to be no more than cheap trickery, so that the claims made for it can be contradicted. At the same time, it must present a genuine threat to true religion, since if it were harmless there would be no need to oppose it. Both scepticism towards and belief in witchcraft are therefore required of the audience. The tricky question of whether Idolatria's magic actually works is avoided altogether.

The most interesting play to touch on witchcraft prior to the professional Elizabethan theatre is *Gammer Gurton's Needle* (*c*.1550–53?), written by an author identified only as Mr. S.[129] The play – whose plot turns on a lost needle – does not contain any witchcraft, but it is packed with witchcraft belief, mainly in the person of Hodge, Gammer Gurton's servant, who is desperate to find the needle in order to repair a hole in the seat of his trousers (which, some of his lines imply, would have been displayed to the audience in performance on several occasions). Many of Hodge's statements about his beliefs and perceptions anticipate later texts on witchcraft, suggesting highly specific beliefs about what counted as evidence of bewitchment, or at least of the supernatural, that date back before the re-criminalisation of witchcraft in 1563. For example, Hodge is amazed to witness an event that may seem less than magical to modern readers:

> ich saw such a wonder as ich saw not this seven year:
> Tom Tankard's cow, by Gog's bones, she set me up her sail,
> And flinging about his half-acre fisking with her tail
> As though there had been in her arse a swarm of bees – (1.2.30–33)

Hodge is, within the play, a ridiculous character, and it seems likely that the well-educated original audience of the play[130] would have regarded him as foolish for thinking that an unusually lively cow

---

129 The most likely author is William Stevenson, but cases have been made for John Bridges and John Still; see Charles Whitworth's introduction to *Gammer Gurton's Needle* by Mr. S, edited by Charles Whitworth (London: A. & C. Black, 1997), p. xiii–xv. References, given in parentheses, are to this edition.
130 Assuming the quarto's title page can be trusted, the play was acted 'in Christes Colledge in Cambridge'.

was a 'wonder'. Nevertheless, similar testimony would later come up in one of the most infamous early trials. In the 1582 trial of witches as St Osyth in Essex, Elizabeth Ewstace was accused of making hogs 'skippe and leape aboute the yarde in a straunge sorte'.[131]

The credulous Hodge almost becomes a witch himself at one stage, when he swears to serve the trickster Diccon and seals the bargain by placing his hand on Diccon's buttock and kissing his 'breech'. The play's editor considers this to be a '[c]oarse parody of a solemn oath taken on a cross' (II.1.68–76 SD and note), and it can be read as such; but as Bruce Boehrer points out, it also resembles the oaths of allegiance sworn by witches to the devil, which often featured buttock-kissing in European sources.[132] In the conjuring scene that follows, Diccon insists that Hodge remain inside a magical circle for protection from the devil, who Diccon proposes to summon in order to find the needle.[133] In his fear, Hodge loses control of his bowels, and when Diccon comments that he can smell the devil coming, Hodge flees. This is medieval jest-book treatment of the diabolical, and in that sense follows established tradition. Importantly, however, the devil is not really present in this scene.

The obscene oath taken by Hodge is one aspect of a wider concern with oaths and swearing within the play, a concern which is linked to the play's anti-Catholic stance. Throughout the play, a variety of the characters swear various colourful oaths: Dame Chat swears by several saints (II.2.33–34), and Hodge and Diccon repeatedly swear by 'Gog's soul' or 'Gog's bones'. The unsympathetic and aptly named curate Dr Rat, a representative of the Catholic Church of whom the play is obviously critical, is most telling when he refuses to believe Dame Chat because she has not sworn an oath: 'Only upon a bare "nay" she saith it was not I' (V.2.39). Gammer Gurton, similarly, seems to think a bare assertion is not enough, saying of Dame Chat 'Ye know she could do little and she could

---

[131] W. W., *A True and Just Recorde, of the Information, Examination and Confession of all the Witches, taken at S. Oses in the countie of Essex* (London, 1582), sig. C7ᵛ.

[132] Bruce Boehrer, 'Gammer Gurton's Cat of Sorrows', *English Literary Renaissance* 39:2 (March 2009), 267–89 (p. 270). See also Clark, p. 14.

[133] This incident seems to be modelled on the story of Henry of Falkenstein; see Russell, pp. 89–90.

not say nay!' (v.2.161). The insistence on the swearing of an oath is similar to Diccon's, and perhaps similarly mock-diabolical; it is certainly in conflict with the scriptural authority so important to early modern Protestants.[134]

Despite – or because of – his continual swearing of oaths, Hodge is evidently untrustworthy. In the following act, Hodge's story about the summoning of the devil is embroidered considerably. Discussing Diccon, Hodge tells Gammer Gurton that

HODGE	By the mass, ich saw him of late call up a great black devil! 'O!' the knave cried, 'Ho, ho!' He roared and he thundered! And ye 'ad been here, cham sure you'ld murrainly ha' wondered.
GAMMER GURTON	Was not thou afraid, Hodge, to see him in this place?
HODGE	No, and he 'ad come to me, chwould have laid him on the face. (III.2.12–16)

Whether Hodge is understood to be lying or merely allowing his imagination to run away with him, the audience can be sure that his claims are inaccurate since they have already witnessed the incident. The idea that Hodge might successfully defeat the devil in a physical fight also appears ridiculous, and not just because Hodge is a clown. One writer on witchcraft, Richard Galis, later wrote that he had attacked the devil with a sword, but this was an unusual claim to make. The idea of physical confrontation with the devil was regarded with great scepticism by Scot, who as noted mocked the idea of St Dunstan taking the devil by the nose.[135]

---

134 See, for example, Matthew 5:37: 'But let your communication be, Yea, yea; Nay, nay: for whatsoever is more than these cometh of evil.' Protestant authors tend to recommend great caution in the swearing of oaths; see, for example, William Perkins, *A Direction for the Government of the Tongue According to God's Word* (Cambridge, 1603), pp. 84–87.

135 Scot, v.8, p. 108; Richard Galis, *A brief treatise containing the most strange and horrible cruelty of Elizabeth Stile alias Rockingham* (London, 1579), sig. C4ᵛ. Scot comments of Galis that 'if you will see more follie and lewdnes comprised in one lewd booke, I commend you to Ri. Ga. a Windsor man; who being a mad man hath written according to his frantike humor' (I.8, p. 17).

One of the most revealing features of the play, in relation to the attitudes towards witchcraft which inform it, is the way in which the characters use the word 'witch'. Gammer Gurton is repeatedly called a witch by her rival Dame Chat, but the term is used simply as an insult rather than as an accusation of any supernatural crime. Nobody ever takes up Dame Chat's suggestion, or accuses Gammer Gurton of using magic, nor does anybody (including Gurton herself) feel that it is necessary to defend her against this accusation. The word 'witch' seems, in the absence of any law against witchcraft, to be no more significant than the word 'whore', which Gurton regularly throws back at Dame Chat.

Nonetheless, it is not clear that Dame Chat is wrong: there is something of the witch about Gammer Gurton, not least because of the intriguing presence of her cat, Gib. Although not a speaking part, Gib is a significant presence in the play, and there are intimations that there might be more to the cat than meets the eye. At line 1.4.28, Gib is counted as one of the people present in the house. Hodge, fearing that the house is haunted by a 'felon sprite' (1.3.3), sees the cat's eyes and reaches the conclusion that the fire is bewitched, eventually chasing Gib up the stairs (1.5.14–27). References to Gib's specialness continue throughout the play. Believing the needle to be in Gib's throat – as if the cat were itself demonically possessed – Hodge claims that 'ich know there's not within this land / A murrainer cat than Gib is, betwixt the Thames and Tyne; / Sh'as as much wit in her head almost as chave in mine!' (III.4.6–8). Of course, this line pays ironic tribute to Hodge's intelligence more than Gib's, but Hodge is not the only character to mention Gib with respect. At the end of the play, Diccon is sworn by Master Bayly to be 'of good abearing' to Gib, Gammer Gurton's 'great cat' (V.2.283).

Gammer Gurton's Needle does not deny the existence of witches; in fact, it seems to feature a 'witch' – that is, a person understood by her community to be a witch – as a character. But the play does present a highly sceptical attitude towards magic in general and towards oath-swearing Catholic 'magic' in particular. It is also remarkable for its charitable attitude towards the eponymous witch. Gammer Gurton is an absurd, and not particularly commendable, character, but at the same time she is certainly not unlikeable or threatening, let alone evil. Even her accuser, Dame Chat, does not seem to regard her supposed status as a witch as very blameworthy, even if the word can serve as an insult which conveniently rhymes with 'bitch'. The play, which probably dates from the 1550s, suggests what the attitudes of the educated gentry towards witchcraft might have been in the absence of laws making it a criminal offence. But it is also another example of a play which associates a witch, or witch-like character, with superstition, ignorance, and Catholicism.

Protestant debunking of implicitly or explicitly Catholic 'witchcraft' further complicates an evidently ambiguous attitude towards witchcraft and the possibility of supernatural events. The widespread Protestant conviction that miracles had ceased, or at least were not to be expected,[136] would seem to leave little room for the supernatural in early modern life, and it appears to have been important to the early reformers to demonstrate that miracles, which seemed to legitimate the teaching of the Catholic Church, were in fact no more than trickery. Under the iconoclastic Protestant regime of Edward VI's protector, Somerset, the Spanish ambassador van der Delft wrote as follows to Emperor Charles V:

> Many persons who still persevere in the holy ancient faith murmur greatly at the casting down of the images from the altars, and consequently a sermon was preached in the cathedral by a bishop, who explained to the people the reasons for the abolition of the images: and in order the better to persuade them he produced and exhibited to them publicly certain artificial figures which moved their heads, arms and legs, these figures having formerly been visited and venerated as miraculous.[137]

The exposure of what had been thought to be supernatural as trickery is a strand in Protestant thought which has obvious resonance with

---

136 D. P. Walker, 'The Cessation of Miracles', in *Hermeticism and the Renaissance*, edited by Ingrid Merkel and Allen G. Debus (Washington: Folger Books, 1988), pp. 111–24 (p. 111). However, Keith Thomas points out that the idea that miracles had ceased 'took some time to establish itself' (p. 147). The author of the manuscript referred to above writes that 'for trew and godly myracles ... although we are not now to requyre or looke for any for the confyrmation of o[u]r faythe bicause the myracles already done and mencyoned in ye scriptures are suffycient yeat ys ther nothinge yt I knowe in dyvynytie to p[er]swade vs that God hathe so vtterly determyned to cease fro[m] all suche myracles yt he will never shewe any after Christs tyme & the tyme of his Apostles for yf we wyll not dyscredyt the hystories of all tymes & ages we can not ... deny but yt God hathe shewed some Myracles in all ages' (MS Harley 2302, fols 67ᵛ–68ʳ).

137 CSP Spain, ix (5 December 1547). www.british-history.ac.uk/cal-state-papers/spain/vol9/pp218–236 (accessed 11 June 2015). On van der Delft's and other contemporary assessments of the impact of the Edwardian Reformation see Diarmaid MacCulloch, *Tudor Church Militant* (London: Penguin, 1999), pp. 107–9.

the sceptical witchcraft writings of, for example, Reginald Scot. This attitude towards Catholic miracles has a protracted literary afterlife. Long after the Renaissance, Matthew Lewis's lurid Gothic novel *The Monk* (1796) features a statue of St Clare in the vault of a convent, a statue which is believed by the nuns to have miraculous powers. Dashing, aristocratic Lorenzo, the Spanish but crypto-Protestant hero of the novel, reveals the nuns' belief to be mere superstition:

> the Saint underwent a thorough examination. The Image at first appeared to be of Stone, but proved on further inspection to be formed of no more solid materials than coloured Wood. He shook it, and attempted to move it; But it appeared to be of a piece with the Base which it stood upon. He examined it over and over ... and discovered a small knob of iron ... This observation delighted him. He applied his fingers to the knob, and pressed it down forcibly. Immediately a rumbling noise was heard within the Statue, as if a chain tightly stretched was flying back.[138]

It transpires that Lorenzo has discovered a sensational, but not supernatural, secret passage, at the other end of which is his sister, who has been imprisoned by the Prioress. The ability of Protestants to cut through the darkness of papist trickery and superstition with the clear light of God-given sceptical reason was an important cultural trope which continued well into the eighteenth and nineteenth centuries. Seen in this light, Reginald Scot, who has often been seen as a radical figure within the debate on witchcraft, is actually quite orthodox.[139] While his view of the nature of spirit is certainly unusual, his anti-Catholic rhetoric and his dedication to the exposure of superstition and trickery are reassuringly mainstream. As has often been pointed out, Samuel Harsnett – certainly an orthodox figure, since he eventually rose to become Archbishop of York – produced arguments influenced by Scot in his dispute with John Darrel.[140] It has also been shown that Calvin himself, in his role as the leading

---

138 Matthew Lewis, *The Monk* (London: Bibliolis, 2010), p. 263.
139 The view of Scot as unorthodox has recently been called into question, however: see Glyn Parry, *The Arch-Conjuror of England* (New Haven: Yale University Press, 2011) pp. 207–08; Elmer, *Witchcraft, Witch-Hunting, and Politics*, pp. 18–24; and Pierre Kapitaniak, 'Reginald Scot and the Circles of Power: Witchcraft, Anti-Catholicism and Faction Politics', in Marcus Harmes and Victoria Bladen (eds), *Supernatural and Secular Power in Early Modern England* (Farnham: Ashgate, 2015).
140 Davies, p. 387.

member of the Genevan Consistory, seems to have displayed considerable scepticism towards accusations of witchcraft.[141]

However, while the Protestant Reformation in England had a strongly sceptical strand to it, it is also associated with greater emphasis being placed on the role of the devil. The devil had been a less important feature of medieval religion; in fact, the medieval mystic Julian of Norwich, encountering the devil in a dream, laughed contemptuously at his weakness.[142] Medieval jestbooks and plays often treated the devil as a buffoonish character, easily tricked or even defeated in physical combat by a human being. The Reformation saw the devil adopt a more central role in Christian thought – not least because Catholic and Protestant polemicists kept accusing each other of serving him.[143] In England, the devil's role as a tempter became increasingly prominent, and the danger that he posed became more pervasive because he was able to win men and women to him by exploiting everyday means, especially the temptations of the flesh. These developments in attitudes towards the devil came to form part of a characteristically Protestant conception of evil.[144]

Witches, according to the theorists who described them, were servants of the devil, a kind of anti-Christian fifth column who had made their pact with Satan and, in doing so, broken with Christ and with God. It was intellectually tenable to hold both that witches themselves were powerless – that genuinely supernatural magic was impossible – and that witches were servants of the devil capable of causing great harm indirectly by virtue of their relationship with their master. The devil sought to win the souls of witches by carrying out, or appearing to carry out, their sinful commands, thereby binding them to him all the more securely. Once again, scepticism and credulity about witchcraft turn out to be much more compatible than they might at first seem.

---

141 Jeffrey R. Watt, 'Calvin's Geneva Confronts Magic and Witchcraft: The Evidence from the Consistory', *Journal of Early Modern History* 17 (2013), 215–44. The Consistory was a 'quasi-tribunal' responsible for 'the enforcement of Reformed morality' in Geneva (p. 215).
142 Darren Oldridge, *The Devil in Tudor and Stuart England* (Stroud: The History Press, 2010), p. 37. However, Russell points out that the devil, while becoming less important to theologians in the late medieval period, simultaneously became more important in popular culture and art (p. 161).
143 Oldridge, p. 20.
144 Nathan Johnstone, *The Devil and Demonism in Early Modern England* (Cambridge: Cambridge University Press, 2006), p. 19. See also Chapter 4 of the present book.

2
Witchcraft in Elizabethan drama

Witchcraft is more frequently associated with the Jacobean theatre than the Elizabethan, despite the fact that, outside the theatre, witchcraft persecution in England seems to have peaked in the 1580s and 1590s. This focus on the later period is partly a matter of modern perceptions and the canonical status of *Macbeth*, whose witches have overshadowed those in earlier plays in many critical discussions. However, it is also the case that witchcraft in Elizabethan drama is curiously absent, even in those plays in which it is present. The witches that appear in Elizabethan theatre are distanced from those represented in the purportedly factual texts of demonologists and pamphleteers, ensuring that it would have been possible for contemporary audiences to interpret stage witchcraft as fictional, and unrelated to the type of witchcraft they encountered outside the theatre. In consequence, both belief in and scepticism about the phenomenon of witchcraft remain, for the most part, submerged. Nonetheless, latent scepticism about witchcraft – magic carried out by women – can be seen to have shaped the representation of stage witches to a considerable extent.

The issue of scepticism in Elizabethan attitudes to witchcraft intersects with questions of gender, class, and attitudes towards magic more generally. While the fear of witchcraft was seemingly at its highest point in Elizabethan England, this was also a period in which the power of magic – understood as a branch of learning open only to an educated male elite with specialist knowledge – was something that governments (including Elizabeth's) sought to exploit. This ambiguity about magic helped to shape the theatrical representation of both female witches and male magicians. The orthodox demonological view of magic that emerged in the early modern period tended to represent all magic as demonic. Distinctions between different types of magic, according to this view, were illusory, and all of the supposed 'varieties' of magic were equally blameworthy.

But a wider range of views are evident in the Elizabethan period, both in drama and in writings on magic. This chapter begins with a discussion of the relationship between gender and magic in early modern England, arguing that 'male' magic tended to be taken more seriously than 'female' witchcraft, and that representations of witches on stage tended to avoid 'realism' partly for this reason. The following sections develop and exemplify this claim, beginning with one of the earliest plays to stage a 'witch', *Fedele and Fortunio* (1584), which provides a particularly interesting example of the female witch as learned magician.

Another way to avoid provoking derision by representing ignorant and impoverished women performing powerful magic was to base witches on classical models. The use of such models has a distancing effect, allowing a controversial subject to be buried in a display of classical learning. Classical models also provide a way of avoiding awkward questions about the reality and efficacy (or otherwise) of witchcraft, since it was possible to regard the witches of classical antiquity as fictional. The witches of John Lyly and Robert Greene are primarily classical in inspiration, and an important classical source of witchcraft stories was translated into English at the start of Elizabeth's reign, *The Golden Asse*. The transformation of Apuleius's witches into fairies in *A Midsummer Night's Dream*, however, suggests an early modern capacity for non-demonological readings of classical myth.

It has often been remarked that witchcraft in Elizabethan drama is not taken as seriously as in several Jacobean plays.[1] Witches are not usually treated as unforgivably evil; in several plays, characters that could be described as witches are treated mercifully and ultimately forgiven, or even given a happy ending of their own. In several plays they are among the more sympathetic characters to appear. Part of what enables forgiveness to be extended to the witches in most Elizabethan plays is that they tend to be involved in comedies with strong romantic elements. A love comedy, by its generic nature, precludes the meting out of harsh punishments. Love magic is a phenomenon with obvious comic and dramatic potential, and one which tends to diminish the guilt of those carrying it out, since love leads to the matrimonial resolution demanded of early

---

1 Katherine M. Briggs, *Pale Hecate's Team* (London: Routledge & Kegan Paul, 1962), p. 59; Harris, p. 31.

modern comedy. This more lenient attitude towards love magic may have prevailed outside the theatre as well: when John Coxe, a Catholic priest, confessed to having used love magic in 1561, he may have made that confession as a means of self-defence, thereby anticipating potential allegations that he had used magic for more sinister purposes, perhaps even threatening the Queen's life: Michael Devine comments that at this time 'Coxe's admission of using love magic was not in itself a serious issue'.[2] Sympathy for at least one Elizabethan stage witch, Medusa in *Fedele and Fortunio*, is made possible on similar grounds. Love, so often described in terms of a metaphorical enchantment, defuses the potential threat of literal bewitchment.

While a seemingly sympathetic attitude towards witches holds for most of the period, the situation changes abruptly in the early 1590s, in a way analogous to, and coincident with, the change in the nature of witchcraft pamphlets detected by Marion Gibson and Barbara Rosen.[3] Hostile depictions of witches appear in several plays of similar date, and these witches are strikingly unlike the previous depictions of classically inspired hags. The witches in the *Henry VI* plays are not presented as fictional, since they represent historical people who were widely believed, or at least reputed, to have been witches with genuine magical power. At around the same time, *Dr Faustus* presents the first – and arguably also the last – depiction in English drama of a witch as a tragic protagonist (also, not coincidentally, the first and last male witch). *Dr Faustus* explores the psychology of its witch in detail and presents the first demonologically informed witch in English theatre – one for whom the characteristics of scepticism and credulity are essential features. With Faustus and the witches of the chronicle histories, witchcraft in the theatre becomes less fictional, less distanced from the contemporary world by the use of classical models, and considerably more hostile to witchcraft and witches.

---

2 Michael Devine, 'Treasonous Catholic Magic and the 1563 Witchcraft Legislation: The English State's Response to Catholic Conjuring in the Early Years of Elizabeth I's Reign', in *Supernatural and Secular Power in Early Modern England*, edited by Marcus Harmes and Victoria Bladen (Farnham: Ashgate, 2015), pp. 67–91 (p. 77).
3 Gibson, *Reading Witchcraft*, pp. 113–17; Barbara Rosen, *Witchcraft in England 1558–1618* (Amherst: University of Massachusetts Press, 1969), pp. 213–14.

Gender, scepticism, and magic in Elizabethan England

The reign of Elizabeth I saw the reintroduction of laws against witchcraft and the most intense period of witchcraft persecution in English history. Between 1570 and 1600, almost 400 people were indicted for witchcraft in the Home Circuit Assizes.[4] The people who were the subjects of these indictments do not form a representative cross-section of early modern English society. The accused witches were disproportionately poor, and disproportionately female: almost 90 per cent of them were women.[5]

That English witches tended to be female will not surprise many people now, but the case could be made that it ought to. As Norman Jones has shown, the witchcraft Acts were probably passed in response to a specific Catholic plot against the Queen in 1561; the conjurers involved in this plot were men. Conjuring and witchcraft were, at the start of Elizabeth's reign, not offences recognised by secular courts, and the punishments available to the ecclesiastical courts were 'too slender', as Edmund Grindal, the Bishop of London, put it.[6] The wording of the statute does not target women specifically,[7] nor does it refer solely to witchcraft. It uses the terms witchcraft, conjuration, and enchantment, seemingly interchangeably and without defining them.[8] The looseness of the Act's wording provided flexibility to an Elizabethan regime that was fearful of a wide variety of real and imagined threats to itself: a revealing phrase used by Elizabeth's spymaster, Sir Francis Walsingham, held that 'there is less danger in fearing too much than too little'.[9] No threat to the Queen herself could be ignored.

Before the Act against witchcraft had been passed, and perhaps afterwards too, many people may not have felt that magic was

---

4 James Sharpe, *Instruments of Darkness: Witchcraft in England, 1550–1750* (London: Hamish Hamilton, 1996), p. 109.These figures cover the counties of Essex, Hertfordshire, Kent, Surrey, and Sussex. The surviving assize records for the rest of the country are, unfortunately, much less comprehensive.
5 Sharpe, *Instruments of Darkness*, p. 108.
6 Quoted in Norman Jones, 'Defining Superstitions: Treasonous Catholics and the Act against Witchcraft of 1563', in *State, Sovereigns and Society in Early Modern England*, edited by Charles Carlton (New York: St Martin's Press, 1998), pp. 187–202 (p. 192).
7 Jones, p. 198.
8 v Elizabeth c. 16.
9 Quoted in Stephen Alford, *The Watchers: A Secret History of the Reign of Elizabeth I* (London: Penguin, 2013), p. 54.

particularly blameworthy. A poem published in 1563, coinciding with the passage of the new Act, seems to propose a change in how the moral status of magic should be understood. John Hall's *Poesie in Forme of a Vision* represents a meadow filled with herbs and plants (that might be used as magical ingredients), which the speaker visits when unable to sleep in order to indulge his love of astronomy (a subject associated with magic). But during his latest visit, he is warned by Theologus that the meadow is no longer safe to visit. In an unpleasantly vivid metaphor, the speaker is told that a 'heron foule' has ruined the meadow. Having eaten what it thought was an eel from the river Styx in hell, the heron developed a stomach ache and flew to the meadow to relieve itself, '[t]hinking as he was wont with Eles, / the same againe to eate'. Unfortunately, the eel, actually a serpent, slithers off into the meadow. The process is repeated until the meadow is overrun with evil, and Theologus warns all the unwary not to visit the meadow, now associated with 'Astrologie iudiciall' and 'Necromancye'.[10] The status of the meadow has been transformed, reflecting a view of magical activity as evil which the authorities may have wished to encourage. It is striking, however, that no blame is attached to the speaker of the poem for his previous activities in the meadow – provided that he stops visiting it from now on.

Once the laws against witchcraft had been passed, and despite the great scepticism shown by the Elizabethan authorities towards cases of demonic possession, questioning the reality of witchcraft could be regarded as a threat to order. One complaint recorded in state papers against 'Dr Brown the Phisition' states:

> He ys corrupte in iudgmente and obstinate and impudente in maynteyninge yt namely that there are no witches contrary to the lawes of god & the lawes of the lande from tyme to tyme executed and that openly before the benche at the maiors table, to breed contempte & mislikinge both of magistrayte & lawe.[11]

It is Brown's willingness to express his scepticism towards witchcraft, together with his reputation as a 'p[ro]fessed obstinate Papiste', that is said to constitute a threat to order. This claim suggests that Reginald Scot's work on witchcraft – entirely orthodox in its declarations of Protestant faith, opposition to superstition, and

---

10 John Hall, *A Poesie in Forme of a Vision* (London, 1563), sigs A7ᵛ, A8ʳ, A8ᵛ.
11 SP xv.25, fol. 212 (5 November, 1578).

anti-Catholic rhetoric – might also have been seen as troubling, and even politically subversive, in its main conclusions.

Witchcraft prosecutions in Elizabethan England overwhelmingly targeted women, but magic in general was far from being a female preserve. 'Cunning' or 'wise' folk – people who provided magical services for hire – included a large proportion, probably a majority, of men.[12] Higher up the social scale were magicians like John Dee. Dee was a mathematician, astrologer, and alchemist who offered his expertise to the royal courts of Mary and Elizabeth. Some of his services may have been genuinely useful, such as when he advised the explorers Humphrey Gilbert and John Davis on navigation.[13] But he was also consulted for his knowledge of alchemy and magic. According to his most recent biographer, Dee corresponded with Robert Cecil on a scheme to use spirits to enable spies to communicate instantaneously from overseas.[14] Despite his notoriety and his reputation as a conjurer, Dee was never tried for witchcraft; Parry suggests that he was under Elizabeth's protection because of her own interest in alchemy.[15]

One example of scepticism towards witchcraft, expressed by a member of the Elizabethan social elite, is revealingly qualified. Henry Howard, a younger son of the aristocratic poet of the same name, eventually became earl of Northampton and was a powerful courtier under James I. Howard wrote a *Defensative against the Poyson of Supposed Prophecies* (1583), in which he records the words of a curing spell he says was used by 'Mother Ioane of Stowe':

> Our Lord was the first man,
> that euer thorne prickt upon:
> It neuer blysted, nor it neuer belted,
> and I pray God, nor this not may.[16]

Perhaps unsurprisingly, Howard does not believe this spell to be effective, but the reasons he gives for his scepticism are not those that might occur to most modern readers. Howard's first objection is that Christ is unlikely to have been the first person ever to have

---

12 Sharpe, *Instruments of Darkness*, p. 189.
13 Glyn Parry, *The Arch-Conjuror of England: John Dee and Magic at the Courts of Renaissance Europe* (New Haven: Yale University Press, 2011), pp. 24, 84.
14 Parry, p. 50.
15 Parry, p. 213.
16 Henry Howard, *A Defensatiue against the Poyson of Supposed Prophecies* (London, 1620), p. 139.

been pricked by a thorn, and he points to the concrete example of Eurydice, Orpheus's wife. (Howard is uncertain about whether this legend is historical or fictional, and he concedes that it might not actually have occurred.) Howard's second line of attack is to suggest that Christ was in fact injured by the thorns that pricked him, arguing that 'Christ was perfect man in euery point, excepted only sinne, and therefore, men had neede be warie, that they scant not any parcell of his suffering.'[17] The assumption behind Howard's reasoning is that the words of the charm need to be an accurate statement of historical fact in order for it to be effective in curing disease; why this should be the case is left unexplained. Howard goes on to argue that

> as for the manner, it is altogether childish and ridiculous; and so much the worse to be liked as it runnes in rime, according to the course of Apollos olde weather-beaten Oracles ... the Woman is so fond and simple, as she speaketh onely like a Parrat, and is not able to deliuer any reason of her dealing.[18]

While the charm may in some sense be poetic, it does not rhyme and is not metrical, so part of Howard's claim is misplaced. But his main objection is to the general impression created by the charm, and, perhaps even more importantly, by the charmer. Mother Joan's 'fondness' and 'simplicity', and her inability to explain her supposed abilities in a suitably learned manner, undermine any confidence that Howard might otherwise have had in her. Howard is sceptical in this passage, but the reasons he gives for his scepticism indicate that he might reach a different conclusion in a different case.

Howard also stresses that Mother Joan is a woman, and this may itself have contributed to his lack of faith in her magical abilities. Howard's claim elsewhere that 'worthy Socrates' was in command of a spirit who brought him news of imminent danger reinforces this impression. Socrates was a learned man, and his relationship with a familiar spirit seems to Howard not only plausible but, apparently, laudable.[19] Furthermore, his scepticism towards female magic need not imply scepticism towards witchcraft, if witchcraft is understood

---

17 Howard, p. 140.
18 Howard, p. 140. A possible counter-argument appears in the Harley MS, whose author points out that 'the most exqysyte phylosophers wh[o] laboured all yt they myght to fynd owt the causes & reasons of all things do confess that many things are done of the wh[ich] no reason can be rendered' (Harley MS 2302, fol. 62ʳ).
19 Howard, p. 85.

as a bargain with demonic powers. He describes the execution of a witch at Cambridge, and claims that the devil demanded 'one droppe of blood' from her in exchange for his services.[20] It is the involvement of the devil, and his desire to obtain the witch's soul, that allows Howard to believe this story. While magic requires skill and learning – and therefore ought to be practised by men – all human souls are of equal value to God and the devil, which implies that the devil would be just as interested in acquiring the soul of an ignorant woman as that of a learned man.[21] Magic, in other words, is an impressive and dignified activity suitable for 'worthy Socrates', while any fool can become a witch.

A number of the earliest printed texts on witchcraft and magic suggest that those practising magic (certainly at the upper end of the social spectrum) were, if anything, more likely to be men than women. One such text is of particular interest in that its author wrote from experience. Francis Coxe, a self-confessed necromancer who got into trouble for his magical activities before the passing of the Elizabethan witchcraft laws,[22] wrote a confession in order to dissuade others from making the same mistake. Coxe provides a list of historical figures who practised various forms of magic, only one of whom (Joan of Arc) is female. He also supports his position with reference to the Bible, but Coxe does not quote Exodus 22:18 ('Thou shalt not suffre a witche to liue' in the 1560 Geneva Bible) which was probably the most cited scriptural comment on witchcraft. Instead he chooses the more gender-neutral passages from Leviticus 20:27 (Coxe renders this as 'if a man or woman have a spirite of diuination or soothsaying in them: they shall dye the death') and Deuteronomy 18:10–12 (which refers, according to Coxe, to 'wythcraft' but also to a variety of users of magic, including the male form 'sorcerer').[23]

---

20 Howard, p. 90.
21 The doctrine of 'equal souls' established that men and women of all social classes, while not equal in terms of their rights on earth, were equal in terms of their value in the sight of God. Scriptural support for this position can be found in, for example, Galatians 3:28, which encompasses what Terry Eagleton has famously called the 'leftist Holy Trinity' of race, class, and gender: 'There is neither Jew nor Greek, there is neither bond nor free, there is neither male nor female: for ye are all one in Christ Jesus.' See Terry Eagleton, *Myths of Power: A Marxist Study of the Brontës* (Basingstoke: Palgrave Macmillan, 2005, first published 1975), p. xiv.
22 Coxe's story is told in Jones, pp. 193–96.
23 Francis Coxe, *A Short Treatise Declaringe the Detestable Wickednesse of Magicall Sciences* (London, 1561), n.p.

The first demonological texts to be printed in English are translations of two works by Protestant theologians. These texts have frequently been overshadowed by Reginald Scot, the first 'native' English demonologist, but they make interesting reading, not least with regard to the issue of gender. The first of the two texts is *A Dialogue of Witches, in Foretime Named Lot-tellers, and now commonly called Sorcerers* (1575), a translation by Thomas Twyne of the French Calvinist theologian and demonologist Lambert Daneau's *Dialogus de veneficiis* (1564). The full English title of this work uses both masculine and feminine terms for magic-users, seemingly making no distinction between them. The main text frequently refers to 'witches, and sorcerers' rather than just witches, and the very first page specifies that 'both men & women' are guilty of the crime – no indication is given that women are the more likely culprits. When a pronoun is used to describe a witch or sorcerer it tends to be a male one.[24]

Some writings by Flemish theologian Andreas Hyperius relating to witchcraft were published a few years after Daneau's text. Hyperius, who eventually became professor of theology at Marburg, had lived in England for several years during the reign of Henry VIII, and several of his works were translated into English; others were published in Latin in London. One anonymous translation, *Two Common Places Taken out of Andreas Hyperius* (1581), repeatedly refers to users of magic as male.[25] But Hyperius also distinguishes between different types of magic, identifying three broad categories: 'witchcrafte or iugling', which is concerned with 'deluding the sences'; predicting the future; and what he describes as 'a certaine generall facultie of wryting diuers signes and miracles by the helpe of euill Spirites'.[26] All three categories are condemned, but it seems that the first type of magic is predominantly female, while the third relates to the kind

---

24 Lambert Daneau, *A Dialogue of Witches* (London, 1575), sig. B2r. Daneau refers to witches/sorcerers as 'wretched and detestable men' (sig. C2r), 'men' who have fallen into wickedness (sig. C2v), and 'wicked men' (sig. F3r), to take a few examples.

25 See, for example, Andreas Hyperius, *Two Common Places Taken out of Andreas Hyperius, a Learned Diuine* (London, 1581), pp. 75, 76, 81 (marked 44).

26 Hyperius, pp. 77–78. Within these three broad categories are a variety of specific types of magic that are very similar to those identified by the seventh-century author Isidore of Seville, one of the most important early Christian authorities on magic: see Valerie Flint, *The Rise of Magic in Early Medieval Europe* (Oxford: Clarendon, 1991), pp. 50–53.

of magic practised by learned magicians like John Dee, although Hyperius never explicitly says so. In his discussion of witchcraft, Hyperius uses Circe as an example of a witch and retells the Canon *Episcopi*'s story of women deluded into thinking themselves able to fly at night on the backs of animals.[27] When discussing the third type of magic, Hyperius refers to the male magicians of Egypt described in the Bible, who were able to produce false miracles.[28]

Hyperius is clear that all three types of magic involve some kind of demonic pact. He acknowledges the religious content of some magical ceremonies, but denies that this in any way condones magic:

> although otherwhile in such kind of prayers there seeme to be mingled certaine wordes that be godly, religious, and somewhat agreeing with lawfull inuocation of God, yet somwhat is alway found either in the words themselues, or els in ye rites and circumstances … that tendeth to the reproche of God, and wherewith God is tempted, blasphemed, mocked, despised, and therefore the deuill reioyceth.[29]

Hyperius regards the use of religious language and props in magical ceremony as blasphemous. This would presumably cover the activities of a witch like Mother Joan, whose charm referred to Christ, but it would also apply to learned magicians like the pious John Dee, who believed himself to be in communication with angels with the help of his scryer, Edmund Kelley.[30] Daneau, too, seems to target learned magicians rather than witches when he identifies ambition as the motivation behind witchcraft, referring to the 'vanitie' present in 'the harts of men' – the hearts of women are not specifically mentioned.[31]

While accused witches were usually female from the very beginning of the period of prosecutions, the first English text on the subject to draw attention to the issue of gender is Reginald Scot's. As Diane Purkiss has pointed out, Scot uses gender as part of his sceptical

---

27 Hyperius, pp. 79–80, 95 (marked 55). On the Canon *Episcopi*, see Stephens, *Demon Lovers*, pp. 127–34.
28 Hyperius, p. 103.
29 Hyperius, pp. 81–82 (marked 44 and 42); see also p. 98.
30 Parry, p. 174.
31 Daneau, sig. B8^v. While using masculine forms to refer to people in general is not uncommon in early modern – and indeed much later – texts, later witchcraft treatises often assume a female witch and consequently use feminine forms. George Gifford, for example, consistently refers to witches as 'she'.

argument.³² Where previous witchcraft texts used examples of male witches and sorcerers to emphasise the seriousness of their subject, Scot insists that witches are always poor, female, and ignorant in order to highlight the absurdity of crediting them with any power. Unlike previous authors, Scot presupposes that witches are female, describing them as

> women which be commonly old, lame, bleare-eied, pale, fowle, and full of wrinkles; poore, sullen, superstitious, and papists; or such as knowe no religion: in whose drousie minds the divell hath goten a fine seat ... They are lean and deformed, shewing melancholie in their faces, to the horror of all that see them. They are doting, scolds, mad, divelish; and not much differing from them that are thought to be possessed with spirits.³³

It might seem surprising to find this apparently hostile description in the book that, more than any other, attempted to undermine belief in witchcraft. But Scot's rhetorical strategy may have been more effective than it now appears: rather than attempting to generate sympathy for those who are 'known' to be witches – probably a hopeless task – he seeks to turn fear into contempt, later asking 'what an unapt instrument is a toothles, old, impotent, unweldie woman to flie in the aier?'³⁴ This approach to the question would probably have been persuasive to many – including, presumably, Henry Howard, who objected to Mother Joan's claims to magical power for very similar reasons.

In fact, even Scot accepted the possibility of some kinds of magic – natural rather than ceremonial magic.³⁵ The anonymous manuscript response to Scot's arguments points to this as an inconsistency in his thinking. The author complains that

> y[ou] confess a trew transubstancyatinge of woode into stones by the qualytie of certayne waters here in England, & that Coralle of hearbes in the sea become stones beinge taken thensse & why then can not he yt gave this forse to these insensyble things [i.e. God]

---

32 Purkiss, *The Witch in History*, pp. 64–65. It should be noted that Scot, while turning misogynistic attitudes to his rhetorical advantage on occasion, also criticises a double standard in the treatment recommended for witches and (male) conjurers, pointing out that 'though a conjurer be not to be condemned for curing the diseased by vertue of his art: yet must a witch die for the like case' (II.5, p. 26).
33 Scot, I.3, p. 7.
34 Scot, I.6, p. 13.
35 Scot deals with natural magic in book XIII of the *Discoverie*.

geave (yf he please) the lyke forse of transubstanciatinge things fro[m] that they were into things wh[ich] before they were not to wytches or dyvels[?][36]

While Scot regards the kind of 'magic' described here as operating according to the laws of nature, he is also prepared to believe claims which he acknowledges to be extremely implausible – such as the idea that the remora fish is able to bring ships to a halt – on the authority of 'so manie and so grave authors' (all of whom are of course male).[37] Scot may even have reinforced perceptions of what was already the reality of witchcraft trials; English witchcraft treatises published after his book tend to address the question of gender more explicitly.[38] Clearly, however, Scot regarded the fact that most of the people accused of witchcraft were female as grounds for an effective argument *against* the reality of witchcraft.

The foregoing discussion points to the existence of a gender gap in credibility between (usually male) magicians and (usually female) witches. Not everyone in early modern England would have accepted that this perceived gap had any real basis; as Robert H. West puts it, the 'only universally accepted distinction between the magician and the witch was that the former was more pretentious in his procedure'.[39] Some authors, especially those who were Calvinists, denied that there was any real difference between magic and witchcraft. George Gifford, for example, denies the significance of such a distinction, writing that, 'A Witch is one that woorketh by the Deuill … The coniurer, the enchaunter, the sorcerer, the deviner, and whatsoeuer other sort there is, are in deede compassed within this circle.'[40] Gifford's *Discourse* refers in its title to both witches and sorcerers; when his *Dialogue* was published six years later, its title referred only to witches and made even less reference to typologies

---

36 MS Harley 2302, fol. 57^v; cf. Scot XIII.5–6, pp. 292, 294. A more sceptical early modern discussion of the nature of coral can be found in Thomas Browne's *Pseudodoxia Epidemica* (London, 1646), II.5, p. 91.
37 Scot, XIII.4, p. 292. Remora fish are associated with witches as early as Lucan's *Pharsalia*, translated by Jane Joyce Wilson (Ithaca: Cornell University Press, 1993), VI.673–75: here they are used as a magical ingredient, and the idea that one remora fish is able to stop a ship 'despite a gale-force wind ripping through her rigging' is also mentioned.
38 See, for example, James I, p. 43.
39 Robert Hunter West, *The Invisible World; a Study of Pneumatology in Elizabethan Drama* (Athens: University of Georgia Press, 1939), p. 31.
40 Gifford, *Discourse*, sig. B2^r. Gifford does acknowledge that differences are perceived to exist, however, and dedicates a chapter to discussing the different terms employed for users of magic in the Bible.

of magic. William Perkins, in a work published posthumously just after the reign of Elizabeth, distinguishes between different types of witchcraft but makes no distinction at all between witch and magician, referring to all users of magic as witches.[41] For Perkins, all that is needed is an explanation as to why most witches are women.[42] The distinctions between different types of magician and magical practice made by Hyperius tend to receive less attention from later demonologists, in favour of more reductive positions which place greater emphasis on the demonic pact as the only source of any magical power.[43]

However, even those authors who refuse to accept that there is any real difference between (male) magicians and (female) witches accept that this distinction is *perceived* to exist. James I discusses two types of magic in his *Daemonologie* (1597). His terminology differs from that of Hyperius; he refers to 'Magie or Necromancie' and 'Sorcerie or Witch-craft'.[44] James establishes that the major difference between the two is a matter of motive rather than technique; practitioners of both are in league with the devil. Witches are motivated either by desire for revenge or 'greedie appetite of geare, caused through great pouerty', while magicians are seduced by their own curiosity. This establishes a class difference between witches and magicians: the learned magician can afford to be driven by curiosity, while the impoverished witch's 'greed' ('hunger' might have been a more suitable word) is what motivates her. The class difference, as the formulation above implies, is linked to a gender difference: witches are much more likely to be female than magicians. According to James's mouthpiece in the dialogue, Philomathes, female witches outnumber males by a ratio of 20:1.[45] There is also a gap in credibility:

---

41 William Perkins, *A Discourse of the Damned Art of Witchcraft* (Cambridge, 1610), p. 167. Perkins also refers to 'certain Popes of Rome ... who for the attayning of the Popedom ... gaue themselues to the deuil in the practise of witchcraft' (p. 10), showing that he understands elite male users of magic to be witches as well.
42 Perkins, pp. 168–69.
43 Stress on the powerlessness of the witch herself was a characteristic feature of most Calvinist writings on witchcraft in England: see Clark, *Thinking with Demons*, p. 449.
44 James I, p. 7.
45 James I, p. 43. A later author claims the ratio is 100:1; Alexander Roberts, *A Treatise of Witchcraft* (London, 1616), p. 40. Both authors appear to overestimate the gender imbalance, which on the basis of surviving records was closer to 10:1.

James acknowledges the existence of scepticism about witchcraft, writing that 'manie can scarcely beleeue that there is such a thing as Witch-craft'.[46] He does not acknowledge any such scepticism about 'magic or necromancy', presumably because he believes it to be less widespread among his readership, including at the very highest levels of society: James criticises those 'Christian Princes' who punish witches but employ magicians.[47]

The magicians themselves, in contrast to witches, were able to articulate an alternative point of view in print. The epistle to the reader in Heinrich Cornelius Agrippa's *Three Books of Occult Philosophy* (1650) claims that

> a Magician doth not amongst learned men signifie a sorcerer, or one that is superstitious, or divelish; but a wise man, a priest, a prophet ... the Sybils were Magicianesses, & therefore prophecyed most cleerly of Christ ... Magicians, as wisemen, by the wonderful secrets of the world, knew Christ the author of the world to be born, and came first of all to worship him.[48]

Agrippa stresses the holy character of magic, in a line of defence used long before by the second-century Platonist Apuleius.[49] He refers to perhaps the only part of the Bible that could conceivably be construed as supporting the practice of magic, especially since astrology was usually considered to be a branch of magic: the story of the wise men or magi who follow the star to Jesus in the Gospel of Matthew.[50] He even makes an unusual case for the existence of female magicians – 'magicianesses' – who are not witches.

Purity and piety, Agrippa claims, are essential characteristics of the successful magician. Among many other things, he recommends abstinence, fasting, and chastity to the aspiring magician, who must be a kind of ascetic[51] – which is perhaps unsurprising given that a

---

46 James I, p. 28.
47 James I, p. 24.
48 Heinrich Cornelius Agrippa, *Three Books of Occult Philosophy*, translated by J. F. (London, 1650, first published as *De Occulta Philosophia Libri Tres* in 1531–33), sig. A1^r.
49 See the discussion of Apuleius in the section '*The Golden Asse* and early modern witchcraft' esp. fn. 131.
50 A more orthodox view, put forward by Isidore of Seville, was that astrology was once permitted, but only until the birth of Christ, after which it was forbidden. See Flint, p. 53. Nonetheless, even Isidore considered the magi to be astrologers.
51 Agrippa, pp. 522–24.

number of reputed medieval magicians were members of religious orders.⁵² Another text provides the reader with a prayer that is to be recited as part of the ritual summoning of spirits. The prayer calls directly on God for aid in controlling the 'obstinate and pernicious' spirits.⁵³ The pious magicians are understandably eager to distinguish their own activities from witchcraft. The unknown author of the *Fourth Book of Occult Philosophy* (purportedly by Agrippa but usually regarded as spurious) accepts that witchcraft involves a covenant with the devil, and goes so far as to depict magic as the opposite of witchcraft, writing that 'the art of Magick is the art of worshipping God'.⁵⁴

Other magicians voiced similar views. Paracelsus, also translated into English during the Interregnum, protested in his work on *Occult Philosophy* that '[i]t were therefore very necessary that the Divines would learn to know something of this Art, and be experienced in Magick what it is; and not so unworthily, without any ground at all to call it Witchcraft.'⁵⁵ However, even though he defends magic, Paracelsus goes on to admit that

> it is a thing chiefly necessary to looke into this ART, that it be not turned into superstition and abuse, and to the destruction or damage of men; and hereby it is made Nigromancy, and Witch-craft; and at length, not undeservedly, so called by all men, because Witches and Sorcerers have violently intruded themselves into the Magicke Art, like Swine broke into a delicate Garden.⁵⁶

Paracelsus is a more ambivalent defender of magic than both Agrippa and his imitator. While he wishes to maintain that magic is lawful

---

52 One of many was John of Morigny, a Benedictine monk whose fourteenth-century text *The Flowers of Heavenly Teaching* is explored in Claire Fanger's *Rewriting Magic* (Pennsylvania: Pennsylvania State University Press, 2015). Other celebrated examples include Albertus Magnus (d. 1280), a Dominican friar, Roger Bacon (1214–92?), a Franciscan friar, and Johannes Trithemius (1462–1516), a Benedictine abbot.

53 Unknown author, *Henry Cornelius Agrippa His Fourth Book of Occult Philosophy*, translated by Robert Turner (London, 1655, first published as *Henrici Cornelii Agrippae Liber Quartus de Occulta Philosophia* in Marburg in 1559), p. 84.

54 *Henry Cornelius Agrippa His Fourth Book of Occult Philosophy*, sig. A2ʳ–A2ᵛ; cf. Apuleius, *Apologia*, translated by H. E. Butler (Oxford: Clarendon Press, 1909), xxv and the discussion of Apuleius in this book.

55 Paracelsus, *Of the Supreme Mysteries of Nature*, translated by Robert Turner (London, 1655, first published as *Archidoxa* in Krakow in 1569), p. 81.

if stripped of 'superstitious' ceremonies and based on faith alone, he cannot avoid admitting that the art can be abused. When it is abused, it cannot really be distinguished from witchcraft.

Paracelsus's concerns are understandable, since some of the practices outlined by the learned magicians themselves are remarkably similar to witchcraft – not the witchcraft that tended to be alleged in actual accusations, which were usually short on details as to the mechanics of the art, but the kind of witchcraft represented on stage, especially in Jacobean drama. Agrippa, for instance, provides recipes for what he calls 'suffumigations' corresponding to various planets:

> For the Moon we make a suffumigation of the head of a Frog dryed, the eyes of a Bull, the seed of white Poppy, Frankincense, and Camphir, which must be incorporated with Menstruous blood, or the blood of a Goose.
>
> For Saturne take the seed of black Poppy, of Henbane, the root of Mandrake, the Load-stone, and Myrrh, and make them up with the brain of a Cat, or the blood of a Bat.[57]

This peculiar list of ingredients mixes the biblical (frankincense and myrrh) with the vaguely scientific (the loadstone) and the gruesomely anatomical (brains and blood), and reflects some very widespread and long-lived beliefs about the dangerous and possibly supernatural properties of menstrual blood; Leviticus 15:19–33 handles the subject in detail. The recipe as a whole is also linked to astrology, as each suffumigation corresponds to a planet (in the medieval and early modern sense of the word). There is no evidence that Agrippa's text was a direct source for any dramatic representation of a witch. But the list of ingredients presented by Agrippa bears much greater resemblance to later depictions of witchcraft than do the descriptions of 'real' witches' activities in English trial pamphlets. Even when stage witches, like those in *Macbeth*, are female, they are modelled on male magicians as well as on female witches, and it may be that this was done in order to lend stage witches greater seriousness, despite the apparent silliness, from a present-day perspective, of their potions.

Distinctions in class and gender also made their presence known in the drama of the period. The existence of scepticism about witchcraft does not imply that nobody believed in the power of witches; the numerous prosecutions suggest otherwise. Nevertheless,

---

56 Paracelsus, p. 83.
57 Agrippa, p. 88.

most Elizabethan playwrights did not take *realistic* female witches seriously as dramatic characters. As Luce in *The Wise Woman of Hogsdon* (1604) puts it, in describing the title character:

> What can this Witch, this Wizard, or old Trot,
> Doe by Inchantment, or by Magicke spell?
> Such as professe that Art should be deepe Schollers.
> What reading can this simple Woman have?
> 'Tis palpable grosse foolery.[58]

The wise woman of the title is not a 'genuine' witch but a trickster who makes her living out of the credulity of her clients. Luce's speech is not sceptical about magic in the least – it is sceptical about the wise woman.

As H. W. Herrington suggests,[59] magic, if it were to be taken seriously by early modern audiences, needed to be practised by male characters, or by female witches who were clearly distinct from the 'real' witches, like Howard's Mother Joan, that people might have encountered in their daily lives. Despite the passage of anti-witchcraft legislation at the beginning of Elizabeth's reign, there are no extant plays from the first two decades of it to feature a witch. Scholars of witchcraft drama have remarked on the apparent absence of stage witches in Elizabethan drama, arguing that witchcraft drama is primarily a Jacobean phenomenon.[60] But the latter part of the Elizabethan period looks quite different. In fact, as Graph 1 shows, female magic users in drama are actually more numerous in the 1590s than they are throughout James's reign.

The perception presumably rests on the greater familiarity of the plays in which they appear rather than on the actual number of characters. When twenty-first-century scholars think of stage witches they think of *Macbeth*, not *Fedele and Fortunio*. Furthermore, witches in Elizabethan drama tend to be minor parts. Witches were not usually the focus of drama in Elizabethan England, but were present enough in society as a whole to appear in the background of the drama. This is evident in the work of the best-known Elizabethan dramatist of all. William Shakespeare's plays are packed with

---

58 Thomas Heywood, *The Wise Woman of Hogsdon* (London, 1638), II.2, n.p.
59 H. W. Herrington, 'Witchcraft and Magic in the Elizabethan Drama', *The Journal of American Folklore* (1919), 447–85 (p. 465).
60 Purkiss, *The Witch in History*, p. 185; Briggs, p. 77.

Witchcraft in Elizabethan drama

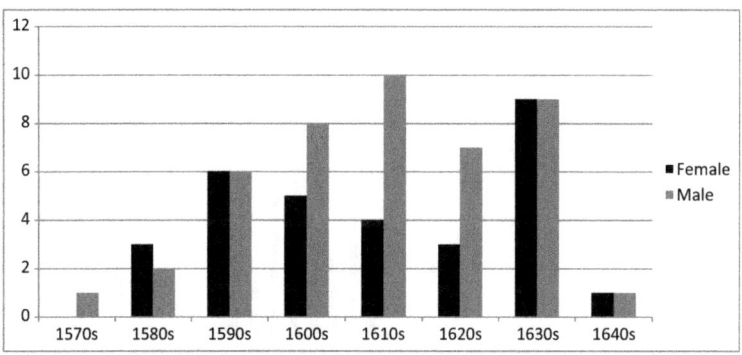

Graph 1 Printed plays featuring magic users, by gender
Source: Figures are compiled on the basis of the entries for 'witch', 'wizard', and related terms in Thomas L. Berger, William C. Bradford, and Sidney L. Sondergard, *An Index of Characters in Early Modern English Drama: Printed Plays, 1500–1660* (Cambridge: Cambridge University Press, 1998). Plays surviving only in manuscript – including Middleton's *The Witch* and Munday's *John a Kent and John a Cumber* – are excluded.

references to witchcraft, as both Diane Purkiss and Garry Wills have pointed out.[61] At the same time, however, 'real' witches only play a significant onstage role in three of those plays: *Macbeth* (discussed in Chapter 3), and the first and second parts of *Henry VI* (discussed in the section, 'Joan of Arc, Margery Jourdain, and the historical witch').

H. W. Herrington argues for a 1597 'vogue' for plays specifically featuring witches, and more recently Diane Purkiss seems to follow Herrington on this point, referring to 'the 1597 boom'.[62] However, Herrington's argument is based on assumptions about the content of three lost plays, chiefly on the basis of their titles – *Mother Redcap*, *The Witch of Islington*, and *Black Joan* (all 1597). The first two titles are certainly suggestive of witchcraft, but there is no

---

61 Purkiss, *The Witch in History*, p. 189; Garry Wills, *Witches and Jesuits: Shakespeare's Macbeth* (New York: Oxford University Press, 1995), p. 35.
62 Herrington, 478; Purkiss, *The Witch in History*, p. 181.

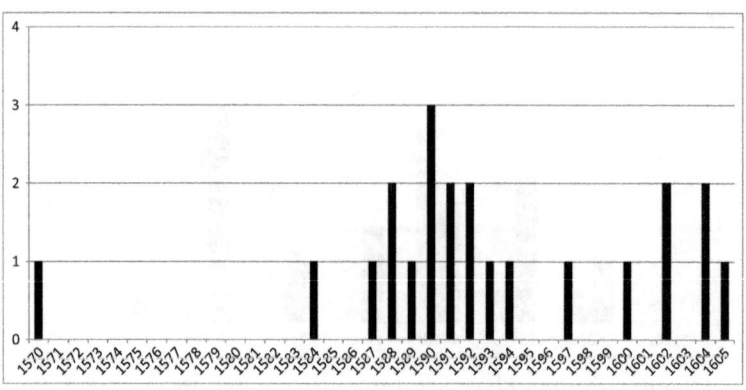

Graph 2 Printed plays with one or more character(s) identified as a user of magic, 1570–1605
Source: Figures are compiled on the basis of the entries for 'witch', 'wizard', and related terms in Thomas L. Berger, William C. Bradford, and Sidney L. Sondergard, *An Index of Characters in Early Modern English Drama: Printed Plays, 1500–1660* (Cambridge: Cambridge University Press, 1998). Plays surviving only in manuscript – including Middleton's *The Witch* and Munday's *John a Kent and John a Cumber* – are excluded.

reason to conclude that *Black Joan* was a witch play.[63] Whether three plays in one year really constitute a 'boom' or a 'vogue' is, in any case, doubtful. It is possible, however, to detect a cluster of extant plays featuring magic generally a little earlier than 1597, as Graph 2 shows.

Extant plays featuring users of magic in Elizabethan drama are clustered around the end of the 1580s and the start of the 1590s. While magic users of either sex seem to be few in number in the theatre of the 1570s, this is probably largely the result of the poor

---

63 Marina Warner, 'Old Hags', in *London: City of Disappearances*, edited by Iain Sinclair (London: Hamish Hamilton, 2006), pp. 431–39, notes that the name Mother Redcap is associated with witchcraft from the seventeenth century, although the play predates this (p. 432). The significance of the name endured for a very long time; C. L. Ewen cites a newspaper article from 1928 which reports the death two years earlier of a Mother Redcap who was apparently widely believed to be a witch: *Witch Hunting and Witch Trials* (London: Kegan Paul, 1929), p. 114, footnote 2.

survival rate of the romance plays that were frequently performed at the newly established public theatres at this time. Most of these plays, unfortunately, are no longer extant, but titles like *Herpetalus the Blue Knight and Perobia* (1574) and *The History of the Solitary Knight* (1577) leave little doubt that the plays bearing them were tales of knights errant and chivalry.[64] One surviving example of this type of play is the anonymous *Sir Clyomon and Sir Clamydes* (1570), which features a villainous enchanter, Brian Sans Foy. Sans Foy, as a character, owes very little to contemporary ideas about witchcraft. It seems likely that many of the lost romance plays of the 1570s contained similar characters.

It is therefore unclear whether the number of magic users on stage increased significantly in the 1580s, but the ways in which these characters were represented do seem to have changed. While the romance plays of the 1570s may have featured many characters like Brian Sans Foy, the cluster of plays from 1588 to 1592 presents a wider variety of magic users, from learned male magicians (Friar Bacon) to romance enchanters (Sacrapant) to classically inspired witches (Dipsas) to historical witches (Margery Jourdain). It also seems clear that after about 1594, magic seems to feature somewhat less than it had done at the turn of the decade; this difference cannot be accounted for in terms of the poor survival of plays, unlike the gap in the 1570s. The theatrical representation of magic in the later 1590s, if anything, seems to experience a slump rather than a boom.

Fedele and Fortunio: the female witch as male magician

It has been argued that the depiction of Elizabethan stage witches owed more to contemporary ideas about learned magic than to beliefs about witches and witchcraft as manifested in actual witchcraft trials. This can be seen particularly clearly in the case of a play from the decade following the boom in stage romances: *Fedele and Fortunio*. The play is remarkable for treating its female magician with a degree of sympathy that is absent in Jacobean dramatic treatments of witchcraft. Usually attributed to Anthony Munday, *Fedele and Fortunio* is an adaptation of Luigi Pasqualigo's *Il Fedele* (1575). The play is not

---

64 Cyrus Mulready, *Romance on the Early Modern Stage: English Expansion before and after Shakespeare* (Basingstoke: Palgrave Macmillan, 2013) provides an appendix listing titles and dates of stage romances, also indicating the prose source of each play where this is known or can be guessed.

well known, even among specialists in sixteenth-century drama: as recently as 2014, one scholar has described it as 'a play much neglected by critics of early modern drama and witchcraft alike'.[65]

The main interest of the play from the point of view of the present study is the character Medusa. Medusa is described in the text as an '[e]nchantresse' rather than a witch, and her literary pedigree is decidedly mixed. Medusa has learned her magical skills rather than bargaining with spirits for them, and she has an array of magical equipment which she displays to the gentlewoman Victoria and her maid:

> MEDUSA Heer's thinges will make men melt in fittes of looue,
> A wanton Goates braine, and the Liuer of a purple Dooue.[66]
> A Cockes eye, and a Capons spurre, the left legge of a Quaile:
> A Goose bill, and a Ganders tung, a mounting Eagles tayle.
> But sith they must be taken in thincreasing of the Moone:
> Before the rising of the Sun, or when the same is down.
> And closely wrapt in Uirgin parchment on a Fryday night:
> I will not trouble you with these.
> VICTORIA   Of more lets have a sight.
> MEDUSA Heer is the Image of a man, made out in Uirgin waxe,
> Which beeing prickt, or roasted in the flame of burning Flaxe.
> Hee that you looue shall come and throwe him selfe before your feet:
> More humble than a Lambe, to doo what you shall think is meet.[67]

Medusa's long list of magical paraphernalia – only a small part of which is reproduced here – includes items similar to those found in magical manuals like Agrippa's. In this respect she resembles later stage witches, like those of *Macbeth*; unlike them, however, Medusa displays her expertise in how these items are to be used.

---

65 Brett D. Hirsch, 'Three Wax Images, Two Italian Gentlemen, and One English Queen', in *Magical Transformations on the Early Modern English Stage*, edited by Lisa Hopkins and Helen Ostovich (Farnham: Ashgate, 2014), pp. 95–108 (p. 95).

66 The word 'purple' is presumably a mistake for 'turtle', since the turtle dove was associated with love.

67 Anthony Munday, *Fidele and Fortunio, the Two Italian Gentlemen* (London: Malone Society, 1910), l.369–81. Subsequent references to this edition are given in parentheses.

This suggests learning on her part – a suggestion that the play later confirms. At the same time, one of Medusa's practices, unusually for the extant plays of this period, does suggest activity usually associated with witches. The wax image of a man described above, which is ultimately used in a magical rite carried out after dark in a chapel, may have had topical significance when the play was first performed, coming quite soon after the scare caused by the reported discovery of wax images of Elizabeth I and the privy council in 1578. As Brett D. Hirsch points out, the parallels between the reports and the play are numerous.[68] However, the threatening nature of image magic is softened somewhat by its purpose, which in this play is to procure a husband. Image magic was more commonly used to cause harm and even death to its targets than to make them fall in love.[69] Furthermore, the ceremony is disrupted in comical fashion by the buffoon Captain Crack-stone, who frightens all the participants away when they mistake him for the devil rising from a tomb. This part of the action appears to be modelled on an incident in Horace's *Satires*, and the classical reference frames and perhaps distracts from any contemporary significance the scene might have had.[70]

Medusa tries to help Victoria attain the love of Fortunio, and in order to do this she tries to command spirits in the ceremony mentioned, which resembles the activities of learned magicians rather than witches. Many of the elements outlined by Agrippa are present in the rite she carries out – the use of water and oil, for example. Medusa invokes ancient deities: 'I coniure thee thou waxen Image here, / By *Venus* fruitfull wombe that *Cupid* bare' (527–28), and finishes her incantation with the words, 'Amen, *fiat, fiat*, in *Cupidoes* name' (550). The invocation of pagan deities again associates Medusa with elite ritual magic.[71] Although she attempts to summon spirits in this part of the play, Medusa later reveals that she was taught the art of magic by a 'doctor' rather than having

---

68 Hirsch, 'Three Wax Images', p. 155.
69 As Hirsch points out (p. 161), Reginald Scot claims that image magic can be used to induce love (XII.16, p. 257).
70 In Horace's poem, the god Priapus scares off a group of witches with 'a resounding fart'; the witches run away so quickly that they leave a wig and some false teeth behind them. See Valerie Flint (ed.), *Witchcraft and Magic in Europe: Ancient Greece and Rome* (London: Athlone Press, 1999), pp. 122–23.
71 Ronald Hutton, *The Witch* (New Haven: Yale University Press, 2017), pp. 237–38.

made a pact with demonic forces. She even hints at a romantic involvement with this man:

> O happie is I trust that Doctours soule by whom I learned,
> This famous Arte, and easely by it my liuing earned.
> O that he knew how deere his life and learning was to me,
> O y^t he could but for his death my griefe and sorrowe see. (1099–1102)

An audience member versed in demonology might have taken the view that this sentiment betrays Medusa's ignorance: the doctor's soul is unlikely to be happy, since he has probably sinned unforgivably in using magic. But such a view is not made explicit in the play, and subsequent events seem not to support it. Medusa goes on to defend magic stoutly when the maid Pamphila suggests that its use might destroy her reputation. Medusa rebukes her, saying: 'What talkst thou of thy name, and honour likely to be lost, / By learning of myne Arte? Which should be honord of the moste' (1107–8). Like the male magicians, Medusa is not slow to defend the reputation of her 'Arte'.

Medusa's defence of magic does, however, turn out to be mistaken. She is wrong to think that magic can provide her with a reliable income, as is later revealed when she complains that, 'My toyle so great, rewarde so small, / that euery man dooth giue, / hath made me weary of my trade, uncertaine how to liue' (1247–49). What appears to be an inconsistency is better understood as character development: Medusa has realised her mistake. This realisation happens implausibly quickly, since the action of the play fits into a couple of days, but such temporal inconsistencies are quite common in early modern drama. Medusa does not explicitly renounce magic, but when she helps Fortunio win Virginia she uses trickery rather than magic, and in the final scene she embarks on a new career. Following the marriage of Fortunio to Virginia, Fedele to Victoria, and Victoria's maid Attilia to Captain Crack-stone, Fedele unexpectedly 'gives' his servant Pedante to Medusa as her husband.

Several of the characters in *Fedele and Fortunio* are inspired by stock characters derived from classical theatre: Captain Crack-stone is a clear example of the 'braggart soldier', while Pedante is a 'clever servant'. Intriguingly, in helping Fortunio at the end of the play with trickery rather than magic, Medusa resembles a female version of the clever servant. The other three couples are married first, with various degrees of coercion for the female characters; Virginia, for example, has declared her love for Fedele throughout the play, but is ultimately married to Fortunio instead, despite her protests. The

Witchcraft in Elizabethan drama

marriage of Medusa and Pedante happens last, and it is presented as entirely consensual. Medusa may have found in Pedante a suitable partner; as he describes it, their marriage is one of '[l]ike vnto like, and learning to skill' (1783). After Medusa consents to marry Pedante, he sets out plans for their future together:

> Giue me thy hand, I'le set vp a great Grammer schoole by & by,
> We shall thriue well ynough, it will tumble in roundly.
> I'le teach boyes the Latin tongue, to write and to reade,
> And thou little wenches, their needle and thred. (1792–95)

Medusa and Pedante are not equal partners in this venture, of course, but of all the female characters Medusa is the only one whose situation is improved at the end of the play: from being 'uncertaine how to live' she gains an apparently sympathetic husband and a more respectable profession. It has been noted that Elizabethan stage witches tend to be let off lightly when they are brought to justice,[72] but *Fedele and Fortunio* is probably unique in giving its witch as happy an ending as any other character in the play. If the generally accepted date of the play is correct, then this play was performed during a year (1584) in which fourteen witches were accused at the Essex assizes alone – the highest annual figure on record for the county until the Hopkins witch-hunt.[73] The most sympathetic portrayal of a witch in all of early modern English literature was thus written and performed during a peak year in witchcraft prosecutions, and 1584 was also the year when Reginald Scot's highly sceptical *Discoverie of Witchcraft* was published. Whether or not *Fedele and Fortunio* is regarded as expressing scepticism about the possibility of magic, its unusually forgiving treatment of Medusa might be taken to imply scepticism about the persecution of witches. Such scepticism could have been provoked by the relatively high levels of witchcraft persecution that form part of the play's immediate social context.

Classical witches and Elizabethan prophecy

Elizabethan stage witches tend to be based on classical models to a greater extent than both pre- and post-Elizabethan examples. Robert Greene's *Alphonsus, King of Aragon* (1587) features a witch

---

[72] Katherine Briggs, for example, points to the 'gentleness' of Dipsas's treatment in Endymion (p. 65).
[73] Alan Macfarlane, *Witchcraft in Tudor and Stuart England* (London: Routledge & Kegan Paul, 1970), p. 26.

named Medea. Although this character has little in common with the Senecan or Euripidean infanticide, she bears a strong resemblance to another classical witch: Erictho from book VI of Lucan's *Pharsalia*. Like Erictho, Greene's Medea is a necromancer, summoning spirits of the dead in order to predict the outcome of a battle. Instructed by a stage direction to 'do ceremonies belonging to coniuring', Medea summons the spirit of Calchas, a seer mentioned in the *Iliad*, who objects to being disturbed:

> CALCHAS Thou wretched witch, when wilt thou make an end
> Of troubling vs with these thy cursed Charmes?
> What meanst thou thus to call me from my graue?
> Shall nere my ghost obtaine his quiet rest?
> MEDEA Yes Calchas yes, your rest doth now approch
> Medea meanes to trouble thee no more,
> When as thou hast fulfild her mind this once.[74]

This exchange, including the complaint of the spirit who simply wants to be left in peace and the promise of the 'wretched witch' to do so in return for information, resembles the discussion between Erictho and the shade of the soldier she summons in order to prophesy. The story of necromancy being used before a battle in order to predict the result (which turns out to be a defeat) is a powerful and enduring myth, one which appears in the biblical story of the witch of Endor in I Samuel 28. The necromancy scene in *Alphonsus* is closer to Lucan's version of the myth, however, since both texts emphasise the desire of the dead to be left in peace. Like Erictho, too, Medea is undeniably powerful;[75] the spirit of Calchas complains that he is 'Forst by thy charme though with vnwilling minde' to do Medea's bidding.

However, while Medea appears at first to be evil, her character is complicated in later scenes. Medea is praised as 'wise' by the goddess Venus, who speaks with particular authority by virtue both of her divinity and of her role as chorus in the play. She is also contrasted with a more straightforwardly unsympathetic oracle: the 'cursed god' Mahomet. Mahomet speaks through a brazen head

---

74 Robert Greene, *Alphonsus King of Aragon* (Oxford: Malone Society, 1926), l. pp. 953–59. Subsequent references, given parenthetically, are to this edition.

75 Whether or not the witch of Endor had any real power was a disputed point in early modern Europe, as was the nature of the apparition that spoke to Saul; see Stuart Clark, *Vanities of the Eye* (Oxford: Oxford University Press, 2007), pp. 242–44, and the section on *Macbeth* in Chapter 3.

(presumably the same prop was used in Greene's *Friar Bacon and Friar Bungay*), and delivers false prophecies which lead directly to the death of the various kings who worship and consult him.[76] Despite the name and setting of the play, Mahomet obviously has more to do with ancient Greek ideas about oracles than with Islam.

The contrast between Medea's honesty and Mahomet's deceit seems, by the end of the play, to establish her as a female magician working in the service of the state. This is particularly clear when she makes a second prophecy without the use of conjuration, as does Friar Bacon in another of Greene's plays after he repents his use of magic (discussed in the final section of this chapter), predicting the marriage of Iphigina and Alphonsus. Furthermore, all of Medea's prophecies, indeed all of her speeches, are aimed at securing peace and the marriage of Alphonsus to Iphigina, the daughter of Amurack and Fausta. Like Medusa in *Fedele and Fortunio*, she begins the play engaging in dubious activities, but is ultimately a force for good within the dramatic framework, helping to secure the happy ending that makes the play a 'comical history'.

Greene's classical witch was soon followed by several witches and prophetesses in John Lyly's plays. Lyly's only malevolent witch is Dipsas in *Endymion* (1588). Dipsas has been seen as one example of an Elizabethan stage witch who conforms to the stereotype established in the literature outside the theatre.[77] This judgement is largely based on the lengthy poetic tributes to Dipsas's ugliness, by the foolish knight, Sir Tophas, who is enamoured of her:

> O, what a fine thin hair hath Dipsas! What a pretty low forehead! What a tall and stately nose! What little hollow eyes! How harmless she is, being toothless! Her fingers fat and short, adorned with long nails like a bittern! In how sweet a proportion her cheeks hang down to her breasts like dugs, and her paps to her waist like bags![78]

---

76 This aspect of the play also draws on Lucan's *Pharsalia*. In book v, Appius is lulled into a false sense of security by the 'riddling oracle' of Apollo at Delphi (120–236). Apollo's deceitful prophecies put him in the position of the devil from an early modern perspective; cf. Syphax's appeal to 'hot-brained Phebus' in *Sophonisba*, mentioned in Chapter 3. (Phoebus is an alternative name for Apollo). In the German version of the *Song of Roland*, Muslims are said to worship Apollo (Russell, p. 84).
77 Christine M. Neufeld, 'Lyly's Chimerical Vision: Witchcraft in *Endymion*', *Forum for Modern Language Studies* 43:4 (October 2007), 351–69 (p. 355); Purkiss, *The Witch in History*, p. 188.
78 John Lyly, *Endymion*, edited by David Bevington (Manchester: Manchester University Press, 1996), III.3.55–61.

While this description does at first sight appear to align Dipsas with the 'village witch', it is equally applicable to the classical sources – Latin rather than Greek[79] – that permeate Lyly's work as a dramatist. Dipsas's unattractiveness alone need not imply that she was meant to be a 'realistic' portrait of a witch, and it is clear from other aspects of her character that the inspiration for her is classical. Her claim that 'I can darken the sun by my skill and remove the moon out of her course' aligns her with Medea.[80] All that separates her from the gods, in fact, is her inability to control love: this aside, she is able to transform her maid into an aspen tree, and is acknowledged by all the other characters, even Cynthia, to be genuinely powerful and wise in her knowledge of 'simples' – meaning magical ingredients, particularly herbs – unlike the stereotypically ignorant village witch. Nor is there any indication in *Endymion* that Dipsas is reliant on the devil or a familiar spirit for her power, which further distinguishes her from the kind of witches found in trial pamphlets.

Some of Lyly's other plays feature prophecies delivered by characters who are witch-like in many respects. In *Sapho and Phao* (1584), the character Sybilla has been granted a long life – but not eternal youth – by the god Phoebus.[81] She lives in a cave, and as she says to Phao, has 'wrinckles and furrowes in my tawnie face'.[82] She also appears, as her name suggests, to be a prophetess, and makes a long and cryptic speech to Phao predicting his future – a speech which, as G. K. Hunter points out, has no connection to the plot

---

79 As Kimberly B. Stratton and Dayna S. Kalleres, *Daughters of Hecate: Women and Magic in the Ancient World* (New York: Oxford University Press, 2014) point out, Greek 'witches' such as Circe are typically represented as young and beautiful, while Roman witches, such as Erictho, tend to be described as old and ugly (p. 46); Hutton points out that Circe and Medea are not really witches, or even human, and contends that pre-Roman Greece had no concept of the witch (pp. 58, 281). Some Roman witches, such as Meroe in *The Golden Asse*, are old and ugly but are able to appear young and beautiful. This characteristic reappears in Renaissance literature as well, for example in Spenser's Duessa in *The Faerie Queene* and, interestingly, in the male enchanter Sacrapant in Peele's *Old Wife's Tale* (1590). In Sacrapant's case the direct influence of *The Golden Asse* is evident, as he declares himself to be Meroe's son.

80 Lyly, 1.4.22–24 and note.

81 On the potential association of Phoebus/Apollo with the devil, see note 76 above and the section on *Sophonisba* in Chapter 3.

82 John Lyly, *Sapho and Phao* (Oxford: Malone Society, 2002), l. 390.

and may have had a topical significance which is now lost.[83] Many of Sybilla's characteristics – old age, ugliness, living outside of society, the gift of prophecy, and a bargain with supernatural powers – are all highly suggestive of common ideas about witches. But despite the obvious potential for presenting this character as a witch, and making her prophecies sinister, Lyly makes Sybilla something quite different. She is not malevolent, although her advice may be of questionable value, and no character accuses her of witchcraft, or any other kind of wrongdoing. In the pattern of contrasts within the play which Hunter describes, it is not Sybilla but Venus who is opposed to the virtuous Elizabeth-figure, Sapho.[84] In naming his character after the sibyls of ancient myth, Lyly associates Sybilla with holiness. Hyperius, for instance, regards the sibyls as divinely inspired, and St Augustine went as far as to pronounce the Erythraean Sibyl 'a citizen of the city of God' who had prophesied the coming of Christ.[85]

Lyly also produced a non-classical 'English' witch in the title character of *Mother Bombie* (1589). Mother Bombie of Rochester is a dramatic character, based on a folkloric figure, who may have been inspired by a historical person.[86] She is referred to in later plays – Heywood's *Wise Woman of Hogsdon* and *The Witch of Edmonton* – as well as in various other texts from the period. Reginald Scot claims that she was a cozener or trickster, while other sources describe her as a diviner, or as a witch.[87] She thus appears to have been someone about whom opinion was divided, as Scot acknowledges. Lyly's play, interestingly enough, presents her as benevolent, and blessed with the gift of prophecy. Mother Bombie is a sympathetic character, and the

---

83 G. K. Hunter, *John Lyly: The Humanist as Courtier* (London: Routledge & Kegan Paul, 1962), pp. 176–77.
84 Hunter, p. 173.
85 Hyperius, p. 94. St Augustine, *The City of God*, translated by John Healey, 2 vols (London: Dent, 1945), XVIII.23 (pp. 196–97). The witchcraft sceptic Johannes Weyer, however, suggests that the Sibyls were inspired by the devil: George Mora (ed.), *Witches, Doctors and Devils in the Renaissance* (Binghampton: Medieval & Renaissance Texts and Studies, 1991), I.8, pp. 21–22.
86 Scot claims that the historical Mother Bungie was a cozener, saying that he knows this 'partlie of mine owne knowledge, and partlie by the testimonie of hir husband, and others of credit, to whome (I saie) in hir death bed, and at sundrie other times she protested these things' (XVI.3, pp. 473–74).
87 See Almond, pp. 52–53, for a discussion of the relevant sources.

play makes a point of allowing her to deny the charge of witchcraft explicitly:

SILENA   They say you are a witch.
MOTHER BOMBIE   They lie. I am a cunning woman.[88]

Mother Bombie acknowledges her genuine magical power by calling herself a cunning woman, but (like a learned magician) posits an ethical distinction between witchcraft and benevolent magic. This distinction was denied by demonologists such as William Perkins, who regarded 'good' witches such as Mother Bombie as worse than harmful witches, since they harmed the soul rather than the body by leading the faithful astray.[89] The character Maestius in *Mother Bombie* expresses a similar view, but it is clear by the end of the play that he is wrong.[90] Bombie conforms in other ways to the witch stereotype: she is old and, as Silena unkindly comments shortly after the lines above, 'foul'. Nevertheless, it is clear that while Mother Bombie can easily be *mistaken* for a witch, she is not one.

Even Mother Bombie is not an entirely 'English' witch, or cunning woman. While she bears a much greater resemblance to the popular idea of a cunning woman or good witch than any of Lyly's other characters, Mother Bombie and the play she appears in are also influenced by the classical sources that suffuse Lyly's other works. Her prophecies are all delivered in a cryptic and punning style:

> In studying to be over-natural,
> Thou art like to be unnatural,
> And all about a natural.
> Thou shalt be eased of a charge,
> If thou thy conscience discharge;
> And this I commit to thy charge.
> (v.2.17–22)

Mother Bombie is a marginally better poet than Howard's Mother Joan, and it would seem that in her case 'Apollo's olde weather-beaten oracles' really have provided some inspiration. As the play's most recent editor points out, the play is set in a kind of Graeco-Roman version of England, with characters named Candius, Dromio, Lucio, and so on, and including servants who are actually slaves working

---

88 John Lyly, *Mother Bombie*, edited by Leah Scragg (Manchester: Manchester University Press, 2010), II.3.98–99.
89 Perkins, pp. 174–75.
90 Lyly III.1.61–63.

to secure their liberty.[91] Even in *Mother Bombie*, classical models are never far from Lyly's dramatic vision.

With the exception of Dipsas in *Endymion*, most of the witch characters in the drama of the 1580s predict the future rather than engaging in acts of *maleficium*. This tends to distance them from the village witches who were being tried in courts at this time, but it also connects them to a broader concern with prophecy in court circles. In December 1580, Edward de Vere, the Earl of Oxford, accused his former friends Henry Howard and Charles Arundel of sedition and involvement in a pro-Catholic conspiracy in which de Vere also confessed his own part.[92] Arundel's written rebuttal of the specific accusations made by de Vere reveals that the one he took most seriously related to 'a certayne boke of pictures, after the manner of a prophesie', which predicted the date of the Queen's death and the identity of her successor.[93] Soon afterwards, in the parliament that sat from 16 January until 18 March 1581, tougher laws against Catholics were passed, as well as legislation prohibiting anyone from seeking to predict the date of Queen Elizabeth's death or the identity of her successor 'by setting or erecting of any Figure or Figures, or by casting of Nativities, or by calculacion, or by any Prophecieng Witchcrafte Cunjuracions or other lyke unlawfull meanes'.[94] Howard and Arundel were never tried, and nor was de Vere, despite their counter-accusations; but the incident does seem to have provided the impetus for Howard's polemic against prophecy, published a few years later.[95]

Following these events, state papers record a number of potentially threatening incidents involving prophecies over the course of the decade. In 1586, at another moment of high political tension, two separate cases of people predicting the death of the Queen took place shortly after the discovery of the Babington plot.[96] It would seem that the court continued to disapprove of prophecy, judging by the peculiar dedications printed in John Harvey's 1588 work. His

---

91 Leah Scragg, introduction to Lyly, *Mother Bombie*, p. 11.
92 Nelson, p. 249.
93 Nelson, pp. 218, 274.
94 XXIII Elizabeth I c. 5.
95 Nelson, p. 220; see also Elmer, *Witchcraft, Witch-Hunting, and Politics in Early Modern England*, p. 26.
96 CSPD CXCII.51 (24 August 1586) and CXCIV.57.1 (22 October 1586). The Babington plot was a conspiracy to assassinate Elizabeth and replace her with Mary Stuart. Mary Stuart herself was subsequently executed.

Discoursive Probleme concerning Prophesies includes two dedicatory epistles, both addressed to the powerful courtier Sir Christopher Hatton. Oddly, the first of these refers to an entirely different work, a book on astrology with a 'short Astrologicall Prognostication, thereunto appending'.[97] This epistle is dated 20 August 1587. It is followed by a second, briefer epistle, in which Harvey explains his reasons for writing the later work:

> in modest hope of like Honorable fauour, I continue the like boldness in presenting your Lordship with a treatise [that] ... in regard of certaine speciall circumstances, both publique and priuate, may respectively minister some reasonable occasion, if not of more fauourable acceptation, yet haply of more inward liking. No man either knoweth better, or can deeplier consider, than your Lordship, how notoriously and perilously the world hath continually from time to time been abused, and in sort cosened with supposed prophesies, and counterfet soothsayings.[98]

The work that follows this grovelling semi-apology is a warning against credulity as regards prophecies, including astrological prophecies of the kind that Harvey had recently sent Hatton, who had obviously not appreciated Harvey's initial effort to impress him.

Prophecy was often perceived as a threat by the Elizabethan government during the 1580s, and was frequently connected to witchcraft.[99] But the Tudor monarchs had also traditionally seen prophecy as an opportunity. From Henry VII onwards, the Tudors made use of sibylline prophecy in order to support their legitimacy, and to justify some of their more controversial decisions, including Henry VIII's break with Rome.[100] As Jessica Malay has pointed out, Elizabeth herself was depicted as a wise sibyl in poetry in the 1580s.[101] This might explain the apparent interest in, and sympathy

---

97 Harvey, sig. A3r.
98 Harvey, sig. A4r.
99 On the threat of prophecy in general in Elizabeth's reign, see Tim Thornton, *Prophecy, Politics and the People in Early Modern England* (Woodbridge: Boydell Press, 2006), pp. 24–25. On the connection between witchcraft and prophecy see Daneau, 1 (n.p.); Hyperius, p. 77.
100 Jessica L. Malay, 'Performing the Apocalypse: Sibylline Prophecy and Elizabeth I', in *Representations of Elizabeth I in Early Modern Culture*, edited by Alessandra Petrina and Laura Tosi (Basingstoke: Palgrave Macmillan, 2011), pp. 175–92 (p. 177).
101 Malay, p. 187. Malay also notes that the earliest depiction of Elizabeth as a sibyl in extant poetry dates from 1585, and that the sibyl of Cumae was known for her virginity (p. 186).

for, wise prophetesses in the drama of the period, particularly that of the court playwright Lyly.[102]

While the role of prophetess and that of witch can potentially be filled by the same person, the 'witches' in the plays of Lyly and Greene are a far cry from those of witchcraft pamphlets in Elizabethan England. The use of classical sources allowed playwrights to generate a gap between the onstage representation of witchcraft and the perceived reality of it. This gap between stage and 'real' witches would have been evident to audiences, and even in a play like *Mother Bombie*, which made reference to a witch who was believed to have been real, the introduction of classical elements into present-day Rochester heightens the sense of this dramatic work as fictional, and the witch portrayed is thereby removed from the lived experience of witchcraft. To the extent that witches in plays of the 1580s might have had contemporary political significance for early modern audiences, this significance seems related specifically to prophecy rather than to witchcraft in general. The presence of both good and bad prophets reflects the ambiguous character of prophecy, which presented both a threat to stability and a means to ensure it.

The following sections study one of the main classical sources of witchcraft lore, the *Metamorphoses* of Apuleius, and a play which drew inspiration from it: Shakespeare's *A Midsummer Night's Dream*. Both works suggest surprising ways of reading what most demonologists considered to be the core element of witchcraft: the pact made between witch and devil. This important idea could be considered in isolation from witchcraft, and presented not as sinful and blasphemous but as light and harmless matter for comedy. Together with the evidence already considered, these texts suggest an Elizabethan theatrical and literary culture which typically preferred to avoid engagement with the assertions and ideas of demonology.

The Golden Asse and early modern witchcraft

Stories from the ancient world began to be disseminated in large numbers during the Elizabethan period. Between 1550 and 1660, there were around 200–400 literary translations into English per

---

102 On Lyly's status as 'court playwright', see Hunter, esp. pp. 132–58. However, Andy Kesson, *John Lyly and Early Modern Authorship* (Manchester: Manchester University Press, 2014) contends that Lyly's status as a court writer has been exaggerated (p. 12).

decade, with peak years during the Elizabethan era (1570–1600). Around 40 per cent of these translations are from a Latin original, making Latin the biggest source language for English translations during this period.[103] Not all Latin texts were necessarily ancient, of course, but a large number of classical works became available in English during Elizabeth's reign, and many of these works were influential as sources for stage plays.

Many of these sources are well known to scholars of early modern drama, and many of them represent witches, including several that were translated in the 1560s, at around the time of the anti-witchcraft legislation.[104] One of the richest classical sources on witchcraft is Apuleius's *Metamorphoses*, available in English after the publication of William Adlington's translation, which was entitled *The Golden Asse* (1566). In print just a few years after the Elizabethan Act against witchcraft was passed (in 1563), Adlington's text is a fairly free translation which, according to one scholar, 'does not so much represent Apuleius's words as transform them into a new and wonderful shape of [Adlington's] own creation'.[105] The novel contains a number of stories which were represented on the early Elizabethan stage. As well as the lost play *Cupid and Psyche* (1580–82?), Robert Carver refers to examples of a number of pre-Shakespearean Elizabethan plays which draw on Apuleius, including Lyly's *Sapho and Phao* and Greene's *Menaphon* (1589).[106]

---

103 Gordon Braden, 'An Overview', *The Oxford History of Literary Translation in English*, edited by Gordon Braden, Robert Cummings and Stuart Gillespie (Oxford: Oxford University Press, 2010), vol. 2, pp. 3, 9.

104 For example, Ovid's *Metamorphoses* (available in a translation by Arthur Golding in 1565), familiar to Shakespeare scholars, tells the story of Medea, and a number of Seneca's tragedies, most of which were translated and published in the 1560s by John Studley, Jasper Heywood, Alexander Neville, and Thomas Nuce, also touch on witchcraft.

105 Julia Haig Gaisser, *The Fortunes of Apuleius and the Golden Ass: A Study in Transmission and Reception* (Princeton: Princeton University Press, 2008), p. 293.

106 Robert H. F. Carver, *The Protean Ass: The Metamorphoses of Apuleius from Antiquity to the Renaissance* (Oxford: Oxford University Press, 2007), pp. 331–32. Brief references to the novel are fairly common in early modern drama: in *Endymion*, Sir Tophas expresses his desire for Dipsas to turn him into an ass, saying: 'I honour her for her cunning, for now, when I am weary of walking on two legs, what a pleasure may she do me to turn me to some goodly ass and help me to four!' (v.2.87–89); George Peele's *The Old Wife's Tale* (London: A. & C. Black, 1996) refers to Thessaly and to Meroe, who Sacrapant says is his mother (ll. 328–29).

The most famous example, however, is *A Midsummer Night's Dream* (1595), which will be discussed at greater length in the next section.

The witches in *The Golden Asse* are female and old, but in other respects they are completely unlike the village witches represented in English pamphlets of the late sixteenth century.[107] The first witches introduced in the novel are the sisters Panthia and Meroe. Meroe stabs her former lover, Socrates, in the neck and pulls out his heart with her bare hands, before Panthia recites a charm and seals the wound with a sponge; Socrates sleeps all night and does not die until he later drinks from a river, causing the sponge to fall out. The witches also urinate on Socrates' terrified companion Aristomenes, apparently for their own amusement. Nothing to match this was ever reported in an Elizabethan witchcraft pamphlet. The powers Meroe is said to command in the novel are virtually limitless, even including 'power to rule the Heavens, to bringe downe the skie, to beare up the earth, to turn the waters into hilles, and the hilles into runninge waters, to lift up the terrestriall spirites into the ayre, & to pull the Goddes out of the heauens'.[108] Meroe is also represented as lustful, a characteristic which is usually absent in English witchcraft pamphlets, where witches are more commonly represented as motivated by a desire for revenge.[109]

The Golden Asse's witches are certainly powerful, but it is unclear whether these witches were taken very seriously by its author, its

---

107 The difference between ancient and modern witches was often invoked by sceptical authors, and denied by those in favour of witchcraft persecution. Henry Holland, for example, denies any difference between the witches of Horace and Ovid and those of sixteenth-century England: Holland, *A Treatise Against Witchcraft*, sig. B3ʳ. See also Roberts, 'The Descendants of Circe', p. 187.

108 Lucius Apuleius, *The XI Bookes of the Golden Asse*, translated by William Adlington (London, 1566), p. 4. These claims are typical of ancient witches in Latin texts; cf. Medea's monologue in Ovid's *Metamorphoses*, translated by David Raeburn (London: Penguin, 2004) VII, 200–9 and Lucan's description of the Thessalian witches' powers in *Pharsalia* (VI, 461–506).

109 Charlotte-Rose Millar, 'Sleeping with Devils: The Sexual Witch in Seventeenth-Century England', in *Supernatural and Secular Power in Early Modern England*, edited by Marcus Harmes and Victoria Bladen (Farnham: Ashgate, 2015), pp. 207–31, argues convincingly for a sexual element in the familiar-witch relationship, but this did not emerge until the seventeenth century.

translator, or any of its early modern readers.[110] A degree of scepticism appears to be built into the text. The opening of the novel – like the opening of *The Late Lancashire Witches*, discussed in Chapter 5 – features a debate about the possibility of witchcraft. The narrator overhears a conversation between two travellers. One of them has been talking about witchcraft, and his companion openly mocks his credulity, calling the stories 'absurde & incredible lies'. The narrator – who is named Lucius Apuleius, but need not be identified with the author – takes the side of the believer, chiding the sceptical traveller for his 'obstinate minde and grosse eares'.[111] But whether Lucius is to be trusted as a source of intellectual authority is open to question; for much of the novel his main function is to be the butt of various cruel jokes. Lucius observes another Thessalian witch, Pamphile, transform herself into a bird by rubbing herself with a magical ointment; Lucius's attempt to copy her is what causes his own transformation into an ass. After his initial transformation – which he frequently blames on fortune, but which readers might conclude is entirely his own fault – the narrator is regularly beaten, threatened with castration, and at one point even scorched under his tail with a burning log. When in serious trouble, Lucius is usually able to escape by defecating on his tormentors.[112] His transformation into an ass, rather than a bird, is indicative of his basically clownish nature in the novel. Of course, within the stories, witches are certainly real. But in the brief debate about the reality of witchcraft staged at the start of the fictional work, readers might not wish to align themselves with the opinion of a character who turns out to be, both literally and figuratively, an ass.

The theme of transformation within the novel is further complicated by the numerous other 'transformations' that take place in it. Ovid's *Metamorphoses* depicts a range of divine, and therefore supernatural, transformations. Apuleius, on the other hand, depicts transformations of humans into animal form with entirely naturalistic (although not necessarily plausible) explanations. The robber Thrasileon, for example, is disguised with a 'Beares skinne, whiche

---

110 The case of Robert Burton suggests that early modern readers – with the exception of many demonologists – were less likely to believe in classical witches. Burton takes modern witches quite seriously, but dismisses the classical variety as 'poetical fictions'. See Burton, 1.2.1.2, p. 190.
111 Apuleius, p. 1.
112 See, for one of many examples, Apuleius, p. 77.

fitted him finely in euery pointe ... in such sorte that he seemed a very liuely & naturall beast'.[113] While Apuleius's transformation may be genuinely supernatural, the novel also acknowledges the existence of what Reginald Scot and other sceptics would later describe as cozening.

Despite these sceptical elements, and despite the evidently fictional nature of the narrative, stories derived from Apuleius's text were among those used in support of the existence of witchcraft by European demonologists. One version of the central story – the transformation of a man into an ass by a witch – is retold in the *Malleus Maleficarum*, often regarded as the most influential of all witchcraft treatises across Europe.[114] In Elizabethan texts, too, literary evidence was used in proving the existence of witchcraft; Gareth Roberts has pointed out the frequent references to Circe in demonological texts,[115] while Hyperius quotes from Ovid's version of the story of Medea,[116] and later goes on to mention the transformations of Odysseus's companions and of Diomedes. Agrippa, too, cites *The Golden Asse* in his discussion of the power of sorcery.[117] The ointment used by Pamphile may also have found its way into demonological theory. A number of early European writings on witchcraft tell stories of ointments used by witches for the purposes of transforming themselves and others into animals, as well as to facilitate transvection (witches' flight).[118] As Walter Stephens points out, witchcraft theorists tended to accept *The Golden Asse* 'as if it were scientific testimony',[119] and this attitude, while strange to modern readers, was based on perhaps the most solid of all theological authorities, St Augustine. Augustine does not quite embrace *The Golden Asse* as true, but he is at least prepared to consider the possibility that Apuleius's transformation genuinely took place.[120] For Augustine, the story is either true or it is false – in his comments on the book, he seems not to recognise the category of

---

113 Apuleius, p. 39.
114 Institoris and Sprenger, II.166C–167C, pp. 432–34, and footnote 547.
115 Roberts, 'The Descendants of Circe', p. 192.
116 Hyperius, pp. 79–80 (p. 80 is incorrectly marked 40).
117 Agrippa, p. 80.
118 Stephens, *Demon Lovers*, pp. 249–56. Stephens identifies Apuleius as the earliest source of stories about non-witches being transvected (p. 162).
119 Stephens, *Demon Lovers*, p. 162.
120 Augustine, *The City of God*, XVIII.18, p. 192.

fiction at all.[121] His authority led later medieval authors to follow his assumption that Apuleius's story was autobiographical.[122]

Adlington's attitude to *The Golden Asse* is quite different from Augustine's – more open to the idea of it as fiction, but also seemingly contradictory. In his dedicatory epistle, Adlington refers to *The Golden Asse* as Apuleius's 'fable or feigned ieste', which implies that he recognises it to be fictional. However, shortly after this comment, Adlington seems in his summary of the novel to accept it as true. He writes that

> the Author him selfe, traveled into Thessaly (being a region in Grece, where all the women for the most parte, be such wonderfull witches, that thei can transfourme men into the figure of beastes) weare after he had continued a fewe daies, by the mighty force of a violent confection, he was chaunged into a miserable Asse, and nothinge might reduce him to his wonted shape, but the eatinge of a Rose, whiche after endurance of infinite sorow, at length he obtained by praier. Verely under the wrappe of this transformation, is tared the life of mortall men, when as we suffer our mindes to be drowned in the sensuall lustes of the fleshe, and the beastly pleasure thereof: (whiche aptly may be called, the violent confection of witches) that we leese wholy the use of reason and virtue (which properly should be in man) & play the partes of bruite and sauage beastes.[123]

Adlington relates Apuleius's story as if it really happened to 'the Author him selfe', and he goes on to cite other examples of transformations, at least one of which he cannot have considered to be fictional – that of Nebuchadnezzar in Daniel 4:33 – as if to convince potential sceptics of the possibility that Apuleius's story really happened. However, Adlington also imposes an allegorical meaning on the novel. This supposed moral of the story is probably put forward partly in order to excuse the sexual and scatological content of the novel, but it also serves to cover Adlington's apparent confusion about the relationship of the novel to historical reality. Both Augustine and Adlington avoid a clear position on the question

---

121 Augustine does seem to recognise the category of fiction in his *Confessions*, however, where he writes disapprovingly of Greek myths as 'lying fables' [*falsis fabellis*] (1.10, p. 10) and 'poetic fictions' [*poetica illa figmenta*]: (1.13, p. 14). See also Nelson, pp. 14–15.
122 Gaisser, pp. 68–75.
123 Apuleius, sigs A2^v–A3^r.

of whether Apuleius's story really happened, but while Augustine simply reserves judgement, Adlington expresses both scepticism *and* belief, and ultimately turns witchcraft into a metaphor: a rhetorical figure which is simultaneously true and false.

Perhaps the most intriguing part of Adlington's translation is Lucius's eventual transformation back into human form. Having travelled and suffered much, Lucius sees a full moon and is moved to call on a goddess – at first referred to as Ceres but later called Isis – for aid. The goddess appears to him in the following form:

> first she had a great abondance of heare, disparsed & scattred about her necke, on ye crowne of her head she bare many garlandes enterlaced with flowres, in the middle of her forehead, was a compasse in fashion of a glasse, or resembling ye light of the moone, in one of her hands she bare serpentes, in the other, blades of corne, her vestment was of fine silke yelding diuers colours, sometime white, sometime yelow, sometime rosie, sometime flamy & somtime (which troubled my spirit sore) darke & obscure.[124]

This highly ambiguous description might have troubled some of Adlington's readers as well as Lucius. That she appears bearing serpents would have been a potentially sinister detail for any Christian reader,[125] as would the unexplained darkness and obscurity of her clothing. The goddess's association with the moon, seen both in her appearance and in the time at which she appears, could link her to various benevolent deities, in particular Diana, but there are other possibilities. She tells Lucius that 'the Phrigiens call me the mother of the Goddes: the Atheniens, Minerue: the Cipriens, Uenus: the Candians, Diana: the Sicilians, Proserpina: the Eleusians, Ceres: some Juno, other Bellona, other Hecate'.[126] The name Hecate, for Adlington's readers, aligns this apparition with witchcraft, and later in the text, Ceres is more consistently referred to as Isis – another goddess associated with magic and necromancy. The variety of names by which the goddess is known would not have troubled the readership of the Latin original, which would have been comfortable with

---

124 Apuleius, p. 117.
125 Snakes could represent wisdom as well as evil, but they were always a potentially disturbing symbol – one portrait of Elizabeth I from the last decades of the sixteenth century was repainted to replace the snake she was holding with a small bunch of roses; 'Portrait of Queen Elizabeth I (1533–1603) with a hidden serpent', www.npg.org.uk/assets/files/pdf/displays/concealedandrevealed/panel1.pdf
126 Apuleius, p. 117.

the rather chaotic nature of ancient religion.[127] But readers of the early modern English translation with monotheistic religious views, and familiar mainly with a clearly defined pantheon of Greek and Roman gods, might have wondered about who or what this goddess really was when presented with such an ambivalent description.

While she appears benevolent in so far as she restores Lucius to human form, Ceres also demands service from him in return. The act of 'unwitching' Lucius could be perceived as sinister, since this was, according to many English demonologists, precisely what witches did in order to win more converts to the devil.[128] The pact Ceres offers Lucius bears some resemblance to the bargain supposedly offered by the devil to prospective witches:

> [T]hou shalt liue blessed in this world, thou shalte liue glorious by my guide and protection, and when thou descendest to hell, where thou shalt see me in that subterren pace, shininge (as thou seest me now) in the darknes of Acheron, and reiginge in the deepe profunditte of Stix, thou shalt woorship me ... if I perceaue that thou art obedient to my commaundment ... I will prolonge thy daies aboue the time that the fates haue appointed, and the celestiall planetes ordeined.[129]

Adlington translates mythological terms from Apuleius's Latin into Christian-era English – the Greek underworld becomes 'hell'. Presumably most, perhaps virtually all, of Adlington's readers would have known this was not the hell ruled over by Satan, but the connotations of the English word may not have been entirely erased by this knowledge, especially given the Renaissance tendency to interpret Greek myth through a Christian lens.

Ceres offers Apuleius a charmed life in return for his devotion on earth and in hell; she even offers to extend the duration of his life. Both Marlowe's Faustus and Middleton's Hecate have been granted an extended life, having reached an agreement with the devil on this point. Ceres also refers to the lake of Acheron, which is mentioned quite frequently in early modern drama, often in an

---

[127] Deities with very similar functions and characteristics were represented by different names in different places, while the same name could refer to a variety of apparently different gods. See Walter Burkert, *Greek Religion*, translated by John Raffan (Cambridge, MA: Harvard University Press, 1985), pp. 119–20, and John A. North, *Roman Religion* (Oxford: Oxford University Press, 2000), p. 35.

[128] See, for example, Perkins, pp. 174–76; Gifford, *Dialogue*, sigs E4ʳ–E4ᵛ; Bernard, pp. 141–47.

[129] Apuleius, p. 118.

infernal context: Faustus swears an oath by Acheron, and *Macbeth*'s witches agree to meet there. Both the actual bargain Ceres offers and the imagery she uses offer support for an interpretation of this scene as a bargain between prospective witch (Lucius) and devil (Ceres). Many early modern authors interpreted the gods of the ancient world in precisely this way: the gods worshipped by the ancient Greeks were really devils in disguise.[130] That Lucius might have bargained with infernal powers would not have surprised any early modern readers who were aware that the author, Apuleius, was accused of, and put on trial for, using magic.[131]

The Golden Asse has the potential for an interpretation along distinctively early modern lines as a story about witchcraft featuring a demonic pact as its climax. The authors of the *Malleus Maleficarum*, after all, had used stories from Apuleius's novel to prove the existence of witches, and witchcraft ought to have been topical in England, having been the subject of legislation three years before Adlington's translation was published. Nevertheless, neither Adlington himself nor any of the dramatists inspired by *The Golden Asse* seem to have picked up on this aspect of the novel. Adlington saw the story as a moral allegory, or even as a piece of light entertainment. He draws no attention to Apuleius's bargain with Ceres as potentially infernal, but regards his transformation back into human form as an uncomplicatedly happy ending: evidence of Lucius's moral development, or even a religious rebirth. Dramatic use of *The Golden Asse* likewise tended to avoid the often grotesque and sensational witchcraft elements of the story, focusing instead on exploiting the comic potential of the various stories that the novel contains.

A Midsummer Night's Dream: witchcraft without witches

The best example of the tendency to lighten Apuleius's witchcraft material is *A Midsummer Night's Dream*. The play has frequently been linked to *The Golden Asse*, primarily on the basis of the

---

130 See, for example, Howard, p. 84. This interpretation dates back to St Augustine; see Stephens, p. 61.
131 In his *Apologia*, Apuleius argues both that 'magic is no other than the worship of the gods' and that magic is 'as mysterious an art as it is loathly and horrible', relying on a distinction between pious and impious magic also made in early modern Europe by learned magicians like Paracelsus: Apuleius, *Apologia and Florida* translated by H. E. Butler (Oxford: Clarendon Press, 1909); xxv, p. 56 and xlvii, p. 84.

transformation of Bottom into an ass, or at least an ass-headed man,[132] although there are certainly other Apuleian elements present. But one feature of *The Golden Asse* that is absent from Shakespeare's play is witchcraft. *A Midsummer Night's Dream* takes Apuleian witchcraft and transforms it, turning witches into much more sympathetic fairies in a process of sublimation.

It is difficult to judge how seriously fairy beliefs were taken in early modern England. Reginald Scot held such beliefs to be a thing of the past, and he appears to have expected his readers to accept without question his claim that fairies existed only in stories told by 'our mothers maids'.[133] However, other authors – among them King James – did feel the need to argue explicitly against the real existence of fairies. There can be little doubt that some people believed in fairies, given that the confidence tricksters John and Alice West succeeded in tricking several people out of their money by posing as 'the King and Queene of Fayries', apparently leaving one victim sitting naked in a garden, 'with a pot of earth in her lap, promising her it should be turned to gold in the morning'.[134] Intriguingly, while the pamphlet telling the Wests' story reveals trickery, it also claims that some of this trickery was carried out by means of witchcraft.[135] While the existence of evil spirits could not really be openly denied by any Christian, fairies did not fit comfortably into any theological category, and could safely be considered fictional. This does not mean that everybody considered them to be fictional, but it does mean that unbelief in fairies was a less controversial position to adopt than denying the existence of witches.

---

132 D. T. Starnes, 'Shakespeare and Apuleius', *PMLA* 60:4 (December 1945), 1021–50 (p. 1031); Carver, pp. 430–37. As Carver points out, several lines in the play suggest that the ass-head is meant to suggest Bottom's complete transformation. Using the head alone makes sense for practical reasons; having an actor dressed as an ass from head to foot would have been tricky to stage without resorting to a pantomime horse.

133 Scot, vii.15, p. 152. Interestingly, Chaucer also thought of fairy beliefs as outdated centuries earlier: Richard Firth Green, *Elf Queens and Holy Friars* (Philadelphia: University of Pennsylvania Press, 2016), pp. 197–98; Purkiss, *At the Bottom of the Garden*, p. 159.

134 Anon., *The Seuerall Notorious and Levvd Cousnages of Iohn Vvest, and Alice Vvest, Falsely Called the King and Queene of Fayries* (London, 1613); sigs A3^r, B3^r.

135 One of Alice West's victims was said to be 'stroke lame by her sorceries' (sig. B1^v); ironically this 'real' witchcraft helped to prove the reality of the 'fake' fairies. She was also able to produce 'some strong illusion' representing the king and queen of fairies (sig. B2^r).

Witchcraft in Elizabethan drama 99

As well as being less 'real', fairies were typically regarded as less sinister than other spirits. One of the earliest records of an Elizabethan witchcraft case details the interrogation of a sorcerer called John Walsh. According to this document, Walsh began by denying that he was in possession of a familiar spirit, but was apparently happy to say that he was able to tell whether people were bewitched with the help of fairies, probably in the hope that less blame would be attached to this admission.[136] A passing comment made in the *Daemonologie* of James I also suggests that working with fairies was generally considered less blameworthy than working with familiar spirits: when witches admit to using fairies it is said to provide 'a cullour of safetie for them, that ignorant Magistrates may not punish them for it'. James disapproves of this attitude and makes clear that fairy beliefs are delusions of the devil and that fairies themselves may be devils in disguise; nevertheless, he acknowledges that working with fairies tends to be judged more leniently.[137] The distinction between a fairy and a witch's familiar spirit was therefore less clear in early modern England than it would now appear.[138] This was even more so in Scotland, and it is no surprise that James writes about fairies in his work on witchcraft.[139]

A Midsummer Night's Dream replaces Apuleius's witches with fairies, and while this is a significant difference, it is perhaps not as drastic a change as it might seem to modern readers, used to thinking of these (if at all) as two entirely separate categories. Robin Goodfellow, the Puck in *A Midsummer Night's Dream*, illustrates the existence of this grey area when he admits his responsibility for many of the everyday misfortunes that could with equal ease be blamed on a witch. Specifically, he 'bootless make[s] the breathless housewife churn, / And sometime make[s] the drink to bear no

---

136 Anon., *The Examination of John Walsh* (London, 1566), n.p.
137 James I, p. 75. This strategy, of course, is the one used by John Walsh in his examination. James's view of fairies as either devils in disguise or diabolical illusions was the orthodox view of the medieval church by the thirteenth century (Green, pp. 14–15); however, as Green also points out, 'pastoral theology' was partly responsible for the view that fairies were 'less culpable' than other devils (pp. 22–23).
138 On witches and fairies see Hutton, pp. 215–42, and Emma Wilby, 'The Witch's Familiar and the Fairy in Early Modern England and Scotland', *Folklore*, 111 (2000), 283–305.
139 For a detailed discussion of fairies in Scottish witchcraft trials see Purkiss, *At the Bottom of the Garden*, pp. 85–115.

barm'.[140] Interfering with the churning of butter and the brewing of beer were two of the more mundane crimes of which witches were often accused, according to Reginald Scot and others.[141] Such activities could be attributed either to witchcraft or to fairies, perhaps depending on whether a suitable scapegoat presented him- or, more frequently, herself. The difference is that Robin's tricks are good-natured, and are balanced by his capacity to reward humans with good luck. Robin himself describes his activities as leading to merriment among humans. While possessed of the powers of a witch, Robin is freed from any real guilt, and is of course far beyond the reach of human laws. Blaming him for the failure to churn milk is, in effect, a way to avoid blaming anybody for what might have been perceived as an 'unnatural' event.

Titania's activities are also, in some respects, reminiscent of witchcraft. She and her fairies are said to meet

> on hill, in dale, forest, or mead,
> By paved fountain or by rushy brook
> Or in the beached margin of the sea
> To dance our ringlets to the whistling wind.
> (II.1.83–86)

These meetings take place in wild places, far from civilisation, just like witches' sabbats. The circular dancing described here also matches depictions of witches' meetings, including Shakespeare's witches in *Macbeth*, who dance an 'antic round'. But if these fairy meetings do represent something similar to witchcraft, it is witchcraft in reverse. While witches were thought to be able to cause natural disasters and disturbances in the weather, in *A Midsummer Night's Dream* it is the cessation of Titania's 'sabbats' with her fairies, and her dispute with Oberon, that have disrupted nature, causing 'Contagious fogs', the rotting of the corn while it is still green, and an abundance of 'rheumatic diseases'.

Oberon, like Ceres in Apuleius's novel, is a somewhat ambiguous figure, and his exact relationship with the 'damned spirits' mentioned by Robin Goodfellow is open to question. Robin clearly implies that Oberon and he need to work quickly to disenchant Titania and Bottom before the sun rises. Oberon denies that this is necessary,

---

140 William Shakespeare, *A Midsummer Night's Dream*, edited by Peter Holland (Oxford: Oxford University Press, 2008), II.1.38–39. Subsequent references to this edition are given in parentheses.
141 Scot, I.5, p. 11.

stressing the difference between the fairies and the spirits of the night:

> But we are spirits of another sort.
> I with the morning's love have oft made sport,
> And like a forester the groves may tread
> Even till the eastern gate, all fiery red,
> Opening on Neptune with fair blessed beams
> Turns into yellow gold his salt green streams.
> But notwithstanding, haste, make no delay;
> We may effect this business yet ere day.
> (III.2.388–95)

Oberon, in other words, tells Robin 'there is no rush – but hurry up'. The speech seems to have no dramatic purpose other than to state explicitly – in case anyone doubted it – that Oberon is not evil. This being the case, he cannot be allowed to fear the daylight; nevertheless, he cannot be other than a creature of the night, so he cannot actually appear on stage during the day.[142] It is impossible to believe that Oberon could share a stage with Theseus in the daylight; the fairies are associated with the night throughout the play, while Theseus is the ruler of the daytime world. Theseus and his court are associated with reason and light, while Oberon and Titania's world is linked to dreaming, magic, and madness. But these potentially sinister associations of the fairy world are redeemed and rendered unthreatening by the way in which they are consistently linked to romantic love; the age-old idea of love as a kind of madness turns the literal and figurative madness brought about by the fairies into a laughing matter.

The love affair between Bottom and Titania is another aspect of the play which suggests the influence of *The Golden Asse*, in particular its story of Cupid and Psyche (in which Psyche, like Titania, is made to fall in love with what seems to be a monster). It can also be linked to the scene in which Lucius, while in the form of an ass, is seduced by a 'fayre matron', although Bottom and Titania's relationship is more chaste.[143] But a more important parallel to the relationship between Titania and Bottom in *The Golden Asse* is the relationship between Lucius and Ceres. Titania, like Ceres, is represented in the play as a deity of some sort. Also like Ceres,

---

142 A previous dramatic representation of Oberon, in Greene's *James IV*, 'cannot endure the coming of morning light': Purkiss, *At the Bottom of the Garden*, p. 176.
143 Apuleius, p. 110.

Titania appears to offer Bottom, or perhaps impose upon him, a kind of Faustian pact:

> I do love thee. Therefore go with me.
> I'll give thee fairies to attend on thee,
> And they shall fetch thee jewels from the deep
> [...] I will purge thy mortal grossness so
> That thou shalt like an airy spirit go.
> (III.1.147–52)

This pact bears great resemblance to that of Faustus with Mephastophilis. Bottom is offered fairies to serve him, just as Mephastophilis is assigned to serve Faust. Titania's fairies will fetch 'jewels from the deep' for Bottom, just as Faustus intends to command his spirits to 'Ransacke the Ocean for orient pearle'.[144] Most striking, however, is Titania's promise to transform Bottom into a spirit. This is at the top of the list of Faustus's conditions to be fulfilled in exchange for his soul in the agreement he makes with Mephastophilis: 'First, that *Faustus* may be a spirit in forme and substance' (v.96). Neither Faustus nor Bottom actually receives this dubious reward; nonetheless, it is part of what they are offered.

Of course, the witch-pact Bottom is offered is a mock witch-pact, one with (almost) all of the horror taken out of it. Nevertheless, as Carver points out, there is a faint trace of threat left in the scene; Titania tells Bottom he cannot leave even if he wishes to, and binds him to silence.[145] Bottom himself rarely responds directly to Titania, usually addressing the fairy servants rather than her. He never indicates that he wishes to accept her offer of love, although he is happy to allow Titania to pamper him. In fact, Bottom barely acknowledges Titania's presence, preferring to eat hay and hold forth to his peers in the fairy world, the servants Peaseblossom, Mustardseed, Cobweb, and Mote. The play stops short of representing an actual pact between Bottom and Titania, but the possibility of such a bargain – and a faint sense that it might be a dangerous one for Bottom to enter into – lurks just beneath the surface of the exchanges between them.

The presence of witchcraft in *A Midsummer Night's Dream* is no more than a suggestion or an undertone, but it is an undertone

---

144 *The Complete Works of Christopher Marlowe*, vol. 2, edited by Roma Gill (Oxford: Oxford University Press, 1990), I.83. Subsequent references, given in parentheses, are to this edition.
145 Carver, pp. 441–42.

that a Renaissance audience would have sensed. The witches of Apuleius, themselves never taken entirely seriously, are transformed into fairies – which were more likely to be seen as fictional creatures in early modern England. The threatening aspect of witchcraft in the fairy world is never entirely neutralised – the fairies are, after all, supernatural – but it is sublimated to such a degree that even a witch-pact can be transformed into matter for gentle, mock-romantic comedy. *A Midsummer Night's Dream* demonstrates both how pervasive ideas central to witchcraft were in early modern theatre and literary culture, and how the demonological associations of such ideas could be rejected in favour of other, gentler, interpretations.

Joan of Arc, Margery Jourdain, and the historical witch

The discussion of witchcraft in the Elizabethan theatre thus far has suggested a theatrical culture which avoided representing 'real' witches in favour of classically inspired female magicians, prophetesses, or female characters who more closely resembled learned male magicians than stereotypical witches. It has also touched on one occasion when the representation of witches is avoided altogether, while retaining most of the elements of witchcraft. The witches discussed so far are evidently both fictional and stylised, in the sense that they do not aim for mimesis but retell stories which were often understood to be fictional rather than historical accounts.

The observation that Elizabethan stage witches tend not to be severely punished – *Endymion*'s Dipsas is forgiven, *Alphonsus*'s Medea is almost heroic, and *Fedele and Fortunio*'s Medusa is rewarded with marriage – was once explained by Katherine Briggs in terms of greater tolerance towards witchcraft during the Elizabethan period by comparison with the Jacobean, despite C. L. Ewen's pioneering work demonstrating that prosecutions actually peaked in Elizabeth's reign.[146] Ewen's conclusions were later given further support by Alan Macfarlane, and Briggs's position is now untenable.[147] But the 'masculine' nature of the magic practised by characters like Munday's Medusa and Greene's Medea suggests why it is treated as less blameworthy than witchcraft; they can be forgiven for the same reason that Howard does not condemn 'worthy Socrates' for his dealings with spirits.

---

146 Briggs, pp. 27, 76–77.
147 Ewen, *Witch Hunting and Witch Trials*, pp. 100–12; Macfarlane, *Witchcraft in Tudor and Stuart England*.

Witches in Elizabethan drama, in other words, are forgiven not because Elizabethan people had forgiving attitudes towards witches, but because they are not really witches. The exceptions that prove this rule are some of very few 'real' witches to appear in English drama during this period, and in these cases the usual leniency is suspended. It has been suggested that 'real' witches, understood to be poor and ignorant women, lacked sufficient gravitas to be considered fit subjects for theatrical representation. But the genre of the chronicle history play, which developed in the early 1590s, could accommodate genuine witches. In fact, some plays could not easily avoid including witches, since they were found in the sources which the plays depended on. The witches of the history plays are the closest thing in English drama to the witches of the trial pamphlets, although some important differences remain.

The most obvious example of a play representing a person widely acknowledged at the time of its performance to have been a 'real' witch is *1 Henry VI* (1592), in which Joan la Pucelle (Joan of Arc) appears and is ultimately tried (offstage) and executed as a 'sorceress'.[148] In presenting Joan as a witch, the play follows the authority of several chronicle histories, most notably Holinshed. Joan's identity as witch, however, is not entirely clear at the start of the play. She presents herself to the Dolphin as blessed rather than charmed:

> Dolphin, I am by birth a shepherd's daughter,
> My wit untrained in any kind of art;
> Heaven and Our Lady gracious hath it pleased
> To shine on my contemptible estate.
> [...]
> In complete glory she revealed herself.
> And, whereas I was black and swart before,
> With those clear rays which she infused on me,
> That beauty am I blest with, which you may see.
> (1.2.72–86)

There is a hint here of what is to come; Joan declares herself to be 'untrained in any kind of art', perhaps protesting her innocence of witchcraft before any accusation has been made. The transformation of Joan's appearance from dark to light – which she credits to 'Our Lady' – hints at the transformation of Satan into an angel of light

---

148 William Shakespeare, *King Henry VI Part 1*, edited by Edward Burns (London: Arden Shakespeare, 2000). v.3.217. Subsequent references to this edition are given parenthetically.

from II Corinthians 11:14, a familiar theme in witchcraft treatises. The French, though, are taken in by Joan's successes, praising her as divine and a 'prophetess' (I.5.47). They acknowledge that her power goes beyond the natural, but regard it as holy rather than demonic.

The difficulty of knowing whose side God is on, however, is summed up in a brief exchange between two of the French commanders:

> BASTARD   I think this Talbot be a fiend of hell.
> REIGNIER If not of hell, the heavens sure favour him.
>   (II.1.46–47)

Both the English and the French claim the support of heaven and condemn their enemies as instruments of the devil, making the play appear, in the early scenes, almost even-handed in its treatment of the conflict. But as the play progresses, it becomes clear that Joan is indeed a witch. Talbot refers to her as a 'witch', a 'damned sorceress', and even a 'railing Hecate' (III.2.37, 63). Even more tellingly, the French themselves seem either to be aware of Joan's witchcraft or, at least, to be drawing the audience's attention to it with dramatic irony – as when the French king asks Joan to 'enchant him [Burgundy] with thy words' (III.3.40), and, more subtly, with references to Joan's 'cunning' and 'secret policies' (III.3.10, 12) – ambiguous words which could in early modern usage be understood to refer to witchcraft, as well as the primary meanings. Indeed, there are moments when such use of irony appears to condemn all the French as demonic. Asked by Sir William Lucy where the English prisoners are held, the French king Charles replies: 'For prisoners ask'st thou? Hell our prison is' (IV.4.170). Charles means that he has sent the English prisoners to hell by killing them, but the line might also imply that the French will soon be imprisoned in hell themselves. Charles has a touch of Mephastophilis about him in this line, and audiences might have recognised the resemblance, as *1 Henry VI* is very close to *Dr Faustus* in date.

By the end of the play, Joan is captured and the truth is revealed. For the first time in the play, her familiar spirits appear on stage, gesturing helplessly when she asks for their help. Interestingly, she has not already concluded a full Faustian pact, although she has fed her spirits with drops of her blood. In order to save herself – and to frustrate the English – she offers to lop off a limb for them; when this is refused, she offers them her soul. The offer is again refused, but the fact that it can be made at all suggests that it has not been made before. If the representation of Joan in this scene is influenced by any textual source, it is not likely to be the writings of learned demonologists. The idea that a drop of blood might be enough for a demon is repeated by Howard, as mentioned, and similar ideas appear in Elizabethan trial pamphlets. It was even claimed that familiar spirits could be contented with being given milk to drink and wool to rest on.[149] The reformed necromancer Francis Coxe, too, suggested that magical power might be granted in exchange for the sorcerer giving up certain types of food.[150] Such ideas are obviously incompatible with the more theologically respectable positions adopted by James I, Gifford, Perkins, and others, which held that the devil would only ever be interested in obtaining the body and soul of the witch or magician. Joan's representation as a witch is closer to popular than to demonological views.

There is at least some doubt, then, about whether Joan's magical activities have necessarily led to her forfeiting her soul. Meanwhile, Joan's motivation might serve to mitigate her crimes to a certain extent, in that she is clearly a patriot, albeit a French patriot. Joan's relationship with the audience is more complex than the final scenes, on their own, would suggest. She sometimes makes ironic comments on the behaviour of the French, as when Burgundy agrees to betray the English. Joan says '[d]one like a Frenchman: turn and turn again' (III.3.85). In making this statement, Joan acts almost as a chorus, expressing a view that comes from a perspective distinct from that of her own character. In doing so, she guides the audience and takes

---

149 George Gifford has no truck with such beliefs but reports their existence (*Discourse*, sig. G3^r). Various pamphlets offer support for, and variations on, Gifford's claim. In Anon., *A Detection of Damnable Driftes* (London, 1579), Mother Smith is said to have kept three spirits: 'greate Dicke' in a 'wicker bottle', 'Little Dicke' in a 'Leather Bottle', and 'Willet' in a 'Wolle Packe' (sig. A7^v). Mother Smith, like Gifford, was from Maldon in Essex. The same pamphlet claims that a spirit was persuaded by Elizabeth Fraunces of nearby Hatfield to harm her neighbour in exchange for a 'crust of white bread' (sig. A4^v). In Windsor, according to *A Rehearsall both Straung and True* (London, 1579), Mother Deuell and Mother Margaret fed their spirits with blood, but also with milk and bread (sigs A5^v–A6^r). *The Apprehension and Confession of Three Notorious Witches* (London, 1589) similarly claims that Joan Cunny fed her spirits with 'white bread and milke' (sig. A4^v). Many Elizabethan pamphlets make no mention of any explicit agreement for the witch's soul.
150 Coxe, n.p. Coxe gives the example of a priest living near Bridgwater who promised to eat cheese instead of bread. Perhaps aware that this might strike some readers as quite a good deal, Coxe later adds that the sorcerer's soul was also part of the bargain.

them into her confidence, establishing the kind of closeness between villain and spectators that also appears in *Richard III*. While she may be a villain, Joan is also the most entertaining character on stage. She is even allowed to pass comment on some of the excessive hyperbole of the English. When Sir William Lucy, who is looking for Talbot, praises him at great length in rather conventional verse, Joan cuts him short with a much pithier speech – one of the most memorable in the play:

> Here's a silly stately style indeed:
> The Turk, that two and fifty kingdoms hath,
> Writes not so tedious a style as this.
> Him that thou magnifiest with all these titles
> Stinking and fly-blown lies here at our feet.
> (IV.4.184–88)

It is hard to guess how a patriotic early modern English audience might have responded to this speech. Booing and hissing might be one possibility, but Joan's occasional function as a kind of jester-cum-vice and choric truth-teller sits uneasily with such a response. Joan is right, too; Talbot is dead and Lucy is long-winded.

In her final scene, however, Joan is suddenly diminished as a character. Having been captured and condemned to death by the English, Joan is sought out by her father, a shepherd, whom she repudiates:

> Decrepit miser, base ignoble wretch,
> I am descended of a gentler blood.
> Thou art no father, nor no friend of mine.
> (V.3.7–9)

At the beginning of the play, when she joined the French camp, Joan drew attention (truthfully) to her low birth, specifically identifying herself as a shepherd's daughter – shepherds being, of course, holy as well as lowly. After her capture, however, she pointlessly lies to contradict what she told the French about her parentage. Soon afterwards, York calls her an 'ugly wench', implying that the beauty she claimed to receive from the Virgin Mary has been taken away again.

But Joan has been much more than a witch throughout the play. She does not fit the witch stereotype established in texts like those of Scot and Gifford; she is not based on ideas about learned male magicians; nor does she match classical models of witches, or the accounts of village witches given in trial pamphlets. The play acknowledges her to be awkward and unclassifiable, with its repeated punning on her name: she is a puzzle, as well as a puzzel (whore) and a pucelle (maid).[151] This puzzle is, however, drastically and jarringly simplified at the end of the play. Joan is pushed into a category to which she does not really seem to belong, hastily forced by the text into conformity with a witch stereotype that cannot easily accommodate her.

In an attempt to save her life, which is itself at odds with the defiant language she uses prior to her capture, Joan claims to be pregnant. In early modern England, this was a valid plea for any woman condemned to death and, if accepted, would result in a postponement of execution which, in practice, often turned out to be a reprieve. Perhaps surprisingly, pleas of pregnancy were quite rare.[152] It seems likely that Joan is merely stalling, but nevertheless, the extreme callousness of the English lords is jarring to modern readers: 'Strumpet, thy words condemn thy brat and thee', says York (v.3.84). York seems, in defiance of English law, not to care whether Joan is pregnant or not. How an early modern audience might have felt about this is open to conjecture, but it seems that Joan's exposure as a witch who has bargained with demons has severely compromised her position, transforming her into someone who can be disposed of without a second thought.

The treatment of Joan in *1 Henry VI* – the reduction of a complex and ambiguous character to a crude stereotype – may be a dramatic analogue of what happened in a number of actual witchcraft trials and the pamphlets associated with them.[153] *1 Henry VI* is perhaps the closest the stage gets to the reality of witchcraft trials. Despite all the awkward questions that Joan's execution raises, there can be little doubt that the play presents that execution as a desirable

---

151 Edward Burns, 'Introduction' to *King Henry VI Part 1*, pp. 25–27.
152 Sharpe, *Instruments of Darkness*, p. 111. Sharpe notes that 'some of the pregnancies recorded by the courts ... were legal fictions designed to allow the judge to extend clemency'. Alice Samuel, one of the witches of Warboys, was said to have induced laughter in court by claiming to be pregnant in an attempt to avoid execution; her age at the time was apparently 'neere fourscore'. Her unmarried daughter Agnes, according to the same source, did not plead pregnancy despite being urged to do so, on the grounds that she refused to be known as 'both a Witch and a whoore'. It might be suspected that this part of the anecdote, which provides an interesting contrast with Joan's behaviour, was added for its literary and didactic value (Anon., *The Most Strange and Admirable Discoverie of the Three Witches of Warboys* (London, 1593), sigs P3^r–P3^v).
153 See Gibson, 'Understanding Witchcraft?' and the introduction to this book.

outcome. Joan's rapid degeneration from the most entertaining character on stage to a caricature villainess who crudely advertises her own evil appears designed to encourage her scapegoating. It is hard to square Joan's representation with the widespread idea that the theatre tended to work against witchcraft persecution.

There are limits to the similarities between Joan and the 'real' witches tried in English courts. The most important is that Joan's witchcraft takes place in the realm of high politics rather than that of village-level disputes. Another of Shakespeare's chronicle histories, *2 Henry VI*, stages a similarly political act of witchcraft, when the Duke of Gloucester's wife, Eleanor Cobham, consults with the witch Margery Jourdain and the conjurer Roger Bolingbroke to predict the fortunes of the King and her husband's aristocratic rivals. As mentioned, it was this type of prophecy that had been made illegal earlier in Elizabeth's reign. This lends some topical significance to the scene while deviating from Holinshed, who writes that Bolingbroke and Jourdain were executed for practising image magic in order to 'waste and destroie the kyngs person'.[154] The cryptic predictions made by the demon Asmath[155] turn out to be both misleading and accurate, anticipating a similar use of prophecy in *Macbeth*. The magic is clearly effective and presented without any obvious condemnation, although Bolingbroke is not allowed to protest his innocence, which according to Holinshed he took 'upon his death'. The interest of the scene, apart from the spectacular presentation of the demon, lies not in the magicians but in their customer, Eleanor. Bolingbroke and Jourdain are only there to serve her interests – and in fact, it is revealed earlier in the play by Sir John Hume that she has been manipulated into consulting them in order to secure her downfall by the devious Cardinal, Winchester, and the Duke of Suffolk (1.2.94–99).

Shakespeare's chronicle histories demonstrate that witchcraft could be represented in a way that must have been perceived by some as relatively accurate, given that it was based on chronicles. Witches could be taken seriously in Elizabethan drama, and witchcraft could

---

154 Raphael Holinshed, *The Third Volume of Chronicles* (London, 1587), p. 623.
155 The demon's name is emended to 'Asnath' by most editors from the Folio's 'Asmath' on the grounds that the name could be an anagram of 'Sathan'; see William Shakespeare, *King Henry VI Part 2*, edited by Ronald Knowles (London: Arden Shakespeare, 1999), 1.4.24n. However, this appears to be no more than a rather wild guess. In the Quarto of 1594 the spirit is named Askalon.

be presented as genuinely efficacious and threatening, but only when dignified by aristocratic or royal patronage – an important point of contact with *Macbeth* and many other witch plays of the Jacobean theatre. La Pucelle and Margery Jourdain, unlike the various stage witches who precede them, are not purely fictional characters; they are characters based on historical people who really were executed, although not for witchcraft – Joan of Arc was burned at the stake for heresy and Jourdain for treason. The important thing about their crimes was not that they supposedly made use of witchcraft, but that in doing so they had been perceived to threaten the monarchical and religious order. This is why – like the plots of Catholic conjurers against the Queen – their crimes are treated without any trace of scepticism.

Magic and demonology in *Dr Faustus* and its competitors

The cluster of Elizabethan plays featuring magic users in the late 1580s and early 1590s includes a number of plays featuring male magicians as protagonists. Anthony Munday's *John a Kent and John a Cumber* (1589), Robert Greene's *Friar Bacon and Friar Bungay* (1589), and Christopher Marlowe's *Dr Faustus* (1592) were first performed in close proximity to one another.[156] But while the

---

156 I have followed the dates given in the most recent *Annals of English Drama* for all three plays, but the dating of *Dr Faustus* is a rather contentious issue. Arguments for an earlier date for *Faustus* are hampered by the absence of solid evidence for any pre-1594 performance, and tend to rely on unprovable assumptions about how the play's main author would have behaved. For example, John Henry Jones writes that Marlowe, once he had seen the play's source, the English Faust Book, 'would have fastened upon it at once. He must have felt it was made for him ... any delay on his part would have given the prize to a rival. It is quite preposterous to suppose that if the EFB appeared in 1588 the play was not written until 1592' (John Henry Jones (ed.), *The English Faust Book* (Cambridge: Cambridge University Press, 1994), p. 53). I fail to see anything preposterous about such a supposition. Referring to similarities between *Dr Faustus* and other plays, Scott McMillin and Sally-Beth MacLean, in *The Queen's Men and Their Plays* (Cambridge: Cambridge University Press, 1998), briefly consider the possibility that Marlowe borrowed from Greene rather than vice versa, but conclude that this 'would not seem at all characteristic of Marlowe's artistic temperament' (p. 158). But Marlowe's 'artistic temperament', as imagined by people writing more than 400 years after his death, is not evidence of anything, except perhaps a modern predisposition to regard Marlowe's work as unusually original.

plays are close in time, they are far apart ideologically – or rather, *Dr Faustus* is far apart from the other two. Greene and Munday represent magic as an activity that is in some respects admirable, almost endorsing the kinds of views held by learned magicians themselves. *Dr Faustus*, for the first time in the English theatre, puts forward the views of the demonologists in detail.

Greene's and Munday's plays can be considered as examples of the 'magical contest' story, as Richard Levin argues.[157] Friar Bacon's antagonist in *Friar Bacon and Friar Bungay* is the German magician Vandermast, whose learning and power are first emphasised when he defeats Bacon's sidekick, Friar Bungay. Bungay and Vandermast begin their contest, tellingly, with a debate rather than immediately resorting to magic: as Henry Howard would have recognised, the learning of the magicians is what establishes their credibility. The men argue about whether geomancy or pyromancy is superior. The obvious answer would be pyromancy, since fire is the 'best' of the four elements, but Bungay chooses to argue on behalf of geomancy. Vandermast, scoffing at his choice, tells Bungay that

> when proud Lucifer fell from the heavens,
> The spirits and angels that did sin with him
> Retain'd their local essence as their faults,
> All subject under Luna's continent.
> They which offended less hang in the fire,
> And second faults did rest within the air;
> But Lucifer and his proud-hearted fiends
> Were thrown into the center of the earth,
> Having less understanding than the rest,
> As having greater sin and lesser grace.
> Therefore such gross and earthly spirits do serve
> For jugglers, witches and vild sorcerers;
> Whereas the pyromantic genii
> Are mighty, swift, and of far-reaching power.[158]

Vandermast's speech posits gradations of guilt among fallen angels and links different orders of spirits to the ancient elements of earth, air, and fire (hydromancy and aeromancy are not mentioned, although

---

157 Richard Levin, 'My Magic Can Lick Your Magic', *Medieval & Renaissance Drama in England*, 22 (2009), 201–28, discusses the history of this type of episode in literature, identifying the contest between Moses and the magicians of Egypt in Exodus as one of the earliest examples.
158 Robert Greene, *Friar Bacon and Friar Bungay* (London: Edward Arnold, 1964), IX.58–71. Subsequent references to this edition are given in parentheses.

Agrippa discusses them along with geomancy and pyromancy).[159] The most corrupt spirits are those associated with the earth, and these are the spirits used by witches, jugglers, and sorcerers. The view Vandermast expresses dates back to the third century in the writings of Origen,[160] and seems to be endorsed by the play, in so far as he wins the contest with Bungay. Agrippa also argues that devils can be divided into four groups corresponding to the four elements.[161] It is, however, a view explicitly contradicted by at least one demonologist, King James, who writes that

> all Devils must be lyars; but so they abuse the simplicitie of these wretches, that becomes their schollers, that they make them beleeve, at the fall of Lucifer, some Spirites fell in the air, some in the fire, some in the water, some in the lande: In which Elementes they still remaine. Whereupon they build, that such as fell in the fire, or in the aire, are truer then they, who fell in the water or in the land, which is al but meare trattles, and forged be the author of al deceit.[162]

Friar Bacon and Friar Bungay advances the ideas of magicians rather than those of demonologists, suggesting that the latter were not quite as unambiguously 'orthodox' in the period up to 1590 as they may later have become.[163]

However, the play also implies that working with the most evil spirits is necessary for very powerful magic. Bacon himself has undoubtedly done so, and he associates himself with witchcraft when he describes the work that went into the creation of the brass head that he hopes will provide protection for the country – an idea with obvious appeal in the immediate aftermath of the attempted invasion of England by the Spanish Armada:

> I have dived into hell
> And sought the darkest palaces of fiends;
> That with my magic spells great Belcephon

---

159 Agrippa, pp. 125–27.
160 Russell, p. 237.
161 Agrippa, p. 21.
162 James I, p. 20.
163 Keith Thomas argues that 'continental concepts of witchcraft' were not 'widely disseminated' in England until after the publication of Scot's *Discoverie*; he dates the beginning of this process to around 1590, with the publication of Henry Holland's *Treatise Against Witchcraft* (Thomas, pp. 523–25). As I have argued, important and analogous changes take place at around this time both in the pamphlet literature of witchcraft and in the theatre.

> Hath left his lodge and kneeled at my cell;
> The rafter of the earth rent from the poles,
> And three-form'd Luna hid her silver looks,
> Trembling upon her concave continent,
> When Bacon read upon his magic book.
> With seven years' tossing nigromantic charms,
> Poring upon dark Hecat's principles,
> I have fram'd out a monstrous head of brass,
> That, by th'enchanting forces of the devil,
> Shall tell out strange and uncouth aphorisms,
> And girt fair England with a wall of brass.
> (XI.7–20)

Bacon, by his own admission, has 'dived' into hell, used 'nigromancy' or black magic, plans to harness the power of the devil – not that of the angels – to protect England, and for good measure mentions Hecate, goddess of witchcraft. The important difference between Bacon's magic and witchcraft, however, is that Bacon commands the evil spirits that he works with, rather than making any kind of bargain with them. In Bacon's contest with Vandermast, the spirit in the form of Hercules is so frightened of Bacon that he refuses to follow Vandermast's commands, and ends up carrying him back to Germany on Bacon's orders. The presentation of magicians as commanders rather than servants of spirits supports the claims of magicians, and contests those of the demonologists.

Friar Bacon does, in the end, repent his use of magic and promises to give it up, but the lesson he claims to have learned is the result of a highly contrived series of events. Bacon shows two scholars their fathers engaged in a duel via his magic mirror; the duel results in both fathers' deaths, and the two young men promptly kill each other as well, while Bacon – normally in command in all situations – looks on passively. The audience or reader is presented with a very stylised pair of tragedies. Bacon laments that his magic has caused the deaths of the scholars, but all it has really done is speed things up: the scholars would surely have found out about their fathers' fight eventually anyway. Having blamed himself for something that was not really his fault, Bacon goes on to repent his use of magic for unrelated reasons: because the practice of magic is blasphemous. This was equally true before the scholars killed each other, and audiences watching Greene's play will have known that magic was usually supposed to be morally questionable. But the play incorporates real-world consequences, however clumsily, *before* Bacon's magic is understood to be in any way reprehensible. Blasphemy alone is not enough. Furthermore, even after his repentance, it is not entirely clear that the humbler and more contrite Bacon is altogether changed. He is last seen making a prophecy, and prophecy is usually seen as a type of magic.

Anthony Munday's *John a Kent and John a Cumber*, roughly contemporary with Greene's play, is even kinder to its magicians. Both the male magicians of the title are masters of disguise and illusion, but it is also made clear that they master the spirits they work with, and not vice versa. John a Cumber, the eventual loser of the contest between the two rivals, is said to have gone 'beyond the Devill / And made him serve seaven years prentiship', and the final line of the play, partially lost as a result of damage to the manuscript, ends with the words 'overmatchde the Devill'.[164]

Neither of the two Johns has any particularly noble aim to justify his working with magic, as Friar Bacon does, nor do they seem to feel any need for such justification. John a Kent, in particular, seeks disharmony for his own amusement. Far from being committed to the ends of the noble couples he ostensibly serves, he treats their needs and desires as irrelevant and even seeks to undermine his own work, simply in order to make things more interesting:

> But must these joyes so quickly be concluded?
> Must the first Scene make absolute a Play?
> No cross, no chaunge? What! no varietie?
> [...] by my troth, to sport myselfe awhile,
> The disappoynted brydegroomes, these possest,
> The fathers, freendes, and other more besyde,
> That may be usde to furnish up conceite,
> Ile set on woorke in such an amorous warre,
> As they shall wunder whence ensues this jarre.   (p. 22)

John's real allegiance lies only with himself – and with the audience, who will also be 'sported' by the events he sets in motion. Things improve even further with the arrival of John a Cumber. At this point, the contest between them becomes of overriding importance to both magicians.

Neither magician repents, expresses the slightest regret for working with magic, or, for that matter, treats any other character as more than a pawn in the game between the two of them. This cavalier

---

164 John Payne Collier, Introduction to Anthony Munday, *John a Kent and John a Cumber*, edited by John Payne Collier (London, 1851), vii–viii and p. 39. Subsequent page references, given parenthetically, are to this edition.

attitude to the rather two-dimensional characters with whom they share a stage is unlikely to have cost them the audience's sympathy. Like Prospero in *The Tempest*, they are in complete control of the events unfolding on stage, and to make the parallel between theatre and magic as clear as it can be, John a Cumber spends much of the play trying to organise a play – ostensibly in order to celebrate the wedding of the aristocratic couples, but mainly to glorify himself. The magicians treat their social superiors in a far from deferential manner, sometimes ordering them about as if they were servants – treatment which the aristocratic characters supinely accept. This mastery of the magician over his 'betters' is also apparent in *Friar Bacon and Friar Bungay*, with Bacon addressing the emperor of Germany as 'thee' (IX.244) and even pointing out to the English king, Henry, the intolerable poverty of scholars, by mockingly offering him the kind of food the friars usually eat. The German emperor takes Bacon to task for this: 'Presumptuous friar, what, scoff'st thou at a king?' (IX.228), but Bacon ignores him. The ability to command spirits seems to go hand in hand with the ability to command one's social superiors.

The situation in *Dr Faustus* could hardly be more different, even though Faustus is, in some respects, quite similar to Friar Bacon. He has major ambitions, including the kind of military and political goals Bacon describes. Faustus, in language which must have been borrowed from Greene or his hypothetical source,[165] also speaks of his desire to 'wall all *Jermany* with brasse' (I.88). In fact, Faust goes into greater detail than Friar Bacon about the kinds of achievements he seeks, such as 'chas[ing] the Prince of Parma' from Germany and acquiring the 'golden fleece' of treasure from the Americas that enriches Philip of Spain (I.93, 131). None of these goals are achieved, although they are all, in themselves, as laudable from a Protestant perspective as is Bacon's desire to protect England. Faustus also seeks to raise himself above his humble origins, and indeed above royalty, declaring that 'The Emprour shal not live but by my leave' (III.110). Friar Bacon, John a Kent, and John a Cumber do not

---

165 Even if *Dr Faustus* does predate Greene's play, such borrowings could easily have found their way into the published version. The A-text of *Dr Faustus*, published in 1604, post-dates the alterations to the play made by William Bird and Samuel Rowley recorded in Henslowe's diary. The extant prose romance of Friar Bacon postdates Greene's play, although it has been suggested that an earlier version of it may have been the source of the play. See Jones, p. 55.

express these kinds of social ambitions in words, but they behave as if they did not accept anyone as their superior. By the end of the play in which he appears, Faustus is ingratiating himself with a duchess by bringing her grapes out of season. Faustus's servility, which ironically results from his excessive ambition, is as far as it could be from the mastery of magicians over both demons and social superiors in the other magician plays.

Faustus's abject failure to command emperors is linked to his initial failure to command spirits. The summoning scene, as is frequently noted, puts paid to any suggestion of Faustus establishing mastery over Mephastophilis in the way Friar Bacon would.[166] Indeed, Mephastophilis explicitly rules out the very possibility of ceremonial magic as described by most authors on magic. After Faustus has summoned Mephastophilis he immediately, and prematurely, congratulates himself on his apparent success:

> How pliant is this *Mephastophilis*?
> Full of obedience and humilitie,
> Such is the force of Magicke and my spels,
> No *Faustus*, thou art Conjurer laureate
> That canst commaund great *Mephastophilis*.
> (III.29–33)

On re-entering, Mephastophilis explains that Faustus's magical ceremonies only attract him because they are blasphemous, rather than compelling him to come, and Faustus abandons the idea of 'commaunding' Mephastophilis with comical rapidity upon being told to 'pray devoutly to the prince of hell' (III.34). In the next scene in which he appears, it is Faustus who is full of obedience and humility as he proclaims his devotion to Beelzebub, for whom he will 'build an altare and a church, / And offer luke warme blood of new borne babes' (v.13–14). The language of worship and sacrifice that Faustus employs here and elsewhere is only used in relation to the devil. Faustus never entertains the idea of worshipping God, even when he tries to repent. Nevertheless, he often uses the language of religiosity – language which is conspicuously absent in *John a Kent and John a Cumber* and, for almost the entire play, *Friar Bacon and Friar Bungay* – although Friar Bacon's late speech of repentance

---

166 Robert H. West, 'The Impatient Magic of Dr. Faustus', *English Literary Renaissance*, 4 (1974), 218–40, draws attention to 'the important distinction between the coercive magic which Faustus abortively attempted and the witch pact for which he readily settled' (p. 225).

performs the ideologically important task of establishing his piety and his refusal to give in to despair.

As Ryan Curtis Friesen points out, Marlowe presents Faustus as a kind of anti-Agrippa.[167] Cornelius, one of the magicians who advise Faustus as he sets about learning magic, tells his protégé that '[h]e that is grounded in Astrologie, / Inricht with tongues well seene in minerals, / Hath all the principles Magicke doth require' (I.138–40). It has been suggested that the name Cornelius was chosen in reference to Agrippa, who, like the character in the play, was 'infamous through the world' for his practice of the 'damned art' (II.32–33). But unlike the works of the historical Agrippa, Cornelius fails to mention piety as one of the prerequisites for learning to use magic. The magicians in *Dr Faustus* are not even allowed to pretend to be godly, a point emphasised in the ceremony Faustus carries out when he summons Mephastophilis:

Faustus, begin thine incantations,
And trie if divels will obey thy hest,
Seeing thou hast prayde and sacrific'd to them.
Within this circle is *Jehovahs* name,
Forward and backward, Anagramatis'd,
The breviated names of holy Saints,
Figures of every adjunct to the heavens,
And characters of signes and erring starres,
By which the spirits are inforst to rise.
(III.5–13)

In some respects the ceremony described here is similar to those presented in magical manuals. Faustus has, after all, prayed before he begins his incantations – but he states that he has addressed his prayers and sacrifices not to God but to the devils he hopes to command. Faustus is not a pious magician but a devil-worshipper.

Other details of the ceremony are also designed to emphasise Faustus's culpability, in particular his use of the names of God. Some magical treatises do say that the names of God should be used in ritual magic. The *Fourth Book of Occult Philosophy*, for example, specifies that the magician's pentacle should be sanctified as follows: 'let there be written about it the ten general names, which are, El, Elohim, Elohe, Zebaoth, Elion, Escerchie, Adonay, Jah, Tetragrammaton, Saday'.[168] The name Jehovah, which Faustus

---

167 Friesen, p. 109.
168 *Fourth Book of Occult Philosophy*, p. 49.

uses, is present only in the shortened form Jah, which is permitted to be spoken in the Judaic tradition.[169] Uttering the full form of God's personal name, however,[170] was considered blasphemous on the authority of Leviticus 24:16. While the word can be found in Elizabethan texts, 'Jehovah' tends to be used with caution in early modern England as well. English translations of the Hebrew bible, for example, tend to replace occurrences of it with the phrase 'the LORD'. The name is repeatedly used by Faustus in his ceremony, however, and Faustus's repeated and casual misuse of the holiest name of God emphasises the sacrilegious nature of the ceremony he performs. Friar Bacon, by contrast, refers with regret to his 'wresting' of the names 'Sother, Eloim, and Adonai, / Alpha, Manoth, and Tetragrammaton' – but not Jehovah.[171] Rather than the pious prayer recommended by Agrippa, Faustus gives a Latin speech in which he bids farewell to – again – Jehovah, and offers greetings to Beelzebub; he does not attempt to command Beelzebub, neither does he call on God for protection.

In all these details, *Dr Faustus* misrepresents the kind of ceremonial magic described by Agrippa in order to undermine any pretensions to holiness on the part of the magicians. In the process, the play emphasises Faustus's guilt, making the matter more clear-cut than in Marlowe's source, the English Faust Book.[172] In Marlowe's version of the legend, Faustus is happy to abandon his initial hopes of commanding Mephastophilis, all but tripping over himself in his eagerness to give his soul away. Gareth Roberts argues that the variety of different discourses about magic in early modern Europe complicates the arguments of critics who assume that audiences would automatically have disapproved of Faustus's use of

---

169 Clifford Hubert Durousseau, 'Yah: A Name of God', *Jewish Bible Quarterly*, 42 (2014), 21–26 (p. 24).
170 'Jehovah', more properly 'Yahweh' or 'Yahveh', is a guess at God's personal name, which is known to contain four consonants – Y-H-V-H – although the vowels are unknown. The 'tetragrammaton' is the name given to these four letters.
171 Greene, XIII.92–94. Greene does use the word 'Jehovah' in another of his plays, *A Looking Glass for London and England* (1590), but this play seems to have been a special case owing to its biblical setting; it tells the story of Jonah and the fall of Nineveh, which might justify the use of God's personal name.
172 Sara Munson Deats, '*Doctor Faustus*: From Chapbook to Tragedy', *Essays in Literature*, 3 (1976), 3–16. Deats points out, among other things, that in the EFB Faustus tries to get Mephastophilis to agree to a deal that does not involve the loss of his soul (p. 8).

magic.[173] But *Dr Faustus* is not a blank slate upon which audiences can project their own beliefs; it is itself a form of discourse. The magic in *Dr Faustus* is presented in an unremittingly hostile light; every detail is made to conform to the views of writers against magic rather than those of the magicians themselves.

Dr Faustus therefore denies the reality of the widely recognised, but disputed, distinction between witch and magician.[174] Faustus's relationship with Mephastophilis has a historical analogue in what Norman Cohn identifies as one of the early legal precedents for witchcraft persecution: the posthumous trial of Pope Boniface VIII, who, like Faustus, was said to have had a personal demon at his service.[175] The difference between Faustus's Mephastophilis and the witch's familiar is one of grandeur rather than kind, and Faustus himself is a male witch – more serious and possessed of greater dignity (at least to begin with) than a female witch would be, but a witch nonetheless.

Dr Faustus is the first play in the English canon to represent a demonologically orthodox witch. In doing so, it may have been significant in both disseminating and contributing to demonological theory. Gareth Roberts notes in passing that there are a number of parallels between *Dr Faustus* (and, of course, the English Faust Book) and King James's *Daemonologie*.[176] Roberts goes on to express reluctance to use *Daemonologie* as 'an exegetical tool', but the great similarity between the texts suggests not just ideological affinity but direct influence. *Daemonologie* repeats the idea that the devil sometimes demands of his followers a contract signed in the magician's own blood.[177] It stresses the ineffectiveness and blasphemy of

---

173 Gareth Roberts, 'Marlowe and the Metaphysics of Magicians', in *Constructing Christopher Marlowe*, edited by James Alan Downie and J. T. Parnell (Cambridge: Cambridge University Press, 2000), pp. 55–73 (pp. 60–62).
174 One demonologist, for example, argues that the conjurer, who is believed to be '[t]his great bynder and commaunder of Deuils, hath his own soule bound and commaunded by them, and is in miserable and uile captiuity' (Gifford, *Discourse*, sig. G1^v).
175 Norman Cohn, *Europe's Inner Demons* (London: Heinemann, 1975), pp. 180–85.
176 Roberts, p. 64.
177 James I, p. 23. The earliest known appearance of the contract signed in blood is in the story of Theophilus of Adana, the best-known version of which is in the thirteenth-century *Golden Legend* of Jacobus Voragine. See Marguerite de Huszar Allen, *The Faust Legend: Popular Formula and Modern Novel* (New York: Lang, 1985), p. 19. Contracts signed in blood are rare in English witchcraft pamphlets.

magical procedures, even adding that the devil 'mockes the Papistes' by demanding that magicians use holy water in their rituals, as some magical manuals do indeed recommend.[178]

Mockery of the papacy by the devil is, of course, a prominent feature of the Faust myth. James claims that conjurers raise spirits because they wish them to 'resolue them of their doubts'.[179] Faustus, in the first scene of the play, uses a strikingly similar phrase: he wants spirits to 'Resolve me of all ambiguities' (1.80). Perhaps most tellingly, James's treatise points to unlawful curiosity as the motivation for magicians, and in particular to an excessive interest in astronomy and astrology as the beginning of this curiosity.[180] Astronomy is the only intellectual pursuit which Faustus does not dismiss. The idea of dealing with the devil in order to satisfy intellectual ambition is an old one, but the close chronological proximity of James's text and the Faust story suggests that the similarity may be more than coincidental.[181] Furthermore, it is not only James's text that bears traces of the influence of the Faust myth: Richard Bernard's *Guide to Grand Jury Men* explicitly refers to Faustus as an example of a witch, making no distinction between this case and others recorded in witchcraft pamphlets.[182] Given that elements of the Faust myth seem to have been absorbed into demonological writings, it it difficult to argue that *Dr Faustus* could have encouraged scepticism about witchcraft.

There is, however, one sense in which *Dr Faustus* – along with many demonological works – is sceptical about magic. The play refuses to accept the possibility of commanding demons that Greene and Munday imagined. The magical-contest plays of Greene and Munday are, in essence, fantasies: plays written from a perspective that knew magic was supposed to be wrong but could not quite resist its dubious glamour. These plays are not sceptical in any overt way, but they present magic in such a way as to remove most of the threat from it. They suggest that magic can be treated lightly, and that it might be forgiven, even if it is sinful. *Dr Faustus* rejects

---

178 James I, p. 17. The use of holy water is recommended by the author of the *Fourth Book of Occult Philosophy* (p. 55).
179 James I, p. 10.
180 James I, p. 10.
181 Gebert of Aurillac, who reigned as Pope Sylvester II from 999–1003, is one important predecessor of Faustus in this respect. See also the discussion in Chapter 1.
182 Bernard, pp. 98, 107. Bernard even explains why the devil appears in the shape of a friar for Faustus, but in animal form for common witches.

all such wishful thinking. While Faustus is capable of the same kinds of tricks as John a Kent and Friar Bacon – all three magicians are able to prevent other men from drawing their swords, for instance – the 'real', ceremonial magic that he wishes to perform is impossible. Not only is Faustus incapable of commanding demons, Mephastophilis makes clear in the summoning scene that nobody can do so. Almost equally important is the play's demonstration that Catholic 'magic' does not work either – the attempts of the friars to exorcise Mephastophilis and Faustus are presented as farcical. *Dr Faustus* represents a specifically Protestant style of scepticism about magic, referred to in Chapter 1: it denies the possibility of genuine magic – magic that is anything more than mere 'juggling' – while accepting with deadly seriousness the reality of the devil and his power to help his disciples perform false miracles. When Faustus performs magic that is more than mere trickery – as when he fetches real grapes out of season for the Duke of Vanholt's wife – it is clear that he is only able to do so with Mephastophilis's aid. While the play is sceptical in that it suggests that both magic and Catholic ritual are ineffective, it is at the same time credulous in its uncompromising assertion that magic is always demonic.

Quite apart from the play's own standpoint in terms of scepticism and credulity towards witchcraft, however, it has often been recognised that scepticism and credulity, more generally, are important themes of the play. The significance of the Renaissance rediscovery of philosophical scepticism within *Dr Faustus* has been noted by William Hamlin, who points out that a phrase used in one of Sextus Empiricus's texts is also used in the play.[183] Faustus himself is the first in-depth dramatic study of the psychology of a witch, and his wild swings from elation to despair are also connected to his attitudes of doubt and credulity. Faustus's scepticism is directed primarily towards the claims of religion, but also to those of all human learning, and this scepticism is represented as wilful. His credulity is most evident in his conviction that his own damnation is inevitable, and this conviction appears, on the face of it, to be equally groundless. For the most part, the play uses Faustus's irrational credulity and scepticism to present an orthodox picture of the witch as a deluded tool of the devil. There are moments, however, when the play seems to complicate this simple picture by subtly raising the possibility that Faustus might be right to believe in the inevitability of his own

---

183 William M. Hamlin, 'Casting Doubt in Marlowe's *Doctor Faustus*', *Studies in English Literature, 1500–1900*, 41:2 (Spring 2001), 257–75 (p. 258).

damnation – a possibility that is particularly significant in the light of the Calvinist theology that was, at the time of the play's first performances, still dominant in the Anglican Church.[184] However, while such moments can be seen as uncomfortable, they need not have troubled early modern Calvinists, who were committed to believing both that reprobate sinners were predestined to be damned and that they deserved this fate. Even if he is right to doubt that God's grace has been extended to him, in other words, Faustus remains blameworthy from a Calvinist perspective.

Faustus is sceptical – in a qualified sense – from the very start of the play. In his opening scene he dismisses the various branches of learning, one by one, in this respect resembling Agrippa, whose Latin treatise *De Incertitudine et Vanitate Scientiarum* (1526) was translated by James Sandford and published in London as *Of the Vanitie and Vncertaintie of Artes and Sciences* in 1569. As Popkin points out, Agrippa's work is not so much one of philosophical scepticism as 'a long diatribe against all sorts of intellectual activities'.[185] Faustus and Agrippa reject various disciplines on similar grounds: for Agrippa, logic is merely 'a skilfulnesse of contention',[186] and Faustus rejects it because 'to dispute well [is] Logickes chiefest end' (I.8). Throughout his soliloquy, Faustus rejects learning not on sceptical grounds but because he feels that the achievements it offers are insufficient. He is not so much a sceptic in this scene as a parody of a sceptic, driven largely by vanity and a desire for self-aggrandisement; but he also resembles Agrippa in his conviction

---

184 The other characters in the play seem to share Faustus's certainty that he will be damned; in particular the Old Man's attitude is peculiar, as he holds out the possibility of redemption – to which Faustus responds in a promising manner – only to depart expressing the opinion that Faustus's soul is 'hopelesse' (XII.42). The young scholars also seem convinced that it is too late for Faustus to repent at a very early stage of the play, at which point he has not even summoned Mephastophilis (II.38). More detailed discussion of this aspect of the play can be found in Lars Engle, 'Marlowe and the Self', in *Christopher Marlowe in Context*, edited by Emily C. Bartels and Emma Smith (Cambridge: Cambridge University Press, 2013), and David Riggs, *The World of Christopher Marlowe* (London: Faber & Faber, 2004), especially chapter 11.
185 Popkin, p. 28.
186 Heinrich Cornelius Agrippa, *Of the Vanitie and Vncertaintie of Artes and Sciences*, translated by James Sandford (London, 1575, first published as *De Incertitudine et Vanitate Scientiarum Atque Artium Declamatio Invectiva* in 1527), p. 21 (marked 23).

Witchcraft in Elizabethan drama

that human learning is ultimately pointless. Unlike Agrippa, however, who recommended a fideist turn to God in the face of the inadequacy of human knowledge, Faustus turns to the devil.

Turning to God does not occur to him because Faustus is convinced that there is no hope of mercy from God from the very start of the play. In Faustus's opening soliloquy, in which he rejects theology along with other branches of learning, Faustus reads from the Vulgate Bible, concluding that since all of us sin we must all 'die an everlasting death' (1.46). This conclusion, as has often been noted, is based on false premises, since Faustus ignores the words of the biblical passages immediately following those he reads; he ignores the second part of Romans 6:23 and the verse following 1 John 1:8.[187] Faustus, learned as he is, must know that he is wilfully misinterpreting scripture – or perhaps he understands that the passages he ignores do not apply to him. In either case, he remains convinced throughout the play that he cannot possibly be saved from damnation. Even Mephastophilis attempts to persuade him to change his mind, saying: 'O *Faustus*, leave these frivolous demaunds, / Which strike a terror to my fainting soule' (III.81–82). But Faustus is determined, telling the spirit: 'Learne thou of *Faustus* manly fortitude, / And scorne those joyes thou never shalt possesse' (III.85–86). It is Faustus's conviction that he will never possess the joys of heaven that makes him so determined; he knows, or wilfully convinces himself, that he has nothing to lose.

As well as despairing of salvation, Faustus is credulous in ascribing too much value to the kind of humanistic learning which he seems to consider to be superior to the academic disciplines dismissed in his opening scene. Paying homage to the devil quickly slips into praising the ancient Greeks:

> There is no chiefe but only *Belsibub*,
> To whom *Faustus* doth dedicate himselfe,
> This word damnation terrifies not him,
> For he confounds hell in *Elizium*,
> His ghost be with the olde Philosophers.
> (III.56–60)

---

187 See note on 1.41. Romans 6:23, in full, reads: 'For the wages of sin is death; but the gift of God is eternal life through Jesus Christ our Lord.' 1 John 1:8–9 are as follows: 'If we say that we have no sin, we deceive ourselves, and the truth is not in us. / If we confess our sins, he is faithful and just to forgive us our sins, and to cleanse us from all unrighteousness.'

The speech moves swiftly from Faustus's pledging allegiance to 'Belsibub' to his devotion to the 'olde Philosophers'. Faustus appears to have been deceived by devils in the same way that the ancient Greeks were often believed to have been. Faustus says he will 'confound' hell in Elysium, playing on the double meaning of the verb – Faustus means 'defeat', but an alternative sense would suggest that he has actually confused the Christian hell with the mythical heaven of the Greeks. Faustus is made to ironically acknowledge his own credulity, and to establish a link between the demonic and the ancient learning recovered during the Renaissance – a link which is maintained throughout the play, most memorably in the conjuring of an evil spirit masquerading as Helen of Troy.

Faustus repeatedly ignores a variety of supernatural warnings which force themselves on his senses. At one point he declares, 'O something soundeth in mine eares: / Abjure this Magicke, turne to God againe' (v.7–8), but the advice is ignored because Faustus cannot or will not believe that God will forgive him. Later, when Faustus tries to sign the agreement with Lucifer, his blood will not flow, and Faustus tries to understand the significance of this event:

> What might the staying of my bloud portend?
> Is it unwilling I should write this bill?
> Why streames it not, that I may write afresh?
> Faustus gives to thee his soule: ah there it stayde,
> Why shouldst thou not? is not thy soule thine owne?
> Then write againe, Faustus gives to thee his soule.
> (v.64–69)

Of course, Faustus's soul is *not* his own, as he must know. Reginald Scot tells the story of a woman who became convinced that she had 'giuen hir soule to the diuell' and was comforted by her husband, who pointed out that 'thy bargaine is void and of none effect: for thou hast sold that which is none of thine to sell; sith it belongeth to Christ, who hath bought it, and deerelie paid for it, euen with his bloud'.[188] Scot's view that such a pact can never happen in reality was unconventional, but the husband's observation was not. Faustus

---

188 Scot, III.10, p. 56. There are dramatic parallels in the characters of Elizabeth Sawyer and Mistress Generous, who both try to avoid promising their souls to the devil on similar grounds: 'What interest in this Soule, my selfe coo'd claime / I freely gave him, but his part that made it / I still reserve, not being mine to give' (*The Late Lancashire Witches*, ll. 1707–09); 'I am thine, at least / So much of me as I can call mine own' (*The Witch of Edmonton*, II.1.142–43).

must know this, and he should also be able to interpret the omen of his blood refusing to flow.

Perhaps the most important thing that Faustus does not want to believe in is the idea of eternal damnation – which, as has been remarked, is also the thing of which he is most convinced. Faustus is completely inconsistent on this point, at one moment dismissing the idea of hell entirely:

> FAUSTUS   Thinkst thou that *Faustus* is so fond,
> To imagine, that after this life there is any paine?
> Tush these are trifles and meere olde wives tales.
> MEPH.   But *Faustus* I am an instance to prove the contrary
> For I am damnd, and am now in hell.
> (v.136–40)

Faustus continues to scoff, despite the evidence presented by the testimony of Mephastophilis and that of his own senses: as Engle points out, the very existence of Mephastophilis and Lucifer would seem to prove the existence of hell.[189] Faustus is an extreme sceptic in that he seems willing to doubt all knowledge, whether it is grounded in empirical evidence or authority, but his scepticism is in this passage presented as foolish to the point of being incomprehensible.

Faustus's incredulity not only coexists with his fear of God's judgement, it is a direct consequence of it. Faustus has to mock and dismiss the tenets of religion in order to deal with his overwhelming fears. In the starkest of heaven's warnings to Faustus, writing appears on his arm:

> But what is this inscription on mine arme?
> *Homo fuge*, whither should I flie?
> If unto God hee'le throwe thee downe to hell,
> My sences are deceiv'd, here's nothing writ,
> I see it plaine, here in this place is writ,
> *Homo fuge*, yet shall not *Faustus* flye.
> (v.76–81)

Faustus is both sceptical and credulous: he is sceptical of the writing's obvious meaning, and even tries to imagine that the writing is not there, ignoring the evidence of his senses. In this he resembles the sceptical opponents of witchcraft, as they were depicted by Bodin and James I: 'fools or madmen' who 'do not want to believe',[190] or

---

189 Engle, pp. 203, 206.
190 Bodin, p. 38.

the 'stiff-necked' people of Exodus 32:9. Faustus's sceptical refusal to believe in what is obviously a heaven-sent warning is connected to his unshakeable belief in God's anger and the certainty of his own damnation.

All of this suggests that Faustus is not merely credulous; he is also superstitious, in a specific sense of the word. The idea of superstition was often used in early modern England to describe excessive ceremony in religion, particularly by reform-minded Protestants, but it could also be used to denote an unhealthy fear of the supernatural, and especially of the afterlife. One seventeenth-century writer on the subject, the royalist clergyman Henry Hammond, explained superstition as follows:

> The Atheist thinks there are no Gods, but the superstitious wishes there were none, but in spight of his Teeth beleeves that there are. An argument whereof is, that he is unwilling to dye [...] Unbeleife and contempt of all that is Divine is a shrewd fault indeed but on the other side Superstition is a shrewd fault too, the shrewder of the twaine.[191]

The fault of the superstitious person is the opposite of the atheist's fault, according to Hammond. In the play, Faustus seems to oscillate between these two faults, boldly denying the existence of hell in one moment, then falling into despair at the thought of his certain damnation in the next. Faustus never manages to achieve the happy medium of the pious man, who according to Hammond 'reveres' God but does not fear him. Faustus's excessive fear of God and his fixed conviction that he is already damned – evident from the first scene in the play – is what keeps driving him deeper into his pact with Mephastophilis.

Faustus's final speech is devoted to his dread of the afterlife, a further token of his superstition: 'The feare of death, or any ill thing after it', according to Hammond, is the defining characteristic of superstition.[192] In this speech, Faustus yearns to 'be changde / Unto some brutish beast: al beasts are happy, for when they die, / Their soules are soone dissolvd in elements' (XIII.103–5). Like the superstitious man described by Hammond, however, Faustus knows 'in spight of his Teeth' that the doctrine of metempsychosis is not true; he remains convinced throughout the play of the existence of God. Faustus's credulous superstition and his sceptical atheism are

---

191 Henry Hammond, *Of Superstition* (Oxford, 1645), pp. 5, 7.
192 Hammond, p. 7.

mutually contradictory, but they are also inseparable, and together they form a closed circuit from which he cannot escape.

Most of the witches in the Elizabethan theatre, I have argued, are not really witches in the early modern sense. While some audience members may have taken characters like Dipsas or Mother Bombie as serious representations of historical or at least realistically imagined people, it seems more likely that these characters would have been appreciated for the entertainment they provided and, perhaps, the moral instruction their stories offered. The question of whether they were, or could have been, real seems unlikely to have arisen, because such a question is out of place within the genre of these plays. However, witches in Elizabethan drama could sometimes be treated more seriously, and these witches are the most realistic, in the sense of corresponding to early modern ideas about witches. In the cases of Joan la Pucelle and Margery Jourdain, the inclusion of 'real' witches – usually avoided in Elizabethan theatre – is justified by a commitment to the source material, and by associating those witches with aristocratic or royal characters whom the witches could serve and other high-ranking characters whom they could threaten. That these witches were much less likely to have been understood as purely fictional is likewise evident from the genre of the plays.

With Faustus, for the first time, a witch becomes a protagonist in his own right. In contrast to most previous dramatic treatments of witchcraft, Faustus is identified as a real person in the source of the play and, implicitly, in the choric comment on him which ends the play (as well as in near-contemporary demonological works). Hostile though the play generally is towards its witch, *Dr Faustus* takes a bold step in putting a witch at the centre in the first place. It is, of course, significant that the first witch to occupy centre stage is male, and in some respects possessed of greater dignity than the stereotypical female witch. As has been argued, masculine magic was always taken more seriously in Elizabethan England than female magic. Faustus is both a rebellious and a submissive character – as women were often paradoxically thought to be – and it is perhaps his maleness and his learning that make his 'effeminate' version of magic dignified enough to be possible to represent on stage. Conversely, earlier witches – or female magicians – like Medusa and Medea were lent greater credibility by practising a supposedly masculine version of magic.

Had Friar Bacon been a real person rather than a character in a play, he might have found himself out of favour after the death of Queen Elizabeth. He would, to begin with, have been guilty of an offence punishable by death under the Witchcraft Act of 1604, passed in the first year of James I's reign. This Act replaced the Elizabethan law of 1563, and its first substantive paragraph is aimed at those who deal with evil spirits:

> if any p[er]son or persons ... shall use practise or exercise any Invocation or Conjuration of any evill and wicked Spirit, or shall consult covenant with entertaine employ feede or rewarde any evill and wicked Spirit to or for any intent or purpose ... [he or she] shall suffer pains of deathe as a Felon or Felons, and shall loose the priviledge and benefit of Cleargie and Sanctuarie.[193]

This provision illustrates a shift of emphasis in the Jacobean Act; the 1563 law places much more stress on the question of *maleficium* – the harm caused by magic – while the new act highlights contact with evil spirits as the basis of the crime and expands its discussion of invocation and conjuration. The idea of feeding spirits – suckling familiars with a witch's teat – is incorporated into the law for the first time.

The 1604 Act seems, in the event, not to have had any great impact on legal practice. As Clark, Gibson, and others have shown, court cases involving witchcraft continued to focus on the issue of *maleficium*.[194] But this might not have been clear at the time of the Act's passing, neither does it prove that nothing at all happened as a result of the new laws. The legislation may have brought about or been accompanied by a more hostile climate for magicians in elite circles. John Dee seems to have regarded the Act as a threat to his safety, since he petitioned both King and Parliament in an attempt to establish his innocence of any such crimes.[195] The Act would seem to reflect a change in attitudes, if nothing else, which may have affected the dramatic representation of magic as well. The most famous Jacobean magician, Prospero, does not deal with the 'evill and wicked' spirits proscribed by the Act, but with the

---

193 1 James I c. 12.
194 Marion Gibson, 'Applying the Act of 1604: Witches in Essex, Northamptonshire and Lancashire before and after 1604', in *Witchcraft and the Act of 1604*, edited by John Newton and Jo Bath (Leiden: Brill, 2008), pp. 115–28 (p. 127); Stuart Clark, 'King James's *Daemonologie*: Witchcraft and Kingship', in *The Damned Art: Essays in the Literature of Witchcraft*, edited by Sydney Anglo (London: Routledge & Kegan Paul, 1985), pp. 156–81 (p. 161 and note 16).
195 Parry, pp. 265–67.

benevolent Ariel; Caliban is not characterised as a spirit, despite his association with earth and water, which neatly complements Ariel's association with the 'superior' elements of air and fire. If Friar Bacon and John a Kent are the theatrical case for the defence of magic, Faustus is the prosecution, and the prosecution seems to have won out in England with the accession of the new king. As Chapter 3 argues, the change of monarch had profound consequences for the theatrical representation of witchcraft.

3
Witchcraft in Jacobean drama

The accession of James VI of Scotland to the English throne was once seen as the beginning of a period of severe witchcraft persecution in England. Largely based on the published opinions of the new monarch, this view always had its critics – an early defender of James's record was the historian of witchcraft and Shakespeare scholar George Lyman Kittredge – and it has since been discredited on the basis of the more empirical approach pioneered by C. L. Ewen and developed further by Alan Macfarlane.[1] James's public attitude to witchcraft was, in practice, a good deal more complex than *Daemonologie* would make it appear, and his later involvement in exposing fraudulent cases of demonic possession by witchcraft is well documented.[2]

But while fewer witches were brought to trial under James than under his predecessor, witches do appear to have become more important on stage, and this change is likely to have been a direct response to his accession to the throne. James is often described as having an 'interest' in witchcraft, which makes his engagement with the phenomenon sound very harmless and scholarly. It would be more accurate to say that the new king had a track record of putting witchcraft belief to political and polemical use. James's writings on witchcraft, and his interventions in cases of it, made a significant contribution to the image of a wise and benevolent king which he attempted, with mixed success, to project. James's later activities in exposing 'impostures' constitute a continuation of, rather than a break with, his previous encouragement of witch-hunting in this

---

1 Elmer, *Witchcraft, Witch-Hunting, and Politics*, pp. 47–53; Kittredge, pp. 276–328; Ewen, *Witchcraft Hunting and Witch Trials*; Macfarlane, *Witchcraft in Tudor and Stuart England*.
2 Kittredge, pp. 319–23; Sharpe, *The Bewitching of Anne Gunter* provides a book-length case study of one well-documented example.

respect. The theatrical representation of witches in the early part of James's reign can be seen to complement (and compliment) his highly political interest in witchcraft, in view of the significance of the witch characters within the plays in which they appear. Above all, it is the way these characters become associated with, or opposed to, the court, and their connection with royal and aristocratic characters, that makes them newly important – and newly serious, in contrast to the predominantly light and comical Elizabethan witches.

If James's reign did not, as was once believed, lead to higher levels of persecution, it does seem to have inspired a theatrical mini-genre which could be termed the royal witch play. Beginning with either Shakespeare's *Macbeth* (1606) or John Marston's *The Wonder of Women*, better known as *Sophonisba* (1606), this type of play was characterised by the use of witchcraft in association with, and in contrast to, the idea of divinely ordained monarchy. There are, as I have argued, Elizabethan precedents for this juxtaposition in some chronicle history plays; but they differ from the Jacobean examples considered here. The Jacobean plays' use of witchcraft is much more stylised, aiming for a clarity of contrast between witchcraft and royalty that is absent in the Elizabethan examples, and they also make more extensive use of learned demonology. These distinctive features are at their most visible in Ben Jonson's *Masque of Queens* (1609), in which the contrast between witchcraft and royalty is built into the dramatic structure – masque versus anti-masque – of the entertainment.

Scepticism and belief in witchcraft itself is not always easy to detect directly in the Jacobean witchcraft drama, because it is not often at issue in these plays. The plays are not in any real sense *about* witchcraft; they are really about kingship and tyranny, or good and bad rule.[3] All of the plays seek to draw a line between rightful kings and tyrants, or between order and chaos. *Macbeth* and the *Masque of Queens*, in particular, serve to glorify James's court in rather obvious ways. But even *Sophonisba*, which is not known to have been performed at court, seems to flatter the king indirectly by combining two of his intellectual interests: demonology and political theory. (James's works on these subjects had recently been made available in England when *Macbeth* and *Sophonisba* were first performed: *Daemonologie*, *The True Law of Free*

---

3 For a general study of the stage tyrant in early modern drama, see Rebecca W. Bushnell, *Tragedies of Tyrants* (Ithaca: Cornell University Press, 1990).

Monarchies and *Basilikon Doron* were all published in London in 1603.) Witchcraft plays a vital part in these plays on royal authority, by highlighting everything that royal authority is not.

However, if kings are diametrically opposed to both tyrants and witches, opposites can sometimes look rather similar. As Stuart Clark points out, with reference to the practice of touching for the 'king's evil', or scrofula:

> For all the huge disparity in moral value, kingcraft and witchcraft displayed, in this instance, certainly a gestural, but also a conceptual affinity. Armed with the categories of Weber and the findings of political anthropologists, we are apt to stress the similarities and treat the differences as a matter of cultural taste. But ... contemporaries too realized that the actions of kings and witches could be sufficiently cognate for them *both* to be suspected of demonism. In seventeenth-century England it was reported as a popular belief that scrofula was called the 'King's Evil' because the king caused, rather than cured it.[4]

The plays discussed here, like the kingship theorists discussed by Clark, are obviously concerned with the distinction between witchcraft and king- or queencraft. But the success of the plays in demonstrating this distinction is tempered by the fact that the monarch's role also contains traces of the supernatural. The quasi-magical nature of the idea of divinely ordained kingcraft, as James and several playwrights understood it, left it vulnerable to a satirical attack which, rather than stressing the differences between witchcraft and kingcraft, highlighted the similarities. This attack came in the form of a brilliant satire by Thomas Middleton, whose play *The Witch* (1615–16?) exploited the previous dramatic associations of court and witch in ways which were considerably less flattering to the former.

Sophonisba

John Marston's *Sophonisba* may have been written and performed shortly before *Macbeth*, as some scholars have speculated;[5] the two plays are at any rate very close in date. Marston's play is discussed first here because it is, in one sense, more conventional in its representation of witchcraft; it follows the pattern, already well established in the Elizabethan theatre, of using witches based on classical models which were far removed from the witch stereotype

---

4 Clark, *Thinking with Demons*, p. 666.
5 See, for example, Harris, p. 64, and Purkiss, *The Witch in History*, p. 274, footnote 39.

familiar from trial pamphlets. Marston's Erictho borrows heavily from the classical witch of the same name in Lucan's *Pharsalia*. Once dismissed as an extraneous distraction from the main action of the play, Erictho has more astutely been recognised as an important symbol of, and complement to, the tyrant Syphax's reckless depravity.[6]

Lucan's Erictho provided some inspiration for Greene's depiction of Medea in *Alphonsus*, but Marston uses the source much more extensively: some passages of the play, including the quotation below, are translations of it. Unlike Greene, who keeps his depiction of Medea quite dignified, Marston exploits some of the most lurid parts of Lucan's description of the Thessalian witch:

> she bursts up tombes
> For half rot searcloathes, then she scrapes dry gums
> For hir black rites: but when she findes a corse
> New gravd whose entrailes yet not turne
> To slymy filth, with greedy havock then
> She makes fierce spoile and swels with wicked triumph
> To bury hir leane knuckles in his eyes.
> Then doeth she knaw the pale and or'egrowne nailes
> From his dry hand: but if she find some life
> Yet lurking close she bites his gelled lips,
> And sticking her blacke tongue in his drie throat,
> She breathes dire murmurs, which inforce him to beare
> Her banefull secrets to the spirits of horror.[7]

This drastic change in tone from the comparatively gentle Elizabethan witches makes Erictho a more horrifying witch than any previous or subsequent theatrical depiction. (*Macbeth*'s witches are, of course, also gruesome in some of their speeches, probably not coincidentally.) Even Joan in *1 Henry VI*, probably the most malevolent of Elizabethan stage witches, is a very different order of witch compared to the demonic Erictho. The extreme nature of Erictho's evil is in keeping with the exaggerated characterisation in *Sophonisba* as a whole. As an editor of the play has pointed out,

> Sophonisba is not merely a good woman; she is the perfect woman. Syphax is not merely evil in a conventional political or ethical sense; he is completely depraved ... The logic of the play is the logic of

---

6 Peter Corbin and Douglas Sedge (eds), *Three Jacobean Witchcraft Plays* (Manchester: Manchester University Press, 1986), pp. 12–13.
7 John Marston, *Sophonisba*, edited by William Kemp (New York: Garland, 1979), IV.1.111–23. Subsequent references to this edition are given in parentheses.

the excluded middle; there is the divine and the satanic, but not the human, so that the characters become prototypical, even allegorical.[8]

Erictho is a fitting partner for the tyrant Syphax, who is presented as even more evil than the witch. In Marston's play, Erictho's necrophilia is projected onto Syphax as well. When Sophonisba threatens suicide in order to avoid rape, Syphax tells her: 'Doe strike thy breast, know being dead, Ile use, / With highest lust of sense thy senselesse flesh' (IV.1.58–59). Syphax's lust anticipates, and is associated with, Erictho's own.

In Marston's source, Erictho is visited by the general Sextus Pompey, who wishes to know the outcome of his coming battle in the ongoing civil wars (an incident closely resembling the story of Saul and the witch of Endor in I Samuel 28). In *Sophonisba*, however, Syphax comes looking for a love charm. Had Marston followed his source, this would have been easy enough for Erictho to provide. Lucan writes that

> A Thessalid's spell can make passion unintended
> by Fate flow into hardened hearts, make crabbed old men
> burn with illicit flames. Theirs is a skill beyond mere
> noxious concoctions [...] Couples bound
> neither by conjugal bliss nor by sweet beauty's allure—
> these they have tied with the mystic spinning of a twisted thread.[9]

Lucan's standpoint is ancient rather than early modern, of course, and it has been suggested that literary attitudes to love magic had changed by the time of Marston's play. Anthony Harris claims that the idea that love magic was impossible was an 'established concept',[10] but it is not difficult to think of dramatic exceptions to this supposed rule (among them *Fedele and Fortunio*, *A Midsummer Night's Dream*, *The Witch*, and *The Late Lancashire Witches*). It is far from clear that love magic was widely agreed to be impossible outside the theatre either.[11] In any case, Marston's play departs, in terms of witch lore, from a classical source which it closely follows in terms

---

8 Marston, p. 23.
9 Lucan, VI.452–60.
10 Harris, p. 67. Dipsas in *Endymion* and Erictho in *Sophonisba* provide some support for Harris's contention.
11 According to Richard Bernard, witches 'can worke vpon the minde of men and women to stirre vp lusts and ill passions' (p. 159); Roberts's *A Treatise of Witchcraft* refers to witches stirring up passions including lust, hatred and love (p. 17).

of verbal resemblance. The departure from the source seems to be based on greater scepticism towards witchcraft – but it is a qualified scepticism.

Erictho does not help Syphax, instead tricking him by magically disguising herself as Sophonisba and sleeping with him herself.[12] Later, having revealed her trickery, Erictho chides Syphax for imagining that she could help him: 'Why foole of kings, could thy weake soule imagin / That t'is within the graspe of Heaven or Hell / To inforce love?' (v.1.4–6). In this play, love magic is impossible – and Syphax's credulity in believing in it is mocked. This particular example of scepticism, however, limits rather than denies the witch's power, and in doing so makes Erictho more credible for an early modern audience. Erictho is instead given the essential witch's power, from an early modern demonological perspective – the power to deceive – which is not characteristic of Lucan's Erictho. Erictho deludes Syphax into thinking she is Sophonisba, but even more importantly she succeeds in persuading an impious man of her great power: Syphax places his faith in her and is thereby led into the sin of idolatry.

After the witch has disappeared, Syphax, having decided that after sleeping with Erictho he 'can no lower fall', offers a prayer to unnamed evil spirits at 'an Aultar sacred to black powers' (v.1.38, 27). Syphax invokes these powers in order to predict the outcome of a battle. Having dealt with a witch, Syphax turns to some form of witchcraft or conjuring himself. Erictho has won a royal convert to the devil, which is the purpose of early modern, rather than ancient, witchcraft. After Syphax's invocation the ghost of Sophonisba's father, Asdruball, appears to him. Asdruball predicts that Syphax will suffer more but, despite being asked, does not predict the outcome of the coming battle, claiming to be ignorant of anything but his own suffering. This is another departure from Marston's source, and again one which reflects early modern rather than ancient beliefs about magic: the author of the Harley MS referred to in previous chapters mocks the idea of asking for advice from the dead, pointing out that it is 'foolyshe to aske councell wher none ys to be had'.[13] The effects of the changes are to downplay the

---

12 Anthony Harris contends that Erictho uses 'straightforward trickery' rather than magic. While her face is veiled, she re-enters, according to the stage direction, 'in the shape of Sophonisba', which to my mind suggests illusion rather than disguise. See Harris, pp. 66–67.
13 MS Harley 2302, fols 86^v–87^r.

efficacy of magic while emphasising the degeneracy of the witch and her client. Scepticism about witchcraft operates within a particularly lurid view of it as threateningly demonic.

A final point to make about the summoning of Asdruball's ghost is that the status of the apparition is also questionable, and also suggests a demonological reading of the scene. While Erictho herself is said to work with the spirits of the dead, Syphax has not specifically asked for Asdruball to appear. Instead, he calls on apparently demonic forces: 'thou whose blasting flames / Hurle barren droughes upon the patient earth' and 'Hot-brained Phebus'.[14] When the ghost of Asdruball appears, Syphax asks: 'What damn'd ayre is form'd / Into that shape?', rejecting the idea that the apparition is really the ghost of Asdruball. The phrase 'damn'd ayre' makes it clear that an evil spirit has taken the shape of Sophonisba's dead father.[15] These words lend subtle support to the orthodox view that necromancers cannot really summon the spirits of the dead, only demonic illusions. *Sophonisba* therefore hints at a set of underlying assumptions very much in tune with the demonological position of King James.[16]

While Sophonisba is the 'perfect' character in the play – the wonder of women – characters in the play repeatedly describe her perfection as excessive, and even threatening, as Rebecca Yearling has pointed out.[17] Furthermore, Sophonisba is described in language which might raise some concern in a play which associates witchcraft with demonic evil. When Syphax is captured by the Roman general Scipio after his defeat by Massinissia, he explains his treachery to Rome by blaming Sophonisba:

> T'was Sophonisba that solicited
> My forc'd revolt, t'was hir resistles sute,
> Hir love to hir deare Carthage 'tic'd mee breake
> All faith with men: t'was shee made Syphax false,
> Shee that lov's Carthage with such violence
> And hath such moving graces to allure
> That shee will turne a man that once hath sworne
> Himselfe on's fathers bones hir Carthage foe

---

14 As mentioned in the discussion of *Alphonsus, King of Aragon* in Chapter 2, this is not the first play to connect Apollo with demonic forces.
15 On the connection between air and spirits, see Chapter 6.
16 The first topic to be discussed in James's *Daemonologie* is the witch of Endor, and by p. 4 James has established that the apparition summoned by the witch was an 'vnclean spirit' and not the ghost of Samuel.
17 Rebecca Yearling, 'John Marston, Stoic?: *Sophonisba* and the Early Modern Stoic Ideal', *Ben Jonson Journal* 18:1 (2011), 85–100 (p. 93).

> To be that citties Champion and high friend.
> Hir Himeneall torch burnt downe my house.
> Then was I captivd when hir wanton armes
> Threw moving claspt about my neck. O charmes
> Able to turne even fate.
> (v.2.70–82)

Syphax is, of course, a villain making excuses for himself, and his criticism of Sophonisba need not be taken seriously in one sense. However, the language in which he frames his excuses is significant. Sophonisba, he claims, has 'solicited / My forc'd reuolt' – creating the rebellion that is, according to 1 Samuel 15:23, the sin of witchcraft. She – not Erictho – has made him 'false' and a breaker of his faith. Sophonisba is described as being possessed of 'charmes / Able to turne even fate'. Obviously, these 'charms' are those of beauty rather than magic – but the word nonetheless recalls 'Hels charmes', with which Erictho cannot seduce Syphax (v.1.16). Sophonisba's 'charms' are actually more powerful than those of Erictho, who is forced instead to fall back on mere trickery, or 'Braine sleightes'. Erictho's boast to Syphax that she can command charms which 'Ioue dare not heare twice' is an empty one; unlike her ancient namesake, she has much more limited powers than she claims. The inability of Erictho's magic to command love serves the purpose of demonstrating that the powers of the virtuous princess, Sophonisba, are greater than those of the evil witch. But such a comparison can only be made by aligning the two characters, and describing them both in similar terms, problematising the otherwise sharp distinction drawn between the good and the evil characters.

Macbeth

The association of witchcraft and tyranny in *Sophonisba* is established even more clearly in *Macbeth*, and with greater personal relevance to King James. The issue of whether or not *Macbeth* is a 'royal play', in Henry Paul's phrase, has divided critics.[18] Sandra Clark, one of the editors of the recent Arden edition of the play, is sceptical about such claims and provides a long list of critics who have disputed the idea that *Macbeth* would have been flattering to James.[19]

---

18 Henry N. Paul, *The Royal Play of Macbeth* (New York: Macmillan, 1950).
19 Sandra Clark, 'The Critical Backstory', in *Macbeth: A Critical Reader*, edited by John Drakakis and Dale Townshend (London: Bloomsbury, 2013), pp. 18–54 (pp. 48–50).

But while Paul's conclusions and, more recently, Alvin Kernan's[20] may seem disappointingly straightforward to scholars in search of fresh readings, there are very good reasons for understanding *Macbeth* as a play written with a royal audience at least partly in mind.

Macbeth is almost universally dated 1606 on the basis of the numerous topical references within the play, and Alvin Kernan follows Paul in suggesting that it was 'probably' written especially for performance during a visit by the King of Denmark to England.[21] Some scenes – most notably the procession of kings, but also the praise of James's supposed ancestor, Banquo, in the third act – are best understood as flattery of the new king. The reference to 'Norweyan' banners, in place of the Danish invaders described in Shakespeare's source, is also suggestive of attention tactfully being paid to the sensitivities of a specific audience.[22] If, as Kernan believes, the play was written specifically with a court performance in mind, the inclusion of witches in the play – and, especially, their association with a rebellious nobleman – was of obvious relevance to its royal auditors, in view of their own first-hand experience of alleged witchcraft.

The series of events that has become known as the North Berwick witch-hunt are, from the beginning, tied up with the marriage of James VI of Scotland to Anne of Denmark in 1589.[23] Anne's planned voyage to Scotland was plagued by various mishaps, and eventually called off altogether, while in Scotland storms led to the drowning of Jean Kennedy, who was to have been one of Anne's gentlewomen. James then decided to sail to Norway, where Anne had been left stranded. Having finally married Anne in Oslo, James and his new wife went on to Denmark, where they stayed for six months as the guests of Christian IV. Just after the royal couple had arrived safely in Scotland in May 1590, a witch was convicted in Denmark, having confessed to using magic to interfere with the ships that had originally been intended to take Anne and her party to Scotland; the extraction

---

20 Alvin Kernan, *Shakespeare: The King's Playwright* (New Haven: Yale University Press, 1995), pp. 71–88.
21 Kernan, p. 76. Paul is much less circumspect than Kernan, and simply states this as a fact (p. 1). There is no direct evidence for this claim, likely though it may seem.
22 Paul, pp. 343–44; Kernan, p. 76.
23 The brief summary that follows is heavily indebted to the account given in Lawrence Normand and Gareth Roberts, *Witchcraft in Early Modern Scotland* (Exeter: University of Exeter Press, 2000), especially pp. 29–49.

of this confession seems to have formed part of an attempt by Danish officials to avoid being blamed for the fiasco. News of the Danish trial reached Scotland in July. What happened in the cases of witchcraft in Scotland is less clear, but by the end of 1590, Agnes Sampson had confessed, under torture and apparently in James's presence, to acts of *maleficium* and to knowledge of the devil's involvement in preventing the arrival of the Queen. Soon afterwards, a group of witches were accused of attempting to harm the King through magic. One of the accused witches, Donald Robson, had specifically mentioned 'my Lord Bothwell' as providing food and money to the group.[24]

Francis Stewart, fourth Earl of Bothwell and James's cousin, had a troubled relationship with the King – especially after having plotted an armed uprising against him in 1589. Whether or not there was any truth to the confessions made by the various witches is impossible to determine, but the accusation certainly played into a well-established political narrative in early modern Scotland.[25] Accusations of witchcraft had frequently been used as a political weapon, and Bothwell's subsequent defence of his conduct blamed his political enemies, especially James's chancellor, John Maitland. When Bothwell was finally tried, an observer reported that 'divers honest men of Edenbroughe ... deposed that Richard Greyme [one of the accused] said to theme that he must eyther accuse the Erle Bothwell falselye, or els endure such tormentes as no man were able to abyde'.[26] According to Bothwell's version of events, he was the victim of a conspiracy, one which used the emerging witch-hunt as an opportunity to settle old scores.

The similarities between Bothwell's alleged involvement with witches and Macbeth's have frequently been noted.[27] Bothwell might well have become king had James died without an heir, as Macbeth does after Duncan's death and his sons' flight. Bothwell also possessed the kinds of 'virtues' associated with Macbeth – he was bold, bloody, and resolute. At the age of 21, according to one contemporary report, Bothwell attacked three members of the rival Hume family, killing all three and hacking one of the men 'all to pieces'.[28] Even

---

24 The examinations and depositions are reproduced in Normand and Roberts, pp. 135–41, 158–63.
25 Normand and Roberts, p. 41 and p. 51, note 80.
26 Quoted in Normand and Roberts, p. 128.
27 See, for example, Harris, pp. 42–43; Kernan, pp. 85–87.
28 Normand and Roberts, p. 39.

after he had been declared a rebel for his alleged part in the witches' activities, he continued to enjoy support; and he posed a serious threat to James's reign, launching a series of violent attacks on James's household. In 1593 he even staged what Normand and Roberts describe as 'a successful coup'. It was after this that his trial finally took place, at his own request, and unsurprisingly he was cleared of the charges of witchcraft. (Bothwell was later out-manoeuvred by James – who by this time hated him implacably – and was in the end banished from Scotland.) That the eponymous villain of *Macbeth* is an accomplished and daring soldier need not be seen as mitigating his villainy – certainly not from the perspective of James, whose motto was 'blessed are the peacemakers'.

James's identification of opposition to him with witchcraft necessitated a kind of anti-witchcraft, the ascription of supernatural power to the rightful monarch – James himself. Following his marriage, James insisted on an elaborate coronation ceremony, complete with the anointing of Anne, in the face of opposition from much of the Protestant clergy, who regarded this as superstition. As Normand and Roberts point out,

> [m]onarchy here uses the resources of theatre – ceremony, costume, action, words – to perform its power and demonstrate its legitimacy, but it is not theatre as illusion. The theatrical elements of the ceremony perform a kind of royal magic. The queen completes the ceremony by speaking the oath of allegiance to, and entering into a covenant with, God, whose power, present in the ceremony, has effected her transformation into a consecrated queen.[29]

Just as witchcraft (and rebellion) is a pact with the devil, true monarchy is a pact with God, and just as witches have magical powers, so do kings. This aspect of James's theological and political thought finds dramatic expression in *Macbeth* in the various partly idealised portraits of kingly characters – Duncan, Banquo, Malcolm, and Edward the Confessor – who collectively present an alternative vision of just kingship, in opposition to the tyranny of Macbeth.[30]

---

29 Normand and Roberts, pp. 37–38.
30 The flaws of Duncan in particular have often been pointed out, but these flaws are notably absent in Macbeth's description of Duncan: throughout the play the tyrant and his speeches are used to emphasise the goodness of the good king.

If the rhetorical purpose of the witchcraft in *Macbeth* is fairly clear, the precise nature of it is much less so. *Macbeth* is by far the best-known play to deal with witchcraft; but demonologically speaking the play seems a mess, and the status of its witches has provoked much debate. It might even be asked whether there are any witches in *Macbeth*. The three characters who are described as witches in the Folio's stage directions are never referred to as such by any character in the play, although one of them reports that she was *called* a witch by another woman – the 'rumpe-fed Ronyon' who never appears on stage. The 'witches' are most frequently called the 'weird sisters' in modern editions of the play, and their exact nature and identity is a matter for debate by the characters on stage – Banquo and Macbeth – as well as for critics of the play. The critics – like the characters – have been unable to agree on anything much in relation to the weird sisters. They may not even be 'weird' sisters: the Folio text consistently describes them as 'weyard' or 'weyward': most modern editions render this word as 'weird', but Davenant's adaptation of the play calls the witches 'wayward' rather than weird.[31]

In fact, *Macbeth* provides plenty of evidence for anyone wishing to make the argument that the sisters, whether weird or wayward, are merely metaphorical – that they represent Macbeth's state of mind or his repressed desires, for example. The witches suddenly 'vanish' according to a stage direction, they anticipate Macbeth's thoughts, some of their speeches are verbally close to his, and they arguably have no real effect on the outcome of events. Nonetheless, while arguments for the unreality of the witches have been made,[32] they have always been oddly implausible even in modern-day performances of the play. Audiences tend to feel the witches to be real within the framework of the dramatic fiction, as do a large majority of critics. This is not to say that the witches are *not* symbolic of Macbeth's state of mind, merely that they are also real.

---

31 Harris suggests that this might indicate 'contemporary double syllabic pronunciation' of the word 'weird' (pp. 33–34). However, Macbeth himself is described as a 'wayward Sonne' by Hecat in III.5.
32 See, for example, Margaret Lucy, *Shakespeare and the Supernatural* (Liverpool: Shakespeare Press, 1906), p. 16. More recently, Ryan Curtis Friesen has suggested that 'the reality of the witches beyond Macbeth's psyche is questionable' (p. 125).

When they first appear to Banquo and Macbeth, the witches resemble the Fates of Greek myth, or similar beings from other mythological traditions, as has often been observed:

> MAC. Speake if you can: what are you?
> 1. All haile Macbeth, haile to thee Thane of Glamis.
> 2. All haile Macbeth, haile to thee Thane of Cawdor.
> 3. All haile Macbeth, that shalt be King hereafter.[33]

Here the sisters, identified in the Folio text only by numbers, present three brief glimpses of past, present, and future: Macbeth is already Glamis, is in the process of becoming Cawdor, and will eventually become king. In this respect the wayward sisters most closely resemble the Norns of Norse mythology: three sisters who are respectively associated with the past, the present, and the future. However, regardless of what their reply might suggest, the witches do not actually answer Macbeth's question, so there is no explicit indication of what the witches 'are', and their characters appear in a very different light in other passages of the play.[34]

Just before delivering their prophetic greeting to Macbeth, the witches have been discussing their recent activities – including 'killing swine' and begging for chestnuts. The trivial nature of their concerns undermines their later representation as Norns or Fates. The point is strengthened by the first witch's desire for revenge on the sailor's wife who has refused her charity. This connection to the stereotypical motive of the witch identifies the weird sisters as 'ordinary' witches. But while the conclusion that the wayward sisters are witches seems fairly obvious in terms of a typical seventeenth-century audience member's frame of reference, it is not the conclusion reached by Macbeth and Banquo. In fact, neither Macbeth nor Banquo reaches any firm conclusion. Banquo suggests that the witches might be 'bubbles' in the earth, or perhaps hallucinations, but he does not consider the apparently obvious answer.

The ambiguous representation of the witches has led to a variety of interpretations. The theory that the witches are in fact Norns,

---

33 William Shakespeare, 'Macbeth', in *Comedies, Histories and Tragedies* (London, 1623), 1.3, p. 132. Further references to the Folio text are given parenthetically.

34 Another perspective on this exchange is offered by Laura Kolb, who interprets the witches' greeting as an answer: 'The suggestion that the witches somehow *are* Macbeth reverberates throughout the play. The weird sisters' prophetic speeches are coextensive with, if not indistinguishable from, Macbeth's own ... thoughts' (p. 346).

originating with Fleay in the nineteenth century, has already been mentioned. A. C. Bradley disagreed, arguing that there is 'not a syllable in *Macbeth* to imply that they are anything but women'.[35] (Perhaps the oddest comment on the nature of the witches is offered by Harold Goddard, who asks himself whether the witches are women before answering, '[o]f course – and who has not seen and turned away in horror from just this malevolence in some shrunken old crone?')[36] W. C. Curry argued that the witches are demons pretending to be witches.[37] Henry Paul argued that the weird sisters are distinctively Scottish witches, which are more serious than the 'stupid and vulgar' stories about English witches.[38] This view steers a middle course between the mundane, swine-killing witches and the apparently omniscient Fates or Norns, but in doing so cannot account satisfactorily for either. More recently, Diane Purkiss starts by claiming that the play is a sensationalist mess, before arguing that the 'indeterminacy' of the witches is precisely the point: their lack of a stable identity aligns them with chaos and disorder.[39] Neat though this argument is, it seems to me to miss an important point about the witches – which is what the wayward sisters are.

The witches are only treated seriously, or rather only present themselves seriously, when others are present, and this is because their appearance before Banquo and Macbeth is a carefully prepared performance. It is evident from the opening scene of the play that the witches are expecting to meet Macbeth. Immediately before the entrance of Banquo and Macbeth, the witches chant: 'Peace, the Charme's wound vp.' It is unclear what this charm is, or whether it has any effect on subsequent events, but the word 'peace' commands silence, as the witches turn from their own affairs to the business

---

35 A. C. Bradley, *Shakespearean Tragedy* (Basingstoke: Macmillan, 1992, first published 1904); p. 299.
36 Harold Goddard, *The Meaning of Shakespeare* (Chicago: University of Chicago Press, 1951), II, p. 127.
37 W. C. Curry, *Shakespeare's Philosophical Patterns* (Baton Rouge: Louisiana State University Press, 1937), pp. 60–61.
38 Paul, pp. 256–57. For more recent variations on this argument see Mary Floyd-Wilson, 'English Epicures and Scottish Witches', *Shakespeare Quarterly* 57:2 (Summer 2006), 131–61 (pp. 147–48) and Alisa Manninen, "The Charm's Wound Up': Supernatural Ritual in *Macbeth*', in *Magical Transformations on the Early Modern English Stage*, edited by Lisa Hopkins and Helen Ostovich (Farnham: Ashgate, 2014), pp. 61–74 (p. 67).
39 Purkiss, *The Witch in History*, p. 211. Deborah Willis also refers to the 'hybridity' of the witches (*Malevolent Nurture*, p. 215).

at hand. Quiet now, he's coming, the witches seem to tell one another – it is time for them to stop their relaxed, backstage chat and get into character. Like their charm, the witches themselves are 'wound up' and ready to perform.

While the witches among themselves relax into informality and speak in doggerel and prose about their everyday activities, their language when speaking to Macbeth is markedly different. As well as slipping almost entirely into pentameter, the witches' tone is noticeably elevated when they are making their prophecies. They even address Macbeth and Banquo as 'thou', placing themselves above the noblemen by using the familiar pronoun rather than the more respectful 'you'. When they speak to Banquo, the witches revert back to tetrameter, perhaps allowing their masks to slip a little, but they are successful enough as performers to conceal their nature from both of their baffled auditors. Curry's view of the weird sisters – which sees them as demons impersonating witches – seems to me to have it backwards; the witches are not more but *less* powerful and mysterious than they appear. Evil is actually weak, not strong, and it puffs itself up to disguise its weakness. Purkiss describes the witches as 'Macbeth's missing comic sub-plot',[40] but they could equally be described as a rather subtle play within the play.

This view of the witches would have been entirely in keeping with King James's documented scepticism towards mythological and folkloric creatures. In his *Daemonologie*, James had discussed the nature of various kinds of spirits. He divides spirits into four types for convenience, but is careful to point out that

> although in my discourseing of them, I deuyde them in diuers kindes, yee must notwithstanding there of note my Phrase of speaking in that: For doubtleslie they are in effect, but all one kinde of spirites, who for abusing the more of mankinde, takes on these sundrie shapes, and vses diuerse formes of out-ward actiones, as if some were of nature better than other.[41]

James goes on to give short shrift to the concept of good and evil genii, an idea which is dramatically represented in *Dr Faustus* and taken seriously later in the seventeenth century by Joseph Glanvill. James's own position is reductive: all such spiritual phenomena are manifestations of the devil, and any appearance of diversity is merely a trick to deceive the unwary. He goes on to make a similar point

---

40 Purkiss, *The Witch in History*, p. 214.
41 James I, p. 57.

in relation to fairies, as noted in Chapter 2. The witches in *Macbeth*, like all servants of the devil, mimic their master's strategies: they pretend to be powerful and mysterious, but when the audience sees them in Macbeth's absence, they are revealed to be no more than ordinary witches.

That the witches might wish to present themselves as agents or personifications of a non-Christian fate or destiny, with the ability to see into the future, is in keeping with what a later author suggested about the devil's tactics. Arguing that the devil's ultimate aim is to persuade humans of the non-existence of any god, Thomas Browne writes that

> [w]here hee succeeds not thus high, he labours to introduce a secondary and deductive Atheisme, that although they concede there is a God, yet should they deny his providence ... to promote which apprehensions ... he casteth in the notions of fate, destiny, fortune, chance and necessity ... Whereby extinguishing in mindes the compensation of vertue and vice, the hope and feare of heaven or hell, they comply in their actions unto the drift of his delusions.[42]

The witches in *Macbeth* could be read as a theatrical representation of how the devil actually carries out a plan resembling the one Browne ascribes to him. They persuade Macbeth that they can tell him his 'destiny', and after meeting the witches he specifically mentions his indifference to the afterlife.

While the witches are not mythological Fates or Norns, it is nonetheless true that they are seemingly able to predict the future. James addressed this question in *Daemonologie*, arriving at the conventional answer that the devil is often able to make accurate predictions based on his great learning and ability to observe events unseen.[43] These predictions are passed on to Macbeth for the purpose of sealing his fate, but the choice of Macbeth is not made at random. Part of the devil's cunning is that he chooses his targets well. The play hints that Duncan's murder has already been conceived of before the witches are encountered. Macbeth's reactions to the witches' prophecies make little sense otherwise: having been promised the kingship, Macbeth might not need to do anything to bring the prophecy about, as he himself realises – 'If Chance will haue me King, / Why Chance may Crowne me, / Without my stirre' (1.3, p. 133). But this sounds like wishful thinking. Macbeth realises it will

---

42 Thomas Browne, *Pseudodoxia Epidemica* (London, 1646), 1.10, p. 38.
43 James I, pp. 21–22.

not in fact happen without his 'stirre' because he has already contemplated Duncan's murder, and has guessed how he is to become king. This being the case, he learns from the witches that his murder will be successful – something that the devil correctly judges to be very likely. The devil's instruments would not make the prophecy if they did not realise that the decision to murder Duncan was ready to be taken.

The witches are, therefore, both allied to Macbeth and the trigger for his self-destruction, and this is because the instruments of darkness are also the instruments of God. The devil was frequently described as God's executioner,[44] and could only torment or test human beings with God's permission – and even then, only within the limits set by God. What happens in *Macbeth* is God's destruction, using the instruments of darkness, of a man who has been deservedly marked out for hell. The involvement of supernatural forces contributes to the sense of inevitability, present from the very start, about the outcome of the play. The idea that the forces of hell are genuinely in control is part of Macbeth's delusion – Malcolm, in pointed contrast, ascribes Macbeth's coming downfall to 'the Powres aboue' (IV.3, p. 148).

Reading the witches as tricksters, who pretend to much greater power than they in fact have, suggests a reading of Hecat as the devil, pretending to be a pagan deity.[45] While there is nothing in the text that makes such a reading of the Hecat scene explicit, it is unlikely that auditors with a grounding in demonology (such as James I) would have needed any prompting in order to reach this conclusion. An interesting parallel is provided by the interpretation of the biblical story of the witch of Endor, in which Saul consults a witch (or, strictly speaking, a pythoness) who summons the spirit of Samuel for him. The appearance of Samuel was frequently interpreted (especially in Protestant Europe) to be a story about demonic illusion, including by James I, despite the fact that the

---

44 Johnstone, p. 70.
45 Hecat's appearance at the end of the third act has struck many critics of the play as anomalous, and is frequently ascribed to Middleton. The question has been debated by Gary Taylor and Brian Vickers; see Taylor's introduction to *Macbeth* in the *Collected Works* of Middleton and the essay in the accompanying *Textual Companion* and Vickers, 'Disintegrated', *Times Literary Supplement* (28 May 2010), 14–15. Taylor responded in his article 'Empirical Middleton: *Macbeth*, Adaptation and Microauthorship', *Shakespeare Quarterly* 65:3 (2014), 239–72.

biblical text itself gives no grounds for such an interpretation.[46] In his discussion of the witch of Endor, James maintains that what appeared to be the ghost of Samuel was in fact an 'vnclean spirit'. James goes on to conclude that the devil was, in this instance, permitted by God to trick Saul for his sin in consulting a witch:

> God will not permit him so to deceiue his own: but only such, as first wilfully deceiues them-selues, by running vnto him, whome God then suffers to fall in their owne snares, and justlie permittes them to be illuded with great efficacy of deceit, because they would not beleeue the trueth.[47]

This logic can be applied to both Macbeth and the witches themselves; having deserved to be deluded by trusting in demonic forces, they are fooled by the devil throughout the play. As Clark points out, the parallels between the story of Saul and the story of Macbeth would have been hard for contemporary audiences to miss, so it seems reasonable to suppose that interpretation of Hecat in *Macbeth* might have been guided by interpretations of the witch of Endor story.

Equivocation – the act of simultaneously speaking the truth and deceiving – is an important theme of the play, and the fact that evil often speaks the truth does not mean it does not also set out to deceive. The witches frequently do this, most famously in the prophecies given in the cauldron scene; but Macbeth also equivocates once he has become a servant of the devil himself. After the murder of Duncan has been revealed, Macbeth expresses his anguish:

> Had I but dy'd an houre before this chance,
> I had liu'd a blessed time: for from this instant,
> There's nothing serious in Mortalitie:
> All is but Toyes: Renowne and Grace is dead,
> The Wine of Life is drawne, and the meere Lees
> Is left this Vault, to brag of.
> (II.3, p. 138)

As Bradley pointed out long ago, this is both disingenuous and true: although he seeks to deceive the other noblemen, the murder really has ruined Macbeth.[48] His declaration of despair is repeated, this time with unambiguous sincerity, later in the play, when Macbeth declares that 'my way of life / Is falne into the Seare, the yellow

---

46 Stuart Clark discusses the connections between Macbeth and Saul in *Vanities of the Eye*, pp. 240–44.
47 James I, *Daemonologie*, p. 4.
48 Bradley, p. 314.

Leafe' (v.3, p. 149). Macbeth is not a witch any more than Saul was,[49] but he is certainly witch-like in important respects: himself deluded, he attempts to trick others, and he deceives even when speaking the truth.

Lady Macbeth is not a witch in the literal sense either, but she too is linked to witchcraft. Like her husband, she is both a deceiver and a self-deceiver, deluding herself that Duncan's murder can be carried out without consequences, and deceiving others as to her guilt. She also invokes the aid of infernal powers, as does her husband. It is not clear that anything results from Lady Macbeth's invocation of the spirits – just as it is not clear that the witches' prophecies actually affect Macbeth's actions – but the mere speaking of the words constitutes an act of blasphemy and expresses trust in the power of evil spirits to aid Lady Macbeth's nefarious purposes. In this respect, she makes precisely the same mistake as her husband – trusting in hell rather than heaven. Both Lady Macbeth and her husband are brought down by their credulity, in the sense that they foolishly hope that evil forces can help them to achieve their aims, when in fact these forces merely seal their fate.

But while the Macbeths seem to be brought down by their credulity, they also display inappropriate scepticism. Macbeth, having decided on Duncan's murder, famously sees a ghostly dagger pointing to Duncan's bedchamber. What is most interesting about Macbeth's encounter with the dagger is his interpretation of it. When Macbeth asks the dagger:

> Art thou not fatall Vision, sensible
> To feeling, as to sight? or art thou but
> A Dagger of the Minde, a false Creation,
> Proceeding from the heat-oppressed Braine?
> (II.1, p. 136)

Macbeth does not seem to consider the possibility that there might be anything supernatural about the dagger: that it might, for example, be a warning sent by God, or a further incitement to crime sent by the devil. Instead he thinks that the dagger must either be real or that it is a hallucination with a physiological basis, which would seem to be a purely naturalistic explanation. Most critics of the

---

49 For a recent argument to the contrary, see Wills, p. 74. Paul also claims that Macbeth is a 'conjuror' (p. 279). If nothing else, Macbeth's apparent invocation of the spirits that appear late in the play bears some resemblance to Syphax's less ambiguous prayers to evil spirits in *Sophonisba*.

play, including those with an interest in demonology, have assumed Macbeth to be correct.[50] This ignores the possibility, outlined by Browne, that the devil, seeking to conceal his own existence, 'maketh men believe that apparitions, and such as confirm his existence are either deceptions of sight, or melancholly depravements of phansie'.[51] Like the writing which appears to Faustus as he signs his soul over to Mephastophilis, the vision of the dagger may be evidence of the involvement of infernal forces, and it is certainly a final opportunity for Macbeth to turn back from the murder he is about to commit. Instead, he ascribes the opposite purpose to the dagger, telling it, 'Thou marshall'st me the way that I was going, / And such an Instrument I was to vse.' Also like Faustus, Macbeth fails to heed the warning; blood appears on the dagger, but Macbeth dismisses its significance, and it disappears. The dagger scene is not there to display the great imaginative power with which some critics have credited Macbeth,[52] but to point to his inability to interpret the supernatural apparitions by which he is tormented.

Throughout the play, Macbeth consistently wishes for less awareness, less sensory perception, rather than more. He wants the eye to wink at the hand, the stars to hide their fires, and later in the dagger speech he makes a plea for the sense of hearing to be suspended:

> Thou sowre and firme-set Earth
> Heare not my steps, which they may walke, for feare
> Thy very stones prate of my where-about,
> And take the present horror from the time,
> Which now sutes with it. Whiles I threat, he liues:
> Words to the heat of deedes too cold breath giues. [*A Bell rings.*]
> I goe, and it is done: the Bell inuites me.
> Heare it not, Duncan, for it is a Knell,
> That summons thee to Heauen, or to Hell.
> (II.1, p. 136)

---

50 Paul, for example, confidently states that both the dagger and Banquo's ghost are 'purely imaginary' (p. 69).
51 Browne, *Pseudodoxia Epidemica*, I.10, p. 42.
52 A. C. Bradley was the most influential exponent of this view, crediting Macbeth with 'the imagination of a poet' (p. 308), although he went on to acknowledge the limited nature of Macbeth's imagination. Harold Bloom continues this tradition; see his 'Introduction' in *William Shakespeare's Macbeth* (New York: Infobase, 2010), pp. 1–7. Clark rightly points out that Macbeth is 'a man who cannot see properly' (*Vanities of the Eye*, p. 257).

Macbeth asks both the earth and Duncan not to hear, but he also seems to wish not to hear anything himself, preferring deeds to words. Macbeth's senses provide him with ample warning – the whole world seems to scream at him not to do what he has set out to do – but he wilfully blinds and deafens himself to the most vivid of portents. Macbeth is a doer, not a seer; he cannot bear to look at Banquo's ghost and tells his wife that 'Strange things I haue in head, that will to hand / Which must be acted, ere they may be scand' (III.4, p. 142). Not only vision and hearing, but even the passing on of information seems to trouble him by the end of the play: 'Bring me no more Reports' he tells his servants before the battle in which he is defeated, turning his back on sensory evidence entirely and placing all his trust in the witches' prophecies.

Stories about Edward the Confessor – one of the idealised monarchs in *Macbeth* – provide a counter-example to Macbeth's demonstration of how not to respond to a vision. According to an anonymous biographer, Edward was reluctant to collect taxes, but his advisers eventually prevailed upon him to do so, and proceeded to extort as much money as they could from the country. When they brought the proceeds to Edward in a chest, he astonished them by declaring that he saw the devil sitting on top of the chest, and demanded that they return all of the money to the people they had collected it from.[53] None of Edward's advisers were able to see the devil, but there is no suggestion in the text that it was not really there – Edward, the best of kings, was simply able to perceive the supernatural, which ordinary people cannot. Macbeth, the worst of kings, also does so, but he is not able to respond as he should, and in fact dismisses the visions he is subject to – even after he is terrified by Banquo's ghost, he calls it an 'Vnreall mock'ry' (III.4, p. 142).[54]

Lady Macbeth is even more sceptical of the evidence of her husband's senses, dismissing the significance of the 'Ayre-drawne Dagger' and the ghost of Banquo. Her attitude towards the sights

---

53 The story is told in the anonymous *Lyfe of saynt Edwarde confessour and kynge of Englande* (London, 1533), sig. A4^v–B1^r.

54 Early modern audiences probably perceived such apparitions to be real within the fictional work, and were likely to accept the ghost's selective invisibility. A passing reference to ghosts appears in Francis Beaumont and John Fletcher's *Knight of the Burning Pestle* (1607), in which Jasper threatens to haunt Venturewell as a ghost 'Invisible to all men but thyself' (London: J. M. Dent, 1913; v.1.27).

produced by her and her husband's actions is rather different from Macbeth's: instead of being unable to look at the murdered body of Duncan, she dismisses the reality of what she will soon see:

> the sleeping, and the dead,
> Are but as Pictures: 'tis the Eye of Child-hood,
> That feares a painted Deuill. If he doe bleed,
> Ile guild the Faces of the Groomes withall,
> For it must seeme their Guilt.
> (II.2, p. 137)

Once life has left Duncan's body, Lady Macbeth reasons, there is nothing left to fear. 'Pictures' – visions and appearances – can safely be ignored, as there is no reality behind them. Lady Macbeth might seem to have a point in relation to the dagger and the ghost of Banquo, but why the sleeping and the dead should be considered mere 'pictures' is less clear. Her words seem to call into question the reality of the world she sees, at a moment when the seriousness of her actions demands a vivid appreciation of it. The speech evokes not merely scepticism about the supernatural but a broader philosophical scepticism towards an external reality existing behind sensory phenomena. Having dismissed the importance of appearance, Lady Macbeth immediately reaffirms it, declaring that she will transfer the appearance of guilt to the grooms, by 'gilding' their faces with Duncan's blood. There is a touch of moral relativism in her speech, with its easy transfer of guilt, and the reference to a 'painted Deuill' hints at the possibility that she may not believe in a real devil, despite her invocation of evil spirits. As noted in Chapter 2, such a seemingly contradictory combination of scepticism and credulity is expressed by Faustus, who summons demons while advancing the opinion that hell is a fable. Like her husband, Lady Macbeth would seem to be prepared to 'iumpe the life to come' (I.7, p. 135) – if she believes in an afterlife at all.

Macbeth and his wife both have a relationship with the instruments of darkness, but their experiences move them in opposite directions. Lady Macbeth calls, unprompted, on evil spirits but does not encounter them, while Macbeth meets the witches without having invoked them. While Macbeth has visions – of the dagger and Banquo's ghost – Lady Macbeth does not, and dismisses her husband's visions as illusions or delusions. She herself starts to hallucinate later in the play, seeing blood on her hands, but only after Macbeth's visions have stopped. Although they do so in markedly different ways, both characters see both too much and too little. Most importantly, they both display misguided credulity *and* misguided scepticism, trusting the things they should be wary of and dismissing the warnings they should heed. The impious scepticism that Macbeth displays when he ignores the visions he should know how to interpret is the consequence of his foolish credulity.

The reading of the witches and other instruments of darkness given here is based on a conventional early modern demonology like the one expressed in James's own work (although that need not have been a direct source for the play). Together with the apparent rhetorical purpose of *Macbeth* – to highlight the contrast between kingship and tyranny in a manner particularly appealing to the King at the time – this would seem to require that the witches are taken as seriously, and with as little scepticism, as possible. This might raise a problem, since scepticism about witchcraft and the supernatural in general does exist in *Macbeth*. Both Macbeth and Banquo express scepticism in relation to the witches' very existence; and Macbeth and his wife display scepticism about the other apparitions in the play. All these expressions of scepticism, however, are part of a wider sense of unreality; as Stephen Greenblatt has put it, much of the action of the play 'transpires on the border between fantasy and reality'.[55] The potential unreliability of the senses, perhaps even of all knowledge, has long been recognised to be a major theme of the play. That the reality or otherwise of the apparitions – the dagger and Banquo's ghost – is never explicitly clarified and remains open to debate is typical of the play's indeterminate representation of supernatural phenomena.

But while Greenblatt argues that 'Shakespeare's theatre ... is on the side of a liberating, tolerant doubt',[56] he also acknowledges that Shakespeare's work is not written from the perspective of a Scotian sceptic. In fact, it is precisely the aspect of the play described – that its epistemology is so doubtful – that prevents *Macbeth* from being a sceptical play in this sense. Scotian scepticism is anything but doubtful – Scot himself is convinced of his position, and presents naturalistic explanations in order to dismiss any apparently supernatural event. This certainty is what is lacking in *Macbeth*: Macbeth and Banquo's conversation about the witches contains more *dis*belief than genuine *un*belief, the kind of disbelief anyone might feel when presented with events completely outside the scope of their previous experience. The type of naturalistic explanation Scot would demand

---

55 Greenblatt, p. 124.
56 Greenblatt, p. 127.

– such as that offered by 'physic' – is thrown to the dogs. It is precisely the great uncertainty felt by Macbeth and Banquo about the witches' nature, and even their very existence, that makes the witches so credible as dramatic creations.

Of course, not all critics share the view that the witches are credible: this is probably why the wayward sisters' scenes have so frequently been dismissed as spurious. Diane Purkiss outlines her case against the witches on these grounds:

> [T]he witch-scenes brazenly refuse any serious engagement with witchcraft in favour of a forthright rendering of witches as a stage spectacular. These all-singing, all-dancing witches bear about as much relation to the concerns of village women as *The Sound of Music* does to women's worries about childcare in the 1990s ... Learned interpretations of the play which eagerly make sense of the witches and relate their activities cogently to the main action are untrue to the play's unbridled sensationalism.[57]

According to Purkiss, witchcraft in *Macbeth* should not be taken seriously, because the 'all-singing, all-dancing' nature of the witches' performance undermines any sense of reality about them. Although Purkiss approaches the play from a very different angle from that of those Victorian Shakespeare scholars who disputed Shakespeare's authorship of the insufficiently serious (and worryingly superstitious) witchcraft scenes, the feelings behind these two different objections are perhaps related: the witches are just not serious enough.

But Purkiss's objection seems misguided to me, particularly in blaming the singing and dancing of the witches for undermining their seriousness in *Macbeth*. It is surprising for Purkiss to criticise the play on these grounds, since her own ground-breaking work highlights the fact that 'real' witchcraft could be all-singing and all-dancing, too. Quoting from *Newes from Scotland*, Purkiss points out that the North Berwick witches confessed to playing music and dancing in the kirk – the kinds of activities that were reminiscent of the witches' sabbat as it was often represented in other parts of Europe, but that English witches did not usually engage in.[58] These accused witches were said to sing 'all with one voice: Commer ye

---

57 Purkiss, *The Witch in History*, p. 207.
58 Purkiss, *The Witch in History*, p. 199. James Sharpe, 'In Search of the English Sabbat: Popular Conceptions of Witches' Meetings in Early Modern England', *Journal of Early Modern Studies* 2 (2013), 161–83, has recently suggested that the sabbat, while largely absent from demonological writings, legislation and trial pamphlets, may have existed in some form in the

go before, commer go ye / If ye will not go before, comer let me.'[59] (It is tempting to detect a faint echo of this in the Folio's 'Come away, come away &c.') Purkiss also draws attention to James's demand, as reported by the pamphlet, that one of the accused witches, Gillis Duncan, dance for his entertainment. The witches' songs and dances in *Macbeth*, and the stage directions calling for 'Infernall Musique' in *Sophonisba*, would appear to be a case of art imitating life – or at least, life as it appears in a piece of Stuart propaganda.[60] The singing witches point to a new development in the representation of the stage witch. Apparently taking its cue from *Newes from Scotland*, *Macbeth* imports a literary view of witchcraft from Scotland into England.

Macbeth is unusual for a play featuring witches in that witchcraft itself is not subjected to an examination of any kind. No limits are explicitly set on the powers of witches; there is little in the way of discussion of what they can or cannot do. While Macbeth's witches recite a list of magical ingredients, like many other stage witches before them, they do not reveal what these ingredients are actually *for*. *Macbeth* raises no questions about the nature and extent of witches' powers in the manner of, for example, *The Witch of Edmonton*, nor does it present a strong sceptical voice on the question within the play like *The Late Lancashire Witches* or *The Lancashire Witches*. Unlike these plays, *Macbeth* is not in any sense about witchcraft. The witches are real within the action of the play, but they are only important for the light they throw on Macbeth and his crime; the audience may be deceived by them along with the characters. In *Macbeth* as in 1 Samuel 15:23, rebellion is as the sin of witchcraft, and it is the rebel, not the witch, who is always in focus.

This is not to say, however, that rhetorical scepticism is irrelevant to *Macbeth*. In fact, *Macbeth* could be said to take its scepticism further than any other witchcraft play. The world of the play is one in which all knowledge is undermined – a world in which nothing is, but what is not. Within such a world, witches and witchcraft are hardly even surprising, let alone impossible; almost everything in *Macbeth* is shrouded in mystery in order to create a suitable backdrop for the supernatural. *Macbeth* avoids regurgitating

---

popular imagination (pp. 164–66). It is striking that the earliest piece of evidence Sharpe presents for this view is *Macbeth*.
59 *Newes from Scotland*, reprinted in Normand and Roberts, p. 315.
60 Purkiss, *The Witch in History*, p. 200.

demonological debates through the medium of characters' speeches, in favour of bringing to life the deceptive power of the devil. The sheer scale of the doubt raised by the play, in fact, comes dangerously close to overwhelming its apparent purpose of glorifying the king, whose divinely ordained power hardly seems adequate to take control of such an uncertain world.

The Masque of Queens

Discussions of Ben Jonson's *Masque of Queens* (1609) often touch on or even revolve around the question of whether the entertainment flatters the King at the expense of the Queen, flatters the Queen at the expense of the King, or attempts to achieve a balance between these two possibilities.[61] But regardless of how it was perceived by individual members of the royal family, there can be little doubt that flattery is the masque's primary function. The means by which this end is achieved is contrast: *The Masque of Queens* was the first masque to present a fully fledged anti-masque as part of the entertainment, with a group of witches (played by men) ultimately defeated by the eponymous queens, whose parts were performed by the Queen and various noblewomen. Once again, the contrast with royalty is provided by witches. If the formal innovation – the anti-masque – which *The Masque of Queens* introduced was indeed suggested by Anne, as Jonson's preface claims, this would hardly

---

61 Stephen Orgel's 'Jonson and the Amazons', in *Soliciting Interpretation*, edited by Elizabeth D. Harvey and Katharine Eisaman Maus (Chicago: University of Chicago Press, 1990), pp. 119–39, points out that the queens are ultimately subordinate to the male figure of Heroic Virtue and the King, while Barbara K. Lewalski, *Writing Women in Jacobean England* (Cambridge, MA: Harvard University Press, 1993), stresses Anne's personal involvement in and influence over the masque, which she regards as subtly subversive of James's patriarchal authority (pp. 24–38). Lawrence Normand, 'Witches, King James, and *The Masque of Queens*', in *Representing Women in Renaissance England*, edited by Claude J. Summers and Ted-Larry Pebworth (Columbia: University of Missouri Press, 1997), offers a similar reading, while Peter Holbrook, 'Jacobean Masques and the Jacobean Peace', in *The Politics of the Stuart Court Masque*, edited by David Bevington and Peter Holbrook (Cambridge: Cambridge University Press, 1998), pp. 67–87, claims that 'Jonson ... plainly found it necessary to bear in mind Anne's views about gender and politics while at the same time producing a public entertainment that would not openly offend the King' (p. 79).

be surprising.[62] Her husband had periodically used witches as the backdrop for his divinely ordained kingship since shortly after their marriage.

The focus of the masque, as its title suggests, is not on the King but on the feminine virtue of queens, a point of contrast with *Macbeth*'s focus on masculinity. Consequently, there is no need to associate the witches with a male tyrant, as happens in *Sophonisba* and *Macbeth*: they are directly opposed to the queens. The witches, who appear on stage before the queens, are an odd mixture of stage witch and personified vice. The head witch is simply called the Dame, but her followers are, in order of appearance, Ignorance, Suspicion, Credulity, Falsehood, Murmur, Malice, Impudence, Slander, Execration, Bitterness, Rage, and Mischief. While the witches are said to be 'all differently attired' by the published text of the masque,[63] the description of the costumes does not individuate them, but emphasises their chaotic and disharmonious nature. The witches are not characters so much as a collective principle of chaos. Their names can readily be associated with stereotypes about witchcraft: they deceive (Falsehood, Slander, Mischief, Murmur), they are themselves deceived (Ignorance, Credulity, Suspicion), and they are motivated by an angry desire for revenge (Malice, Bitterness, Rage, Execration, Impudence). But the names can also be read as politically threatening, in that they suggest a potential for the creation of popular disorder.

Once again, witchcraft is not represented for its own sake, but as a symbol of something else. In the case of this entertainment, however, the witches do not represent tyranny so much as anarchy. The witches are 'differently attired', they make 'a confused noise' and 'strange gestures' (ll.27–30); they eventually perform a 'dance full of preposterous change and gesticulation' (328). Order is restored only by the appearance of Heroic Virtue and the queens, who at their first appearance are seen 'sitting upon a throne triumphal erected in the shape of a pyramid' (340). The throne – monarchical power – restores order and drives away an evil that has been portrayed in terms of an unnatural lack of control over vices – vices associated in elite circles both with the populace in general and with witches

---

62 Anne's patronage of the theatre and her involvement in the masque are discussed by Lewalski, esp. pp. 24–28.
63 Line 27. References, given in parentheses hereafter, are to the text in *Ben Jonson: The Complete Masques*, edited by Stephen Orgel (New Haven: Yale University Press, 1969).

in particular (especially Ignorance and Credulity). The conquered vices are later shown bound to the chariots ridden by the queens. Royal power over the unruly populace is the happy resolution of the threat presented by the anti-masque. The key to this victory is reputation, and consequently power over information.

Heroic Virtue – the only male character – appears dressed as Perseus and describes himself as the father of Fame.[64] Monika Smialkowska shows that 'Fame', in an early modern context, is a highly equivocal term; by no means straightforwardly 'good', it is sometimes equated with the idea of rumour. As Smialkowska also notes, this important point is acknowledged, briefly but explicitly, in the masque.[65] Line 368 makes reference to 'all rumours and reports, true or vain' existing in the palace of Fame. Both ignorant and suspicious witches and virtuous queens give rise to fame, it is just that they create fame of different kinds. The good Fame created by Virtue is opposed to the kind of false fame that is motivated by Malice, Suspicion, and all the rest. It is difficult not to perceive a response to dissatisfaction with Stuart rule in the allegory of the masque.

Fame, for queens, is an unavoidable condition, one way or another. As the masque puts it, Fame 'only hangs great actions on her file' (370), and the actions of the great are always, by definition, great actions, whether they become famous or infamous. The ambiguity of fame need not be seen as implying criticism of the queens; it could simply derive from a recognition that Ignorance, Credulity and other vices, as well as the virtues of the heroic queens, can create reputations too – bad ones. It is often noted that Jonson points to the poet's role in preventing this by creating and eternising good reputations for royal patrons; indeed, as Orgel points out, this function of poetry was communicated by the architecture of the set.[66] In a world where 'all rumours and reports, true or vain' abound, there is an obvious need for a strong voice to ensure that the 'true' reports – or the most convenient ones – are heard above

---

64 Orgel, 'Jonson and the Amazons', discusses the significance of Perseus in detail, pp. 128–31.
65 Monika Smialkowska, '"Out of the authority of ancient and late writers": Ben Jonson's Use of Textual Sources in *The Masque of Queens*', *English Literary Renaissance* 32:2 (2002), 268–86 (p. 276).
66 Orgel, 'Jonson and the Amazons', p. 131. The façade featured statues of great heroes, underneath which were statues of great poets. As Orgel points out, 'the heroes' fame is supported and preserved by the immortal poets',

the clamour of witch-like Suspicion. Anything or anyone that seeks to cast aspersions on Queen Anne – unpopular in England as a result of her poorly concealed Catholicism – is not only deluded but demonic.

However, the glory of the queens is less clearly distinct from the evil of the witches than at first appears. The queens, supposedly historical characters, are in some cases associated with the use of magic; others were supposedly responsible for extreme acts of violence, all of which is made clear by Jonson's own notes. As Kathryn Schwarz puts it, 'the drama of masque and antimasque opposes two myths of female power, and the visible result ... is not difference but assimilation'.[67] This blurring of the apparently sharp distinction between good and evil power follows from the difficulty of distinguishing between witchcraft and kingcraft (or, in this case, queencraft).

A masque, by its nature, is a highly artificial form of entertainment, and the artificiality of Jonson's witches renders the question of scepticism and belief in witchcraft moot. An attitude from outside the dramatic fiction does, however, shine through in Jonson's extensive marginal notes. Jonson is clearly interested in displaying his own expertise, which he does by reference both to classical myth and to early modern demonology. He also adopts a demonologically orthodox attitude towards witchcraft. Throughout his notes, Jonson's statements about witches are worded as statements of fact. Jonson writes about what witches (really) do, and what they (really) believe. To take one brief example, he writes, in reference to actions related by the witches in the main text, that: 'This throwing vp of ashes, and sand, with the flint stone, crosse sticks, and burying of sage &c. are al vs'd (and beleev'd by them) to the raysing of storme and tempest.'[68] While Jonson may be dubious about this specific power of witches, his doubt is compatible with more general witchcraft belief. Whatever the precise extent of their powers, Jonson never implies that witches do not, in fact, exist. He also attempts to identify ancient witches with modern witches,[69] an attitude which aligns him with those demonologists who wrote to encourage the persecution of witches, rather than with the sceptics. Given that masques are always allegorical, a witch in a masque is not really a

---

67 Kathryn Schwarz, 'Amazon Reflections in the Jacobean Queen's Masque', *Studies in English Literature 1500–1900* 35:2 (1995), 293–319 (p. 308).
68 Jonson's note to line 249.
69 Smialkowska, 284.

witch at all (she is, instead, Ignorance or Credulity). But Jonson's notes allow the printed text to emphasise that the topic of witchcraft, though necessarily symbolic or allegorical in the masque itself, is not merely fictitious.

But as well as citing Ovid and Del Rio, Jonson makes use of less serious sources in explaining his witches' declarations: he would not have been aware, when writing the performance version of the masque, that his sources would later have to be revealed in the annotated holograph that Prince Henry requested of him.[70] As Smialkowska points out, Jonson

> sometimes uses hearsay, popular stories, or even gossip alongside the more 'respectable' sources, yet he is slightly embarrassed by this: 'Of the green cock we have no other ground (to confess ingenuously) than a vulgar fable of a witch that with a cock of that color and a bottom of blue thread would transport herself through the air, and so escaped, at the time of her being brought to execution, from the hand of justice. It was a tale when I went to school' (annotation to l. 59).[71]

There is nothing unusual about Jonson's use of gossip and hearsay, given the precedent set by supposedly respectable demonological sources like the *Malleus Maleficarum*. But Jonson's admission that the green cock mentioned in the masque is taken from a story he heard as a schoolboy is made with a degree of sheepishness. Jonson's embarrassment might be heightened by the irony that a work which attacks rumour and slander, and associates it with witches, nevertheless uses similarly groundless gossip as if it were possessed of authority. Ignorance and Credulity might be the villains of the masque, but they also seem to have helped to write it. *The Masque of Queens* is left in the uncomfortable position of both relying on and rejecting popular rumour and 'credulity', suggesting a double-edged quality to the Jacobean theatre's rhetorical and propagandistic use of witchcraft.

As noted, the opposing forces of kingcraft and witchcraft have much in common. The opposition of witchcraft to the court which James had done so much to inspire carried risks. One such risk is evident in *The Masque of Queens*. The masque treats queenly virtue

---

70 Lynn Sermin Meskill, 'Exorcising the Gorgon of Terror: Jonson's *Masque of Queenes*', ELH 72:1 (2005), 181–207 (p. 181).
71 Smialkowska, 285.

as indissolubly linked to feminine reputation, or good fame, a connection made explicit in the following lines:

> Sing then good Fame that's out of Virtue born,
> For who doth Fame neglect doth Virtue scorn.
> (487–88)

The appearance of virtue is so important that it can almost be equated with virtue itself. A bad reputation is in itself evidence of lack of virtue, since virtuous people – especially, perhaps, virtuous women – take care of their reputation. But as well as being a particular view of what feminine virtue consists of, the lines are a call to action. Fame, the words imply, must not be neglected, and this is the function of the poet. The Ignorance and Credulity of the people will listen to any Falsehood or Slander, and this threat must be countered. In the masque this is an easy matter, with the virtue of the queens banishing the witches as soon as they appear on stage. In reality, however, the witchcraft of Suspicion and Murmur were not so easily defeated, and Impudence, in the person of Thomas Middleton, was to take the dramatic representation of witchcraft in a new direction. In doing so, Middleton was inspired by the activities of one of the queens in the masque – not the pseudo-historical character, but the performer: Frances Howard, Countess of Essex, who appeared alongside Queen Anne on stage. The concluding lines of the masque are triumphant:

> Force greatness all the glorious ways
> You can, it soon decays,
> But so good Fame shall never:
> Her triumphs, as their causes, are forever.
> (523–26)

Frances Howard, however, was soon to demonstrate that 'good Fame' could decay quite rapidly, and that a 'queen' could easily turn into a witch. The connections between witchcraft, reputation, and rumour remain important in the next major Jacobean work of witchcraft drama, Middleton's *The Witch*.

Frances Howard, court scandal, and *The Witch*

Frances Howard, daughter of the Earl of Suffolk, had married the Earl of Essex when both were in their early teens, but they did not live together as a couple until several years later. When the time came for this to happen, at around the same time as Frances danced in Jonson's masque at court, the marriage proved not to be a success. Eventually Frances, having become romantically and politically linked to the King's favourite Robert Carr, sought an annulment of the marriage, with Essex's acquiescence. The couple claimed that the marriage should be annulled on grounds of non-consummation, and that, despite their best efforts, the marriage not only had not been but could never be consummated, because Essex suffered from selective impotence. He was unable to have sexual intercourse with his wife, although he suffered no such impediment with other women. It was claimed, although not very confidently or consistently, that this infirmity was the result of witchcraft.

Despite considerable opposition, the annulment had James's personal support and was eventually granted. Soon afterwards, Frances Howard and Robert Carr were married, amid lavish celebrations, including a performance of the *Masque of Cupids* (1613), written especially for the occasion by – ironically, in view of what was to come – Thomas Middleton. The text of the masque is unfortunately lost.[72] Another masque written in celebration of the wedding is Thomas Campion's *Masque of Squires* (1613), which features 'curst Enchanters' and enchantresses named Error, Rumor, Curiosity, and Credulity, presumably in reference to the scandal that had preceded the marriage.[73] Campion's use of these characters would seem to owe something to *The Masque of Queens*, and the continuing concern of this elite genre with public discontent, reflected in the depiction of such discontent as a form of evil magic, is evident.

While popular unrest could figure as witchcraft in elite drama, actual cases of witchcraft among the populace were the subject of more frequent, and sceptical, intervention in James's reign. James's relish for unmasking fraudulent cases of demonic possession has already been referred to, and state papers reveal a number of pardons given for witchcraft, as well as a warrant 'to pay ... such sums as the Earl of Salisbury shall require, for the charges of two maids suspected to be bewitched, and kept at Cambridge for trial'.[74] But

---

72 A thorough discussion of the masque is provided by M. T. Jones-Davies and Ton Hoenselaars, 'Masque of Cupids', in *Thomas Middleton: The Collected Works*, edited by Gary Taylor and John Lavagnino (Oxford: Oxford University Press, 2007), pp. 1027–33.

73 Thomas Campion, *The Description of a Maske: Presented in the Banqueting Roome at Whitehall, on Saint Stephens Night Last at the Mariage of the Right Honourable the Earle of Somerset: And the Right Noble the Lady Frances Howard* (London, 1614).

74 CSPD, xiv, 21 May 1605.

what appears to have been a generally sceptical attitude on the part of James and his councillors towards cases of witchcraft in the populace at large was not displayed towards the claim that Essex had been bewitched. In the case of this claim, it was the populace that seems to have been sceptical, while James personally wrote to the most outspoken critic of the nullity, George Abbot, Archbishop of Canterbury, in order to argue that this particular type of maleficent magic was possible, pointing out that 'if the Devil hath any power, it is over the flesh, rather over the filthiest and most sinful part thereof, whereunto original sin is soldered'.[75] Elite scepticism about popular witchcraft was replaced by belief – sincere or otherwise – when it was the elite themselves who were threatened by it. A dramatic analogy can be seen in the treatment of witchcraft in most of the plays discussed so far. Where witchcraft is taken seriously, it is only because it is dignified by the involvement of royal or aristocratic characters.

A large proportion of the general public, frequently depicted (and not only in *The Masque of Queens*) as credulous and ignorant, seem to have been outraged by the Essex divorce, and their views were represented by Abbot who, in his objections to the nullity, took aim at what he seems to have regarded as the weakest part of the case – the claim that Essex's impotence was caused by maleficent witchcraft:

> [A]mongst a million of men in our age, there is but one found in all our country, who is clearly and evidently known to be troubled with the same. And if there should be any which should seem to be molested, we are taught to use two remedies, the one temporal physic, the other eternal ... Now admit the earl might be imagined to be troubled with *maleficium versus hanc*; I demand what alms hath been given, what fasting hath been used, and what prayers have been poured forth to appease the wrath of God towards him or his wife; or what physic hath been taken, or medicine hath been applied for three years together? Not one of these things: but the first hearing must be to pronounce a nullity in the marriage.[76]

---

75 T. B. Howell (ed.), *A Complete Collection of State Trials* (London, 1816), vol. 2, p. 801. James's argument finds support in the most famous of witch-hunters' manuals, the *Malleus Maleficarum*, which claims that God gives permission to the devil to hinder 'the sexual act, through which the first sin is spread'. The *Malleus* also allows for the dissolution of a marriage in cases of selective impotence in an unconsummated marriage: see II.2.161D–163B (pp. 421–24). If James did base his argument on this (Catholic) authority, he does not mention it to Abbot.

76 *State Trials*, p. 795.

Considering that Abbot is addressing himself to the King, his tone is surprisingly blunt. His scepticism about the witchcraft claim is close to the surface; he is barely willing to concede that the Earl of Essex can even be 'imagined' to be bewitched. The failure to try to find any kind of remedy, Abbot feels, makes a mockery of the institution of marriage, and in other sections of his written opinion he worries about the precedent that will be set.

The annulment of the Essex-Howard marriage was eventually granted without explicit reference to *maleficium versus hanc* in the text of the decision, which referred instead to 'some secret, incurable, binding impediment'.[77] *Maleficium* seems to have been abandoned as a convincing rationale for the nullity, probably because of the widespread scepticism with which the claim seems to have been greeted by the public. The topic seems to have induced considerable mirth, as well as anger, and people associated with the nullity proceedings were reportedly held in 'perpetual scorn' afterwards.[78] Abbot's written thoughts on the decision, which in the end were not read out in public, show him to have been aware of the embarrassment caused by the witchcraft claim, but unaware that it had been quietly dropped:

> [I]n the very sentence which is this day to be given, it falleth directly upon the description of 'maleficium versus hanc.' So that what should I think of this case of my lord's, which is built on such a foundation as no man will stand to? We are on it, and off it, and avow it we dare not, yet fly from it we will not.[79]

Perhaps the most remarkable thing about this undelivered speech is that the Archbishop of Canterbury – the highest clergyman in England, writing on a matter of national importance for an audience including the monarch and the assembled nobility – felt it appropriate to include a crude joke about erectile dysfunction, describing *maleficium versus hanc* as something that 'no man will stand to'. As is so often the case, scepticism about witchcraft is accompanied by ridicule and laughter. The scepticism towards this particular alleged instance of witchcraft may have been exacerbated by the dithering of those who sought the nullity, which Abbot mocks with gusto.

But the public response to the Essex nullity was not straightforwardly sceptical; it also included a great deal of credulity. Many people, judging by the rumours that circulated, were sceptical about

---

77 *State Trials*, p. 804.
78 *State Trials*, p. 833.
79 *State Trials*, p. 848.

the claims made by the elite in support of the nullity, but highly credulous in their attitudes to alternative explanations. To take one example, the grounds for the divorce were supported by the testimony of a panel of midwives and noblewomen, who were said to have conducted a physical examination of Frances Howard and declared her to be a virgin. Rumours suggested that the panel had been tricked, and that the person examined was not, in fact, Frances Howard. Doubting whether the examination had taken place at all would be a purely sceptical response to this news. Claiming that the examination had indeed taken place, but that the panel had been subjected to an elaborate deception is not (or not only) scepticism but (also) a form of credulity – the kind that would now be called a conspiracy theory.

Furthermore, not everybody doubted the involvement of witchcraft. One manuscript verse libel on the subject claimed that:

Letchery did consult with witcherye
how to procure frygiditye
upon this ground a course was found
to frame unto a nullatye.[80]

In this poem, the claims of *maleficium versus hanc* are taken seriously; but rather than supporting James's desire to grant the nullity, Frances is accused of having procured her own husband's impotence by magical means. One major weakness of the claim made in support of the Essex nullity was that it diagnosed witchcraft without identifying the witch; as far as I am aware, this is a unique circumstance in the history of English witchcraft cases. In such circumstances it is hardly surprising that Frances herself was identified as, if not the witch, then the witch's client – particularly in view of rumours about her marital infidelity and her alleged involvement with a cunning woman from Norwich.[81]

The public credulity demonised by the masques of Jonson and Campion reached new heights after further developments in the growing scandal around Frances Howard. Soon after her marriage to Robert Carr, her new husband's fortunes changed. A new favourite – George Villiers, later to become Duke of Buckingham – rose to prominence, threatening his position at court, and Carr and his

---

80 Anon., 'Letchery did consult with witcherye', *Early Stuart Libels*, www.earlystuartlibels.net/htdocs/essex_nullity_section/F2.html (accessed 16 August 2016).
81 Anne Somerset, *Unnatural Murder: Poison at the Court of James I* (London: Orion, 1998), pp. 119–21.

wife became entangled in accusations of murder. Carr's associate Sir Thomas Overbury, who had been imprisoned by James after refusing a diplomatic post, had died in the Tower before the marriage of Carr and Howard, and in 1615 rumours that he had been poisoned began to be investigated. A number of people were convicted of, and executed for, involvement in Overbury's murder. The final trials were of Frances and Robert Carr. Frances pleaded guilty, while her husband maintained his innocence, but both were convicted. Unlike their accomplices, neither Frances nor Robert Carr was executed, however, as James pardoned them both. As Alastair Bellany has shown, the evidence suggests that James's pardon of the murderers was both unexpected and shocking to many people.[82]

Following the revelation of Overbury's murder, the rumours circulating about Frances and Carr increased in both variety and implausibility. This was partly the result of the investigation into the murder, which was led by the Lord Chief Justice of the King's Bench, Sir Edward Coke. According to the Spanish ambassador, Coke had been chosen with Carr's blessing as his 'creature and intimate friend', but quickly became associated with Carr's enemies.[83] In fact, Coke's zeal in investigating, prosecuting, and executing those involved in the Overbury murder may have been the reason for his eventual replacement by Francis Bacon; a later manuscript account of Coke's role in the prosecutions claims that he angered James by 'peeping in to the secrets of his Prince, & making publick diuers contents pickt out of such letters as Somerset not only minion but principall Secretary of State had in his custody at the time of his apprehension'.[84] The same source says of Carr that 'if posterity mesur his fallt by the gretnes of the Judge Coocks hiperbolicall & reduckulus Crimenations thay say more to his charge then possibly he desarved'.[85] Certainly, Coke did little to play down some of the wilder rumours that circulated concerning Overbury's murder. In open court, he declared:

> The eye of England never saw, nor the ear of Christendom never heard of such poisoning so heinous, so horrible ... You my masters,

---

82 Alastair Bellany, *The Politics of Court Scandal in Early Modern England: News Culture and the Overbury Affair, 1603–1660* (Cambridge: Cambridge University Press, 2002), pp. 244–45.
83 S. R. Gardiner, 'On Certain Letters of Diego Sarmiento de Acuna, Count of Gondomar', *Archaeologia* 41 (1867), 151–86 (pp. 169–70).
84 BL Add MS 25348, fol. 17^v. See also Somerset, pp. 427–28.
85 BL Add MS 25348, fol. 4^r.

shall hear strange, and stupendous things, such as the ears of men never heard of ... God is my witness, and whether it hath brim or bottom I yet know not, I yet cannot find it.[86]

Coke whipped up public concern by linking the Overbury murder to widespread fears of Catholic Spain, a strategy which exploited Carr's recent political manoeuvres. Carr undoubtedly became a part of the pro-Spanish grouping in court by November 1613 – against the wishes of his friend Overbury – and had been the leading voice in attempts to arrange a marriage between Prince Charles and the Spanish infanta.[87] His marriage to a member of the notoriously Catholic and pro-Spanish Howard family cemented these allegiances, and after the murder of Overbury was revealed, it was rumoured that he would be charged with treason as a Spanish spy.[88] Coke fuelled such rumours by referring in court to the attempted Spanish invasion of 1588 and the gunpowder plot, and one of the accused, James Franklin, added to the intrigue by hinting at a larger conspiracy, probably in an attempt to delay his execution. The implausibility of the rumours peaked with stories of a Catholic plot to poison the entire royal family. To this end, it was said that Frances had faked her pregnancy so that the poisoning could be carried out at a banquet celebrating the birth of the baby (which would be borrowed). After the murder of the royal family, English Catholics would have risen up in support of 'King Carr', and the Tower of London was to be taken over by 500 Spaniards who would set London on fire. Mass would then be said, following which Protestants throughout the country would have been massacred. The ultimate goal of this supposed Popish plot was the total destruction of the Protestant religion throughout Europe.[89]

Frances Howard's association with witchcraft was strengthened by such tales. The involvement of poison was significant. Poison was frequently associated with witchcraft in early modern England; and like witches, poisoners were said to have been taught 'cunning' by the devil during the Overbury trials.[90] In the trial of Frances

---

86 Quoted in Bellany, p. 181.
87 Bellany, p. 63.
88 Bellany, p. 192.
89 Bellany, pp. 185–91. The real and perceived threat of various 'Popish plots' in the sixteenth and seventeenth centuries connects with the history of witchcraft drama both at this time and in the case of Thomas Shadwell's *The Lancashire Witches* (1681) – see Chapter 7.
90 *State Trials*, p. 912.

Howard's accomplice Anne Turner, magical paraphernalia such as 'pictures of a man and woman in copulation' and a black scarf 'full of white crosses' were displayed in court – with unfortunate results:

> At the shewing of these, and inchanted papers and other pictures in court, there was heard a crack from the scaffolds, which caused great fear, tumult and confusion among the spectators, and throughout the hall, every one fearing hurt, as if the devil had been present, and grown angry to have his workmanship shewed, by such as were not his scholars; and this terror continuing about a quarter of an hour, after silence [was] proclaimed.[91]

This incident, trivial though it may have been, reveals the genuine fear that witchcraft was capable of generating. During the same trial, Coke ordered that the defendant's conjurations were not to be read out, apparently for fear that the devil might appear.[92]

Following all this excitement, the eventual result of the investigation and trials must have been an anti-climax. While their low-born accomplices were executed, Carr and his wife were found guilty but pardoned, and spent the rest of their lives in relatively comfortable disgrace. Coke, and to a lesser extent Bacon after him, had sought to portray the activities of the poisoners as witch-like, in opposition to the divinely ordained kingship of James. In doing so, they not only followed a narrative of providential deliverance, as Bellany points out,[93] but also an opposition between monarch and witchcraft that had been established in James's own association of his enemy Bothwell with witches – an association which had by this time been reinforced by the theatre. Ultimately, however, such an opposition could not be maintained in the face of the royal pardon and the closeness of the Carrs to the King himself.

The Overbury affair coincided with, and probably caused, a spike in public interest in witchcraft, and three significant English works on the subject were published very soon after the trials: Alexander Roberts's *Treatise of Witchcraft* (1616), John Cotta's *The Triall of Witch-craft* (1616), and Thomas Cooper's *The Mystery of Witchcraft* (1617). Roberts's book was inspired by the trial of Mary Smith in King's Lynn in Norfolk, and would seem to have no connection with the Essex or Overbury scandals (although it

---

91 *State Trials*, p. 932.
92 David Chan Smith, *Sir Edward Coke and the Reformation of the Laws* (Cambridge: Cambridge University Press, 2014), p. 132.
93 Bellany, p. 206.

does contain an intriguing metaphorical use of the word 'nullity').[94] Cotta's book, however, is dedicated to Sir Edward Coke, suggesting that the impetus for its publication may have been the Overbury trials. The dedication could have been a miscalculation on Cotta's part. By June 1616 at the latest, Coke had fallen from favour,[95] and it may be that, by the time the book was actually completed, Cotta had become aware of this. He appears at times to strike a balance between flattering Coke – as he does in his reference to the importance of 'the learned, prudent, and discerning Iudge' in protecting the nation from the threat of witchcraft – and acknowledging that some cases will never be solved, and that this has to be accepted with 'patience and sobriety'.[96] Coke had not displayed these qualities in seeking to portray the Overbury affair as a vast and sinister conspiracy. Cotta's book avoids any direct reference to the Overbury affair, but there is at least one passage towards the end of the book which might have seemed rather pointed to its original readers:

> [I]t is not onely the sauing duety of all priuate men to take more diligent and warie notice thereof, thereby to eschew and flye from it, according vnto Gods expresse charge and command; but it is the charge of Princes & Magistrates also, to fulfill therby the commanded execution of Gods holy wrath and vengeance vpon it.[97]

King James had disappointed public opinion by *not* executing vengeance on the two main culprits in the Overbury case. Cotta says nothing in the passage above that the King could have disagreed with, since James had made similar points himself in *Daemonologie*, but for readers in 1616 the sentiment might have taken on a new layer of meaning.

Thomas Cooper's *The Mystery of Witchcraft* makes no claim to originality. Cooper states that 'I am not ashamed to acknowledge, that which thou canst not but discerne; That *I have borrowed most*

---

94 Roberts, p. 4.
95 Somerset, p. 427. Cotta's book was entered into the Stationer's Register on 26 November 1615, a month which saw four other titles directly related to the Overbury scandal entered into the register, as well as a copy entitled *The reward of the adulterer and adulteresse paid by GODs owne hand* – another topic with obvious potential for application to the Carrs. See Edward Arber (ed.), *A Transcript of the Registers of the Company of Stationers of London* (London, 1875), vol. 3, pp. 266–67.
96 Cotta, p. 18.
97 Cotta, p. 127.

of my Grounds'.⁹⁸ Cooper credits a number of previous writers on witchcraft, including James, but despite his apparent humility there are a number of unusual features of his work – many of which seem much less flattering to the King than Cooper's explicit mention of him would suggest. On one point, Cooper follows James's lead, as he argues for the possibility of witchcraft causing selective impotence.⁹⁹ But Cooper also peppers his work with critical references to the court and to the powerful and wealthy. These references are never to specific people from Cooper's England; but read in the light of the Overbury scandal – probably the most sensational event to take place in England since the gunpowder plot – his attitude towards the social and political elite is revealing.

One of Cooper's more surprising positions on witchcraft is his claim that witches are more devout in their loyalty to the devil than some Christians are to God.¹⁰⁰ Comparing Christians, unfavourably, with witches is an unusual rhetorical strategy for a writer on witchcraft, and Cooper goes on to attack those clergymen who '*leaue the Flocke*, and attend the Courts of Princes, or their Hounds and Hawlkes, or worse'.¹⁰¹ Cooper's dissatisfaction with insufficiently zealous clergymen is maintained throughout his text, and it is significant that he chooses to link them to 'the Courts of Princes'. Cooper's frequent attacks on court corruption and worldly power

---

98 Cooper, p. 363.
99 Cooper, pp. 260–61: 'though the party may haue ability to others, yet to serve one, for the like reasons, he may be impotent, not able to performe the worke of Generation, and so deny that duety of marriage, and so happily [i.e. haply] produce a nullity thereof; vnlesse by *Phisicke*, or some spirituall means his power [i.e. the devil's] may be ouerruled, for which some time is to be graunted, and meanes vsed'. Cooper thus attaches important qualifications to his support for James's position on the nullity, similar to those put forward by Abbot.
100 Cooper asks rhetorically: 'Is *there not more hope of the saluation euen* of these *Witches* … then of many thousands in the world, who are *lulled asleepe in securitie*, and fatted vp. without all sense of danger, euen to vtter destruction?' (pp. 100–1).
101 Cooper, p. 113. The Archbishop of Canterbury, George Abbot, later become notorious for accidentally killing a man while out hunting with his friend Lord Zouche, an incident which raised questions about whether it was lawful for bishops to hunt. Cooper's reference to hunting suggests that, despite his solid Calvinism and his opposition to the nullity, Abbot's close association with the court might have exposed him to criticism from some quarters ('George Abbot', *ODNB*).

might well have raised very specific associations in the minds of Cooper's readers, as might his insistence that justice ought to be carried out 'without respect of persons'.[102] This point, in this context, is unusual, since witches were normally described as dwelling at the bottom of the social scale.[103]

Another unusual claim of Cooper's is that witches may receive real help from the devil – not just in hurting others, but in achieving their own aims and desires. Cooper writes that the devil binds his servants to him 'by his *familiar & carefull dealing* with them, in furnishing them with all meanes, to become maisters of their desires'.[104] Again, this is unusual because most writers on witchcraft stress that witches are, almost without exception, extremely poor and wretched. The devil's bargain, typically, is a trick: he will promise pleasure, wealth, and plenty, but he never delivers it.[105] All the devil is really able to provide is the pleasure of revenge, by harming, or appearing to harm, one's enemies. But if a person like Frances Carr, who had very publicly become mistress of her desires, was to be regarded as a witch, this standard demonological position needed to be modified.

Cooper's attitude to the wealthy and the powerful is hostile throughout his text. In describing the eventual corruption of the early Church, Cooper puts the blame firmly on the influence of secular power:

> [E]uen thus it befell with the deare *Spouse of* CHRIST [i.e. the Church], that as her former afflictions, had now fitted her to some rest, which shee attayned by the meanes of *Constantine*: so this rest and ease, accompanied with *outward honour* and *acceptance* with the greatest: instead of *Godlie simplicitie brought in carnall pompe and wisedome of the flesh.*[106]

---

102 Cooper, p. 314. The point is a conventional one in itself, as God is 'no respecter of persons' according to Peter in Acts 10:34 and many other passages in both the Old and New Testaments. Roberts also stresses that all offenders must be punished, regardless of their social position (p. 75).
103 The exceptions to this rule, according to many English authors, are usually found in the papacy: William Perkins, for example, mentions a number of witches who rose to the position of pope (p. 10).
104 Cooper, p. 112.
105 Cooper is not consistent in his unusual position, elsewhere making the more conventional claim that witches are 'fed with shadowes in steed of substance, with cold and dead delights, in steed of reall contentment of the flesh' (p. 122).
106 Cooper, p. 190.

Corruption is associated with the powerful, and the emperor who brings rest and ease is blamed for the eventual transformation of the virtuous early Church into the Roman Catholic Church, which Cooper, like many Protestants at the time, regards as the Antichrist. The warnings not to seek 'the fauour of earthly Princes', and to avoid *'looseness and profaneness'* and *'worldly pompe and glorie'*,[107] are frequently repeated; and while James is never named, he also prided himself on having brought 'rest and ease' by ending what had seemed to be an interminable war with Spain in 1604. The 'looseness and profaneness' of his court, as well as its 'pompe and glorie', were well known by 1617.

Some of Cooper's claims about the devil's trickery in dealing with witches also seem to be more widely applicable:

> [H]e thereby *Puffs them up with a conceit of some extraordinarie fauour with God* that gives them such power ouer Satan ... And *so prouoketh to horrible blasphemie, and Idolatrie*, to aduance themselues in Gods steed; to saue life and to destroy it at pleasure: And therevpon inferres a further securitie of their estates; That they which can thus dispose of others estates, they are wise enough to secure their owne.[108]

Again, this is unusual language with which to describe witches, who were not typically regarded as believing themselves to be in favour with God (or with anyone else). The Carrs, however, would certainly have regarded themselves as blessed by 'extraordinarie fauour', which was derived mainly from God's representative on earth, King James. Their exalted position enabled them to commit many of the crimes Cooper ostensibly ascribes to witches, in particular that of destroying life 'at pleasure', and their downfall represented a clear case of a misplaced sense of security in their estates.

While Cooper does write about witchcraft in a more conventional way for much of the treatise, his attention frequently wanders on to other topics. Recurring themes include Catholicism, the sinfulness of Christians who merely pay lip service to religion, and the importance of serving God rather than earthly power. Witchcraft is not Cooper's only, nor perhaps even his primary, concern in this text, despite the fact that it is its ostensible subject. It is often treated as a kind of moral yardstick with which to compare a range of other sins – some of which, like the complacency of the 'politike' Christians for whom Cooper reserves particular ire, are far more heinous.

---

107 Cooper, pp. 192–93.
108 Cooper, p. 83.

Cooper's rhetorical use of witchcraft is both similar to and sharply distinct from the way witchcraft is used in *Macbeth* and other early Jacobean witchcraft plays. In these plays, witchcraft is not essential; it is a largely peripheral element presented in order to sharpen the contrast between good and evil. Cooper's text also locates witchcraft within a wider discussion of good and evil; but he does not depict witchcraft as occupying the extreme end of the scale. There are worse sins than witchcraft for Cooper, who even argues (following William Perkins) that some witches may belong to the ranks of God's elect, and so may eventually repent.[109] Witchcraft, for Cooper, is not the epitome of evil: the Catholic Church fills that role. Nor is it clear that witchcraft is necessarily opposed to secular (or church) authority. In fact, the authorities seem more likely to be on the devil's side than God's.

The attitudes present in Cooper's text make it a valuable point of comparison with Middleton's play *The Witch*, a text which has its own place in the tangle of legal, religious, and literary discourse about the scandals surrounding the Carrs, as Anne Lancashire showed in an important article on the play.[110] It cannot seriously be doubted that the play makes reference to the scandals, as even a cursory glance at the events of the drama shows. A wife – Isabella – remains a virgin, despite having two husbands. The second of these husbands, Antonio, is rendered impotent by a witch's spell, but only in relation to Isabella; he is still able to have sex with the courtesan Florida. Another courtier, the relatively low-born Almachildes, buys a love charm from the witch, and seems set to become the second husband of an aristocratic lady. The same aristocratic lady, having committed outrageous crimes, is magnanimously (or preposterously) forgiven by the ruler on the grounds of her supposed repentance – of which the audience sees no evidence until after she is caught. Some of these features, particularly the jarring final scene of reconciliation, struck earlier critics of the play as crippling flaws, which explained its supposed fate as a stage flop. But the ending of *The Witch* can more convincingly be read as satirical, rather than as incompetent.

---

109 Cooper, p. 279; cf. Perkins, who states that 'some one or more of them [i.e. witches] may belong to Gods election and therefore albeit for causes best knowne to himselfe, he may suffer them for a time to be holden in the snares of Satan, yet at length in mercie he reclaims them' (pp. 216–17).

110 Anne Lancashire, '*The Witch*: Stage Flop or Political Mistake?', in '*Accompaninge the Players*': *Essays Celebrating Thomas Middleton, 1580–1980*, edited by Kenneth Friedenreich (New York: AMS Press, 1983).

At the same time, it is also clear that *The Witch* is not just a straightforward dramatisation of the Essex and Overbury scandals. No single character in the play is identifiable as a dramatic representation of a historical person. Lancashire describes Sebastian as 'partially' Carr, since he wins his wife, Isabella, back from her second husband (Antonio) whose magically induced impotence has prevented him from consummating the marriage. But Sebastian could also be understood to represent Essex; after all, he married Isabella first, stating at the very start of the play that '[s]he is my wife by contract before heaven', despite the fact, pointed out by Fernando, that '[a]nother has possession'.[111] This is not to say that Sebastian 'is' Essex any more than he 'is' Carr. The play develops its satire carefully, by incorporating into its plot a series of vignettes which evoke but do not replicate the events of the scandal. Despite the somewhat coded nature of the play's references to the Overbury scandal, it seems very likely, as Lancashire has shown, that performances of the play were put to an end by official interference.[112] Middleton hints at this himself, writing that 'Witches are, *ipso-facto*, by the law condemned and that only, I think, hath made her lie so long in an imprisoned obscurity' in the dedicatory epistle to the play.

Margot Heinemann's depiction of Middleton as a playwright propagandising on behalf of a purported 'Puritan faction' at court, once very influential, is now regarded with greater caution.[113] But while Heinemann may have overstated her case, it is clear that, as a dramatist, Middleton exploited widespread discontent with what were regarded as pro-Spanish policies and a pro-Spanish faction at

---

111 Thomas Middleton, *The Witch*, edited by Elizabeth Schafer (London: A. & C. Black, 1994), 1.1.3–6. Subsequent references to this edition are given parenthetically. The marriage is valid and legally binding, and even has Fernando as a witness (IV.2.4–5), although this was not necessary for the creation of a valid marriage – all that was necessary for a so-called spousal was the consent of both parties: see B. J. Sokol and Mary Sokol, *Shakespeare, Law and Marriage* (Cambridge: Cambridge University Press, 2003), pp. 13–14. Schafer claims that the marriage was 'not legally recognised' because it was not consummated, but as the case of Frances Howard demonstrates this is inaccurate. Non-consummation could provide grounds for the annulment of a marriage, although even this was controversial, but did not automatically invalidate it.
112 Lancashire, p. 161.
113 Heinemann, *Puritanism and Theatre*. For a detailed critique of Heinemann's position see N. W. Bawcutt, 'Was Thomas Middleton a Puritan Dramatist?', *Modern Language Review* 94:4 (1999), 925–40.

court. Middleton's credentials as a Calvinist – established by his religious work *The Two Gates of Salvation* (1609)[114] – as well as his employment with the consistently Protestant city authorities make it unsurprising that he chose to align his work for the theatre with anti-Spanish sentiment: Spain was frequently regarded as the secular wing of the Catholic Church by early modern English Protestants. Middleton's positioning of himself as a populist, Protestant, and anti-Spanish playwright culminated in a warrant being issued for his arrest after performances of *A Game at Chess* (1624) provoked complaints from the Spanish ambassador for its portrayal of his predecessor in the post, Count Gondomar.

The Witch was written a little earlier than the works recognised as Middleton's 'Spanish' plays.[115] But while *The Witch* is nominally set in Ravenna, it could be said that it is much more convincingly 'set' in both Spain and England. Most of the characters' names are either Spanish or more evocative of Spain than Italy: Florida, Francisca[116] (rather than the Italian Francesca), Sebastian and Fernando, for example. Meanwhile, the references to contemporary English politics, the jokes aimed at London audiences, and especially the incongruous Scottish messenger sent by Antonio's 'bonny lady mother' (II.1.171) locate the play in contemporary England. The messenger's Scottishness suggests that Antonio might originally have come from over the border himself – which would naturally have brought Robert Carr's situation to the minds of a contemporary audience. The combination of Spanish and Anglo-Scottish elements in the setting of the play might have added to its politically dangerous nature, implying that Spain was achieving an unhealthy degree of influence in the English court – just as *A Game at Chess* was to do later, even more bluntly.

---

114 See Lori Anne Ferrell's introduction to the text in the *Collected Works* of Middleton.
115 Trudi L. Darby, 'The Obsession with Spain', in *Thomas Middleton in Context*, edited by Suzanne Gossett (Cambridge: Cambridge University Press, 2011), pp. 144–50.
116 The name Francisca is also notable for its audible similarity to Frances Carr, as Elizabeth Schafer and others have pointed out (Introduction to *The Witch*, p. xvi). Another parallel between Francisca and Frances is that Francisca is pregnant and gives birth in secret during the play; Frances Carr was thought to be pregnant during 1616 (Somerset, p. 429). When she actually had been pregnant, in 1615, the pregnancy was rumoured to be faked.

Middleton's play does not merely make use of the actual events of the Overbury scandal. *The Witch* also uses rumour, hinting even at some of the wildest stories that circulated at the time of the Carrs' trial. The Carrs were said to be at the head of a poisoning plot, aimed at the King himself, and in the play the Duke of Ravenna is supposedly poisoned – although it eventually transpires, in the implausibly happy ending, that the poison was merely a sleeping potion. As with the rest of the play, events in the drama and the events predicted by rumour do not match precisely, but the assassination of the monarch is a shared theme. *The Witch* is both sceptical and credulous: utterly sceptical of the court and the moral authority of the ruler, it is at the same time wilfully credulous in its acceptance and recapitulation of rumour – any rumour scandalous enough to fill a theatre. In this respect the play is aligned with the kind of rumour and suspicion castigated in *The Masque of Queens* as the forces of disorder.

The Witch also features rumour and popular discontent in its plot, just as *The Masque of Queens* did, although in a concrete rather than an allegorical fashion. The Duchess, who is the closest thing to a queen in Middleton's play, so provokes the people of Ravenna that they become restive and unwilling to accept her as their ruler. Concerned for her safety, the duchess decides to murder Almachildes and find a new protector:

> My great aim's
> At the lord governor's love; he is a spirit
> Can sway and countenance; these obey and crouch.
> My guiltiness had need of such a master,
> That with a beck can suppress multitudes,
> And dim misdeeds with radiance of his glory,
> Not to be seen with dazzled, popular eyes.
> (IV.1.47–53)

The duchess has dark secrets which she is anxious to hide from 'popular eyes' – the eyes of the people. Jonson's masque had suggested that queenly virtue might banish the Ignorance and Credulity of the populace, but Middleton's duchess wishes instead to dazzle and deceive. The anger of the multitude seems justified, despite Almachildes' claim to the contrary (IV.1.18), and the Lord Governor even explains the 'people's tumult' as the result of the 'rankness of long peace' (IV.1.64–65) in what might be a dig at King James's foreign policy. The populace is not exactly celebrated in *The Witch*, but neither is it characterised as witch-like. It is the duchess who wishes to deceive the people, not their own credulity and ignorance.

The play and Cooper's demonological work both treat witchcraft as one sin among many, and describe a world in which witches are neither the only nor the worst of the devil's servants. Both texts are hostile to the rich and powerful; Cooper unfavourably compares privileged and hypocritical Christians to witches, and Middleton also uses a witch to comment on wealthy people with ugly secrets to hide. Referring to the witch Stadlin's ability to raise storms, Hecate boasts that she

> [f]lies over houses and takes *Anno Domini*
> Out of a rich man's chimney – a sweet place for't!
> He would be hanged ere he would set his own years there;
> They must be chambered in a five-pound picture,
> A green silk curtain drawn before the eyes on't,
> His rotten diseased years.
> (1.2.135–40)

In a sudden digression from the powers of witches, Hecate describes the rich man as someone with secrets to hide, events that, represented metonymically by the years of his life, are said to be 'rotten' and 'diseased'. The dark truth is revealed by an expensive portrait 'chambered' behind closed doors and concealed by silk curtains, like a seventeenth-century Dorian Gray. The obvious, rather comical evil represented by Hecate is considerably less sinister than the concealed evil of the rich man she describes.

Hecate, despite her occasionally gruesome language, is not a particularly frightening witch, and this has prompted some critics of the play to look elsewhere for the 'real' witch referred to in the play's title. As mentioned, representing Frances Howard as a witch became a fairly common satirical practice at this time. She might also be understood to be the witch lurking behind the scenes of Middleton's play. Margot Heinemann argues along these lines in suggesting that Francisca is the 'real' witch, describing her as a dramatic representation of Frances Carr.[117] This view has the similarity of names in its favour, but Marion O'Connor's excellent introduction to the play in the recent *Collected Works* of Middleton argues persuasively for a more sophisticated interpretation. The Hecate of Greek myth, as opposed to the Hecate of the play, is a 'triple goddess', with different aspects representing virginity, maternity,

---

117 Heinemann, p. 111.

and sterility.[118] Similarly, Isabella, Francisca, and the duchess can be understood to represent three different aspects of Frances Howard's fractured public persona. More broadly, the three characters can be seen to represent what might be called the three ages of woman, of which Isabella sings to Antonio and Francisca:

> In a maiden-time professed,
> Then we say that life is best.
> Tasting once the married life,
> Then we only praise the wife.
> There's but one more state to try,
> Which makes women laugh or cry –
> Widow, widow.
> (II.1.127–33)

These three stages of a woman's life are presented on stage by the three major female characters: Francisca is the maid (except that she is not, because of her affair with Aberzanes), Isabella is the wife (except that she is not, because neither of her two marriages is consummated), and the duchess is the widow (except that she is not, because her husband is still alive). As O'Connor points out, the only women who are what they seem to be are Florida and Hecate – the whore and the witch.[119] Witches are conventionally supposed to be deceivers, but in Middleton's play it is the courtly characters who are not what they seem. Middleton suggests that there are always dark secrets to be found behind the outward finery of the powerful, about whom the play encourages its audience to believe the worst.

Another possible witch in the play – and another possible representation of Frances Carr – is Florida. Her portrayal is a reminder that the line between whore and witch had become increasingly blurred by the Overbury affair, with Frances depicted as exemplifying both stereotypes. In *The Witch*, Florida is witch-like in that her purpose is to entrap others in order to win more souls for the devil. Encouraged by Sebastian to use her 'cunning' and 'art' – words highly evocative of witchcraft – to deceive Isabella, Florida replies:

> What need you urge that
> Which comes so naturally I cannot miss on't?
> What makes the devil so greedy of a soul

---

118 Marion O'Connor, Introduction to *The Witch*, in *Thomas Middleton: The Collected Works*, edited by Gary Taylor and John Lavagnino (Oxford: Oxford University Press, 2010), p. 1127.
119 O'Connor, p. 1128.

> But 'cause he's lost his own, to all joys lost?
> So 'tis our trade to set snares for other women
> 'Cause we were once caught ourselves.
> (IV.2.48–53)

After she exits, Sebastian comments that 'Hell and a whore ... are partners'; and while some sympathy for Florida may be extracted from her lines, the main point of them is that she is spiritually dangerous, as is a witch. Sebastian later expresses regret for working with Florida: 'I curse the time now I did e'er make use / Of such a plague' (IV.2.124–25); and he has previously voiced a similar revulsion after having consulted with Hecate: 'grant, you greater powers that dispose men, / That I may never need this hag again!' (I.2.176–77). Even more telling in connecting witchcraft and whoredom is Hecate's exchange with Almachildes:

> ALMACHILDES Is your name Goody Hag?
> HECATE   'Tis anything.
>   Call me the horrid'st and unhallowed'st things
>   That life and nature trembles at – for thee
>   I'll be the same.
>   (I.2.198–201)

Hecate presents herself as a prostitute, willing not only to do anything but to *be* anything to fulfil the wishes of her client. The similarity of whore and witch, less obvious in the pre-Overbury Jacobean witch plays, is made apparent in *The Witch*.

While a variety of characters are figuratively compared to witches in order to stress their sinfulness, the 'real' witches in the play are rarely taken very seriously. Sebastian, reluctantly seeking Hecate's help in breaking up Antonio's invalid marriage to Isabella, says to her, 'Whate'er thou art, I have no spare time to fear thee; / My horrors are so strong and great already, / That thou seem'st nothing' (I.2.119–21). The speech displays a confusion about the nature of the witch, as was the case in *Macbeth*, and the suggestion that the witch might be 'nothing' is reminiscent of Banquo's idea of *Macbeth*'s witches as mere 'bubbles'. But there is also a clear difference between the plays in that Sebastian's deal with the witches involves plenty of disdain on his part, but no existential terror. He explicitly declares himself *not* to be afraid of Hecate, in contrast to Macbeth's frightened reaction to the appearance of the witches in 1.3. Sebastian's problems are firmly rooted in the realm of the social, rather than that of the supernatural. The comic scenes treat the witches even more lightly. Almachildes, seeking a love charm from the witches, stumbles in drunk, knocking over Stadlin and Puckle. Puckle ends up with her 'clothes over her ears' (1.2.187–88) and Firestone considers an attempt to 'throw the cat upon her to save her honesty' (180). For his part, Almachildes, so far from being reverent or afraid, comments scornfully: 'Call you these witches? / They be tumblers, methinks, very flat tumblers' (193–94). It has been argued that the servants of the devil are required to be both powerless and deluded (so that they can be seen as vastly inferior to the servants of God) and at the same time dangerous (so that they constitute a real, not merely an imagined, threat). From this point of view, the witches represented in *The Witch* are all wrong. They are possessed of virtually limitless power, but somehow remain unthreatening to both the other characters and the audience.

The play therefore tends to suggest scepticism about the possibility of witchcraft, but there is one scene which presents an exception. In this scene, the only character to treat the witches with any degree of respect is also the only character to express any doubts about the efficacy of their magic, and the only one for whom they fail to deliver. The duchess, asking Hecate to provide a fast-acting poison with which to murder Almachildes, asks her:

DUCHESS Canst thou do this?
HECATE   Can I?
DUCHESS   I mean so closely.
HECATE So closely do you mean too?
DUCHESS   So artfully, so cunningly?
HECATE Worse and worse! Doubts and incredulities!
        They make me mad.
        [...]
DUCHESS I did not doubt you mother.
HECATE   No? What did you?
        My power's so firm, it is not to be questioned.
DUCHESS Forgive what's past – and now I know th' offensiveness
        That vexes art, I'll shun th' occasion ever.
        (v.2.14–36)

Despite the obvious effectiveness of witchcraft within the play, the duchess expresses doubts about the possibility of Hecate making a poison – which is far from implausible by any standards (Hecate does not, in the event, successfully poison Almachildes; this part of the plot is simply dropped). The duchess really ought to know that magic works, having briefly been the victim of a love charm herself (II.2.82–104); but her questions might be regarded as expressions of anxiety rather than of sceptical doubts about witchcraft. In any case, the duchess is browbeaten by Hecate, who recites Ovid to terrify her,[120] after which the duchess starts to address Hecate respectfully as 'mother'. The sight of the haughty duchess behaving with humility before Hecate can only emphasise Hecate's power. But even in this scene, the point is not to create a fearsome witch character; this is merely the means to a more important end, that of accentuating the duchess's guilt. That she places her faith in witches, as Frances Carr was reputed to have done, condemns her as much as anything else.

Witchcraft in the early Jacobean theatre is always positioned in relation to the court. At the beginning of James's reign, perhaps before many of his subjects had had time to become discontented with the new king, witches are on stage to provide flattery. Witchcraft performed a rhetorical function; it constituted the anti-masque (literally so in Jonson's *Masque of Queens*) which made the virtues of the court shine all the brighter. In *The Masque of Queens*, the witches' connection to vices evocative of popular discontent suggests a court already feeling itself beleaguered and in need of reassurance, a reassurance provided by the characterisation of critical attitudes to the throne as witchcraft. Just a few years after the *Masque of Queens*, however, witchcraft had become a measure for the court's corruption, in comparison with which the court was made to appear monstrous. Middleton's treatment of the Overbury scandal may have been largely responsible for the end of the early Jacobean witch play. After *The Witch*, a play attempting to represent court ladies as moral paragons in opposition to a group of evil witches would probably have been laughed off the stage.

The Overbury trials failed to deliver on all the excitement that they had promised. What had been presented as a sensational plot threatening the security of the country ultimately appeared as a fairly straightforward case of murder. After all of Coke's dark hints and exaggerated claims about the nature of the plot, this was understood by those courtiers still sympathetic to the Carrs as an exposure of Coke's credulity. Others, though, regarded the result as further evidence of a conspiracy: it was suggested that Coke had been disgraced because he had discovered too much. There were even suggestions that the King himself had been involved in the murder.[121] In its imagery of dark secrets and corruption in high

---

120 The passage, omitted above, is from the *Metamorphoses*, VII.199–207.
121 Somerset, p. 428.

places, the play aligns itself with the forces of popular rumour: from the perspective established in Jonson's *Masque of Queens*, the play is witch-like in its alliance with Ignorance and Credulity. It is striking that Middleton's dedicatory epistle refers to the play itself as a witch, telling Thomas Holmes that '[f]or your sake alone she hath thus far conjured herself abroad and bears no other charms about her but what may tend to your recreation'.

For the rhetoric of witchcraft to be turned against the Jacobean court is ironic in view of the theatre's previous use of witchcraft to flatter the King. However, the tension in the idea of demonic witchcraft standing in opposition to divinely ordained monarchy had been present from the start. Sophonisba, for all her (excessive) moral virtue, is presented as a disruptive force in the world of her play, and the murderous and witch-like nature of several of the queens represented in Jonson's masque has been pointed out. The pervasive uncertainty of *Macbeth*, too, threatens to overshadow its support of the monarch. In a world in which fair is foul and foul is fair, distinguishing between the demonic and the divine is no easy matter, as Macduff finds out when Malcolm baffles him with his list of pretended vices. The royal witch play was always potentially vulnerable to the kind of satirical inversion to which Middleton subjected it.

Witches did not disappear from the stage after *The Witch*. Not many years afterwards, in fact, Thomas Dekker, John Ford, and William Rowley wrote their play *The Witch of Edmonton* (1621), inspired by a real-life witchcraft case. But while this play also features a witch, Mother Sawyer is a far cry from Middleton's Hecate. The representation of witchcraft in *The Witch of Edmonton* is, or purports to be, grittily realistic; classical references like those of *Sophonisba* are gone entirely. Just as significantly, king and court are conspicuously absent. The social setting of the play shifts down to the level of the village witch – a character type who, despite her prominence in pamphlet accounts of witchcraft, had yet to appear on stage.

4
The Witch of Edmonton

Thomas Dekker, John Ford, and William Rowley's *The Witch of Edmonton* (1621) departs from the conventions established in previous witchcraft drama in relation to the depiction of scepticism. *Macbeth* and *Dr Faustus* depicted the scepticism and credulity of witches, using the discourse of demonology to illustrate the psychology of witch and devil's servant – a psychology which is characterised by both inappropriate and excessive credulity (towards the devil) *and* inappropriate and excessive scepticism (towards God). While the delusions of the witch are not irrelevant to *The Witch of Edmonton*, the play also examines the credulity and scepticism of its characters in relation to witchcraft itself. In doing so, *The Witch of Edmonton* acknowledges the existence of public credulity about witchcraft. But it is also able to define the boundaries of the possible in relation to witchcraft, and therefore to establish a plausible and coherent vision of witchcraft – one which depends on a particular cultural and theological conception of evil and demonic agency in the everyday world.

The Witch of Edmonton is unlike any other extant play from the period in that it portrays a character matching the stereotype of the village witch, a character who can reasonably be regarded as plausible in terms of her psychology. Prior to *The Witch of Edmonton*, there are sceptical plays depicting tricksters in a more or less realistic fashion (*The Wise Woman of Hogsdon*), and there are plays showing witches as lurid, supernatural agents of the devil (*Sophonisba*, *The Witch*). After it, there are two-dimensional comic witches (*The Late Lancashire Witches*, *The Lancashire Witches*). But Elizabeth Sawyer is the only stage witch who actually resembles a human being, complete with recognisably human motivations and desires. What is more, the play shows the audience how she becomes a witch. In this sense at least, her character actually develops during the play. This is not true of any witch characters in the other plays mentioned: in those plays, the witches are simple, static characters.

Despite her psychological richness, however, Elizabeth Sawyer is not the play's central character, as Frances Dolan has pointed out.[1] Elizabeth Sawyer is absent for the entirety of the first act, which concerns itself with what – despite the play's title – must be regarded as the main plot, the story of Frank Thorney and his bigamous marriage. A great deal of the first scene of the second act is devoted to Sawyer's exchange with Old Banks, to her soliloquising and to the pact she makes with the devil-dog; but in the next scene she has disappeared again, not to return until the fourth act. Sawyer is a major presence in just three scenes – II.1, IV.1, and V.1 – and aside from a few lines before her execution in the final scene (V.3), she is not on stage for the rest of the play. In total, she speaks 12.5 per cent of the lines in the play, compared to 18.5 per cent for Frank Thorney. In fact, Cuddy Banks – the central figure in the other subplot, and a character who has sometimes been ignored entirely by modern critics of the play – speaks more than Mother Sawyer, with 13.2 per cent of the lines. This is not to suggest that the significance of a character in a play can be measured simply by counting lines. But it does seem that the modern critical interest in witchcraft has led to an excessive focus on the character of Elizabeth Sawyer.[2]

It may seem eccentric to downplay Elizabeth Sawyer's importance in a study of the dramatic representation of witchcraft. But the marginality of the witch character, even in the play in which she is at her most central, is itself revealing. By providing a thoughtful, sensitive, and sympathetic depiction of the village witch, the playwrights take witchcraft beliefs as seriously as any other text of the period. However, two other aspects of the play are crucial in making its representation of a witch plausible: first, the less credible views of witchcraft dismissed by Henry Goodcole's pamphlet account, discussed in Chapter 1, are treated with scepticism – a partial and limited scepticism that is necessary to establish a firmer belief. Second, this seriousness about witchcraft is only possible within a larger story about demonic presence and agency, which is why it is necessary to embed a difficult-to-believe witch story in the context of a more

---

1 Dolan, p. 219.
2 Leonora Brodwin's article on 'The Domestic Tragedy of Frank Thorney in *The Witch of Edmonton*', Studies in English Literature, 1500–1900 7:2 (Spring 1967), 311–28, as the title suggests, is one exception.

credible domestic tragedy incorporating widely shared beliefs about the devil's involvement in human affairs.

While the play gives voice to scepticism about particular aspects of popular belief about witchcraft, this scepticism would have supported, rather than challenged, a general belief in the reality of witchcraft for most contemporary audience members. In this sense, the sceptical voices in the play can be regarded as expressing rhetorical scepticism. In this instance, no specific rhetorical aims can necessarily be attributed to the playwrights: a work of drama, after all, is not a polemic. Nevertheless, the play goes to great lengths to make its eponymous character a credible witch. Indeed, the reality of witchcraft as a pact with the devil is powerfully represented by the play in performance in a more visceral way than any pamphlet could hope to achieve. Lisa Hopkins suggests that 'a judge who had seen *The Witch of Edmonton* might well prove more sympathetic and enlightened than one who had not'.[3] More sympathetic, perhaps; but not necessarily more sceptical about the existence of witchcraft.

Scepticism in *The Witch of Edmonton*

The Witch of Edmonton has frequently been regarded as a sceptical play, with a variety of critics admiring the play's exploration of Sawyer's victimisation by her neighbours in Edmonton.[4] Mother Sawyer's early speeches have struck many critics as subversive of the very idea of witchcraft. Her opening lines are especially in tune with modern views of witchcraft as a phenomenon produced by social disharmony:

> And why on me? Why should the envious world
> Throw all their scandalous malice upon me?
> 'Cause I am poor, deformed and ignorant,
> And like a bow buckled and bent together,
> By some more strong in mischiefs than myself,
> Must I for that be made a common sink
> For all the filth and rubbish of men's tongues

---

3 Hopkins, p. 98.
4 To take just two examples, Viviana Comensoli in *Household Business* (Toronto: University of Toronto Press, 1996) claims that the play goes beyond 'the pious indictments of both continental and English sceptics' (p. 126), while Kathleen McLuskie in *Renaissance Dramatists* (Hemel Hempstead: Harvester Wheatsheaf, 1989) writes of the play 'subverting established views of witchcraft by its sympathetic treatment of Mother Sawyer' (p. 72).

To fall and run into? Some call me witch,
And being ignorant of myself, they go
About to teach me how to be one, urging
That my bad tongue, by their bad usage made so,
Forespeaks their cattle, doth bewitch their corn,
Themselves, their servants and their babes at nurse.
  Enter OLD BANKS.
This they enforce upon me. And in part
Make me to credit it.[5]

In the confrontation with Old Banks which follows these lines, Sawyer reveals that she has been gathering firewood, or 'gleaning', on Old Banks's land. According to the social historian Keith Wrightson this practice was, by the seventeenth century, 'beginning, in some places, to be redefined and prosecuted as theft ... One Hertfordshire farmer attacked local women for gleaning on his land "as is usual for all the pore to do" in 1603.'[6] Sawyer's gleaning is the trigger for Banks's attack on her, a detail which hints at the social and economic relationships at the root of their enmity. Sawyer's self-description as 'poor, deformed and ignorant' matches the analyses of many early twentieth-century historians so the speech can be read as sceptical of the idea of witchcraft, supporting instead the idea of witches as scapegoats.

It would have been just as easy for well-informed members of contemporary audiences to interpret the lines in this way, since the situation Elizabeth Sawyer describes tallies so closely with the views expressed by sceptics such as Scot, as well as by cautious believers, like John Gaule, who incorporated Scot's claims about popular credulity into his own work.[7] According to these writers, witches

---

5 Thomas Dekker, John Ford, and William Rowley, *The Witch of Edmonton*, edited by Peter Corbin and Douglas Sedge (Manchester: Manchester University Press, 1999), II.1.1–15. Subsequent references to this edition are given in parentheses.
6 Keith Wrightson, *English Society 1580–1680* (London: Hutchinson, 1982), p. 164.
7 According to Scot, witches are 'old, lame, bleare-eied, pale, fowle, and full of wrinkles; poore, sullen, superstitious, and papists' (1.3, p. 7). John Gaule, in *Select Cases of Conscience Touching Witches and Witchcrafts* (London, 1646), a work confirming the existence of witches but also urging caution in prosecuting them, criticises those who see a witch in 'every old woman with a wrinkled face, a furr'd brow, a hairy lip, a gobber tooth, a squint eye, a squeaking voyce, or a scolding tongue' (pp. 4–5). Samuel Harsnett's *Declaration of Egregious Popish Impostures* (London, 1603) describes the

are people – generally women – who are unpopular, victimised by others because of their appearance and perhaps also their behaviour and religious beliefs, or lack thereof. Sawyer goes on to suggest that she has nearly begun to believe herself to be a witch, which is in line with the arguments of Scot and Weyer, among others, about the relevance of melancholy.[8] The explanation Sawyer offers for her persecution as a witch is therefore a naturalistic one, consistent with thoroughgoing scepticism.

However, as David Nicol has pointed out, all this is said *before* Sawyer concludes her pact with the devil.[9] It is easy to pounce on this speech as evidence of scepticism if one is, as presumably all modern critics are, a sceptic oneself. But contemporary audiences would have included many people who were at least prepared to consider the possibility of witchcraft, and who already knew the outcome of the recent Sawyer case. Such an audience would be more likely to regard the sentiments expressed here, particularly Sawyer's despair, as ominously foreshadowing the conversion to witchcraft which they already knew was to come. While Sawyer denies that she is a witch, her speech apparently acknowledges the existence of actual witches, since she claims she is being pushed into becoming a witch by her ill-treatment at the hands of her neighbours. This stereotype of the witch was also appropriated by those who wished to justify witchcraft persecution. Keith Thomas points out, citing historical cases as well as this passage in the play, that some witches 'confessed that they had taken up witchcraft in order to avenge themselves upon neighbours who had falsely called them witches'.[10]

---

idea of a witch as 'an olde weather-beaten Croane, hauing her chinne, & her knees meeting for age, walking like a bow leaning on a shaft, hollow eyed, vntoothed, furrowed on her face, hauing her lips trembling with the palsie, going mumbling in the streetes' (p. 136).

8 See Scot, p. 30; Mora (ed.), pp. 183–86.
9 David Nicol, 'Interrogating the Devil: Social and Demonic Pressure in *The Witch of Edmonton*', *Comparative Drama* 38:4 (Winter 2004–5), 425–45 (p. 426).
10 Thomas, p. 628. Thomas assumes that the idea predates the writing of the play, but the cases he cites are from 1647, 1664–65, and 1667; all of them therefore postdate the play. While it is not possible to prove that *The Witch of Edmonton* is the first instance of this particular idea, I have not been able to discover any preceding it, and Goodcole's pamphlet account does not suggest that Sawyer became a witch out of frustration at being accused of witchcraft. It is therefore a real possibility that the play created a narrative which was later followed in prosecuting actual cases.

After suffering violent treatment at the hands of Old Banks and being verbally abused by the Morris dancers, but still before she has become a witch, Sawyer's despair deepens. She wishes for the devil to come and take possession of the 'ruined cottage' of her body, adding shortly afterwards: "Tis all one / To be a witch as to be counted one' (II.1.125–26). This statement is open to interpretation. It could conceivably be taken to mean – as the pamphlet on Philip and Mary Flower discussed in Chapter 1 sometimes implies – that there are no real witches; in other words, the state of being a witch is literally identical with having the reputation of a witch. Some contemporary audience members or readers, if they thought about it at all, might have understood the lines in this way. But a much more likely interpretation, taking the lines in their context, is that Mother Sawyer is expressing her anger and despair at the way she is being treated: things have become so bad now that people consider her to be a witch that she feels she has nothing left to lose and might as well become one – which is exactly what happens. Mother Sawyer, in other words, actively chooses to become a witch. What might at first glance appear to be scepticism about witchcraft is better understood as dramatic irony.

Sawyer's opening soliloquy is used to generate a degree of sympathy for the witch-to-be that is unusual, perhaps unique, among extant Jacobean witch plays. This sympathy has frequently been remarked on, often with surprise, and it has itself been seized on as evidence of scepticism. Diane Purkiss takes a dissenting view, but acknowledges that the play is widely regarded as 'sceptical about witchcraft and sympathetic to the witch'.[11] Purkiss, rightly and importantly, identifies two separate issues which are frequently treated as identical:[12] on

---

Brian Gunter, who bullied his daughter into faking the symptoms of demonic possession, seems to have drawn inspiration from the pamphlet account of the witches of Warboys: Sharpe, *The Bewitching of Anne Gunter*, pp. 7–8, 135; Anon., *The Most Strange and Admirable Discoverie of the Three Witches of Warboys* (London, 1593).

11 Purkiss, *The Witch in History*, p. 232. Ronald McFarland, '"The Hag is Astride": Witches in Seventeenth-Century Literature', *The Journal of Popular Culture* 11:1 (1977), 88–97, also comments that the play 'is indeed sympathetic, though it is not altogether sceptical or enlightened' (p. 91).

12 Julia Garrett, 'Dramatizing Deviance: Sociological Theory and *The Witch of Edmonton*', *Criticism* 49:3 (Summer 2007), 327–75, for example, writes that the play's 'sympathy in itself is noteworthy, given the censorious climate for any form of scepticism about witch crimes' (p. 328).

the one hand, the issue of scepticism about witchcraft, and on the other, sympathy for the character of Mother Sawyer. It is perhaps natural for present-day readers to view the two questions as inextricably linked. Modern readers tend to be sympathetic towards witches *because* they are sceptics about the existence of witchcraft, and therefore work from the assumption that witches were innocent victims who were, by definition, wrongfully accused. This being the case, when sympathy for a witch character is expressed, it is tempting to interpret it as grounded in scepticism about the existence of witchcraft – a scepticism as similar to our own as the sympathy seems to be. But sympathy for Elizabeth Sawyer in *The Witch of Edmonton* is not grounded in outright scepticism about witchcraft at all; it serves to make her human, which in turn serves to make her descent into witchcraft comprehensible, if not excusable.

There is, of course, much scepticism on display in *The Witch of Edmonton*, since some aspects of popular belief about witchcraft are denied or even mocked. One example is the supposed power of words. After she has agreed to become the devil's slave, Elizabeth Sawyer is taught a charm by the dog. The charm is a corrupted version of the Lord's Prayer in Latin, a detail taken from Goodcole's account. (The use of Latin is significant since this is the language of specifically Catholic prayer.) Sawyer repeats the phrase several times, getting it slightly wrong each time. There is no indication that the charm itself has any effect. Any mischief brought about by the witch's activities is caused directly by the devil, as the play later demonstrates when his touch is required to drive Anne Ratcliffe to suicide. After the scene in which Sawyer is taught her Latin prayer, it disappears from the play until the fifth act, when Elizabeth Sawyer recites it in an attempt to summon the dog back to her (v.1.25).[13] The words themselves, however, are a prayer to Satan, and therefore blasphemous. Sawyer has been duped by the devil into using a 'spell' which is both ineffective and extremely dangerous to her spiritual well-being.

Scepticism about the effectiveness of spoken charms relates to the play's evidently Calvinist vision of the world.[14] It is not an attempt

---

13 The devil does appear to Mother Sawyer after she recites the charm in the fifth act, but there is no suggestion that he is compelled to do so: he comes in order to torment her.
14 Nicol argues that the outlook of the play is not straightforwardly Calvinist, claiming that the play 'downplays' predestination (435) in favour of social causation, but social causation does not preclude predestination.

to cast doubt on the reality of witchcraft, but is dependent on a particular view of how witchcraft operates. The ineffectiveness of Sawyer's demonic prayer is in line with the views of Calvinist writers on witchcraft such as George Gifford and William Perkins, both of whom denied that charms, including verbal charms, could have any real power.[15] Catholic writers on witchcraft, committed to the view that the sacraments approved by the Church were effective by virtue of the words, objects, and actions involved and the office of the priest, had a more complex view on the efficacy of witches' charms. Jean Bodin and the authors of the *Malleus Maleficarum* are happy to confirm the real effectiveness of various charms (although, as noted in Chapter 1, Bodin also betrays a degree of scepticism towards verbal charms).[16] The play rejects anything which ought to have been regarded by educated Protestants as superstition.

The ability of witches to see into the future is also questioned in the play. After his bigamous marriage to Susan, and desperately resisting her attempts at intimacy, Frank resorts to telling her lies that are dangerously close to the truth: '"Twas told me by a woman / Known and approved in palmistry, / I should have two wives' (II.2.118–20). Susan fails to understand why this troubles Frank so

---

Frank frequently expresses a deterministic attitude, for example at the end of the first act: 'No man can hide his shame from heaven that views him. / In vain he flees whose destiny pursues him' (1.2.235–36).

15 Gifford, *Discourse*, sig. G1ᵛ; Perkins writes that 'a charme is onely a diabolicall watchword, and hath in it selfe no such effectuall power or possibilitie to worke a wonder'. He goes on to devote fifteen pages to proving this claim, suggesting the importance of the issue (pp. 133–48). The anonymous author of *The Witches of Northamptonshire* (London, 1612) expresses a similar view, asking, 'Shall wee be so foolish as to imagine that things are effected by the vertue of words, gestures, figures or such like? All those are doubtlesse but to deceive' (sig. B1ʳ). See also Holland, sig. F2ʳ.

16 See, for example, Institoris and Sprenger, III.215A–B, pp. 553–54, which tells of heretics who could not be executed by either fire or drowning until 'a device for sorcery' was removed from them; cf. Cohn, p. 234. The authors are clear that these magical trinkets are used by the devil purely in order to increase the blasphemous and idolatrous nature of the sin of witchcraft, as Perkins and Gifford would have agreed; nevertheless, the charms are also genuinely effective. The *Malleus* also advises judges to use holy counter-magic: 'they should by all means carry with them salt that was exorcized on a Sunday and a Blessed Palm and Blessed Plants. These objects, along with Blessed Wax that is wrapped up and worn on the neck ... are wondrously effective at keeping a person safe' (III.214A).

much, and in telling him so comments that '[s]uch presages / Prove often false' (II.2.131–32). After reaching her own conclusions about what is troubling Frank – Susan thinks he has arranged to fight a duel with Warbeck – she chides him for attempting to 'flam me off / With an old witch' (II.2.164–65). This is a fairly clear expression of scepticism about the power of witches to foresee future events, and also trivialises the existence of witches. But although these predictions are said to be false 'often', they are not said to be worthless, and immediately after making this suggestion Susan goes on to consider the possibility that the prediction will turn out to be true. That the predictions of witches are often, but not always, accurate also aligns the play with demonological orthodoxy.[17]

The attitudes and credulity of the persecutors of witches are clearly parodied in the play. In the fourth act, a series of characters named in the original stage directions as 'Country-men' – perhaps significantly, since the play would primarily have been performed in London – blame various ills, including the infidelity of their wives, on Elizabeth Sawyer. The lines are packed with bawdy puns about falling, standing, and maypoles, and the absurdity of the accusations is clear. The laughter of the audience would have been at the expense of the countryman who, having caught his wife *in flagrante delicto*, is foolish enough to accept her excuse of bewitchment.[18] Later, Old Banks claims to have been compelled by witchcraft into kissing his cow under the tail, a story borrowed from George Gifford (IV.1.55–61). Gifford's main argument against the persecution of witches is that people blame witches for their problems rather than accepting their misfortunes for what they are – the judgement of God – and praying for forgiveness. The play represents a similar attitude in its depiction of the countrymen, and is similarly critical of it.

Instead of self-examination and obedience to the word of God, the villagers of Edmonton resort to a kind of magic themselves in order to confirm their suspicions. They burn some thatch from Mother Sawyer's roof in order to 'summon' her. Goodcole's account of the case dismisses this as 'an old ridiculous custom'[19] while simultaneously portraying it as having worked. The play follows

---

17 Perkins, for example, writes that 'the predictions of Satan are onely probable and coniecturall' (*Discourse*, p. 65).
18 Claims of witchcraft as an excuse for sexual indiscretions are taken seriously by very few authors – even Bodin refuses to do so (Bodin, p. 169).
19 Goodcole, sig. A4^r.

Goodcole almost to the letter, with the Justice using the word 'ridiculous' (IV.1.48) to describe the test after it has been represented on stage as appearing to have worked. The similarity to Gifford's demonological work is again apparent. Gifford suggests that such measures can work, but only by the power of the devil, and also asks, in relation to those who persecute witches by extra-legal or magical means, 'when as they ascribe power unto such things to driue out deuils, what are they but Witches?'[20] This question is echoed in *The Witch of Edmonton* when Elizabeth Sawyer, accused of witchcraft by Sir Arthur, declares 'A witch! Who is not?' (IV.1.116). Again, the play's levelling vision of the universality of human sinfulness reveals its broadly Calvinist assumptions. It is Gifford's view of what he would regard as superstitious and unchristian behaviour on the part of the accusers of witches that informs the critical depiction of the villagers in the fourth act. The countrymen are correct, albeit for the wrong reasons, in saying that Elizabeth Sawyer is a witch; but it is clear that their credulous excesses are also blameworthy.

Not all of the characters in the play are quite so credulous, however, and the less credulous characters are presented as more deserving of respect. The Justice is certainly sceptical about the burning of thatch as a test for witchcraft (despite the fact that the test appears to the audience to have worked). However, while the Justice is presented as the voice of reason in the fourth act, he is not quite the voice of outright scepticism about the existence of witches. Rather, he is open-minded, judging the claims made by various parties on their merits. He tacitly concedes that witches do exist, and even seems to be convinced that Elizabeth Sawyer is a witch, judging by his brief comments. After Sir Arthur concludes that Sawyer is definitely a witch, the Justice seems happy to take his word for it, telling her to 'mend thy life, get home and pray' (IV.1.162). Sir Arthur's word, as an educated, landowning gentleman, is worth much more than that of the countrymen, regardless of whether or not it is based on anything firmer than their superstitions, and in spite of his ethical shortcomings.

The other character in the play to express scepticism about witchcraft is Cuddy Banks. While he enlists Elizabeth Sawyer in his attempt to win Kate Carter's hand in marriage, Cuddy never seems to take her very seriously. Asked by Sawyer whether he believes

---

20 Gifford, *Discourse*, sig. H3^r.

that her powers can achieve this, Cuddy replies: 'Truly, Mother Witch, I do verily believe so and, when I see it done, I shall be half persuaded so too' (II.2.247–48). Despite his exaggerated asseverations, Cuddy says he will only be 'half' persuaded, even after he has seen it 'done'. He is making fun of Sawyer, but this does not rule out his believing that she *is* a witch, or that she is in league with the devil. When Sawyer says that she learned her charm from a 'learned man', Cuddy comments '[l]earned devil it was as soon!' (l. 270). He also refers to the dog as 'your goblin' (l. 262), revealing his awareness that the dog is in fact a spirit. The scepticism expressed by Cuddy is the solidly Protestant variety which doubts the effectiveness of witchcraft, but not the existence or malice of witches and devils. The seriousness with which the devil is treated is a vital part of the play, which is discussed in the next section.

The devil and sin in *The Witch of Edmonton*

A number of scholars have noted that the devil is the only character that links the three plots of the play.[21] Others have argued that this connection is insufficient, starting with Edward Sackville-West back in 1937:

> We can, if we like, argue that the Dog acts as a sufficient binding force; but I do not think this argument holds, for the reason that that figure is made to do (since the stage is after all a simplifying medium) for two different devils: the revenge-lust of the witch and the self-destructiveness of Frank.[22]

Leonora Brodwin, like Sackville-West, points to the devil as the only point of contact between the Thorney and Sawyer plots, but finds that the Sawyer subplot is 'sketchy' and 'largely unrelated',[23] while David Atkinson feels the need to argue instead for the theme

---

[21] Frances Dolan points to the dog as the 'dangerous familiar' providing a connection between the three plots (p. 220). John Cox, *The Devil and the Sacred in English Drama, 1350–1642* (Cambridge: Cambridge University Press, 2000) refers to 'three plots ... united primarily by the common presence of one devil' (p. 173). Comensoli regards the 'two plots' as 'loosely connected by the influence of the supernatural' (p. 127), and Kathleen McLuskie regards the dog as the 'linking figure' (p. 66).

[22] Edward Sackville-West, 'The Significance of *The Witch of Edmonton*', *Criterion* 17:66 (1937), 23–32 (p. 30).

[23] Brodwin, 311.

of moral knowledge as the unifying element of the play.[24] Sackville-West may have a point – the invisible devil that spurs Frank Thorney on to murder seems very different from the tangible and frightening devil that Elizabeth Sawyer covenants with. But the objection fails to take into account the complex and changing understanding of the devil at the time the play was written and performed. The three different functions served by the devil in the three plots of *The Witch of Edmonton* correspond to different sets of beliefs and cultural traditions that coexisted, perhaps uneasily but certainly simultaneously, in seventeenth-century England.

Recent work by historians on the idea of the devil in early modern England has demonstrated that the concept was increasingly important to Protestants in interpreting their everyday experiences.[25] Protestant theologians developed a view of the devil which emphasised his role in tempting human beings into committing sinful acts. In *The Witch of Edmonton*, just before Cuddy Banks beats the devil out of Edmonton, he is told something about how evil spirits operate:

> I'll thus much tell thee. Thou never art so distant
> From an evil spirit, but that thy oaths,
> Curses, and blasphemies pull him to thine elbow.
> Thou never tell'st a lie, but that a devil
> Is within hearing it; thy evil purposes
> Are ever haunted. But when they come to act—
> As thy tongue slandering, bearing false witness,
> Thy hand stabbing, stealing, cozening, cheating,—
> He's then within thee.
> (v.1.137–44)

The devil presented in this passage is a decidedly Protestant one. He is ever-present, always within earshot of mundane, everyday human transgressions such as lies and curses. He is also – given the opportunity opened up by a sinful act – an internal devil, one who is 'within thee', using the sinners' own corrupted nature against them. While the Protestant devil was usually understood to be capable of physical manifestation (although Reginald Scot denied this capability), this was exceptional rather than the norm.

---

24 David Atkinson, 'Moral Knowledge and the Double Action in *The Witch of Edmonton*', *Studies in English Literature, 1500–1900* 25:2 (Spring, 1985), 419–37 (p. 420 and throughout).
25 Johnstone, pp. 1–2; Oldridge, pp. 58–60. Russell points to the great importance of the sermon in Protestant religious practice as one reason for the increased importance of the devil (p. 275).

The devil as a tempter is central to the story of Elizabeth Sawyer, and even more so to that of Frank Thorney. Frank presents a kind of Rake's Progress of early modern sin, in which each wrong act leads inexorably to a worse act. Nathan Johnstone identifies this process of 'cumulative sin' as characteristic of early modern Protestant ideas about evil and comments that it 'was not a seamless progression, but a series of watersheds, each confirming a further descent into sin until the mind was ready to entertain thoughts of unquestionably diabolic crimes such as murder and witchcraft'.[26] Frank's story presents just such a series of turning points. The significance of this feature of the play, from the perspective of the present study, is that the devil's presence in everyday life – which appears to have been widely accepted by early modern Protestants – is ultimately linked to witchcraft. 'Ordinary' sins are a kind of gateway drug, which can ultimately lead to the worst of crimes, as is demonstrated by the cases of Frank Thorney and Elizabeth Sawyer. Mother Sawyer's story is a cautionary tale – a dreadful warning about the ultimate consequences of what might seem to be trivial sins. But the depiction of cumulative sin also serves to make the end point – witchcraft – plausible, by connecting it in a chain of causal relationships to relatively uncontroversial ideas about the presence of the demonic in more mundane settings.

The frequent references to the devil in the Frank Thorney plot are indicative of this view of evil and its connection to the devil. Even before his first appearance on stage in the second act, even before the start of the play in fact, the devil has been at work on, and in, Frank Thorney. Frank's covert affair with Winnifride is what starts his descent into the evils of bigamy and murder. Wrongly believing himself to be responsible for Winnifride's pregnancy, Frank feels himself honour-bound to make amends by marrying her. Sir Arthur, who is in fact the father of the unborn child, hypocritically chides Frank:

> If the nimble devil
> That wantoned in your blood rebelled against
> All rules of honest duty, you might, sir,
> Have found some more fitting place than here
> To have built a stews in.
> (1.1.78–82)

This may seem to be putting it figuratively, but the statement can also be taken literally. Burton's *Anatomy of Melancholy* suggested,

---

26 Johnstone, pp. 159–60.

quoting the sixteenth-century Dutch physician Jason Pratensis and others, that 'the devil, being a slender incomprehensible spirit, can easily insinuate and wind himself into human bodies' and, once there, could affect both mind and body.[27] The *pneumata* that were believed to be responsible for sensory perception were spirits in the bloodstream, and humoural blood was associated with the sensuousness of the sanguine personality type.[28] In this passage, it would appear that these vital constituents of the blood have been manipulated by another type of spirit – the devil. Frank's sinful relationship with Winnifride has indeed been inspired by a 'nimble devil', and it apparently exercises power over Frank at the physiological level.

From this initial sin follow further sins. Frank's lies lead him into committing the sin of bigamy by fraudulently marrying Susan for her dowry. In II.2, the effects of his sins start to take their toll on his mind. He is so distracted by his troubles that he calls Susan 'Winnifride', confusing his two wives, and in an aside refers to his bigamous situation as if it were a demon: 'the fiend [that] torments me' (II.2.129). The ultimate result of Frank's sins is the murder of Susan in Act III, and it is not until this point that the character of the devil actually appears on stage with Frank. The murder seems to be brought about by the dog's touch, but Frank remains unaware that he has been touched. The dog is not visible to him throughout the scene, despite the fact that it may have provided him with a murder weapon – the knife.[29] Even more remarkably, the dog helps Frank to tie himself up afterwards in order to support his story of an attack by Warbeck and Somerton, without Frank being aware of this demonic aid. This could be seen as requiring the devil's actual corporeal presence, as Nicol suggests;[30] but given that Frank remains unaware of the aid he has received (III.3.72–73), it may simply be a dramatic representation of the devil's proverbial ability to look after his own.

The devil's involvement in the Sawyer plot is, at first sight, quite different. Sawyer's devil, Tom, is visible and tangible, embodied

---

27 Burton, I.2.1.2, p. 199.
28 Noga Arikha, *Passions and Tempers: A History of the Humours* (New York: HarperCollins, 2007), pp. 10, 38–39. See also Chapter 6.
29 According to Corbin and Sedge, '[s]ince he [Frank] has given up his sword and states that he is unarmed (l. 22), it seems most likely that the Dog provides the knife' (III.3.24n). Of course, there is nothing in the text that requires the scene to be staged in this way, but the suggestion does seem fitting.
30 Nicol, p. 432.

and apparently capable of violence. His appearance before Sawyer is a special case; witches provided one of the few occasions on which the devil was required to take on a physical form. As Johnstone argues, the invisible nature of witchcraft necessitated the manufacture of physical evidence of the devil's involvement – witches' marks, for example. Conversely, murder could be proved by normal physical evidence, so the involvement of the devil could simply be taken for granted.[31] That the devil bargains directly and in embodied form with Sawyer does not imply that he is a 'different' devil from the one who touches Frank. The play instead reveals the variety of means through which the devil works.

Like Frank, Sawyer is gradually pushed into her pact with the devil-dog. However, rather than actively sinning as Frank does, Sawyer is driven into sin by what others do to her, in accordance with the passivity that was widely asserted by male authors to be characteristic of women at the time. First, she complains of the way she is spoken of by her neighbours, next she is abused and beaten by Old Banks, before finally being shunned by Cuddy and a group of other villagers. This series of humiliations drives her into the arms of the devil in much the same way as Frank's sins do for him. Frank's sins, however, are represented as both actively chosen and, paradoxically, as an inescapable destiny.

The other character to make an explicit deal with the devil is Cuddy Banks. Following his rough treatment at the hands of the spirit disguised as Katherine, Cuddy and the dog discuss their agreement:

> DOG   I'll help thee to thy love.
> CUDDY   Wilt thou? That promise shall cost me a brown loaf, though I steal it out of my father's cupboard. You'll eat stolen goods, Tom, will you not?
> DOG   Oh, best of all. The sweetest bits, those.
> CUDDY   You shall not starve, Ningle Tom, believe that. If you love fish, I'll help you to maids and soles. I'm acquainted with a fishmonger.
> DOG   Maids and soles? Oh, sweet bits! Banqueting stuff, those.
> (III.1.138–47)

Cuddy's offer of a 'brown loaf' is reminiscent of Ralph's offer to 'feed thy devil with horse-bread as long as he lives' in exchange for

---

31 Johnstone, pp. 143–44.

the love of Nan Spit in the clown subplot of *Dr Faustus*.[32] In both plays, the deal is not carried out, for the same reason; Mephastophilis is merely irritated at having been summoned by 'damned slaves'[33] while the dog, in the end, says of Cuddy, 'I scorn to prey on such an atom soul' (v.1.206). The suggestion that the devil might have any interest in brown bread is part of the comic aspect of this scene: the idea is presented as laughable, in accordance with Gifford's view – although, as noted in Chapter 2, it may not have been laughable to some Elizabethan readers of witchcraft pamphlets.[34] The dog might be interested in Cuddy's offer anyway because the bread will be acquired by sinful means – theft. But there is no sign in the play that Cuddy ever actually steals the bread.

Cuddy is, of course, the play's clown, but there is something clownish about the dog in the Cuddy scenes as well. In the end, he is even beaten out of Edmonton by Cuddy. In these scenes audiences encountered the devil in his guise as a trickster, playing his silly practical joke on Cuddy, and also the physically vulnerable devil who becomes the butt of jokes himself when Cuddy chases him away. Such comic depictions of the devil date back as far as the twelfth century, although they continued to survive in popular culture throughout the Tudor and Stuart periods. Within the play, the various conceptions now seem to sit rather awkwardly together, but they also provide something for everyone in the audience: the godly and the more profanely inclined. Russell suggests that the devil needed to be funny precisely because he was terrifying, and this might explain the need for comic relief from the stories of Mother Sawyer and Frank Thorney.[35]

In any case, the bargain between Cuddy and the dog is never taken seriously by either party, and there is no exchange between them. While the dog makes good on his promise to see misfortune befall Cuddy's rival Somerton, his wrongful arrest for Susan's murder is quickly resolved, and Cuddy never actively seeks any harm to Somerton. As for Kate Carter, Cuddy never even comes into contact with her. Apart from dealing with the devil, Cuddy also makes a deal with the servant of the devil – Elizabeth Sawyer. Asking for

---

32 vi.26–31. Horse bread was low-quality bread, so called because it was usually fed to horses. Brown bread was also perceived to be inferior to white bread, which was labour-intensive and expensive to produce.
33 viii.40.
34 Gifford, *Discourse*, sig. G3^v.
35 Russell, pp. 259–60.

her help in winning Kate Carter, he seems to offer her something more than bread: 'Do, and here's my hand, I am thine for three lives' (II.1.235–36). Virtually all witchcraft theorists condemned such dealings with witches, even if no harm was intended; Gifford and Perkins both regard 'white' witches or cunning folk as worse than workers of *maleficium*, on the grounds that by seeming to do good they draw people into the service of the devil.[36] But Cuddy never takes Mother Sawyer seriously, despite her insistence that he must.

Cuddy is ultimately immune to the threat of the devil, unlike the more serious character Frank Thorney, because Cuddy is a clown, and does not, or cannot, take either devil or witch seriously. This is a consistent feature of clowns in plays with supernatural elements – they never suffer serious harm, although they are generally put through some discomfort. Cuddy in *The Witch of Edmonton*, Robin in *Dr Faustus*, Trinculo and Stephano in *The Tempest*, Robert in *The Late Lancashire Witches* – all follow a similar pattern. They are tricked or made to look foolish, but left basically unharmed. The best way to neutralise the threat of the supernatural is to treat it as ridiculous – a point made by a number of contemplative theologians[37] – and in this respect Cuddy's strategy for dealing with the devil resembles Reginald Scot's strategy for dealing with witchcraft belief.

The play also explicitly provides another reason for Cuddy's immunity to the devil's temptations. The spirit who tricks him into falling into a pond says of Cuddy, '[w]e can meet his folly, / But from his virtues must be runaways' (III.1.85–86). Cuddy's virtue, the spirit claims, makes him immune to supernatural harm, while it is Sawyer's cursing and blasphemy that ensures her damnation. This claim is not entirely convincing; as Nicol points out, Cuddy is not completely blameless or innocent.[38] Late in the play, Cuddy says to the dog: 'I entertained you ever as a dog, not as a devil', and the dog seems to accept this to be true (V.1.116–18). Cuddy

---

36 Perkins, in his *Discourse*, states that 'howsoever both these be euill, yet of the two, the more horrible & detestable Monster is the good Witch'; p. 174. Gifford, *Discourse*, sigs H1ʳ–H1ᵛ; *Dialogue*, sigs D4ᵛ–F3ʳ. See also Gaule, pp. 30–31.
37 Russell, pp. 292–93.
38 Nicol goes so far as to claim that 'Cuddy is prepared to make deals with devils and see an innocent man hanged in order to satisfy his desire for Kate Carter' (pp. 438–39). This is hard on Cuddy, who has not solicited Somerton's death, and is not in a position to help his rival.

has been well aware all along that the dog is the devil; just a few lines earlier he shows that he knows Elizabeth Sawyer to be powerless without the dog's aid (v.1.105–8). But in these lines he suggests that by treating the devil as a dog and reducing the prince of this world to an object of comedy, Cuddy has avoided being trapped by his own sinful urges.

Cuddy cannot be represented as being entirely without sin for the simple reason that Cuddy is a human being, and therefore tainted by sin, as are all human beings. Unlike the two other main characters, however, Cuddy is only ever tempted to commit sinful acts; he never actually succumbs. The three main characters in the play – Cuddy, Frank, and Elizabeth Sawyer – represent three possible responses to the temptations of the devil. Cuddy, despite moments of evident temptation which the comic nature of the scenes does not entirely lighten, ultimately resists sin. This enables him to reject the devil and beat him out of Edmonton. Frank gives in to temptation and sins grievously, but repents before it is too late. Sawyer also sins, and is hardened by her sins to such an extent that she is unable to repent before her execution. While they respond differently, all three characters face challenges of a comparable nature and fit into the same moral schema.

Nathan Johnstone draws a contrast between the 'otherness' of witches and the ordinariness of murderers in the pamphlet literature of the time.[39] The ordinariness of murderers demanded that readers empathise with the criminal, in order to see how they came to commit such terrible crimes and so avoid the same fate themselves. In *The Witch of Edmonton*, this principle explains Frank Thorney's dying wish that 'my example / Might teach the world' (v.3.108–9). But, interestingly, Elizabeth Sawyer expresses a similar sentiment: 'All take heed / How they believe the devil; at last he'll cheat you' (v.3.46–47). It is not surprising that Frank Thorney, a murderer, is held up as an example to demonstrate the terrible end results of what had seemed to be trivial sins. But for Elizabeth Sawyer to be held up as an example to be avoided, rather than as an alien, incomprehensible 'other', is, according to Johnstone's conclusions, unusual. Some early modern evidence suggests exceptions to this rule, however: John Davenport's pamphlet on *The Witches of Huntingdon* suggests on its title page that '[t]he reader may make use hereof against Hypocrisie, anger, malice, swearing, Idolatry,

---

39 Johnstone, p. 154.

Lust, Covetousnesse, and other grievous sins, which occasioned this their downfall.'[40] This appears to be a clear reference to everyday sins leading ultimately to witchcraft; and Goodcole's account of the Edmonton case also stresses that the devil was attracted to Sawyer by her habit of swearing.[41] As discussed in Chapter 3, Thomas Cooper's witchcraft treatise also locates witches within the normal spectrum of human sinfulness, and suggests that other sins may be even more deplorable than witchcraft.

The humanising of Elizabeth Sawyer makes the audience empathise with the witch. But although this might be a bold move on the part of the playwrights, and although it is intuitively appealing to modern readers' feelings of sympathy with historical witches, it is also part of what makes witchcraft in this play less outlandish, less alien, and as a result much easier to believe. The play makes the orthodox conception of witchcraft 'real' in the same way that the influence of the devil over murderers seems to have been widely accepted as real. *The Witch of Edmonton* taps into a widely distributed discourse of human corruption and diabolic agency that was much less controversial than witchcraft belief in early modern England, especially to committed Protestants. Locating Mother Sawyer on the normal human spectrum of sin and repentance is part of what makes her uniquely plausible as a witch in the extant plays of the period. Another important ingredient in the humanising of witchcraft that the play carries out is the integration of Sawyer into the community of Edmonton and into human society in general.

The social and the demonic

Many recent critics of *The Witch of Edmonton* have regarded the play as providing a sophisticated analysis of early modern society, and one which emphasises the social causes of witchcraft persecution. This type of interpretation is intuitively appealing, since a wide range of characters from the community of Edmonton feature in the play, and the differences in outlook between representatives of a range of different social classes are very much in evidence. However, much of this work has identified the play's apparent stress on the social causes of witchcraft persecution as implying an underlying opposition to, or scepticism towards, witchcraft. Viviana Comensoli, for example, argues that '*The Witch of Edmonton* is unusual in

---

40 John Davenport, *The Witches of Huntingdon* (London, 1646).
41 Goodcole, sigs C1^r–C1^v.

that the dramatists deliberately discredit supernatural causation by treating witchcraft as a complex social construction.'[42] David Nicol instead sets out to distinguish between demonic and social causation, finding a place for both in the play. Nicol argues that the play 'stages both social and demonic pressure in order to decide on the boundary *between* the two, and to decide where the blame for evil finally lies'.[43] But the play does not, in my view, distinguish between demonic and social causation. Rather, human society is represented throughout the play as being thoroughly infected by the demonic, in accordance with early modern Protestant ideas about the role of the devil in the human world. It is not merely that social causation does not invalidate a serious belief in demonic causation, as Nicol argues, but that the two things are not separate categories at all.

The most famous example of the play's interest in social causation is Mother Sawyer's frequently quoted speech about society's other 'witches', which provides what looks like firmer ground for arguing that the play is sceptical about witchcraft. Interrogated by Sir Arthur and the Justice, Sawyer objects to being called a witch:

> A witch! Who is not?
> Hold not that universal name in scorn then.
> What are your painted things in princes' courts,
> Upon whose eyelids lust sits, blowing fires
> To burn men's souls in sensual hot desires,
> Upon whose naked paps a lecher's thought
> Acts sin in fouler shapes than can be wrought?
> (IV.1.116–22)

This is the beginning of a long diatribe against various kinds of 'witch', but none of Sawyer's examples of other 'witches' have any kind of supernatural or preternatural power; they are all social parasites. They are the 'painted things in princes' courts', 'city-witches' who ruin their husbands by excessive spending, women who scold their husbands, cheating lawyers who feed on the hopes of their clients, and, finally, rich seducers like Sir Arthur. What all her examples of 'witches' have in common is that they are described as leading others astray, often by some kind of temptation, just as the dog has led Sawyer herself astray, and as Sawyer attempts to lead Cuddy astray. Like Elizabeth Sawyer, these 'witches' mimic the behaviour of the devil.

---

42 Comensoli, p. 121.
43 Nicol, 432.

It is possible for any present-day reader, and perhaps even for some members of contemporary audiences, to understand this extended speech as conveying scepticism about the existence of witchcraft. This is particularly true when Sawyer says 'an old woman / Ill-favoured grown with years, if she be poor / Must be called bawd or witch' (IV.1.135–37). However, even these very sceptical lines do not quite go so far as to deny the existence of witches. Throughout the speech, Elizabeth Sawyer never denies that she herself is a witch – in fact, she tacitly admits it in an exchange with the Justice.[44] Instead, she points out that society is full of a range of other evil characters, all of whom can be characterised as witches too, in the important sense that they serve the ends of the devil by drawing others into danger and temptation. If this speech can be said to have a 'message' for the audience, that message is something similar to Gifford's; rather than scapegoating old women, Sawyer urges, people should closely examine their own sinful behaviour. But neither Gifford nor Sawyer's speech denies the existence of literal witchcraft. Instead, Sawyer's words normalise witchcraft by locating it within a broader context of human sin.

Less frequently remarked upon than Sawyer's speech is one of Cuddy's to his father, in which Cuddy supports the dog against accusations of involvement in Sawyer's witchcraft. The substance of the speech is similar to Sawyer's. Cuddy defends the dog by highlighting the ubiquity of sin in human society, in contrast to which '[t]he dog is no court-foisting hound, that fills his belly full by base wagging his tail; neither is it a citizen's water-spaniel, enticing his master to go a-ducking twice or thrice a week, while his wife makes ducks and drakes at home' (IV.1.244–47). This time the dog, rather than the witch, is favourably compared to the sins induced by a range of other 'dogs' within human society. These are not dogs in the literal sense; the 'court-foisting hound' could be understood as the kind of (human) flatterer widely associated with the court, but in rhetorically giving them the same shape as the devil, Cuddy reveals the demonic nature of human society. Similarly, Sawyer's rage is inspired by someone she describes as a 'black cur / That barks and bites, and sucks the very blood / Of me' (II.1.123–25) – Old Banks. The devil, as the 'prince of this world', has many

---

44 At l.123: 'JUSTICE: But these work not as you do. / ELIZABETH SAWYER: No, but far worse.' This constitutes an admission on Sawyer's part of working by witchcraft, in the usual sense.

means at his disposal, and need not work all his mischief directly when he can more profitably use an intermediary. This is also true of God, who uses the devil as an intermediary.

Any attempt to distinguish between social and demonic pressures is impeded by the language of the play, which repeatedly and consistently equates social ills with the demonic. In Elizabeth Sawyer's speech to the Justice, the mundane London sinners leading others astray are described as witches. Sir Arthur, the villagers, and Old Banks are likened to the devil, as are more abstract threats such as the 'beggary and want' (1.1.18) that Frank Thorney fears, and his own situation as a bigamist (II.2.130). Even the spreading of rumour is ascribed to the actions of demons. When Frank realises his father knows about his marriage to Winnifride, he says in an aside that '[s]ome swift spirit / Has blown this news abroad' (1.2.169–70). It is possible that this speculation is literally true; the devil's ability to pass on information to witches was often ascribed by demonologists to his ability to travel quickly. The devil has an interest in ensuring that Old Thorney hears of the marriage, since this pushes Frank into the additional sin of equivocating to deceive his father. Whether or not the news has literally been spread by a devil, however, gossip and rumour certainly serve an infernal purpose, as the opening speeches of Elizabeth Sawyer have already made clear.

It is, of course, possible to see such linguistic features of the play as purely metaphorical. Discussing the use of demonic language in the play, Dennis Kezar writes that 'the authors of *The Witch of Edmonton* deploy strikingly similar metaphors in an apparent effort to divest witchcraft and demonism of literal power and to distribute guilt across the whole community'.[45] But while the second part of Kezar's claim is surely pertinent – guilt is distributed across the whole community, and indeed the whole of humanity – the play only works to 'divest witchcraft and demonism of literal power' if the reader is not prepared to consider the possibility that witchcraft and the involvement of the devil in daily life are, in fact, realities. A reader who is prepared to consider that possibility – or one who is already committed to it – is more likely to understand the language of the demonic to imply that the working of the devil is present throughout a human society which has been corrupt from the very beginning, as a result of the Fall.

---

45 Dennis Kezar, '*The Witch of Edmonton* and the Guilt of Possession', in *Solon and Thespis: Law and Theater in the English Renaissance*, edited by Dennis Kezar (University of Notre Dame Press, 2007), pp. 124–60 (p. 144).

Elizabeth Sawyer's descent into sin need not be caused directly by the devil in order to be understood as demonically inspired, and the same is true of Frank's own sinful career. Frank may not reach an explicit agreement with the devil, but he does make a deal with a character who might be considered a servant of the devil.[46] Sir Arthur's role in bringing about Frank's marriage with Winnifride in the first act of the play is vital. In his conversation with Frank, Sir Arthur offers to 'make the maid a portion', and Frank mentions in passing: 'So you promised me / Before, in case I married her' (1.1.96–98). Sir Arthur has been encouraging the marriage since before the beginning of the action of the play. His peculiar eagerness to see Winnifride married, and his triumph after Frank has left – 'Have I caught thee, young man? / One trouble then is freed' (1.1.153–54) – suggests that he, not Frank, is responsible for Winnifride's pregnancy. It also suggests that the temptations of the flesh have been central to Sir Arthur's entrapment of Frank; Sir Arthur has used the devil's favourite snare.

The agreement reached by Frank and Sir Arthur is that Sir Arthur will provide a dowry of £200. Like the devil in *Dr Faustus*, Sir Arthur begins to renege on his side of the bargain immediately after having made it; he claims not to be able to make a 'present payment' (in obvious contrast to Old Carter, who uses exactly the same phrase). Sir Arthur also agrees to write to Frank's father and assure him that Frank has not married. It is this letter that enables Frank to go through with the sin of bigamy. His father will not accept Frank's word alone, and it is only the word of the high-ranking, respected Sir Arthur which causes him to back down and allow the second marriage to go ahead (1.2.201–04). At Sir Arthur's suggestion, the letter is first written by Frank, and then signed by Sir Arthur. On stage, the sight of the characters drawing up and signing a document might provide a visual cue, for an audience anticipating the demonic activity that is to come, that what is taking place is a kind of devil's pact, similar to Faustus signing a deed of gift for Mephastophilis.

Sir Arthur's quasi-demonic role in drawing Frank into sin helps to explain the extreme disapproval reserved for him at the end of the play, which could otherwise seem puzzling. Sir Arthur has seduced

---

46 As Helen Vella Bonavita, 'Maids, Wives and Widows: Multiple Meaning and Marriage in *The Witch of Edmonton*', *Parergon* 23:2 (2006), 73–95, writes, '[t]he false bargains made by Sir Arthur with Frank Thorney have had their demonic aspect' (p. 95).

Winnifride and lied to and manipulated Frank, so he is not blameless. After this, however, his actions are for the most part commendable, assisting the Justice, standing surety for the falsely accused Warbeck and Somerton, and promising to make financial amends to Winnifride. Frank has committed bigamy and murdered Old Carter's daughter – acts which by any measure are surely far worse than Sir Arthur's, and certainly in the case of the murder one which Sir Arthur cannot reasonably be thought to have desired or foreseen. Nevertheless, Old Carter tells Sir Arthur he is 'worthier to be hanged of the two', and not only forgives Frank but actually weeps for him (v.2.7–8; v.3.143–45). Old Carter's attitude makes more sense if it is accepted that Sir Arthur can also be seen as an agent of the devil, with Frank, his victim, in the role of the deluded witch who takes the blame for all the harm that his master has caused.

Elizabeth Sawyer also sets out to do the devil's work, the difference in her case being that she is so lacking in power that she requires the devil's direct aid. Sawyer, as Cuddy says to the dog, will 'never thrive if thou leavest her' (v.1.106). When Cuddy Banks approaches her and asks for help in winning Katherine Carter's love, she asks him 'dost thou think that I can do't, and I alone?' (II.1.245–46). Here she mimics her master, the dog, who earlier said to her that in order to get her revenge she must 'put credit in my power, / And in mine only, make orisons to me, / And none but me' (II.1.176–78). Both devil and witch demand allegiance to themselves and themselves only, and ask for belief in their power as a prerequisite for its effectiveness. This mimicry of the devil's methods is typical of the agents of the devil.[47] But diabolical servitude need not involve the kind of explicit pact with the devil that Mother Sawyer makes. Other human beings also do the work of the devil, as the play makes clear.

The idea that all human relationships are corrupt, and corrupting, is so prevalent in the play that no character entirely escapes diabolical influence. Old Carter, who seems at first a benign character, is revealed in Act II to have broken his word to Warbeck, an uncomfortable shortcoming in a play as concerned with oaths and bargains

---

47 Johnstone, p. 157. It should also be noted that the devil mimics Christ, who is said in the gospels to have asked for belief in his power as a condition of its effectiveness: 'And when he was come into the house, the blind men came to him: and Jesus saith unto them, Believe ye that I am able to do this? They said unto him, Yea, Lord. Then touched he their eyes, saying, According to your faith be it unto you' (Matthew 9:28–29).

as *The Witch of Edmonton*. Even the apparently blameless Susan has been seen as culpable in some respects.[48] But one character does appear to stand somewhat outside of human society, a point which helps to explain his ability to resist the devil: Cuddy Banks. Cuddy is a member of the Edmonton community, with relationships to the other characters. He is Old Banks's son, and says that he is in love with Kate Carter. But he never appears on stage with Kate, whose real suitor is Somerton in the Frank Thorney strand of the plot, and has little to do with his father apart from exchanging some cross words in Act IV. He seems almost to inhabit a different Edmonton from the other characters. Cuddy generally only appears in company with the dog, Mother Sawyer, or unnamed minor characters such as the Morris dancers. A large number of his spoken lines are asides, and Cuddy seems frequently to speak as a chorus, detachedly commenting on the action rather than being involved in it: his curious passivity in relation to the dog's offers of demonic help has already been remarked upon. Cuddy's status as of Edmonton but somehow, subtly, outside it is another aspect of his character that enables him to reject the devil, as he is relatively untainted by the human relationships that are so corrupting to all the other characters. It also makes Cuddy appear to be, if anything, less grounded in reality than the witch Elizabeth Sawyer.

Evidence and authority in *The Witch of Edmonton*

It has been argued that the play employs scepticism in order to present a plausible picture of witchcraft, drawing a boundary between those things that can reasonably be believed about witchcraft and those which are the product of an excessive credulity that is itself witch-like in some respects. This means that the scepticism and credulity of the characters themselves, in relation to witchcraft, is an important issue in the play. The unrestrained credulity of the countrymen threatens to overwhelm both reason and order, as their increasingly wild claims almost lead to an illegal burning. It is left to the authority figures, the Justice and Sir Arthur, to restore order with a more measured degree of belief in witchcraft – one tempered by scepticism.

But in one scene, the play seems to extend its concern with scepticism and credulity to touch on broader issues. Frank's father

---

48 Comensoli, p. 129.

has discovered his secret marriage to Winnifride, and Frank is forced to dissemble:

> FRANK   With your licence, 'tis not charitable,
>   I am sure it is not fatherly, so much
>   To be o'erswayed with credulous conceit
>   Of mere impossibilities [...]
> OLD THORNEY Why, canst thou yet deny thou hast no wife?
> FRANK   What do you take me for? An atheist?
>   (1.2.172–78)

When shown the letter from Sir Arthur, Old Thorney apologises by saying: 'Forgive me, Frank. Credulity abused me' (1.2.202). This repetition of the significant word 'credulity' again raises the issue of scepticism and belief. Some of the terms used in the argument are strongly reminiscent of the language of the witchcraft debate, with its talk of credulity, impossibilities, and atheism.[49] The use of such language is incongruous in this context; there is nothing 'impossible' about Frank's secret marriage, nor does it seem especially 'credulous' of his father to believe what he has heard.

The kind of evidence of the marriage in which Old Thorney initially puts his trust is report: second- or third-hand stories that may have become distorted in transmission. These are the kinds of stories that were typically used to prove the existence of witchcraft. In dismissing such evidence as 'mere impossibilities', Frank places himself in the position of the Scotian sceptic. The sceptical position is compromised, of course, by the fact that Frank is lying. In the play, Frank eventually forms an implicit league with the devil, and this fits well with his expression of scepticism. Sceptics like Scot and Weyer were frequently accused either of being witches themselves, or of some form of atheism, a charge which, in the passage quoted, Frank implicitly (and seemingly superfluously) denies. In this scene, the evidence of report – witness testimony – is ultimately overruled by that of authority: the written evidence of Sir Arthur, whose name and social position count for more than rumours. But report, in the event, turns out to be more reliable.

While no character in the play expresses outright scepticism towards witchcraft, this scene touches on the idea of scepticism

---

49 Scot refers frequently to credulity and impossibilities, while according to the first sentence of John Gaule's book on witchcraft, '[h]ee that will needs perswade himself that there are no Witches ... will ere long believe that there is no God' (pp. 1–2).

more broadly, and on the question of evidence. The play evinces a sceptical attitude towards authority, and places trust instead in the 'empirical' evidence of testimony. The play also connects Frank's dismissive attitude towards the kind of evidence often presented as empirical proof of the reality of witchcraft with corruption and sin. Ultimately, it confirms the orthodox opinion that the supernatural and the demonic can offer an explanation of all that lies outside human understanding. But in the process, this exchange between father and son seems tacitly to acknowledge the existence of more sceptical views. With *The Late Lancashire Witches*, the expression of scepticism moves much further into the open.

5
The Late Lancashire Witches

The pioneering journalist and poet Joseph Addison once commented on the subject of witchcraft. Directly addressing the question of belief and scepticism, Addison wrote:

> In short, when I consider the Question, whether there are such Persons in the World as those we call Witches? my Mind is divided between the two opposite Opinions; or rather (to speak my Thoughts freely) I believe in general that there is, and has been such a thing as Witchcraft; but at the same time can give no Credit to any particular Instance of it.[1]

Addison does not so much sit on the fence as attempt to plant a foot on both sides of it. While he does not contradict himself, it is difficult to see how scepticism towards every case of witchcraft that he has encountered can coexist with a professed belief in it 'in general'. Despite what Addison says about his beliefs, he gives the impression of not being prepared even to consider the possibility of witchcraft, or at least of 'any particular Instance of it'.

The ambivalence of Addison's view in this passage is grounded in the acute problems that witchcraft belief presented by 1711. Belief in witchcraft remained a kind of shibboleth for many orthodox Anglicans, but actual witchcraft prosecutions were by this time extremely rare, and there would be no more executions. The total and unquestioning belief demanded by earlier writers on witchcraft like Bodin had to be weighed against the reality that actual accusations of witchcraft were unlikely to be taken seriously by virtually any educated person. Addison's statement is the result of a difficult balancing act: on the one hand, he must say, in effect, 'I am not an atheist: of course I believe in witchcraft!' On the other hand, Addison must also say, 'I am not a fool: of course I don't believe in witchcraft!'

---

1 Joseph Addison, *The Spectator* 117 (14 July 1711).

In 1711, the tensions involved in witchcraft belief were particularly acute. But these tensions emerged in embryonic form much earlier, as a careful reading of Richard Brome and Thomas Heywood's *The Late Lancashire Witches* makes apparent.

This chapter begins with a consideration of the evidence on witchcraft belief and witchcraft persecution in the 1630s, including a discussion of Heywood's own views on witchcraft, a subject which he discussed in his non-dramatic works. I go on to discuss the connections between the play and the case on which it was based before attempting to show how the play exemplifies a shift in attitudes towards witchcraft compared with previous dramatic treatments. I argue that the play is the product of a society in which belief in witchcraft was already starting to develop into the 'dual' attitude that is so evident in Addison's short article on the subject.

Witchcraft in the 1630s

The Late Lancashire Witches was first performed at a time when witchcraft persecution – at least in the Home Counties – had declined dramatically. Nor was witchcraft a major topic for debate among the educated, assuming that their interests can be inferred from the textual remains of the period. The publication of witchcraft-related books and pamphlets during the 1630s fell to almost nothing; the only extant publications from this decade are reissues of earlier works. One of the first historians to point to this dramatic decline in witchcraft literature was R. Trevor Davies, who argued that it was related to William Laud's appointment as Bishop of London in 1628. As Bishop of London, Davies believed, Laud withheld permission for the publication of witchcraft writings.[2] This argument is appealing in many respects. Certainly, the more orthodox wing of the Anglican Church had previously shown itself hostile to belief in the related phenomenon of demonic possession, while some Puritans – like John Darrel – had encouraged such belief among the godly.[3]

---

2 R. Trevor Davies, *Four Centuries of Witch Beliefs* (London: Methuen, 1947), p. 90.
3 On the war of words between John Darrel and Samuel Harsnett see Marion Gibson, *Possession, Puritanism and Print: Darrell, Harsnett, Shakespeare and the Elizabethan Exorcism Controversy* (London: Pickering & Chatto, 2006).

However, there is no direct evidence for Laud's antipathy to witchcraft publications, let alone evidence for any action he might have taken to stamp them out. Davies endeavours to prove that Laud was a sceptic in relation to witchcraft, but the evidence he presents is thin at best.[4] As Laud's most recent biographer, Charles Carlton, points out, Laud questioned all the clergy in his diocese about witchcraft, which hardly suggests a sceptical attitude.[5] A further problem is the fact that while Laud did indeed attempt to strengthen print censorship, these efforts were not entirely successful; Carlton points out that Laud's restrictions 'failed to prevent the appearance of seditious works'.[6] James Sharpe has argued that there are 'occasional shards' of evidence pointing to opposition to witchcraft prosecution on the part of the Caroline authorities, and this is perhaps the most that can safely be said.[7] However, as Peter Elmer has recently pointed out, there is a difference between discouraging witchcraft prosecutions and discouraging belief in witchcraft.[8] It

---

4 See Davies, pp. 90–92. James Sharpe, in *Witchcraft in Early Modern England* (Harlow: Pearson, 2001), tactfully states that Davies's book 'overstates its case' in relation to Laud (p. 29); Ian Bostridge, *Witchcraft and its Transformations, c.1650–c.1750* (Oxford: Oxford University Press, 1997) more bluntly describes Davies's general argument as 'eccentric, even monomaniac' (p. 6). Davies's main piece of evidence is a diary entry in which Laud refers to a conversation about witchcraft. The diary entry gives no indication of what was said in this conversation and therefore does not support Davies's argument. It is more telling that, in the seven volumes of Laud's *Works*, Davies found such a tiny volume of material relating to witchcraft. Laud's near-total silence on the issue of witchcraft seems to me much more significant than his supposed scepticism towards it, which is far from proven. See also Elmer, pp. 72–73.
5 Charles Carlton, *Archbishop William Laud* (London: Routledge & Kegan Paul, 1987), p. 71. Davies acknowledges this (p. 91) but asserts that the questions were 'probably' copied from Laud's predecessor.
6 Carlton, p. 71. According to Carlton, Laud ordered the Stationers' Company to put his imprimatur into all published books in 1631. By 1640, 35 per cent of books appeared with the episcopal imprimatur – an increase compared with the situation previously, but still very far short of 'all' (Carlton, p. 118).
7 Sharpe, *Witchcraft in Early Modern England*, p. 30. Sharpe points to a 1636 case in the Somerset assizes in which a woman who had been accused of witchcraft was not only acquitted, but allowed to bring an action for malicious prosecution *in forma pauperis* (i.e. without paying costs, and with court-appointed legal representation) against her accuser.
8 Elmer, *Witchcraft, Witch-Hunting, and Politics in Early Modern England*, pp. 74–75.

seems likely, therefore, that the sudden decline in witchcraft publications was at least partly due to a decline in interest on the part of authors and the reading public.[9] After all, if the authorities had been particularly concerned to discourage belief in witchcraft at this time, they might have encouraged the writing of sceptical texts like Scot's or Harsnett's.

Witchcraft was mentioned in some texts on other subjects written during the decade, and these texts throw an interesting light on attitudes at the time. One such text is James Hart's medical treatise *Klinike* (1633). Hart is mostly sceptical about claims of what he calls 'effascination' by sight or by voice. Interestingly, his arguments are entirely naturalistic; he considers the possibility of vapours produced from the mouth causing harm but, with some qualifications, dismisses it. Hart does accept, however, that God may suffer the devil to do harm at times, 'for causes best knowne to himselfe'. When he discusses witches, Hart remarks that

> such persons as are by the vulgar suspected of performing such ill offices, are ignorant wicked people, filled with envie and malice, often wishing such harmes to their neighbours, which Satan by his power from above, putting presently in execution, these wicked malicious people are often beleeved to be the actors, and sometimes God in his justice suffereth such to be punished by the sword of the Magistrate, although free from any compact with Satan; God sometimes thus justly punishing their envie and malice, and other sins. And therefore it behooves those in authoritie to be carefull of the lives of such people, where there is no evident and apparent proofe to convince them.[10]

Witches, according to Hart, are deserving of punishment but not guilty. The devil may be responsible for the harms they wished to bring about, but the witches themselves cannot be said to have caused this harm by wishing it to happen. All the elements of witchcraft are still present – hateful witches, the devil, supernaturally inflicted harm – but the causal link between witch and harm has been broken, and the pact between witch and devil is absent. Furthermore, while the punishment of these witches, for their 'envie

---

9 Gibson suggests that the decline in interest in witchcraft stemmed from the publication of more controversial possession pamphlets: see *Reading Witchcraft*, pp. 186–87.

10 James Hart, *Klinike, or the Diet of the Diseased* (London, 1633), p. 356. All other references to Hart's discussion of witchcraft are also to this page.

and malice', may be just, it is also to be avoided; 'those in authoritie' are advised to be careful in prosecuting witches.

Hart's logic, if that is what it is, is convoluted, and his position shifts abruptly and repeatedly within a single page. Immediately after the passage above, the envious and malicious witch is referred to as 'some poore melancholicke woman'. Hart uses the phrase 'poor woman' three times, and comments that she 'is presently accused for a witch; and if it lay in their power (so ignorant, envious and malicious are some of those people) ... they would hang this accused party'. The envy and malice that had been the defining feature of the accused witch are reassigned to her accusers. The confusion Hart evinces may explain why he declares himself, after this brief and baffling discussion, to be unwilling to dwell on the subject.

Sir Thomas Browne's *Religio Medici* (published in 1643, but written and circulated in manuscript in the 1630s)[11] also briefly discusses witchcraft. Browne declares himself to be a believer:

> It is a riddle to me ... how so many learned heads should so farre forget their Metaphysicks, and destroy the Ladder and scale of creatures, as to question the existence of Spirits: for my part, I have ever beleeved, and doe now know, that there are Witches; they that doubt of these, doe not onely deny them, but Spirits; and are obliquely and upon consequence a sort, not of Infidels, but Atheists.[12]

Browne establishes what is at stake in the witchcraft debate in this passage, which constitutes his first words on the subject. Browne ties the existence of spirits (and therefore God) to the existence of witches, and seems in no doubt about either.

Having made this declaration of belief, Browne goes on to undermine all of its practical implications without abandoning the belief itself. First, he establishes his openness to alternative explanations in individual cases, holding that 'the Devill doth really possesse some men, the spirit of melancholy others, the spirit of Delusion others'. Browne even allows for magic in the absence of witchcraft: 'I beleeve that all that use sorceries, incantations, and spells, are not Witches'.[13] This statement would seem to allow that the activities of

---

11 Kathryn Murphy, 'The Physician's Religion and *salus populi*: The Manuscript Circulation and Print Publication of *Religio Medici*', *Studies in Philology* 111:4 (2014), 845–74 (p. 850).
12 Thomas Browne, *Religio Medici* (London, 1643), p. 67.
13 Browne, p. 69.

some magic users – perhaps Browne has wise men and women in mind – are excusable, or at least less blameworthy than witchcraft. But he proceeds to go even further than this. Having established that not all witches are witches, he argues that not all magic is magic:

> I conceive there is a traditionall Magicke, not learned immediately from the Devill, but at second hand from his Schollers; who having once the secret betrayed, are able, and doe emperically practice without his advice, they both proceeding upon the principles of nature ... Thus I thinke at first a great part of Philosophy was Witchcraft, which being afterward derived to one another, proved but Philosophy, and was indeed no more but the honest effects of Nature: What invented by us is Philosophy, learned from him is Magicke.[14]

This statement credits witches with increasing the sum of human knowledge – 'Philosophy' – by learning the secrets of nature from the devil. The knowledge gained by witches, passed on to others, becomes harmless and even beneficial. Witches' magic is not supernatural, according to Browne, but appears to be identical with what writers such as Scot described as natural magic.

Browne's position is in one sense orthodox. As James I also argued, the devil is not capable of performing true miracles (that is, things which are outside the laws of nature): only God can do this. The devil's wonders are not supernatural but merely preternatural – achieved through hidden means but in accordance with natural laws.[15] What is unusual about Browne's discussion of this topic is that he does not draw a sharp distinction between the natural and the preternatural. While the devil's wonders may not break the laws of nature, it is commonly stressed that it is not possible for humans to perform them. James I, for instance, discusses in depth the devil's ability to travel at speeds impossible for humans.[16] This is possible by virtue of his nature as a spirit; and while he may also teach his followers 'manie juglarie trickes at Cardes, dice, & such like',[17] the devil's potential as a source of knowledge useful to humanity is not stressed. Rather, his wonders – which only he can perform – are the important point. Although strictly speaking not supernatural,

---

14 Browne, pp. 69–70. Browne is using an argument previously associated with ritual magicians, and condemned by Thomas Aquinas (Hutton, p. 113).
15 James I, pp. 22–23, argues further that the devil's 'miracles' are illusory, while God's miracles take place in reality. See also Holland, sig. E1^r.
16 James I, pp. 21–22.
17 James I, p. 22.

these wonders are also not 'natural' in the usual sense, neither is it possible for humans to perform them without the devil's aid.

Browne's discussion of 'Witchcraft' and its transformation into 'Philosophy' is as far as it can be from James's demonological view while maintaining the same underlying principles. Things that were once thought to be magical, according to Browne, are eventually revealed as merely natural, simply by virtue of becoming more widely known. The knowledge derived from the devil is not even forbidden knowledge, except in so far as it comes from the devil: learned from some other source, such knowledge can be described as 'honest'. While the avoidance of atheism makes it important for Browne to believe in witches as a guarantee of the existence of spirits, by the end of his discussion these witches have been divested of any real significance, and their magical powers have been transformed into 'Philosophy' – knowledge of the workings of the natural world – for our benefit. There is no sense, in Browne's admittedly brief remarks on the subject, of any real threat posed by witches. In accordance with this absence of threat is the fact that Browne offers no opinion on the legal punishment of witches, still less an exhortation to judges to punish them severely.

Nonetheless, it ought to be stressed that Browne was by no means a sceptic. In fact, it has frequently been asserted that he gave evidence favouring the prosecution in a witchcraft trial that took place in Bury St Edmunds in 1662, apparently on the basis of a pamphlet account of the trial.[18] This pamphlet names the witness as '*Dr. Brown of Norwich*, a Person of great knowledge',[19] but does not identify him as the author of *Religio Medici*. The pamphlet is of questionable reliability in any case, as it was published nearly twenty years after the event and gets the date of the trial wrong on the cover. It seems likely that Browne was called to give evidence by the witches' accusers, but the pamphlet does not confirm this, stating only that he was present and was asked his opinion.

What is interesting in Browne's evidence, however, is his concern to eliminate the supernatural as an explanation. It is difficult to see how a natural disease could result in the victims vomiting pins, as the witches' accusers said had happened; nonetheless this is what Browne claims. The symptoms described in the pamphlet would have been easily recognisable at the time as the classic symptoms

---

18 See, for example, Kittredge, p. 334; Davies, p. 109; Sharpe, *Witchcraft in Early Modern England*, p. 122.
19 Anon., *A Tryal of Witches*, p. 41.

of demonic possession, but the word 'possession' is avoided throughout the pamphlet – instead, the witches' victims are said to be bewitched. Browne's evidence goes even further, presenting the victims as suffering from an entirely natural disease, despite the fact that he also argued that they were indeed bewitched. According to the pamphlet, Browne 'conceived, that these swouning Fits were Natural, and nothing else but that they call the Mother, but only heightened to a great excess by the subtilty of the Devil, co-operating with the Malice of these which we term Witches, at whose Instance he doth these Villanies'.[20] This could indeed be the author of *Religio Medici* speaking, as the reality of witchcraft is simultaneously confirmed and stripped of its supernatural qualities.

Browne's view and Hart's are very different in presentation and, to some extent, in content. Nonetheless, they do share some assumptions. Both authors emphasise the conformity of witchcraft to the normal laws of nature, and they both assume that the actual mechanics of witchcraft can, in principle, be understood. Both place little emphasis on, or in Hart's case actually discourage, the prosecution of people accused of witchcraft. In addition, both continue to maintain the power of the devil and his potential for intervening in human affairs. The two authors were educated people, and the similarities between their texts provide some evidence of what might be termed an 'elite' view of witchcraft during the 1630s. From this perspective, the belief in witchcraft was necessary for reasons of religious orthodoxy. It was supported by important authorities and well established, but many of the details of this belief were rather lurid and may have become embarrassing. The topic was not one to dwell on at length; there was no longer any need to write full-length monographs about it. Furthermore, the theoretical belief in witchcraft had to be maintained without allowing too many practical consequences to follow on from it. Witchcraft prosecutions during the 1630s, as Sharpe points out, 'almost invariably led to an acquittal'.[21] The disruptive impact of high-profile witchcraft cases was not welcome to the authorities.

---

20 *A Tryal of Witches*, p. 42.
21 Sharpe, *Witchcraft in Early Modern England*, p. 30. The situation outside the Home Counties is much more uncertain owing to the patchier survival of assize records; Janet A. Thompson argues in *Wives, Widows, Witches and Bitches: Women in Seventeenth Century Devon* (New York: Peter Lang, 1993) that persecution in that county peaked in the second half of the 1600s (see pp. 101–02). Sharpe makes a similar suggestion about the Western, Oxford, and Northern circuits, although more cautiously, in *Instruments of Darkness*, p. 124.

Thomas Heywood and witchcraft

Another of the few authors to touch on the subject of witchcraft in the 1630s is also a co-author of *The Late Lancashire Witches*. Thomas Heywood, an especially significant figure in the study of witchcraft drama, was also the author of partly demonological works. In *Gynaikeion* (1624), a collection of stories and mythology about women, Heywood devotes about twenty pages to a discussion of witchcraft, in the course of which he relies heavily on Jean Bodin, whose work he had probably read in Latin translation.[22] *The Hierarchie of the Blessed Angels* (1635) is perhaps even more interesting, as it was published so soon after the play. This book is an eclectic mixture of mythology, angelology, theology, and demonology, mostly written in rhyming couplets, with frequent digressions on all manner of topics. It is primarily on the strength of these two works that Heywood has been described as a 'famous witch-lorist',[23] and one who, according to Katharine Briggs, 'believed the witch stories'.[24] But this reputation repays closer examination, because Heywood's beliefs are not quite as straightforward as these writers suggest.

Unlike most previous authors on witchcraft, Heywood took a great many examples from classical myth. He cites, among others, Plutarch, Herodotus, and Pliny, and discusses Circe, Medea, Vitia, Mycale, Locusta, Eriphila, and many other mythological characters.[25] This is perhaps not surprising given his previous interest in mythology, as the author of plays on the *Golden*, *Silver*, *Brazen* and *Iron Ages*. The attitude of Renaissance authors towards classical myth is often difficult to gauge, but some readers would have understood these stories to be fictional.[26] Heywood does not say that the myths he repeats are invented, but he does acknowledge their implausibility, describing the stories told by 'the antient Poets' as 'most strange things, as miraculous to relate as difficult to beleeue'.[27]

---

22 Heywood was probably unable to read much French: see Hirsch, 'Werewolves and Severed Hands', p. 94.
23 Arthur M. Clark, *Thomas Heywood* (Oxford: Blackwell, 1931), p. 121.
24 Briggs, p. 100.
25 Thomas Heywood, *Gynaikeion* (London, 1624), pp. 403–06. Other authors on witchcraft also refer to ancient poets, but much less extensively than Heywood. Gareth Roberts, 'The Descendants of Circe', discusses a number of examples; see pp. 187–92.
26 See the discussion of classical myth in Chapter 1.
27 Heywood, *Gynaikeion*, p. 403.

Heywood professes to believe in witchcraft, but there are several occasions on which his attitude to the material he presents is confused or defensive. He is reluctant to take any position on what he regards as controversial theoretical issues presented by witchcraft. When referring to such points, he does so in order to avoid them: 'The difference betwixt Witches, or to define what *Maga* are and what *Lamia*, were but time misspent, the rather because it hath beene an argument so much handled in our mother tongue.'[28] Heywood refuses to take any position on the possibility of witches transforming their shapes,stating that

> [w]hether this be possible in Nature, or no ... hath beene a Question as well amongst the Theologists, as the Philosophers: It is no businesse of mine at this present to reconcile their Controuersies, my promise is onely to acquaint you with such things as I haue eyther read, or heard related: which if they erre in any thing from truth, blame not me, but the Authors.[29]

Heywood here disowns any responsibility for the stories he is repeating, and it is difficult to see why he would feel the need to do so if he were convinced of their accuracy. Heywood's apparent lack of confidence on this subject is emphasised by his total dependence on authority. Unlike many earlier writers on witchcraft, Heywood appeals solely to authority – other people's stories – and makes almost no reference to the evidence of daily experience. The closest he comes to a personal anecdote is a story he tells about a witch who will stop at nothing in order to be reunited with her kettle, attributing this tale to a 'woman of good credit and reputation, whom I have knowne aboue these foure and twentie yeares'.[30] But even this story takes place far away, on a ship that was sailing to England. (The witch terrifies the crew by creating a storm and appearing on the mainmast to demand the return of her kettle, which had been given as security for a loan that she failed to repay. The witch is only placated when the kettle is thrown over the side of the ship, and she promptly sails away in it.) Many of the other stories that Heywood repeats are distanced from Heywood's England in time and place; many are classical, others concern 'the Witches in Lap-land, Fin-land, and these miserable and wretched cold countries'.[31] One exception is the Warboys case, mentioned in passing

---

28 Heywood, *Gynaikeion*, p. 406.
29 Heywood, *Gynaikeion*, pp. 409–10.
30 Heywood, *Gynaikeion*, p. 414.
31 Heywood, *Gynaikeion*, p. 417.

in *The Hierarchie of the Blessed Angels*. Heywood's only source of information about this case seems to be the pamphlet account published in 1593, but he nonetheless presents it rather proudly, as a story which buttresses the credibility of the other stories he has already told:

> To giue the histories past the more credit, as also those which follow, concerning Witches, Magitions, Circulators, juglers, &c. if we shall but cast our eyes backe upon our selues, and seeke no further than the late times, and in them but examine our owne Nation, we shall vndoubtedly finde accidents as prodigous, horrid, and euery way wonderfull, as in the other. Concerning which whosoever shall desire to be more fully satisfied, I refer them to a Discourse published in English, *Anno* 1593. containing sundry remarkable pieces of Witchcraft.[32]

This story, belonging to the not-so-recent past from Heywood's perspective, is told specifically in order to back up the others. In stating this to be the case, he tacitly admits them to be unconvincing. Furthermore, while this story is described as more credible than the others – perhaps partly because it happened in the more familiar territory of England – Heywood declines to share any of the details with the reader. The really convincing evidence is the evidence he chooses *not* to present.

Jostling with Heywood's belief in witchcraft is his scepticism towards it. Heywood's attitude to the kind of magic users that he might have been encountered in daily life – wise men and women – is revealed in an earlier section of *Gynaikeion* on prophetesses, in which he tells a story revealing the 'imposturous lies' of a cunning woman, and dismisses the claims of all 'Fortune-tellers, Gypsies, Wisewomen, and such as pretend to tell of things lost'.[33] This is very similar to the attitude articulated in one of Heywood's earlier dramatic writings, *The Wise Woman of Hogsdon* (1604?). The everyday witchcraft that members of the audience might actually encounter in their daily lives – the magical services sold by wise folk – are scornfully dismissed in both Heywood's dramatic and non-dramatic writings. His attitude to witchcraft seems to be built on an implicit distinction between the 'real', threatening witchcraft, which always seems to be happening somewhere else, and the familiar, basically harmless fake 'witchcraft' practised by tricksters like the

---

32 Thomas Heywood, *The Hierarchie of the Blessed Angels* (London, 1635), pp. 597–98.
33 Heywood, *Gynaikeion*, p. 103.

wise woman. A similar divide exists in the representation of witchcraft in *The Late Lancashire Witches*.

Heywood, while conceding the difficulty of believing in witchcraft, is nonetheless determined to do so, assuming that the statements in *Gynaikeion* and the *Hierarchie* can be taken as an accurate representation of his views. Interestingly, the tone of his discussion in *Gynaikeion* is rather darker than that in *Hierarchie*; in his discussion of impotence magic in the earlier text, for example, he seems almost angry, making oblique reference to everyday experience when he describes this practice as 'commonly in use now adayes'.[34] By the time of *The Hierarchie of the Blessed Angels*, however, while maleficent witchcraft certainly happens, it has become something that almost always happens somewhere else – not here in London. Another issue on which Heywood takes no stand – in fact, he hardly ever even refers to it – is the legal punishment of witches. Again, this is in contrast to earlier writers on witchcraft like James I, Perkins, and Bodin, who all demand that tougher action be taken against witches.[35] Heywood does not feel the need to make any demand for greater severity, despite the fact that, by the time of the *Hierarchie*, very few convictions were taking place. The stories about witches are recounted simply as stories, not as evidence that action needs to be taken. However genuine Heywood's belief in witchcraft may be, it is a belief devoid of practical consequences, as with his contemporaries, Browne and Hart.

The play and the case

In *The Witch of Edmonton* many popular beliefs about witches are ridiculed or shown to be false. In *The Late Lancashire Witches*, by contrast, everything is true. The powers the eponymous witches are able to command are varied and spectacular: they are able to transform themselves into large cats, summon spirits to impersonate real people, magically steal food from a wedding feast, cause impotence, and make milk pails walk by themselves (this last effect was apparently reproduced on stage in performances). The chief witch, Mistress Generous, is in possession of a magic bridle which transforms the wearer into a horse when a rhyming charm is recited.

---

34 Heywood, *Gynaikeion*, p. 402.
35 Perkins, for example, argues that witches should always be put to death, even in the absence of *maleficium* (pp. 181–84), while James I equates leniency towards witches with witchcraft itself (p. 78).

In *The Witch of Edmonton*, such spoken charms are represented as both serious – in that they are blasphemous – and ineffective, whereas *The Late Lancashire Witches* treats magic spells as comical, but at the same time genuinely efficacious, as did Middleton's *The Witch*. The comic nature of the play was recognised by an auditor of the play's third performance, Nathaniel Tomkyns, whose letter to a friend provides a detailed description and can reasonably be described as the earliest extant theatre review.[36]

As a number of scholars have pointed out,[37] much of this material closely resembles the deposition statements made by people involved in the case. Edmund Robinson, a 10-year-old boy, was the main witness against the witches, and his deposition provides many of the play's plot elements. His deposition described a woman and a boy turning into greyhounds, a gathering of witches where he was given 'Flesh and Bread upon a Trencher and Drink in a Glass', and a fight with a devil-boy whose identity is betrayed by his having a 'cloven foot'.[38] All of these events are also found in the play. Other parts of the play seem to have come from the depositions of the accused. Margaret Johnson testified that 'there appeared unto her a spirit or devill in the similitude and proportion of a man, apparrelled in a suite of blacke, tied about with silke pointes'.[39] There are close resemblances between this statement and the confession delivered by Peg at the end of the play, which even refers to 'blacke points'.[40]

The play's repetition and apparent endorsement of all these allegations is a point of contrast with *The Witch of Edmonton*.

---

36 All critics of the play are indebted to Herbert Berry, who discovered this manuscript. See Berry, *Shakespeare's Playhouses* (New York: AMS, 1987), pp. 123–24.

37 Berry, pp. 129–31; Harris, p. 176; Briggs, p. 102; Heather Hirschfeld, *Joint Enterprises: Collaborative Drama and the Institutionalization of the English Renaissance Theatre* (Amherst: University of Massachusetts Press, 2004), p. 364.

38 Popular belief had it that the devil could take on human form, but would be given away by having one cloven hoof instead of a foot (Oldridge, p. 82). Various versions of the deposition survive (see note 47); I have used the text as reproduced in John Webster's *Displaying of Supposed Witchcraft* (London, 1677), pp. 347–49.

39 Margaret Johnson's deposition is reproduced in Thomas Wright (ed.), *Narratives of Sorcery and Magic*, vol. 2 (London, 1851), pp. 114–17.

40 Thomas Heywood and Richard Brome, *The Late Lancashire Witches*, Quarto Text, edited by Helen Ostovich, Richard Brome online (www.hrionline.ac.uk/brome, 17 January 2010), l. 2646. Subsequent line references, given in parentheses, are to this edition.

This is partly the result of the differences between the main sources for the plays. Goodcole's pamphlet on Elizabeth Sawyer is relatively sober, whereas Edmund Robinson's deposition is fantastic, even by the standards of witchcraft accusations. However, as Goodcole's pamphlet makes clear, there was no shortage of wild stories in circulation about Elizabeth Sawyer, and the playwrights in general did not make use of these; with a few exceptions, *The Witch of Edmonton* follows Goodcole's rejection of the less plausible stories that circulated about Elizabeth Sawyer. Had Dekker, Ford, and Rowley wanted to write a much more comic play, they might have found some way to include scenes involving 'a Ferret and an Owle dayly sporting'[41] for Elizabeth Sawyer's entertainment – this might have been difficult to stage, but such considerations did not prevent the King's Men from presenting a walking pail of milk in *The Late Lancashire Witches*. In fact, *The Late Lancashire Witches* not only represents many of Edmund Robinson's stories about witchcraft in detail, it goes on to add several unlikely stories of its own.

The plot elements that do not come from depositions are drawn from a variety of sources. During the wedding feast, the musicians are first enchanted into playing '*Musicke. Every one a severall tune*' (1337SD), then they are prevented from playing at all (1342), and finally the musicians are magically compelled to smash their instruments (1378). This part of the plot was probably inspired by the failed Morris dance in *The Witch of Edmonton*. Following the wedding, in Act IV, Lawrence is the victim of witchcraft-induced impotence, a topic discussed by Heywood in earlier writings.[42] The 'parade of fathers', in which Whetstone purports to reveal the true parentage of Arthur, Bantam, and Shakestone, is borrowed from the John Teutonicus story which Heywood told soon afterwards in *The Hierarchie of the Blessed Angels*, as Alison Findlay points out.[43] Finally, the episode in which Mistress Generous is identified as a witch by her severed hand, cut off by the soldier-miller when she attacks him in the shape of a large cat, is taken from the *Malleus Maleficarum*, possibly in combination with other sources.[44]

---

41 Goodcole, epistle to the readers.
42 *Gynaikeion*, p. 402.
43 Alison Findlay, *Illegitimate Power* (Manchester: Manchester University Press, 1994), p. 61. The John Teutonicus story is told on pp. 512–14 of *Hierarchie*.
44 See Institoris and Sprenger, II.123C–124B (pp. 339–40). A very similar story is retold in *Gynaikeion*, where Heywood explicitly attributes it to the *Malleus* (see *Gynaikeion*, p. 410), suggesting that this was his source for the play's version

The apparent credulity of the play has led some scholars to claim that it is a piece of witchmongering propaganda. Davies claims that 'the supreme object' of the play 'must have been to intensify public feeling against witches',[45] while Berry writes that

> Heywood and Brome knew that many of the accused persons stoutly denied being witches ... Yet they managed to keep any hint of the denials out of the play, or of the case for the accused otherwise. The play represents the case for the prosecution alone ... all the rational people who have had doubts about the existence or seriousness of witchcraft are convinced that they have been wrong.[46]

The case for the prosecution would have been the only one heard in court as well, since defendants in criminal trials were not entitled to legal representation at the time. Berry makes this claim in the course of an elaborate and highly speculative argument, which links the play to an attempt by the Puritan faction within the Privy Council to push for punishment of the witches. There is no direct evidence for this alleged disagreement; Berry's view is based on his assumption that the playwrights' access to depositions indicates that they had inside information from the Privy Council. But given the relatively large number of texts in which the depositions have survived, it seems unlikely that these documents were a well-kept secret.[47] In arguing for his view, Berry relies primarily on the interpretation of the play outlined here, which is not, in my view, a persuasive one. To begin with, it is not strictly true that the denials of the witches are kept out of the play: 'confession you get none from us', says Mall (2616). Berry argues that the play 'represents

---

of the story as well. Brett D. Hirsch argues that the episode was inspired by a French text, Henri Boguet's *Discours des Sorciers* (1590), which features the specific detail of a wedding ring on a severed hand ('Werewolves and Severed Hands', p. 92). However, this version of the story deals with a werewolf rather than a witch who transforms herself into a cat, so it is probably not the only source, especially in view of Heywood's own reference to the *Malleus*. Kittredge comments that these kinds of stories – in which injuries inflicted on a magician or witch in changed form are used to identify him or her – were very common and date back at least as far as the twelfth and thirteenth centuries (p. 41).

45 Davies, p. 114.
46 Berry, p. 131.
47 The depositions survive in 'several manuscript sources, more or less corrupt', according to Ewen, p. 244, footnote 3, and are also reprinted in Webster's *Displaying of Supposed Witchcraft*. Berry himself acknowledges that the depositions 'sooner or later ... circulated widely' (p. 134).

the case for the prosecution', but this case had been proven in a court of law. By the time the play was first performed, the accused had already been convicted by a jury in Lancashire. This means that the deposition given by Edmund Robinson had been accepted by both a grand jury and a petty jury as substantially true; as far as the legal record was concerned, the guilt of the witches was established fact. One of the witches – Margaret Johnson – had even confessed, as the play shows in lines 2627–46. In view of the confession and the guilty verdict, the play could hardly do otherwise than represent the witches as guilty. As an editor of the play points out, 'it would be most inappropriate (as well as politically dangerous) for the players to tell "Justice" what to do'.[48] In addition, there are dramatic and commercial reasons for presenting the witches as unambiguously guilty. A witch play that represented the witches as innocent would be anti-climactic to say the least, and such a play would have been unlikely to draw the large crowds that went to see *The Late Lancashire Witches*.

That the witches really are witches is to be expected; much more significant than the play's demonstration of the witches' guilt is the effort that goes into depicting them as amusing and, for the most part, harmless. Once again, this is in contrast to Elizabeth Sawyer in *The Witch of Edmonton*, who is shown to be responsible for the death of Agnes Ratcliffe. As Kathleen McLuskie points out, the historical Lancashire witches were accused of murder – accusations which disappear in the play.[49] The witches in the play may scratch the miller, but no one is killed; for the most part, their activities result in situations aimed at making the audience laugh. In fact, the play even makes the witch hunter Doughty explicitly state that the witches have *not* killed anyone: 'I have sought about these two dayes, and heard of a hundred such mischievous tricks, *though none mortall*' (2143–45; emphasis added). This is despite the fact that seventeen of the witches in the case in Lancashire had been found guilty of charges including murder by witchcraft.[50] Even more

---

48 Laird Barber, introduction to *The Late Lancashire Witches*, by Thomas Heywood and Richard Brome (New York: Garland, 1979), p. 71.
49 Kathleen McLuskie, 'Politics and Aesthetic Pleasure in 1630s Theater', in *Localizing Caroline Drama: Politics and Economics of the Early Modern English Stage, 1625–1642*, edited by Adam Zucker and Alan B. Farmer (New York: Palgrave Macmillan, 2006), pp. 43–68 (pp. 62–63).
50 See Ewen, *Witchcraft and Demonianism*, p. 249. The charges are summarised on pp. 246–47.

striking than the omissions of the plot is the way the witches themselves stress their harmlessness; "'Tis all for mirth, we mean no hurt', says Mistress Generous (2000).

The epilogue to the play has also been the subject of much discussion, since it refers explicitly to the fate of the witches, which had yet to be decided at the time of the play's performance:

> Now while the Witches must expect their due
> By lawfull Iustice, we appeale to you
> For favourable censure; what their crime
> May bring upon 'em, ripenes yet of time
> Has not reveal'd. Perhaps great Mercy may
> After just condemnation give them day
> Of longer life.
> (2685–91)

Made in the context of a recent guilty verdict by the jury in Lancashire ('just condemnation'), this speech is highly suggestive in intimating that mercy may be granted to the witches. It is also striking that, as Hirschfeld points out, the witches and the playwrights are associated in the lines above, and throughout the play – perhaps most obviously when they arrange a show for Arthur and his friends, the parade of fathers.[51] In the epilogue, like the witches awaiting the decision of the King and his council, the playwrights and actors anxiously await the judgement of the audience.

That any doubt at all is expressed about the punishment the witches will suffer would be highly presumptuous if their execution were not already in doubt. Even the bishop sent by the King to examine the witches hesitated to push his own doubts about the verdict too far, commenting that 'such evidence being, as lawyers speak, against the King, I thought it not meet without further authority to examine'.[52] Lowly playwrights would have had even greater reason to be cautious than a bishop, and hinting that the witches may receive mercy would not have been a very wise thing for the playwrights to do if they did not already believe this outcome to be likely. It may be that the playwrights did have some inside knowledge of what was going to happen, as Berry suggests. Alternatively, it may have been obvious to everyone that the authorities did not

---

51 Hirschfeld, p. 142.
52 Quoted in Barber, p. 60. Barber adds that 'legally speaking, the King was on the side of the prosecution and the Bishop hesitates to undermine the King's case'.

want to see large numbers of people convicted of witchcraft on the fantastical evidence of 10-year-old boys. As the prologue suggests, the case was 'unto many here well knowne' (l. 7); and given the rarity of successful witchcraft prosecutions at this time, the likely attitude of the authorities was probably no mystery to anyone. Had the Privy Council been willing to allow the execution of the witches, there would have been no need to have them brought to London, so the motives for the intervention were hardly mysterious.

The guilt of the witches is maintained in the play and, as I have suggested, there are two important reasons for this: the simple commercial and dramatic reason that 'real' witches are much more entertaining than wrongly accused women, and the fact that it would be presumptuous for a play openly to question the verdict of an assize court. Nonetheless, coexisting with the guilt of the witches is their innocence, in that they do no real harm. Far from presenting the case for the prosecution, the play goes as far as it can to undermine that case without actually contradicting it. In simultaneously maintaining the reality of witchcraft and its insignificance, the perspective of the play resembles the position of Browne, and even the later view of Addison. Witchcraft is shown to exist, but very little follows from this; it cannot and must not be taken seriously, and it presents no real threat.

Debating witchcraft in *The Late Lancashire Witches*

The play opens with an argument about the existence of witchcraft, as Hirschfeld points out,[53] but it is also an argument about scepticism in a broader sense. The discussion concerns the interpretation of empirical evidence. Three young gentlemen – Arthur, Bantam, and Shakestone – have been hunting, and the hare they were chasing has disappeared without a trace. Their argument is about whether the hare disappeared by witchcraft, or whether there is some as yet unknown natural explanation. Arthur's companions make the case for the latter:

> BANT. She might find some Muse as then not visible to us,
> And escape that way.
> SHAK. Perhaps some Foxe had earth'd there,
> And though it be not common, for I seldome
> Have knowne or heard the like, there squat her selfe,

---

[53] Hirschfeld, pp. 135–36.

> And so her scape appeare but Naturall,
> Which you proclaime a Wonder.
> (36–42)

While most modern readers will probably find this line of thought to be reasonable, the terms in which Bantam and Shakestone state their case put their argument in the worst possible light. In arguing for a natural explanation of the hare's disappearance, the two sceptics are unable to come up with a wholly convincing account. They can only suggest airy possibilities, in contrast to the strong and satisfyingly complete explanation of witchcraft which Arthur puts forward. Even as he argues against his friend's interpretation of events, Shakestone concedes that his case is weak and unlikely. Since they are unable to give a definite account of how the hare disappeared 'naturally', the case for a supernatural explanation is strengthened.

If this last statement does not seem self-evident, it is worth remembering that seventeenth-century views of what might be considered 'natural' often differed from the typical view in the present. In the well-known case of Mary Glover, a young woman supposedly suffering from demonic possession, it was argued by the doctor Edward Jorden that Glover was in fact suffering from a natural disease: hysteria. In the trial of the witch accused of being responsible for Glover's possession, one observer recorded the following exchange between Jorden and the judge, who was the Chief Justice of the Common Pleas, Edmund Anderson:

> The Lord Anderson, hearing Doctor Jordaine to often insinuat, some feigning or dissembling fashions in the maide and withal, so much to beat upon these words; *for these causes, I thinck it may be natural; and these accidents and Symptoms for ought I see bee naturall*: pressed him to answere directly, whether it were naturall or supernaturall. He said, that in his conscience he thought it was altogether naturall. What do you call it quoth the Judge? *Passio Hysterica* said the Doctor. Can you cure it? I cannot tell: I will not undertake it, but I thinck fit tryall should be made thereof. *Lord Anderson*, Doe you thinke she Counterfetteth? *D. Jordeyn* No, in my Conscience I thinke she doth not counterfett: Lord Anderson, Then in my conscience, it is not natural: for if you tell me neither a Naturall cause, of it, nor a naturall remedy, I will tell you, that it is not natural.[54]

---

54 Quoted in Michael McDonald (ed.), *Witchcraft and Hysteria in Elizabethan London: Edward Jorden and the Mary Glover Case* (London: Routledge, 1991), p. 28. See also Sharpe, *Instruments of Darkness*, pp. 215–16.

Jorden claims that the disease is the result of natural causes, but is unable to identify exactly what those causes are or how to treat the disease. To a typical modern reader this may seem reasonable. But a typical modern reader will probably demand any illness to have natural causes; this is the only type of explanation likely to be accepted. If the natural causes of a disease are not currently known, then they can, in principle, be discovered. Anderson's view is different: he appears to regard human knowledge as subject to unvarying limitations. Whatever lies outside the scope of human knowledge is necessarily not natural.[55] In the play, Shakestone and Bantam fail to provide a clear, plausible, and complete explanation of the hare's disappearance, in the same way that Edward Jorden failed to provide such an explanation for Mary Glover's illness. In consequence, the strength of the sceptical case is significantly weakened.

Arthur, the closest character the play has to a hero, argues against Shakestone and Bantam, making the case for a common-sense, empirical approach to the evidence:

> Well well Gentlemen, be you of your own faith, but what I see
> And is to me apparent, being in sence,
> My wits about me, no way tost nor troubled,
> To that will I give credit.
> (43–46)

What is strange about this speech, at least to a modern reader, is that Arthur is arguing *in favour* of the witchcraft explanation for the hare's disappearance. Arthur believes that he has clear, empirical evidence of witchcraft, and he tellingly refers to his companions' contrary belief as 'faith'. Arthur, in other words, is making the obvious inference, the judgement based on the solid ground of sensory experience rather than preconceived ideas about what is and is not possible. The reasons for the hare's disappearance cannot be convincingly explained by reference to known natural causes, therefore they are not natural. His friends are simply clinging to their 'faith' in spite of clear and conclusive evidence. Arthur also feels the need to stress that his wits are 'no way tost nor troubled', and this part of his speech connects the young gentlemen's debate

---

55 The Spanish theologian Pedro Ciruelo likewise argued that, in the absence of a known natural cause, supernatural or spiritual causation must be inferred; see Moshe Sluhovsky, *Believe Not Every Spirit* (Chicago: University of Chicago Press, 2007), pp. 183–84.

not only to scepticism about witchcraft but to philosophical scepticism more generally.

Arthur's statement aligns him with a common response to sceptical arguments against the idea that certain knowledge is attainable through the evidence of the senses. While sceptics stressed the unreliability of the senses, pointing out that sensory perception could be distorted and misleading under certain conditions, one major strand of the anti-sceptical response was to reaffirm the ability of a healthy person with senses operating under normal conditions to reach accurate conclusions about the world, in accordance with established Aristotelian principles.[56] One of the earliest writers against Pyrrhonism was Pierre Le Loyer, who wished to defend his belief in supernatural apparitions by arguing for the reliability of sensory data.[57] Of course, this intuitively appealing but logically inadequate idea did not go without a response from sceptical thinkers. Montaigne, in his *Apologie of Raymond Sebond*, wrote that

> since the accidents of sicknesse, of madnesse, or of sleepe, make things appear other unto us, then they seeme unto the healthie, unto the wise, and to the waking: Is it not likely, that our right seate and naturall humors, have also wherewith to give a being unto things … and our health as capable to give them his visage, as sicknesse? Why hath not the temperate man some forme of the objects relative unto himselfe as the intemperate: and shall not he likewise imprint his Character in them?[58]

We have no more reason to trust the senses of the healthy than we do those of the diseased, according to Montaigne; the important point is that the senses can vary, and this demonstrates that human perceptions of reality are mediated and therefore distorted by our sensory apparatus. But this powerful sceptical argument is not represented in the play, which gives Arthur's common-sense view the last word. While Arthur's view is associated with empirical evidence and distinguished from that of blind faith, his opinion is not sceptical in the philosophical sense; on the contrary, he expresses an anti-sceptical empiricist position.

As well as taking a position in relation to philosophical scepticism, Arthur's view seems to anticipate a common objection of sceptics to witchcraft specifically. Reginald Scot tended to focus on the

---

56 For a general discussion of this debate see Popkin, pp. 105–11.
57 Popkin, p. 78. As mentioned in Chapter 1, Bodin and John Cotta both took the trouble to reject philosophical scepticism in their works on witchcraft.
58 Montaigne, II.12, p. 317.

delusions of witches themselves, claiming that witches believed themselves to have magical powers because they were misled by melancholy which 'depraved' their senses, but he also accused one writer on witchcraft, Richard Gallis, of being 'a mad man'.[59] Later in the seventeenth century, John Webster claimed that those who are not 'perfect in the organs of their sense' or who are 'of a vitiated or distempered Phantasie' are unreliable as witnesses, since they will 'take a bush to be a Boggard, and a black sheep to be a Demon'.[60] It is therefore important for Arthur, in the play, to make clear that no such reservations can be applied to him.

This pattern, stressing the blind faith of sceptics and the common-sense empiricism of believers, is repeated later in the play. Generous, a character who is represented and described by others as admirable, has one flaw: he does not believe in witches. Presented with evidence of witchcraft in the form of the disturbances in the Seely household, he refuses even to consider what Arthur describes as the general opinion, saying: 'They that thinke so dreame, / For my beliefe is, no such thing can be' (286–87). This is not the only reason Generous has to believe in witchcraft – he is at this stage already aware that his tenant, the miller, is being tormented by nocturnal visits from 'Rats, Cats, Wezells, Witches Or Dogges, or Divels' (792–93). Later in the play, his scepticism about witchcraft is explicitly linked to his religious beliefs. Confronted by the claim of his servant, Robin, to have ridden to London and back in a night, Generous again refuses to believe: 'I would have sworne ... it had been the same Wine, but it can never fall within the Christians beleefe, that thou cou'dst ride above three hundred miles in 8. houres' (1163–67). The evidence of sensory experience – the taste of the wine – competes with Generous's faith – 'the Christians beleefe' – and faith beats sensory experience.

The sentiments that Generous expresses associate religious faith with scepticism about witchcraft, rather than with belief in it, inverting the views of a large majority of early modern witchcraft theorists. While most writers on witchcraft claim that empirical evidence demonstrates the existence of witches, they also tend to make a clear connection between atheism and scepticism. Robert H. West regards Generous as one of the characters representing 'Scotian rationalism' in the play.[61] Generous does resemble Scot in

---

59 Scot, I.8, III.9 (pp. 17, 52).
60 Webster, p. 60.
61 West, *The Invisible World*, p. 154.

so far as he holds witchcraft beliefs to be impious, but he is *not* the voice of reason in the play – still less that of empiricism. The voice of empiricism and common sense is Arthur, and, in more complicated fashion, Doughty: characters who judge, apparently without preconceptions and on the evidence of their senses, that witches really do exist. Generous, by contrast, is presented with seemingly incontestable proof of his servant's visit to London – a piece of paper delivered by Robin from the drawer at the Mitre in Fleet Street, where he has bought Generous's favourite wine. The obvious conclusion, suggested by the evidence of the wine and the note, is the correct one: Robin really has travelled to London and back impossibly quickly.

Instead of reaching this conclusion, however, Generous stretches his ingenuity to find an alternative explanation, one which fits his preconceived ideas about the impossibility of witchcraft: 'but why may not this bee a tricke? this Knave may finde it when I lost it, and conceale it till now to come over me withall. I will not trouble my thoughts with it further at this time' (1209–12). Generous will believe anything sooner than believe in witchcraft. Rather than questioning his cherished beliefs, he prefers to stop thinking altogether, dismissing the question from his mind. Generous's thought process resembles that of Jean Bodin, who seems uneasily aware of the implausibility of witchcraft but is determined to believe in it nonetheless. Generous ought to be aware of the reality of the witchcraft that pervades the play, but he refuses to accept it.

At other points in the action, however, the play depicts Generous not as a man blinded by faith but as a hard-headed empiricist sceptic who will trust nothing but the evidence of his senses. 'Ile not perswade you to any thing, you will beleeve nothing but what you see' (1613–14), says Robin to Generous. Robin indicates that the sight of Mistress Generous returning to her normal shape once the magic bridle is removed from her will persuade Generous, but he also implies that Generous is a stubborn sceptic who will take nothing on faith – as he should. This is at odds both with Generous's earlier characterisation as someone blinded by faith and with the favourable characterisation of Arthur as a rational empiricist, simply believing the evidence of his senses: the same quality is rhetorically depicted as admirable in Arthur and deplorable in Generous.

Generous is, in the end, punished for his incredulity rather than his faith. His wife's continued activities as a witch are revealed to him in a gruesome manner when he is presented with her severed hand, complete with wedding ring. Not only does the play punish

Generous, it also makes him acknowledge the reasons for, and the justice of, his punishment:

> Amazement upon wonder, can this be;
> I needs must know't by most infallible markes.
> Is this the hand once plighted holy vowes,
> And this the ring that bound them? doth this last age
> Afford what former never durst beleeve?
> O how have I offended those high powers?
> That my great incredulity should merit
> A punishment so grievous, and to happen
> Vnder mine owne roofe, mine own bed, my bosome.
> (2341–49)

One peculiar aspect of this speech is that this is the second time Generous has had his wife's witchcraft proved to him; at this point in the play he has already witnessed her transformation from horse to woman, and her confession has persuaded him of the existence of witchcraft. Nonetheless, his amazement is repeated in the speech above; he is just as surprised by his wife's witchcraft as he was the first time.

Equally striking is that Generous's 'great incredulity' has been transformed. From having been a key component of his religious beliefs, it suddenly (and incongruously) becomes the sin of intellectual pride which renders him deserving of his punishment. His scepticism has previously been represented as blind faith, but in the passage above he is revealed to have lacked faith. This second, and seemingly contradictory, characteristic of Generous the sceptic – his excessive confidence in his own capacity for understanding, grounded in a lack of faith in God – is a more traditional way of attacking scepticism about witchcraft. The play represents scepticism as both irrational and unchristian; it is grounded in both blind faith *and* a deplorable lack of faith.

Generous's conversion to belief in witchcraft performs the function of rhetorical scepticism within the play. As in supposedly factual texts on witchcraft, scepticism is defeated by incontestable evidence of the reality of witchcraft. But in contrast to *The Witch of Edmonton*, where no character denies the existence of witchcraft, Generous expresses scepticism as to the very possibility of witchcraft, rather than mere doubts about specific aspects of witchcraft belief. Moreover, while Generous's scepticism is a kind of tragic flaw, it does not render him unworthy of the audience's esteem. The other characters in the play offer him almost nothing but praise – the one exception is his wife. Indeed, the majority of the sensible voices within the play – Bantam, Shakestone, Generous, and, at least some of the time, Doughty – are sceptical voices. Arthur believes in witches, but for much of the play the only character who seems to agree with him is the buffoonish Whetstone – hardly promising company. Irrespective of the opinions of the playwrights or the perspective from which the play itself was written, *The Late Lancashire Witches* is the product of a society that had become considerably more sceptical in a period of little more than ten years since *The Witch of Edmonton* was first performed.

There are other traces of this scepticism within the play. The character of Doughty, in the early part of the play, provides another example of rhetorical scepticism as he is gradually convinced that the chaos in the Seely household can only be the result of witchcraft. Later in the play, however, his beliefs change again; Heather Hirschfeld argues that Doughty's shifts from belief to scepticism 'compromise either stance'.[62] Doughty was deluded when he disbelieved in the reality of witches, but it is not entirely clear that he is any less deluded afterwards. His belief in the story told by the miller's boy is a case in point. The audience has seen the encounter between the miller's boy and a witch, but the details of this encounter do not match what the miller's boy tells Doughty in Act V. This is, on the one hand, an example of dramatic economy; the audience does not need to be given the same information twice. At the same time, however, the fact that the audience has not seen the events related by the boy to Doughty raises the possibility that the story is being embellished after the event. This possibility is made more prominent by the way the story is told:

DOUGHTY   Thou art a brave Boy, the honour of thy Country; thy Statue shall be set up in brasse upon the Market Crosse in Lancaster, I blesse the time that I answered at the Font for thee: 'Zookes did I ever thinke that a Godson of mine should have fought hand to fist with the Divell!
MIL.   He was ever an unhappy Boy Sir, and like enough to grow acquainted with him; and friends may fall out sometimes.
DOUGHT.   Thou art a dogged Sire, and doest not know the vertue of my Godsonne, my sonne now; he shall be thy sonne no longer: he and I will worry all the Witches in Lancashire.
MIL.   You were best take heed though.
DOUGH.   I care not, though we leave not above three untainted women in the Parish, we'll doe it.
(2102–16)

---

62 Hirschfeld, p. 137.

Doughty's praise of the boy – whose supposed fight with the devil has not been witnessed by the audience – is wildly excessive, and the boy's father is distinctly sceptical about his son's character and perhaps also his story, at least in this early part of the scene. Doughty ignores the miller's attempt to urge caution, and even goes so far as to imply he will make the boy his heir – a prospect he has previously tantalised Arthur with. Even this faint suggestion that the boy could have a financial interest in making accusations of witchcraft could be significant. In the historical case, according to the sceptic John Webster, 'the boy, his Father, and some others besides did make a practice to go from Church to Church that the Boy might reveal and discover Witches ... and by that means they got a good living'.[63] This 'practice' seems to be more or less what Doughty is proposing, and the chaos it could lead to is suggested by Doughty's reckless boast at the end of the passage.[64]

In this scene, then, considerable doubt is cast on the source of the evidence against the accused witches in the historical case – the miller's boy, who is obviously a dramatic representation of the historical Edmund Robinson. This doubt is first expressed by the boy's own father. Later, Doughty brings the reliability of both father and son into question again, as the miller relates a story of what sounds like demonic possession:

MIL. Till I wondring at his stay, went out and found him in the Trance; since which time, he has beene haunted and frighted with Goblins, 40. times; and never durst tell any thing (as I sayd) because the Hags had so threatned him till in his sicknes he revealed it to his mother.

DOUGH. And she told no body but folkes on't. Well Gossip Gretty, as thou art a Miller, and a close thiefe, now let us keepe it

---

63 Webster, p. 277. Berry points out that there were suspicions at the time that 'the elder Robinson might have profited from his son's accusations by taking money to exclude people' (p. 128).

64 That widespread fear of witchcraft could cause social disruption is suggested by Samuel Harsnett's *Discovery of the Fraudulent Practises of Iohn Darrel* (London, 1599) in which he writes that: 'The pulpets ... rang of nothing but Diuels, and witches: wherewith men, women, and children were so afrighted, as many of them durst not stir in the night ... Fewe grew to be sicke or euil at ease, but straight way they were deemed to bee possessed ... such were the stirres in Nottingham about this matter, as it was feared the people would grow ... to further quarrels and mutinies, or to some greater inconuenience' (p. 8).

> as close as we may till we take 'hem, and see them handsomly
> hanged o' the way.
> (2184–92)

Demonic possession, as has often been pointed out, was typically regarded with much greater scepticism by the authorities than the existence of witchcraft in general. In fact, action was taken to prevent ministers from attempting to exorcise spirits after the Darrell controversy.[65] Doughty does not express any scepticism, but what he says nevertheless casts significant doubt on the miller's character and reliability. The appellation 'Gretty' – gritty – implies that the miller adulterates his flour, which is what makes him a 'close thiefe'.[66] Doughty's statement that the boy's mother told 'no body but folkes' about the witches is intriguing. One editor of the play glosses the word 'folks' as 'relatives', but while this reading works in context, this sense of the word 'folk' is not recorded by the OED until 1715.[67] An alternative, and much older, sense of the word is 'people in general'.[68] It seems likely that Doughty is speaking ironically, and that news of the witches' antics has spread quickly – as it did in the historical case. This interpretation is supported by the fact that Doughty characterises the miller as a 'gossip'. This could simply mean 'friend', but the more usual modern sense of 'one who delights in idle talk' was also present well before the 1630s.[69] The exchanges between Doughty, the miller, and his son are another sign of submerged scepticism about the specific accusations of witchcraft which inspired the plot of the play.

Given the evidence of scepticism towards the specific accusations against the Lancashire witches and the play's acknowledgement of scepticism about witchcraft in general, it is striking that *The Late Lancashire Witches* seems in some respects to be so credulous, especially when compared to the relatively sober account of witchcraft given in *The Witch of Edmonton*.[70] The change in the representation

---

65 Thomas, p. 579.
66 Thomas Heywood and Richard Brome, *The Witches of Lancashire*, edited by Gabriel Egan (London: Nick Hern, 2002), p. 148, note to l.100.
67 See Heywood and Brome, *The Witches of Lancashire*, p. 148, note to l.99 and OED, 'folk', def. 4a.
68 OED, 'folk', def. 3a.
69 OED, 'gossip', defs 2a, 3.
70 Harris, for example, argues that '[p]atently incredible accusations made at the trial are incorporated into the drama, with no apparent attempt to expose their absurdity' (p. 176).

of witchcraft in the two plays is analogous to the changes in the kinds of evidence presented in witchcraft pamphlets during the period. Changes relating to the evidence required for a conviction in criminal courts[71] meant that unambiguous testimony was required in later cases of witchcraft. In the later seventeenth century, the kind of evidence presented in court was often more 'persuasive' than was the case in sixteenth-century trials, in the sense that the only possible explanation for the alleged occurrences was a supernatural one. However, in consequence, the evidence also became less plausible, as it was often plainly impossible.

The classic pattern of witchcraft stories in most Elizabethan pamphlets is a simple one: the witch is offended by her victim in some way (often because she is refused charity), swears revenge, and the victim later suffers illness or misfortune, which is then attributed to the witch.[72] All of these events are entirely plausible, to modern as well as early modern readers; the only thing missing from the narrative is direct evidence of supernatural causation. In Elizabethan and early Jacobean witchcraft cases, many courts were content to assume such causation, resulting in a high rate of convictions. Later, however, a more cautious attitude towards evidence made it necessary to rule out the possibility of merely coincidental harm.[73] A pamphlet of 1682 records witness testimony that left nothing to chance in seeking to demonstrate that a non-natural explanation was the only one possible:

> [S]ome others of the house, went out to see if they could see anny thing; and being out, there were stones thrown at them from every side, and they could not see from whence they came; so that they were forced to retire into the house; and having shut the door, the stones were thrown as fast in at the window, and yet not one Quarrel of Glass broken. Her master swore, that she being in the middle of the Room, she suddenly screamed out, saying, Something is got into my back, when going to her, he pulled out a great piece of Clay from about the middle of her back, stuck as full of pins as ever it could hold.[74]

---

71 Brian P. Levack, 'The Decline and End of Witchcraft Prosecutions', in *The Oxford Handbook of Witchcraft in Early Modern Europe and Colonial America*, edited by Brian P. Levack (Oxford, Oxford University Press: 2013), pp. 429–46 (pp. 438–39).
72 This pattern is described by Keith Thomas, pp. 659–663; cf. Gibson, 'Understanding Witchcraft?', p. 47.
73 Thomas, p. 688; see also Sharpe, *Instruments of Darkness*, pp. 213–34.
74 Anon., *An Account of the Tryal and Examination of Joan Buts* (London, 1682), n.p. Despite the 'strength' of the testimony, Buts was acquitted, a

The witnesses in this case offer a story that would be very difficult to explain in terms of natural causation; other parts of the tale explicitly refer to the accused woman, Joan Buts, to ensure that there can be no doubt about who is responsible for what can only be magic. Edmund Robinson's testimony in the 1634 case also left little to the imagination.

Witchcraft was sometimes described as a secret, invisible crime, but the witches in *The Late Lancashire Witches* do their best to provide their persecutors with as much evidence as possible. Walter Stephens points out that many early witchcraft theorists place a great deal of emphasis on the witch's testimony, requiring her to prove her own guilt.[75] The witches in the play are likewise complicit in their own conviction. Mall is responsible for the ligatory magic that causes Laurence's impotence, and this is known to everyone because she *publicly* gives him the enchanted point which he attaches to his codpiece. Doughty later recalls this: 'Now do I thinke upon the codpeece point the young jade gave him at the wedding: shee is a witch, and that was a charme, if there be any in the World' (1832–34). If further proof were needed, it is provided by the enchanted point's reaction when it is thrown into the fire, described by Parnell:

> Marry we take the point, and we casten the point into the fire, and the point spitter'd and spatter'd in the fire, like an it were (love blesse us) a laive thing in the faire; and it hopet and skippet, and riggled, and frisket in the faire, and crept about laike a worme in the faire, that it were warke enough for us both with all the Chimney tooles to keepe it into the faire, and it stinket in the faire, worsen than ony brimstone in the faire. (2474–80)

Parnell's description of the point's reaction to being burned is a relatively common feature of English witchcraft pamphlets, although more typically the thing burned is a witch's familiar or the transmogrified witch herself, often in the form of a toad.[76]

When the witches are planning to trick more hunters into chasing after phantom hares, they make it clear that they want the hunters

---

circumstance tactfully but unconvincingly ascribed by the pamphlet's author to 'the great difficulty in proving a Witch'.
75 See Stephens, *Demon Lovers*, p. 94.
76 See, for example, *A Detection of Damnable Driftes*, sig. A6ʳ, and *A Tryal of Witches*, pp. 6–8. In this pamphlet, the witch, having been burned in the form of a toad, is discovered the following day because she is suffering from burns – a story similar to that of Mistress Generous.

not merely to fail, but to be aware that their failure is caused by supernatural trickery:

> GILL. Then will we lead their Dogs a course,
> And every man and every horse;
> Untill they breake their necks, and say—
> ALL. The Divell on Dun is rid this way. Ha, ha, ha, ha.
> (575–78)

The witches intend to keep at it until the hunters are left with no choice but to blame the supernatural. In the end, they are even able to persuade Generous of the existence of witchcraft. It takes a lot to persuade him: Generous first sees his wife transformed from horse to woman, then he is presented with her severed hand, complete with wedding ring, proving her to be the 'cat' whose paw was cut off by the soldier-miller. As Generous himself puts it, 'I needs must know't by most infallible marks' (2342). The evidence put to Generous for the existence of witchcraft is completely conclusive, and, at the same time, completely implausible. The greater credulity of the play is, in part, a consequence of increasing scepticism in both the world outside the theatre and the characters within the play.

Two types of witchcraft

It has been argued that the play is sceptical towards the particular instance of witchcraft represented by the Lancashire case which inspired it, but also that it seeks to overcome the general scepticism towards witchcraft that it cannot help but acknowledge. The play resolves this tension by presenting two distinct and very different types of witchcraft, one that the audience is intended to take seriously, and one that is intended to entertain. The serious type of witchcraft is represented in the dialogue between Generous and his wife. Interestingly, however, when Generous first begins to harbour suspicions about his wife, they are not initially concerned with witchcraft:

> I see what Man is loath to entertaine,
> Offers it selfe to him most frequently,
> And that which we most covet to embrace,
> Doth seldome court us, and proves most averse;
> (1538–41)

Generous is discussing his thoughts and fears, and it is significant that he chooses to express himself in the language of courtship. Once again, these lines express something about his attitude to the evidence with which he is confronted. He does not like what his experiences are pointing to, and wishes to ignore it if he can. The grounds of his concern – Mistress Generous's absence – are made clear a few lines later:

> Entring her Chamber to bestow on her
> A custom'd Visite; finde the Pillow swell'd,
> Vnbruis'd with any weight, the sheets unruffled,
> The Curtaines neither drawne, nor bed layd down;
> Which showes, she slept not in my house to night.
> Should there be any contract betwixt her
> And this my Groome, to abuse my honest trust;
> I should not take it well, but for all this
> Yet cannot I be jealous.
> (1556–64)

Generous, once again, seems determined to resist the conclusion to which the evidence is pointing, but this time witchcraft is not the issue. It is the possibility of adultery that Generous fears and tries to repress. It is not entirely clear whether Generous suspects his servant, Robin, of helping his mistress to meet a lover or of actually being her lover, but the latter possibility is suggested indirectly by a recurring motif within the play: women of a high social class conducting illicit affairs with their servants. Immediately before Generous expresses his suspicions, the play has invited bawdy laughter at the circumstance that Mistress Generous has 'ridden' Robin by making him wear the magic bridle, and Robin later turns the tables on her and 'rides' Mistress Generous. Later, the theme of illicit servant–mistress relationships recurs in the 'parade of fathers' arranged for Arthur and his friends.

Of course, Mistress Generous is, as far as the audience knows, innocent of actual adultery. The play does not place great stress on the idea of witches having sexual relationships with demons – the only reference to this comes at the end of the play in lines which are derived from the deposition of Margaret Johnson. But Mistress Generous's witchcraft is only ever treated seriously in the two scenes in which she is confronted by her husband. These scenes, referred to by Tomkyns as 'the onely tragicall part of the story',[77] gain whatever gravitas they may have by representing a husband betrayed by his wife, not by representing a witch. In so far as they do touch on witchcraft, it is a witchcraft far removed from what has been

---

[77] Quoted in Berry, p. 123.

represented on stage. Instead of high-jinks with a walking bucket and disappearing hares, there is a demonic pact:

> GEN. Hast thou made any contract with that Fiend
>   The Enemy of Mankind?
> MRS.   O I have.
> GEN. What? and how farre?
> MRS.   I have promis'd him my soule.
> GEN. Ten thousand times better thy Body had
>   Bin promis'd to the Stake, I and mine too,
>   To have suffer'd with thee in a hedge of flames:
>   Then such a compact ever had bin made.
>   (1694–1702)

As Catherine Shaw comments, in this scene '[a] very serious kind of reality is thrust upon the audience when they have not been prepared for it, and it is in no way parallel or sequential to the other actions'.[78] Mistress Generous has not mentioned the devil; it is her husband who brings up the subject of the demonic. In this exchange, the audience is presented with information that has not only been absent from the rest of the play's depiction of witchcraft, but is completely at odds with it in terms of tone. Familiar spirits have been present on stage, but they are rather negligible presences without any spoken lines, entirely obedient to the witches and far removed from the complex character of the dog in *The Witch of Edmonton*. No diabolic pact is represented on stage, in contrast to both *The Witch of Edmonton* and *Dr Faustus*. As Tomkyns suggests, witchcraft is lifted from farce to tragedy in this part of the play, but it is an entirely different kind of witchcraft, and it remains offstage not only before this exchange but afterwards as well. The only other references to demonic pacts come in the second exchange between Generous and his wife, and in the lines closely resembling Margaret Johnson's confession at the end of the play.

It is clear that the Generouses' marriage is far from perfect in terms of the ideals of early modern English society. The couple have no children – by the end of the play Generous names Arthur his heir – and Generous refers to the fact that the couple sleep in separate rooms. A demonic pact constitutes a betrayal of God by breaking the covenant with him. This betrayal of God bears some resemblance

---

78 Catherine Shaw, *Richard Brome* (Boston: G. K. Hall, 1980), p. 116. Kathleen McLuskie also points to the 'serious dislocation' between the comic and tragic elements of the play (*Professional Dramatists*, p. 152), as does Matthew Steggle, *Richard Brome: Place and Politics on the Caroline Stage* (Manchester: Manchester University Press, 2004), p. 58.

to a wife's betrayal of her husband: as God is king in heaven, so, within the household, should a husband be king over his wife and family. The close proximity of Generous's fears about his wife's possible adultery and the revelation of her pact with the devil does not seem to be coincidental; there is an analogy between the two types of betrayal.

The exchange between Generous and his wife goes on to touch on the issue of whether souls can be sold or not:

> MRS. What interest in this Soule, my selfe coo'd claime
> I freely gave him, but his part that made it
> I still reserve, not being mine to give.
> GEN. O cunning Divell, foolish woman know
> Where he can clayme but the least little part,
> He will usurpe the whole; th'art a lost woman.
> (1707–12)

The interesting feature of this conversation is that Generous moves immediately from not believing in witchcraft at all to having a complete, and demonologically sophisticated, understanding of it. Generous immediately understands, in lines 1694–95, that his wife may have made a pact with the devil. In the exchange quoted above, he seems to understand better than she does what the implications of this pact are. His understanding is not based on, or even connected to, the evidence with which he has been presented. That evidence is indisputable proof of the existence of witchcraft, if witchcraft is understood to be the magical achievement of impossible things (specifically, turning human beings into horses by means of a magic bridle). But it is a considerable leap from accepting the existence of the magic bridle to accepting that such an item necessitates a pact between its owner and the devil. Contrary to appearances, Generous's belief in witchcraft – just like his scepticism – is primarily based on preconceived ideas, rather than empirical evidence.

After her confession and false repentance, Mistress Generous returns to witchcraft, but there is still no sign of the devil: instead, she returns to the harmless type of witchcraft with which the audience has already been entertained. The next piece of trickery she practises will be the 'parade of fathers' for Arthur and his friends, and she describes her purpose to Mall. Asked, 'Of this, the meaning?' Mistress Generous replies:

> Marry Lasse
> To bring a new conceit to passe.
> Thy Spirit I must borrow more,
> To fill the number three or foure;

> Whom we will use to no great harm,
> Only assist me with thy charme.
> This night wee'l celebrate to sport:
> 'Tis all for mirth, we mean no hurt.
> (1993-2000)

Mistress Generous refers to 'spirits' rather than 'devils', as she did in confessing to her husband. Whether there is any difference in meaning between the two terms as used in 1634 is open to question, but there is a difference in tone. Equally marked is the shift from her elegant, simple words to her husband and the garbled doggerel she speaks to Mall. But perhaps most remarkable is the representation of the witches' motivation. The exchange above is between two witches: no one else is present, so there can be no reason for Mistress Generous to downplay the villainy of her plan. Nevertheless, she stresses, twice, that she does not intend to cause any 'harm' or 'hurt'. The speech is hardly put in the kind of language that would tend to justify burning anyone at the stake, as her husband has suggested. There is almost no connection between Generous's conception of witchcraft and the witchcraft that is actually carried out by his wife and her friends.

The play presents witchcraft in the sense of magic as both harmless and ridiculous. But the demonological conception of witchcraft – witchcraft as a pact between a human being and the devil – is taken quite seriously. This is the kind of witchcraft that it was necessary for the 'fine folke' in the audience to believe in, but it is tellingly left unrepresented. The audience is told about this serious witchcraft but not shown it, just as Heywood, in his *Hierarchie of the Blessed Angels*, told his readers about the really convincing evidence that they could find in another text, but did not present in his own. In this respect, the play provides a literary representation of the view that would later be expressed by Addison. Witchcraft in the abstract is to be believed in but is somehow absent; specific instances of witchcraft are not to be taken seriously.

Intriguingly, Nathaniel Tomkyns' letter describing the play seems to acknowledge this, albeit very briefly. Tomkyns writes of the play that 'there be not in it (to my vnderstanding) any poeticall Genius, or art, or language, or iudgement to state or tenet of witches'.[79] The final phrase – 'iudgement to state or tenet of witches' – is somewhat ambiguous. Herbert Berry interprets the phrase as meaning

---

79 Quoted in Berry, p. 124.

that the play – according to Tomkyns – makes no judgement as to 'the state or the "tenet of witches", about, that is, national politics or a matter equally contentious, the current doctrine about witchcraft'.[80] But reading the word 'state' as 'national politics' is to my mind an unlikely interpretation. A more likely reading of Tomkyns' claim is that the play does not make any judgement as to the state, or the tenet, of witches. Tomkyns, seemingly unconsciously, separates the question of the existence of witches, and their precise nature ('state'), from what ought to be believed about them ('tenet'). The unstated assumption which his choice of words expresses implies a distinction between what should be believed and what is actually the case. This attitude is very close to the kind of doublethink that was later expressed by Addison.

The place of witchcraft in English society had changed radically by the 1630s compared to the situation at the height of the persecution in the 1580s and 1590s. The changes in belief can be discerned in the contrast between *The Witch of Edmonton* and *The Late Lancashire Witches* as well as in the strictly historical evidence; one play takes witchcraft seriously, while the other treats it as material for low comedy. But while the later play is radical in highlighting the existence of outright witchcraft denial for the first time on the English stage, it also devotes considerable ingenuity to defeating it. Within the world of the play, witchcraft is trivial rather than threatening, but it remains a Christian duty to believe in it. At this pivotal moment, the eventual abolition of witchcraft as a criminal offence was by no means a foregone conclusion, and in just another ten years things would change, drastically, again.[81] The outbreak of civil war and the resulting collapse of judicial authority enabled the series of prosecutions instigated by Matthew Hopkins and John Sterne in 1645–46. This episode could be regarded as the only genuine witch-hunt – in the sense of a large-scale, active search for witches – in English history. Witchcraft in 1634 had become a comical matter for many people, but the potential for tragedy remained.

---

80 Berry, p. 135.
81 James Sharpe writes that 'it is tempting to argue that, but for the disruption of the Civil Wars and their aftermath, which led to a renewal of prosecutions in the 1640s and 1650s, witchcraft prosecutions on the Home Circuit might well have petered out around the middle of the seventeenth century' (*Instruments of Darkness*, p. 110).

6
Witchcraft in the Restoration

By comparison with the late Elizabethan and early Jacobean periods, there were very few prosecutions and executions for witchcraft during the Restoration. But despite the decline in formal indictments and convictions, lively debate about witchcraft began again during the civil war and continued, and if anything intensified, during the Restoration. Witchcraft belief, at least at the level of educated debate, had become divorced from the issue of witchcraft persecution.[1] Belief in the existence of witches as agents of the devil had been understood by many to be a guarantee of Christian piety, but prior to the Restoration witches had also been said to be a threat to human society over and above the other works of the devil. The authors of the *Malleus Maleficarum* wrote that 'countless acts of sorcery are committed that the Devil would not be permitted to inflict on humans, if he endeavoured to harm humans by himself, but he is permitted by the just and hidden judgment of God to use sorceresses'.[2] A number of treatises on witchcraft in the late 1500s and early 1600s dealt extensively with the legal aspects of witchcraft, such as the rules governing evidence against witches and the degree of proof required in order to find an accused witch guilty. But the urgent threat of *maleficium* and the concern with legal procedure disappear almost entirely from the writings of witchcraft theorists following the Restoration – an indication that the practical aspects of the question were fading into insignificance.[3]

As the witchcraft debate moved away from questions about the extent of witches' power and how they should be dealt with under

---

1 Clark, *Thinking with Demons*, p. 310.
2 Institoris and Sprenger, II.131D–132A (pp. 355–56).
3 Although Richard Bernard's *Gvide to Grand-Ivry Men*, which does deal with such questions, was reprinted in the 1680s: see Bostridge, *Witchcraft and its Transformations*, p. 88.

the law, a much more pronounced concern with the ontological status of spirits emerged.[4] This had always been an important underlying issue, but the Restoration debate on witchcraft dealt with the relationships between witches, spirits, and the physical world more openly than had hitherto been the case. In his *Daemonologie*, for example, James I had made passing reference to 'the old error of the Sadducees, in denying of spirits',[5] but most of the book is devoted to discussing what witches can and cannot do and how the law should deal with them. In contrast, Joseph Glanvill and Henry More's *Saducismus Triumphatus* (1681) moves 'Saducism' into the title, making it clear that the aim of the book is to defeat those who question the existence of spirits – witchcraft is significant primarily as a means to this end. The actual cases of witchcraft which Glanvill provides as evidence are presented in a section of their own in the second half of the book, as if they merely formed an appendix.

The discussion of witchcraft in *Saducismus Triumphatus* is often concerned with what witchcraft implies about spirits, and the witches themselves are sometimes absent from this discussion. *Saducismus Triumphatus* has generally been seen as constituting the final version of the argument on one side of the 'Glanvill–Webster debate', but in the expanded 1689 edition, which reprints a number of earlier writings on the topic by Glanvill and his co-author Henry More, the witchcraft sceptic John Webster is far from being the only target. This is hardly surprising given that Webster was no 'Saducee' – he was an occultist and natural magician, among other things, who believed that spirits were everywhere.[6] Nor is it tenable to claim, as Wallace Notestein did, that all other participants in this debate were a kind of 'Greek chorus' to the main dispute between Glanvill and Webster.[7] Indeed, *Saducismus Triumphatus* was published after Glanvill's death in 1680, put together by More, who wrote the introduction and a fair proportion of the content.

---

4 Heightened interest in such questions originated in the years before the Restoration, and one scholar has recently suggested the 'possibility that Scot's unorthodox conception of spirits found an audience in the radical ferment of the Interregnum' as a reason for the publication of new editions of the *Discoverie*: Davies, 'The Reception of Reginald Scot's *Discovery of Witchcraft*', p. 390.

5 James I, p. 2.

6 Thomas Harmon Jobe, 'The Devil in Restoration Science: The Glanvill-Webster Witchcraft Debate', *Isis* 72:3 (September 1981), 343–56 (p. 343).

7 Notestein, p. 297.

Saducismus Triumphatus takes exception to the views on spirit of materialists such as Thomas Hobbes; 'nullibists' like Descartes (whose definition of spirit, according to More, is tantamount to declaring its non-existence); 'Holenmerians' (for similar reasons); followers of Spinoza; and 'psychopyrists' like Thomas Willis, a founding member of the Royal Society (of which More was also a fellow) who regarded the soul as a kind of flame.[8] While More treats his colleague Willis much more respectfully than he does materialists and Cartesians, he obviously feels the need to defend his concept of spirit from competing views coming from a number of different sources. Some of these challenges originated within the emerging scientific establishment, and More feels that all of them threaten to destroy belief in spirits, and even the concept of spirit more broadly. While More and Glanvill had impressive credentials, it is clear that even their colleagues in the Royal Society did not always share their views, as Barbara Shapiro points out, and in fact Webster's treatise was licensed by the Royal Society, while *Saducismus Triumphatus* was not.[9]

It is widely recognised that the label 'witchcraft' had significant political dimensions throughout the early modern period. Stuart Clark has pointed out that the early years of the Restoration in particular saw a renewal of the connection between rebellion and witchcraft established in 1 Samuel 15:23,[10] while Ian Bostridge has shown that the radicalism of 'fanatics' and 'enthusiasts' was equated with witchcraft by more orthodox thinkers.[11] Thomas Harmon Jobe has identified this as perhaps the key issue in the dispute between Webster and Glanvill: 'Webster opposed the belief in witches because his Paracelsian-Helmontian science and the radical Protestant theology

---

8 More uses the term 'Holenmerian' to refer to 'those scholastics' who had described the soul as existing in 'all parts of the whole body equally' according to his biographer Robert Crocker, *Henry More* (Dordrecht: Kluwer, 2003), p. 172. On Willis's view of the soul, see John Henry, 'The Matter of Souls: Medical Theory and Theology in Seventeenth-Century England', in *The Medical Revolution of the Seventeenth Century*, edited by Roger K. French and Andrew Wear (Cambridge: Cambridge University Press, 1989), pp. 87–113 (pp. 108–09). A more general account of his thought can be found in Arikha, *Passions and Tempers*, pp. 223–27.
9 Barbara J. Shapiro, *Probability and Certainty in Seventeenth Century England* (Princeton: Princeton University Press, 1983), p. 215.
10 Clark, pp. 611–12.
11 Bostridge, p. 63.

linked to it had been attacked as the devil's work.'[12] For sceptics as well as critics, witches themselves are of less interest than the implications of belief in witchcraft. Politics is frequently involved in the Restoration theatre's representation of witchcraft as well.

For orthodox writers like Glanvill and More, the existence of witchcraft served a dual purpose. It was used to attack radicals and freethinkers by associating them with witches, but it was also said to provide empirical evidence for a particular view of the operations of spirit in the material world. This view of the world of spirit was in turn regarded as essential to Anglican Christian belief. These two aims do not necessarily sit comfortably together; as I argue, Glanvill's view of spirit is in fact closer to Webster's than More's. The dispute between Webster and Glanvill may have arisen from their finding themselves on opposite sides of a religious and political divide, rather than from any real disagreement about the relationship between the material and spiritual worlds. Nonetheless, understanding how the people involved thought about this relationship is of vital importance in understanding the significance of the Restoration witchcraft debate. The first section of this chapter discusses the nature of body and spirit as understood in early modern thought and the importance of these concepts within the Restoration witchcraft debate. The following section turns to witchcraft as it was represented in the theatre, highlighting both growing scepticism towards witchcraft and growing interest in the operations of spirit in the material world.

The nature of spirit and body

A great deal was written in medieval and early modern Europe about the nature of spirits and their relationship to the human body and the physical world, but in broad terms there were two basic conceptions of the distinction between body and spirit. One such conception has its roots in Platonist philosophy. The other is based on scholastic thought, especially the writings of Thomas Aquinas, which was heavily influenced by Aristotelian ideas.

The older Platonist conception of the spirit world represents the human world as occupying one extreme of a sliding scale. According to this view, the world is at the centre of the universe because it is made of the heaviest matter, which naturally sinks to the bottom.

---

12 Jobe, 344.

The grossest material makes up the human world, while the areas above our world are made of progressively finer matter. Spiritual creatures have material bodies, as do humans, but they are made of finer – both in the sense that it is less dense and in the sense that it is superior – material than we are. C. S. Lewis summarises the views of the Platonist philosopher Apuleius – who also wrote about witches in *The Golden Ass* – as follows:

> The daemons have bodies of a finer consistency than clouds, which are not normally visible to us. It is because they have bodies that he calls them animals ... They are rational (aerial) animals, as we are rational (terrestrial) animals, and the gods proper are rational (aetherial) animals. The idea that even the highest created spirits – the gods, as distinct from God – were, after their own fashion, incarnate ... goes back to Plato.[13]

The association of the body with earth, and spirits – including the human soul – with air, had great appeal to early Christian theologians, in particular St Augustine, whose work incorporated Platonist ideas into Christian theology. God, after all, had made Adam from soil (earth) and brought this soil to life with a breath – air (Genesis 2:7). Augustine identifies this 'breath' as the soul in his *City of God*.[14] He also accepted the existence of the 'airy spirits' described by Apuleius, but denied that they were superior to human beings or should be worshipped. Rather, these spirits are identified with the fallen angels who were 'thrust out of the glorious heaven for their unpardonable guilt'[15] and are identified in VIII.19 as the source of magical power. But while Augustine disputes the moral status of the Platonists' daemons, giving to the word its Christian sense of an evil spirit, he does not dispute that they are corporeal, although their bodies are 'airy'.

This was not the only way of understanding the concept of spirit. The view that was to become dominant in the medieval Church made an absolute distinction between the spirit and human worlds. Rather than presenting a sliding scale, this view posited a fundamental qualitative distinction between matter and spirit. Spirits' bodies are not made of air; instead, spirits are entirely incorporeal. This conception is present as early as the late fifth or early sixth century in the

---

13 C. S. Lewis, *The Discarded Image* (Cambridge: Cambridge University Press, 1964), pp. 41–42.
14 St. Augustine, *City of God*, XII.23, p. 367.
15 St. Augustine, *City of God*, VIII.22, p. 245.

writings of pseudo-Dionysius,[16] but it was fully developed much later, especially by Thomas Aquinas.

However, this new conception of spirits as non-corporeal did not greatly alter the association of spirits with the air. According to Aquinas, spirits do not have bodies but could 'assume' them by constructing temporary bodies from air.[17] The *Malleus Maleficarum* follows Aquinas, making the rather woolly claim that 'regarding the material and quality of the assumed body, it should be said that he [i.e. the demon] assumes a body made of air and that it is made of earth in some way inasmuch as it has the characteristic of earth through a process of thickening'.[18] Whether the demon is actually made of air, or simply assumes a temporary body which is somehow constructed from air (possibly mixed with earth), spirits are clearly associated with the element of air.

At the root of this association may be a degree of confusion over whether air can really be considered a physical substance, as Hobbes later suggested:

> in the sense of common people, not all the Universe is called *Body*, but only such parts thereof as they can discern by the sense of Feeling, to resist their force ... Therefore in the common language of men, *Aire*, and *aeriall substances*, use not to be taken for *Bodies*, but (as often as men are sensible of their effects) are called *Wind*, or *Breath*, or (because the same are called in the Latine *Spiritus*) *Spirits*; as when they call that aeriall substance, which in the body of any living creature, gives it life and motion, *Vitall* and *Animall Spirits*.[19]

Hobbes feels the need to clarify, explicitly and repeatedly,[20] that air is in fact a physical substance and not incorporeal. His observations about the etymology of the word 'spirit' are also relevant here. It may be that it is inherently difficult for human beings to conceive of air as physical; most of us, despite having learned otherwise, tend not to think of air as occupying space.

Both the view of Apuleius (that spirits are corporeal and have thin, airy bodies) and that of Aquinas (that spirits are incorporeal but can form temporary bodies from air in order to interact with humanity) imply that spirits are capable of directly influencing the

---

16 Lewis, p. 71.
17 Stephens, *Demon Lovers*, p. 62.
18 Institoris and Sprenger, II.105D, pp. 302–03.
19 Thomas Hobbes, *Leviathan* (London: Penguin, 1968), III.34, p. 429.
20 He reminds the reader of this again in IV.45, p. 660, for example. Webster also makes this point repeatedly; see pp. 202–03.

material world. In fact, the Aristotelian natural philosophy of the late medieval period invoked the concept of spirit to explain a wide range of natural phenomena, including the physiological functions of the human body. Aquinas himself was involved in assimilating Galen's ideas into a Christian (and Aristotelian) framework. The resulting synthesis incorporated Galen's three types of *pneumata* or 'spirits' – the principles of life thought to be carried in the bloodstream – and a tripartite soul, only one part of which was incorporeal and rational.[21] In consequence, and despite its denial of the corporeality of spiritual substances (including the rational human soul), the scholastic view involved 'spirits' in a wide range of physical processes. One clear expression of this attitude in layman's terms can be found in Thomas Nashe's *Terrors of the Night* (1594):

> There be them that thinke euerie sparke in a flame is a spirit, and that the wormes which at sea eate through a ship, are so also: which may verie well bee; for haue not you seene one sparke of fire burne a whole towne, & a man with a sparke of lightning made blinde, or kild outright? It is impossible the gunnes should goe off as they doo, if there were not a spirit either in the fier, or in the powder.[22]

Spirits, in Nashe's view, are essential to the functioning of the physical world, a necessary element in any explanation of cause and effect in nature, particularly in relation to the 'superior' element of fire.

The kind of 'spirit' involved in making the physical world function was not always clearly distinguished from the kind of spirits that were angels and devils, as is apparent from a passing comment of Glanvill's. Glanvill notes that 'some have thought that the Genii (whom both the Platonical and Christian Antiquity thought embodied) are recreated by the reeks and vapours of humane blood and the spirits that proceed from them'.[23] The genii are guardian spirits which were thought to be assigned to human beings from birth onwards in order to guide and protect them. The opinion Glanvill notes, without going quite so far as to endorse it, clearly links the *pneumata* thought to be necessary for the functioning of the human body with spirits of another kind. Glanvill goes on to speculate that familiars might inject 'vile vapour' into witches' blood when

---

21 Arikha, pp. 38–39.
22 McKerrow, p. 350.
23 Joseph Glanvill and Henry More, *Saducismus Triumphatus* (London, 1688), p. 75.

feeding from them.²⁴ This requires the belief that spirits of the supernatural variety can physically affect the natural spirits, just as the natural and embodied spirits carried in the blood can generate supernatural spirits.

The supposed interaction between corporeal and incorporeal spirits has struck many modern observers as problematic. C. S. Lewis, despite his confessed nostalgia for what he calls 'the Medieval Model', comments that

> [t]he spirits [i.e. the Galenic *pneumata*] were supposed to be just sufficiently material for them to act upon the body, but so very fine and attenuated that they could be acted upon by the wholly immaterial soul ... This ... seems to me the least reputable feature in the Medieval Model. If the *tertium quid* is matter at all (what have density and rarity to do with it?) both ends of the bridge rest on one side of the chasm; if not, both rest on the other.²⁵

This seems obvious enough, so why did nobody at the time object? Perhaps Lewis, a twentieth-century scholar, had a clearer sense of the materiality of 'fine' substances like air than most medieval thinkers. On the other hand, it has been suggested that Aquinas himself was aware of the problematic nature of his opposition between the material and the spiritual.²⁶

In any case, the problem of the relationship between spirit and matter seems to have become increasingly apparent to a number of seventeenth-century intellectuals. Alternative ideas began to be proposed, the most drastic of which is Hobbesian materialism. Hobbes states unequivocally that

> The World ... is Corporeall, that is to say, Body; and hath the dimensions of Magnitude, namely, Length, Bredth, and Depth: also every part of Body, is likewise Body, and hath the like dimensions; and consequently every part of the Universe, is Body, and that which is not Body, is no part of the Universe: And because the Universe is All, that which is no part of it, is Nothing; and consequently no where.²⁷

---

24 Glanvill and More, p. 76. Reference to this possibility is made much earlier by Johannes Weyer (Mora, III.7, p. 186). Glanvill's explanation of witchcraft in physiological terms concedes much ground to the sceptical outlook of Weyer and Scot. Julie A. Davies discusses Glanvill's views and the background to them at length in her article 'Poisonous Vapours: Joseph Glanvill's Science of Witchcraft', *Intellectual History Review* 22:2 (2012).
25 Lewis, p. 167.
26 Marleen Rozemond, *Descartes' Dualism* (Cambridge, MA: Harvard University Press, 1998), p. 45; Stephens, *Demon Lovers*, pp. 66–67.
27 Hobbes, p. 689.

Anyone foolish enough to depart from Hobbes's uncompromising opinion has been deluded, he declares, by 'the Vain Philosophy of Aristotle',[28] a comment which can leave no doubt that Hobbes is opposed to the dualist scholastic conception of the universe.

Descartes' version of dualism was almost as radical in its implications for the involvement of spirit in the everyday world. Descartes maintained the real existence of spirit, and for this reason is often seen today in opposition to Hobbes, who wrote one of seven sets of objections to the *Meditations*. But in his own time, Descartes' conception of spiritual substance was seen as dangerously restrictive. Descartes excluded spiritual substance from all aspects of physical existence and limited the operations of the human soul to thought – for Descartes, as John Cottingham puts it, '"soul" (Fr. *âme*, Lat. *anima*) and "mind" (Fr. *esprit*, Lat. *mens*) are synonymous'.[29] Spiritual substance, for Descartes, is not characterised by any of the attributes of physical matter: it cannot, therefore, occupy space or even be located in space, contradicting the conventional scholastic view taken by the *Malleus* and coming dangerously close to that of Hobbes. Both views were felt to be extremely problematic by the witchcraft theorists of the Restoration.

Descartes defined spirit partly in terms of what it is not, an aspect of his position which inspired Henry More's term 'nullibist'. The nullibists, More explains,

> affirm Spirits to be *nowhere*; but would be found to do it only by way of an oblique and close derision of their Existence, saying indeed they *exist*, but then again hiddenly and cunningly denying it, by affirming they are *nowhere*.[30]

More cannot accept Descartes' minimalist conception of spirit, which defines spirit by its propensity for thought as *res cogitans*, but also negatively, in opposition to matter. The qualities of matter are, by definition, not present in spirit, which is therefore *not* located or extended in space. More needs something more positive, and he defines a spirit as 'an Immaterial Substance intrinsecally endued with Life and the faculty of Motion'.[31] Perhaps even more importantly, More also defines body as

> Substance Material, of it self altogether destitute of all Perception, Life, and Motion. Or thus: Body is a Substance Material coalescent

---

28 Hobbes, p. 691.
29 John Cottingham, *Descartes* (Oxford: Blackwell, 1986), p. 111.
30 Glanvill and More, p. 135.
31 Glanvill and More, p. 162.

or accruing together into one, by virtue of some other thing, from whence that one by coalition, has or may have Life also, Perception and Motion.[32]

If spirit has historically been identified with air, then body has tended to be identified with earth. Matter has traditionally been conceived of as inert and lifeless – like soil or stone – in the absence of spirit to enliven it. More insists on this ancient view of matter, whereas both Descartes and Hobbes allow for matter to live without the involvement of a soul (since, for Descartes, plants and animals are examples of soulless matter). More also defends the Aristotelian idea of spirit as the form of the body, as it is 'by virtue of some other thing' – a spirit or soul – that matter can 'coalesce' in the first place.[33]

But although More's conception of spirit is very much opposed to the new theories of Descartes and Hobbes, *Saducismus Triumphatus* does accept the need for something more than simply repeating old assertions about the nature of spirit. Both More and Glanvill were aware of the importance of providing empirical evidence in support of their beliefs. More's introduction to the 1689 edition highlights this aim of the book: 'it is of main importance, that we have a true genuine and consistent Notion of the Nature of a *Spirit*, and such as will not beget a misbelief of their Existence in such as consider it'. As well as being 'Erroneous', More argues that it is also 'hurtful' to conceive of 'the Nature of a *Created Spirit* to be such as is inconsistent with the *Perceptive Functions*'.[34] More and Glanvill are united in demanding spirits, and these spirits must not only exist, they must be seen to exist. This requires that they are active in the world, so that they – or at least, evidence of their activities – can be seen and heard: this is where witchcraft comes in.

The notion of spirit that is needed must be a 'true genuine and consistent' one, but it is of at least equal importance that this notion 'will not beget a misbelief of their Existence'. More's search for spirit begins with the assumption that spirit, and spirits, exist – precisely what it seeks to prove. Ian Bostridge, drawing on work by Moody Prior, suggests that Glanvill's position in favour of the possibility of witchcraft is based on a radical scepticism that avoids

---

32 Glanvill and More, p. 161.
33 On the Aristotelian idea of the soul as the form of the body, adopted by many scholastic thinkers, see Rozemond, pp. 44–46.
34 Glanvill and More, p. 8.

ruling anything out.³⁵ This is true of the negative part of the argument – the part that casts doubt on arguments against the reality of witchcraft. But the positive part of the argument, where Glanvill and More offer support for the existence of witchcraft, is a different matter. Here, the sceptical attitude is suspended completely. The authors offer a great deal of speculation about how witches *might* operate; but ultimately, the only way the existence of spirits can be supported with positive evidence is by stretching the concept of empirical observation so that it includes hearsay and evidence from witnesses whose reliability is simply taken for granted. This evidence – in sufficient quantity – is claimed to be indisputable, while all the arguments of the sceptics are characterised as assertions based on unproven theoretical premises. Glanvill and More are only sceptical towards the views of people with whom they disagree.

Perhaps the most obvious objection to More's view of spirit as an 'immaterial substance' is made by Hobbes, who with typical bluntness states that the concept is a contradiction in terms.³⁶ Although More does not deal with this objection, Glanvill responds to it. His answer is to return to the spiritual ontology of Apuleius:

> [T]hough it should be granted them, that a substance immaterial is as much a contradiction as they can fancy; yet why should they not believe, that the Air and all the Regions above us, may have their invisible intellectual Agents, of Nature like unto our Souls, be that what it will.³⁷

Glanvill seems grudgingly to agree, as More does not, that the idea of immaterial substance is a contradiction. Unlike his co-author, in fact, Glanvill clearly believes that those spirits which are capable of interacting with human beings are embodied, an opinion he shares with the witchcraft sceptics Webster and Wagstaffe,³⁸ for two main reasons:

> (1) we perceive in our selves, that all Sense is caused and excited by motion made in matter; and when those motions which convey

---

35 Bostridge, pp. 74–75. See also Popkin, pp. 214–15.
36 Hobbes, for example in I.4, I.12, III.34 (pp. 108, 171, 439). Webster makes a similar argument by a more circuitous route (pp. 198–201).
37 Glanvill and More, p. 69.
38 Webster, unlike Glanvill, believes that *all* spirits, with the exception of God himself, are embodied. See Webster, pp. 204–14. John Wagstaffe, in *The Question of Witchcraft Debated* (London, 1671), argues that devils are 'aerial creatures' (p. 81).

sensible impressions to the Brain, the Seat of Sense, are intercepted, Sense is lost: So that, if we suppose Spirits perfectly to be disjoin'd from all matter, 'tis not conceivable how they have the sense of any thing ... Nor doth it (2) seem suitable to the Analogy of Nature, which useth not to make precipitous leaps from one thing to another, but usually proceeds by orderly steps and gradations: whereas were there no order of Beings between Us, who are so deeply plunged into the grossest matter, and pure unbodied Spirits, 'twere a mighty jump in Nature.[39]

Glanvill concedes a great deal of ground to Hobbesian materialism in his first point. His use of the terms 'matter' and 'motion' seem to echo Hobbes, who uses these words constantly in *Leviathan*. What is more remarkable, however, is that this (neo-Platonist) passage, evidently at odds with More's (Aristotelian) definition of spirit, is included at all in a book in which More intended to present 'a true genuine and consistent Notion of the Nature of a *Spirit*'.[40]

The confusion evident in *Saducismus Triumphatus* is not simply the result of its mixed authorship. More and Glanvill (and, more surprisingly, Webster), in one sense, share the same view of spiritual substance: they want it to be both corporeal and incorporeal.[41] This is why More insists that, although it is incorporeal, spirit must be extended and located in space – possessed, in other words, of properties which both Hobbes and Descartes associate with matter only. Glanvill, by contrast, accepts that spirits must be embodied in order for them to interact with human beings – but he also wants some of them to be 'pure' and 'unbodied'. The co-authors are united in wanting to preserve the simultaneous distinction between, and conflation of, spirit and body which was increasingly being challenged by other thinkers.

To say that this confused spiritual ontology is a necessary condition for the existence of witches (as Wallace Notestein did long ago)[42] is accurate, but it also gets things backwards. Rather, the reality of

---

39 Glanvill and More, p. 92.
40 Glanvill and More, p. 8. *Saducismus Triumphatus* was published after Glanvill's death and was a compilation of previously published writings by both Glanvill and More. The introduction to this work, titled 'An Account of the Second edition', was written by More.
41 As did Thomas Aquinas, according to Walter Stephens: 'Without declaring it in so many words, Aquinas argues that angels and devils have bodies that both are and are not real' (*Demon Lovers*, p. 62).
42 Notestein, pp. 290–91.

witchcraft is offered as *proof* of this particular view of spirits: creatures not of this world, but nevertheless active in it. This, in turn, was widely perceived to be a necessary precondition for the existence of God, a point made clear by Meric Casaubon. Casaubon was an ally of Glanvill's and More's who contributed a detailed attack on the witchcraft sceptic John Wagstaffe to the Restoration witchcraft debate. Casaubon writes elsewhere that

> the abettors of Atheism promote the opinion, as much as they can, that nothing is truly existent, but what is corporeal ... Hence it is, that they that deny, or will not believe any supernatural operations, by witches and magicians, are generally observed to be Atheists, or well affected that way ... if there be false miracles, that is, supernatural operations, by the power of Devils; there must of necessity be true miracles also, by the power of God. Certainly, it is a point of excellent use, to convince incredulity, to know certainly, that there be witches and magicians.[43]

Casaubon reveals his own *desire* for witches to exist, because if this can be demonstrated it is a point of 'excellent use' in a much more important question – the battle against the broader sceptical doubts of atheists. Like Glanvill and More, Casaubon is primarily interested in witches for what they imply about the existence of spirits, which are active within the material world, and therefore the existence of God.

Why, then, was witchcraft gradually abandoned as a defence for the existence of spirits? Part of the reason could be that the debate had moved out into the open by the time of the Restoration. The Civil War and Interregnum had resulted in a huge outpouring of radical political, religious, and scientific ideas, often collectively dismissed as 'enthusiasm' by more orthodox figures like Casaubon.[44] Responding to these 'enthusiasts', as Ian Bostridge has pointed out, was an urgent religious and political goal for Casaubon and More.[45] Many of the 'enthusiastic' ideas that were expressed in the period 1642–60 touched on the nature of the spirit.[46] A number of titles written in the latter half of the seventeenth century deal directly

---

43 Casaubon, *Of Credulity and Incredulity in Things Divine and Spiritual*, pp. 170–71.
44 See, for example, Meric Casaubon, *A Treatise Concerning Enthusiasme* (London, 1654).
45 Bostridge, pp. 55–56.
46 A number of such radical thinkers are discussed in Nigel Smith, 'The Charge of Atheism and the Language of Radical Speculation, 1640–1660',

with the immortality of the soul – a question that had also exercised scholastic philosophers – and at least two of these writers (Henry More and Richard Baxter) had also published on witchcraft.[47]

The changed climate from the end of the Civil War onwards, in which it became possible to express a wide range of views on this sensitive topic, accounts for why the nature of spirit takes up much more space, and is much more openly acknowledged, in the Restoration debate. Before 1642 denials of the existence of spirits were scarce, despite the accusations levelled at Scot (who in fact has a clear position on the existence of spirits, which he affirms).[48] By the time of the Restoration debate, 'enthusiasm' of all kinds had been expressed, and Hobbes had made his terrifying, although certainly not new, point about the world being no more than 'matter in motion'. Judging by the tone of dismay in much of *Saducismus Triumphatus*, More and Glanvill appear to have believed that materialism had won widespread acceptance.

Witchcraft had previously been a kind of Maginot line – if belief in witchcraft was defended, earlier witchcraft treatises implied, the existence of spirit, and ultimately God, could not be questioned.[49] But this line of defence was eventually circumvented, rather than defeated, by the radical ideas brought to the surface in the aftermath

---

in *Atheism from the Reformation to the Enlightenment*, edited by Michael Hunter and David Wootton (Oxford: Oxford University Press, 1992), pp. 131-58. Richard Overton, to take one example, denied the distinction between soul and body and argued that every aspect of a human being was mortal.

47 Titles devoted partly or wholly to demonstrating the immortality of the soul include Walter Charleton's *The Immortality of the Human Soul* (1657), Henry More's *The Immortality of the Soul* (1659), Richard Baxter's *Christianity* (1667), Thomas Wadsworth's *Antipsychothanasia* (1670), a 1675 translation of Plato's *Phaedo*, William Bates's *Considerations of the existence of God and of the immortality of the soul* (1676), Samuel Haworth's *Anthropologia* (1680), Richard Baxter's *Of the immortality of mans soul* (1682), Sir George Mackenzie's *The religious stoic* (1685), and Timothy Manlove's *The immortality of the soul asserted* (1697). A sermon on the subject preached to the King and Queen in 1694 was also published. On the immortality of the soul in scholastic thought, see Stephens, *Demon Lovers*, pp. 356-64.

48 Scot, citing Peter Martyr, explains that 'divels are spirits, and no bodies' and further that 'we find not that a spirit can make a bodie, more than a bodie can make a spirit: the spirit of God excepted, which is omnipotent' (xvii.32, pp. 540-41).

49 See, for example, Gaule, pp. 1-2.

of the English Civil War, ideas which often questioned the nature of spirit directly, without much or any reference to witchcraft. Witchcraft was not immediately abandoned as a badge of orthodox Christianity – More and Glanvill were among those holding on to it – but the debate on spirit had moved past it, and its significance was already dwindling by the time Glanvill and More started to defend it. The supposed position of Glanvill and More at the intellectual cutting edge is itself open to question, as Shapiro points out.[50]

Ian Bostridge observes that 'the disappearance of witchcraft belief cannot be plausibly explained by the supposed triumph of a mechanistic world-view'.[51] Levack, too, expresses his agreement with the 'widely held view ... that a fundamental philosophical scepticism based on or greatly influenced by the mechanical philosophy had little or no impact on the decline of prosecutions'.[52] Nonetheless, it is evident from the sheer amount of space this issue takes up in the Restoration debate that there is a connection between the issues of 'a mechanistic world-view' and witchcraft belief. The direction of the causal link, however, is the reverse. Witchcraft belief did not disappear as the result of the victory of a mechanistic conception of the world; rather, it was one aspect of a continuing attempt to *resist* that victory. Witchcraft belief, as a respectable intellectual position, was gradually abandoned because it had become irrelevant to its original purpose. As Jobe points out,

> the phenomena ascribed to witchcraft gradually lost their attractiveness as empirical proofs for the existence of the spirit world. They were superseded in Anglican science by the panoply of demonstrations set out by the Boyle lecturers, in which only divine and angelic spirits were allowed to stimulate, adjust or refresh the cosmic mechanism.[53]

Although belief in witches eventually faded away, attempts by early scientists to prove the existence of the spirit world continued, from the Boyle lecturers to the Society for Psychical Research, founded in London in 1862. Walter Stephens detects the same desire to believe in a spirit world in academic work on supposed victims of alien abductions,[54] and other scholars with broader concerns have recently called into question the idea that the world has been, in a

---

50 Shapiro, p. 225.
51 Bostridge, p. 105.
52 Levack, 'The Decline and End of Witchcraft Prosecutions', p. 445.
53 Jobe, p. 356.
54 Stephens, *Demon Lovers*, pp. 367–68.

phrase associated with Max Weber, 'disenchanted'.[55] While witches are no longer executed, resistance to the 'triumph of a mechanistic world-view' has never been abandoned and continues to this day. The resistance dates back much further than the seventeenth century, too: mechanistic world-views, after all, were found in the ancient world. The most famous pre-Hobbesian materialist was Epicurus, whose philosophy is best known through Lucretius's infamous poem *De Rerum Natura*.[56] Stories about witchcraft, however, became increasingly marginal in the later seventeenth century, although as Bostridge points out they continued to circulate in print into the eighteenth century.[57]

Perhaps the biggest problem with witchcraft stories as a source of evidence for the existence of spirits was that people kept laughing at them. While the serious works of Webster and Wagstaffe are usually seen as the important sceptical books of the Restoration witchcraft debate, perhaps more telling are a number of less well known satirical works which deal with witchcraft and the supernatural without making an explicit argument on either side of the question. A series of pamphlets appeared during the Civil War in the peculiar war of words that grew up around the Royalist commander Prince Rupert's dog.[58] This animal was ironically said by a Royalist propagandist, in mockery of the Parliamentarians' apparent belief in the military use of witchcraft by their enemies, to be 'no Dog, but a Witch, an Enemy to Parliament ... a meer Malignant Cavalier-Dog, that hath something of the Divel in or about him'.[59] Some years later, *The Devill seen at St Albons* (1648) tells the story of the devil appearing in the cellar of an inn in the shape of a white ram; when the proprietor and his staff are too frightened to do

---

55 Jason A. Josephson-Storm, *The Myth of Disenchantment* (Chicago: University of Chicago Press, 2017), p. 3; see also Egil Asprem, *The Problem of Disenchantment* (Leiden: Brill, 2014), pp. 1–10.
56 Lucretius argues that the universe (*omnis*) consists exclusively of bodies (*corpora*) and void (*inane*) (I.419–420), and that mind (*animi*) and spirit (*animai*) are both corporeal and mortal (III.161–62; III.417–18); Lucretius, *On the Nature of Things*, trans. W. H. D. Rouse, rev. Martin F. Smith (Cambridge, MA: Harvard University Press, 1992).
57 Bostridge, p. 242.
58 Mark Stoyle examines the story of the dog in *The Black Legend of Prince Rupert's Dog* (Exeter: University of Exeter Press, 2011).
59 T. B., *Observations vpon Prince Rupert's White Dog, called Boy* (London, 1642), sig. A4ᵛ. The authorship of the pamphlet is discussed in Stoyle, pp. 62–67.

anything about the situation, the local butcher volunteers to deal with it and kills, roasts, and eats the enemy of mankind. The pamphlet unconvincingly claims to be 'Printed for confutation of those that beleeve there are no such things as Spirits or Devils'.[60] The mockery of credulity continued in the Restoration: two longer works published in 1673 both seek to undermine witchcraft belief with laughter.[61]

Like Bodin before them, the Restoration defenders of witchcraft were well aware of the threat posed by ridicule. In fact, Glanvill felt scorn to be such a problem that he responded to it in a separate work. First printed in 1668,[62] *A Whip for the Droll, Fidler to the Atheist: Being Reflections on Drollery and Atheism* is also included in the second edition of *Saducismus Triumphatus* from 1682, and subsequent editions. Glanvill begins by pointing out that a joke is not an argument, and that laughing at witchcraft does not disprove it. He also intimates that would-be 'wits' who laugh at stories of witchcraft are not 'governed by the Rules of Vertue', before claiming that 'these quibbling debauchees' are not merely foolish or immoral, they are 'the Enemies of Government and Religion'.[63] Glanvill, like Bodin before him, recognises that laughter and mockery are the most dangerous weapons that can be used against witchcraft, and he acknowledges, also like Bodin but more openly, that sceptical laughter may threaten more than just witchcraft belief. Glanvill does not name any specific targets in this attack on wit, but the phenomenon he describes is one that can be associated with fashionable London society, and consequently with the theatre.

Witchcraft in the theatre

The Restoration theatre's audiences, while remaining mixed in terms of social composition, were considerably wealthier than was the case prior to 1642. Charles II was the first English monarch to be a regular theatregoer and attended at least 280 performances in

---

60 Anon., *The Devill seen at St Albons* (London, 1648).
61 Anon., *A Pleasant Treatise of Witches* (London, 1673); Anon., *A Magical Vision, or a Perfect Discovery of the Fallacies of Witchcraft* (London, 1673).
62 See Coleman O. Parsons, introduction to *Saducismus Triumphatus* (Gainesville: Scholars' Facsimiles & Reprints, 1966), p. xx. Parsons provides a helpful discussion of the book's complicated publication history.
63 Glanvill and More, p. 537.

public theatres during his reign.[64] Along with the King, especially in the first decade of the Restoration, came a group of noblemen and courtiers whose influence on the institution of the theatre and the writing of plays was 'out of all proportion to their numbers'.[65] These courtiers and noblemen were regular auditors at the theatre, and a number of them also wrote plays for it. Such people could be described as 'wits', and were in the position to which other 'wits' aspired. Their opinions, and perhaps also their jesting, may have served as an example of which Glanvill disapproved.

Glanvill rather vaguely identifies 'the looser Gentry' and 'small pretenders to Philosophy and Wit'[66] as the main scoffers, but it seems likely that some of the doubters were close to the very top of the social scale. Hobbes's 'wit' was regarded by some of his critics to be a kind of gateway drug that would eventually lead those exposed to atheism,[67] but he had an aristocratic patron who presumably cannot have found his views offensive. The earl of Rochester, too, was undoubtedly both a wit and a sceptic about witchcraft (and much else besides). Rochester was also involved in the theatre, sometimes as more than just an audience member: he adapted John Fletcher's play *Valentinian*, which was performed after his death in the Theatre Royal, and wrote a prologue for Settle's *Empress of Morocco*.[68] The close association of 'wit' and theatrical art suggests that drama may have been aligned with the kind of sceptical mockery that Glanvill regarded as such a threat.

At the same time, however, the connection between witchcraft and rebellion, familiar in the early Jacobean witchcraft drama discussed here, is also evident in the drama of the Restoration, especially early in the period when memories of the Civil War were still fresh. While the rather comical treatment of witchcraft in most Restoration drama reflects a growing tendency to mock witchcraft

---

64 Allan Botica, 'Audience, Playhouse and Play in Restoration Theatre, 1660–1710' (unpublished doctoral thesis, Oxford University, Worcester College, 1986), p. 48.
65 Botica, p. 57.
66 Glanvill and More, p. 62.
67 Roger D. Lund, *Ridicule, Religion and the Politics of Wit in Augustan England* (Farnham: Ashgate, 2012), pp. 33–35.
68 On Rochester and Glanvill, see Marianne Thormählen, *Rochester: The Poems in Context* (Cambridge: Cambridge University Press, 1993), pp. 213–15. Thormählen shows that Rochester was not merely a 'small pretender' to learning, although he was undoubtedly somewhat 'loose'.

belief in society more generally, witchcraft as a symbol of rebellion is often treated seriously. In this limited respect, warnings by Glanvill, More, and Casaubon that dismissing witchcraft was a threat to the civil government as well as to the principles of established religion seem to find some dramatic support.

The later seventeenth century was the last period in which witchcraft was frequently represented on stage. Indeed, references to witches and witchcraft peaked during the Carolean Restoration. Around half of the extant plays first performed in the 1670s, 1680s, and 1690s contain at least one instance of the words 'witch', 'witchcraft', or variant forms. The words occur roughly twice as frequently as in the period during which witchcraft prosecution peaked – the 1580s and 1590s.[69] Witches were therefore mentioned in drama most frequently when they had ceased to be persecuted very much. In the eighteenth century witchcraft, and other aspects of the supernatural world, gradually ceased to be represented on the stage. By 1749, the narrator of *Tom Jones* was able to point out that

> these doctrines are at present very unfortunate, and have but few, if any, believers ... the whole furniture of the infernal regions hath long been appropriated by the managers of playhouses, who seem lately to have lain them by as rubbish, capable only of affecting the upper gallery; a place in which few of our readers ever sit.[70]

Even in the theatre, witchcraft and its accompanying 'furniture' is associated with the lower social classes by the mid-eighteenth century, and may have been abandoned entirely. This was certainly not the case in the Restoration, but it is noticeable that Restoration drama – less socially inclusive than prior to 1642 – often treats witchcraft belief as a matter for ridicule. The frequent references to, and representations of, witches in the dramatic literature of the Restoration do not seem to indicate any great public concern about the issue of witchcraft. Rather, the proliferation of witches on the Restoration stage is probably a sign that the subject of witchcraft

---

69 Based on searches in the *English Drama* database, the percentages of new or adapted plays containing the words 'witch', 'witchcraft', and variants were: 1580–89: 26 per cent; 1590–99: 24 per cent; 1670–79: 52 per cent; 1680–89:50 per cent; 1690–99: 49 per cent. Dates of first performance were checked against those in the *Annals of English Drama*.

70 Henry Fielding, *Tom Jones* (Oxford: Oxford University Press, 2008), p. 581.

had lost a great deal of its urgency, as Anthony Harris suggests.[71] It should be remembered, however, that Restoration theatre audiences were probably not very representative of the English population as a whole, being overwhelmingly urban, wealthier than average, and strongly influenced in taste and ideology by a small group of courtiers.

Charles II's taste in theatre had been influenced by the years he spent in France as a young man,[72] and the innovations imported into the Carolean theatre were an important factor behind the greater number of supernatural characters and events presented on stage. The Restoration theatre utilised machinery to a much greater extent than prior to 1642. One account of an entertainment presented in 1661 at the Cockpit in Drury Lane describes a performance by French actors.[73] It is unclear whether it involved much speech – the focus of the pamphlet is, as its title suggests, on the visual aspects of the production. Other advances in staging, such as moveable scenery, were quickly imported into the new theatrical duopoly established by Thomas Killigrew and William Davenant at the King's and Duke's theatres.[74] The new machinery opened up the possibility of performing convincing stage magic. Stage directions from a number of Restoration plays indicate that spectacular visual display often accompanied stage witches. The epilogue to Thomas Duffett's farce version of *The Empress of Morocco* (1673), for example, requires that 'Three Witches fly over the Pit Riding upon Beesomes.[75] Heccate descends over the Stage in a Glorious Chariot, adorn'd with Pictures of Hell and Devils, and made of a large Wicker Basket.'[76] Of course, the new machines were not reserved exclusively for presenting witches.

---

71 Harris, p. 184.
72 Nancy Maguire, *Regicide and Restoration* (Cambridge: Cambridge University Press, 1992), pp. 54–55.
73 Anon., *The Description of the Great Machines of the Descent of Orpheus into Hell* (London, 1661).
74 Derek Hughes, *English Drama 1660–1700* (Oxford: Oxford University Press, 1996), pp. 1–2.
75 *OED*, n. 1: 'A bundle of rods or twigs used as an instrument of punishment; a birch.'
76 Thomas Duffett, *The Empress of Morocco* (London, 1674), p. 30. A fuller account of witches' flight on the early modern stage is provided by Roy Booth, 'Witchcraft, Flight and the Early Modern English Stage', *Early Modern Literary Studies* 13:1 (May 2007), https://extra.shu.ac.uk/emls/13-1/bootwitc.htm.

A wide variety of supernatural characters, including spirits and devils, but also characters from mythology, are to be found in plays and semi-operas like Shadwell's *Psyche* (1675) and the various adaptations of *The Tempest*.

The tendency of visual effects to distract from the literary aspects of plays had frequently been regretted by playwrights such as Ben Jonson, and Restoration playwrights did not necessarily appreciate the change in audience tastes either. One prologue makes a revealing complaint about the recent history of English theatre:

> Th' Old English Stage, confin'd to Plot and Sense,
> Did hold abroad but small intelligence,
> But since th' invasion of the forreign Scene,
> Jack pudding Farce, and thundering Machine,
> Painted to your grave Ancestours unknown,
> (Who never disliked wit because their own)
> There's not a Player but is turned a scout,
> And every Scribler sends his Envoys out
> To fetch from Paris, Venice, or from Rome,
> Fantastick fopperies to please at home.
> And that each act may rise to your desire,
> Devils and Witches must each Scene inspire,
> Wit rowls in Waves, and showers down in Fire
> With what strange Ease a Play may now be writ,
> When the best half's composed by painting it?
> And that in th' Ayr, or Dance lyes all the Wit?[77]

Rawlins's patriotic complaint identifies the 'thundering machine' as part of the 'invasion' of the foreign into English theatre, an invasion which is linked to a proliferation of witches and devils. But aside from his complaint about the ascendancy of the special effects made possible by machinery and the allure of painted and moveable scenery, the prologue also identifies singing and dancing as a distraction from the playwright's wit – or an excuse for the deficiency of playwrights in that regard.

Singing and dancing was another aspect of the theatre which grew in prominence during the Restoration, the period during which the opera began to emerge as a distinct theatrical form in England. These innovations generated considerable resistance, usually on the grounds that it was unnatural and nonsensical for characters to communicate by singing. As Stephen Plank has argued, supernatural elements countered this objection by providing an excuse for music:

---

77 Thomas Rawlins, *Tunbridge-Wells* (London, 1678), prologue.

'Magical scenes peopled by those from the irrational, supernatural world might rationally proceed in music; where "incantation" is the modus operandi, music would be essential'.[78] Witches in Restoration drama almost invariably sing.

Witches were not the only supernatural characters that could be used to justify a song and dance, and Curtis Price has pointed out that even in the Restoration, '[c]auldron-stirring hags of the sort depicted by Middleton, Shakespeare, and Davenant are rare in both plays and semi-operas.'[79] Nevertheless, references to witches do peak in this later period, and some Restoration plays feature a lot of talk about witches without representing any actual 'cauldron-stirring hags' on stage. One example is Sir Robert Stapylton's *The Step-Mother* (1663). This play has been described by Price as a 'bold attempt to create a novel genre for the English stage' based on its integration of music into the action of the play.[80]

Like most plays of the very early Restoration, the plot of *The Step-Mother* is laden with contemporary political significance. It represents a pseudo-historical Britain peopled by Romans and Britons, and ruled by King Sylvanus, who has unwisely married the scheming Roman lady Pontia, the title character. The mixed population of Roman republicans and monarchical Britons obviously bears little relation to ancient Britain, but it has considerable relevance to the recent division of the country into Cavaliers and Roundheads. The play even features an honourable Roman general, Crispus, whose sense of duty draws admiration from all the other characters. In the first few years of the Restoration, the honourable or king-restoring general was something of a stock character, created in recognition of the role played by General Monck in establishing Charles II as monarch.[81]

While there are no supernatural events in *The Step-Mother*, it seems significant given the political context of the play that the character of Pontia is associated with witches throughout. The association begins when she attempts to commission a witch and a conjurer to murder her husband. Unfortunately for her, the pair

---

78 Stephen Plank, '"And Now about the Cauldron Sing": Music and the Supernatural on the Restoration Stage', *Early Music* 18:3 (August 1990), 392–407 (pp. 395–96).
79 Curtis Price, *Henry Purcell and the London Stage* (Cambridge: Cambridge University Press, 1984), p. 231, footnote 11.
80 Price, p. 9.
81 Maguire, pp. 48–49.

are in fact her husband's men, Fromund and Tetrick, in disguise. Even though these witches are not genuine, they take the trouble to stress that their powers are dependent on a greater power. Rather than the devil, however, the 'great Witch-maker' is identified as a Merlin-like character: 'the British Bard', who later sings a song taken by Pontia to be a prophecy. The 'witch' herself only claims to be able to tell fortunes by palmistry, although, in accordance with the established witch stereotype, she is motivated by the desire for revenge on a 'scurvy proud young widow' who insulted her.[82] The tone of the scene is not particularly sinister, though, and the fact that the witches' power comes from a bard rather than from the prince of darkness emphasises their status as fictive, literary creations. After they have negotiated with Pontia, Tetrick and Fromund 'fall into a Dance, then comes in another Conjurer, and another Witch, and from under his Coat and her Gown, drop out two little familiars, an he and a she' (II, p. 23). Judging by the stage direction, this dance seems unlikely to have inspired much terror in the audience; the fake witches are played mostly for comic effect.

Pontia herself, however, is another matter. Unlike the fake witch Fromund, she does appear to be in league with hell in some sense. Asked to write down the names of those she wishes to die, she writes, Faustus-like, 'DIS MANIBUS. Pontia devotes to hell Filamor, Violinda and Sylvanus' (II, p. 22). Earlier, in declaring her own fitness to rule, Pontia claims that '[a] Crown he merits, who piles Tow'r on Tow'r / To scale the Stars, and ristle Soveraign Pow'r' (I, p. 14). In associating herself and her ambition with the Tower of Babel, Pontia declares herself – like a witch – to be a rebel against God. This rebellion against God is conflated with a challenge to the 'Soveraign Pow'r', associating Pontia with the republican cause, as well as with witchcraft.

While the character of Pontia could easily be understood to represent a particularly pernicious 'enemy within' in the England of the 1660s, *The Step-Mother*, like other early Restoration political tragicomedies, ends with an optimistic reconciliation scene. After Pontia mistakenly stabs her son Adolph she repents, and in the ensuing masque she plays the part of the goddess Diana. The

---

[82] Robert Stapylton, *The Step-Mother* (London, 1664), II, p. 21. Brianella, Pontia's favourite, is also witch-like in her desire for revenge on Crispus: 'Mighty General / 'Twill elevate my Soul to see thy Fall: / There is a Pleasure in Revenge, above / The expectation or the joyes of Love' (IV, p. 71). Subsequent references to this edition are given in parentheses.

association with Diana is significant. As Crispus puts it at the end of the play, '[n]ow Pontia, like the Planet of the Night, / Breaks from her clowd, and shews us her pure light' (v, p. 82). Both Diana, goddess of women, childbirth, and virginity, and Hecate, goddess of witchcraft, are associated with the moon, and Stapylton uses the ambiguity to lend a classical twist to Pontia's transformation. The redemption of Pontia and the reconciliation of Romans and Britons sent an important message in a country still scarred by a traumatic period of civil war.

Both Pontia's association with witchcraft and her ultimate repentance and forgiveness are used to draw attention to the political issues of the day, but witchcraft itself is treated as a joke. The appearance of (fake) witches on stage is the cue for some comic relief, and the only characters who take the predictions of witches seriously are Pontia and Brianella, both of whom are obviously mistaken in doing so. The heroic general Crispus dismisses the witch-making British Bards as 'Juglers' (II, p. 24). The theme of witchcraft performs a dual function, as in *The Late Lancashire Witches*. Witchcraft is only taken seriously as a symbol of rebellion against husband, king and god. In itself, witchcraft is treated as laughable.

The most famous witches on the Restoration stage were of course those in the Davenant adaptation of *Macbeth* (1664). The political appeal of *Macbeth* in a theatre that was partly revived for propagandistic purposes[83] is hard to miss: Macbeth murders a king, whose son flees abroad but later returns to replace the tyrant as ruler. The parallels with the situation of Charles I, Oliver Cromwell, and Charles II could hardly be more obvious. This aspect of the political context could account in part for the cruder and more obvious villainy in Davenant's version of the main character. Davenant's alterations have received some censorious critical comment, including from Anthony Harris, who condemns their 'trivialising effect'.[84] From the point of view of this study, however, they are interesting for two reasons: first, because the most significant change is the expansion of the witches' roles, and second, for the addition of references to the nature of spirits.

Towards the end of the play, when Macbeth is preparing for the battle against the English army that will depose him, the Davenant

---

83 Maguire, p. 17.
84 Harris, p. 187.

text exaggerates the fears of which Shakespeare's Macbeth had almost forgotten the taste:

> MACBETH I am sure to die by none of Woman born.
> And yet the *English* Drums beat an Alarm,
> As fatal to my Life as are the Crokes
> Of *Ravens*, when they Flutter about the Windows
> Of departing men.
> My Hopes are great, and yet me-thinks I fear
> My Subjects cry out Curses on my Name,
> Which like a North-wind seems to blast my Hopes:
> SEATON That Wind is a contagious Vapour exhal'd from Blood.[85]

Seaton's rather baffling choric comment becomes clearer in the light of the passage in *Saducismus Triumphatus* quoted above, which bears repeating: Glanvill states that 'some have thought that the Genii (whom both the Platonical and Christian Antiquity thought embodied) are recreated by the reeks and vapours of humane blood and the spirits that proceed from them'.[86] The genii are guardian spirits, and Seaton's remark suggests the possibility that the blood of Macbeth's victims has unleashed spiritual forces that are now working against the usurper. The terms 'wind' and 'vapour' might seem to suggest naturalistic, physical causation, but the association of air with spirit means that this need not preclude spirits at work. The implication of both these passages – Glanvill's and Davenant's – is that the spiritual and physical worlds interact, and indeed that they might be difficult to distinguish. The 'Crokes Of Ravens', which are also disturbances in the air, are said to have a direct effect on dying men. Macbeth's actions in the physical world, the passage suggests, have consequences in the spirit world, which in turn come back to haunt him in the physical world.

Another reference to spiritual powers and their functioning in the physical world comes when Lady Macbeth, having repented her part in the old king's murder, confronts her husband and urges him to abdicate:

> MACBETH Resign the Crown, and with it both our Lives.
> I must have better Councellors.
> LA. MACB. What, your Witches?
> Curse on your Messengers of Hell. Their breath
> Infected first my Breast: See me no more.
> (IV.1, p. 53)

---

85 William Davenant and William Shakespeare, *Macbeth* (London, 1674), v.3, p. 59. Subsequent references are given in parentheses.
86 Glanvill and More, p. 75.

Davenant's Lady Macbeth appears to identify the witches as responsible for her conversion to evil, suggesting that their 'breath' – which, since it is air, is in the grey area between body and spirit – has somehow 'infected' her, presumably in the same way that Glanvill claimed evil spirits could inject witches with 'vile vapours' when sucking their blood.[87] Her claim is not entirely persuasive, since to the audience's knowledge she has not come into contact with the witches. Nevertheless, the fact that it is possible for her to make this claim at all suggests that she is performing in front of an audience which might consider such a thing possible in principle.

The witches in Shakespeare's *Macbeth* are evil, and seemingly possessed of mysterious powers. Davenant's witches are also evil, most of the time, but their powers are made less mysterious. The witches may be capable of affecting the human body directly, presumably by acting on the spirits or *pneumata* that are carried in the blood. Davenant's *Macbeth* gives more prominence to spirits than Shakespeare's version, and the manner in which it does so includes those spirits within the chain of causal relationships that make up the visible world of 'matter in motion'. Things which had previously been left to the imagination are, in the adaptation, highlighted and even explained. It seems that it has become interesting or necessary to account for the abilities of the witches in mechanistic terms.

The play's references to the operations of spiritual winds and vapours are dealt with seriously, but the same is not always true of the witches themselves. At times, the witches are straightforwardly and exuberantly infernal, as when Heccate appears and demands that the witches meet her 'at the pit of Achæron' in order to summon a spirit (III.1, p. 44). But the witches' songs do not always dwell on their evil:

> Oh what a dainty pleasure's this!
> To sail i'th' Air
> While the *Moon* shines fair;
> To Sing, to Toy, to Dance and Kiss;
> Over Woods, high Rocks and Mountains;
> Over Hills, and misty Fountains;
> Over Steeples, Towers, and Turrets:
> We fly by night 'mongst troops of Spirits.
> No Ring of Bells to our Ears sounds,
> No Howls of Wolves, nor Yelps of Hounds;
> No, nor the noise of Waters breach,

---

87 Glanvill and More, p. 76.

Nor Cannons Throats our Height can reach.
(III.1, p. 45)

The earliest appearance of this song is in Middleton's *The Witch*, and original audiences of that play might have understood it to satirise the apparent impunity with which the Carrs had committed murder.[88] Like the singing witches, the Carrs were unperturbed by earthly threats which could not reach their 'height', leaving them free to concentrate on their dainty pleasures. (The song may have appeared in the Jacobean *Macbeth*, too, but the folio text only reproduces the opening lines.) But by the Restoration, this song must have lost its fleeting political significance: the Overbury murder is unlikely to have been uppermost in auditors' minds in 1664. Stripped of this potential meaning, the significance of the singing witches turns from satire to pantomime.

Witches' songs often undercut the sense of threat that they might otherwise generate. However seriously or otherwise the witches in *Macbeth* were taken by Restoration audiences, it is certain that they inspired at least one parody. Elkanah Settle's tragedy *The Empress of Morocco* (1673), in addition to Dryden's attack in prose (*Notes and Observations on* The Empress of Morocco), prompted a farce of the same title by Thomas Duffett in which Settle and his play are openly mocked. The epilogue to this farce features witches explicitly modelled on those of *Macbeth*. Duffett's witches directly address, and indeed mock, the audience, in words based on Shakespeare's:

> 1. WITCH Fie! Fah! Fum!
> By the itching of my Bum,   {*pointing to the*
> Some wicked Luck shou'd that way come.   *Audience.*}
> HECATE Stand still – by yonder dropping Nose I know,
> That we shall please them all before we go.
> Hail! hail! hail! you less than wits and greater!
>   {*Heccate speaks to the*
> Hail Fop in Corner! and the rest now met here,   *Audience.*}
> Though you'l ne're be wits – from your loins shall spread,
> Diseases that shall Reign when you are dead.[89]

Hecate's prophecy to the audience – predicting their role in spreading venereal diseases but denying them the crown of wit – is obviously based on the witches' words to Banquo. Duffett's version of *The*

---

88 See Chapter 3 on Jacobean drama.
89 Duffett, *The Empress of Morocco*, pp. 34–35.

Empress of Morocco is not an isolated example of witchcraft being made farcical; in fact, Duffett seems to have specialised in absurd witches. *Psyche Debauch'd* (1675) was also written by Duffett in mockery of a Whig playwright's work, in this case Thomas Shadwell's *Psyche* (1675). Shadwell's opera featured Venus, who is replaced in Duffett's burlesque by Woossat, a witch addressed as 'your hagship', who makes her entrance on 'a Charriot drawn by two Brooms'.[90] Despite her malevolence it is difficult to imagine Woossat, or anything else in the play, inspiring much fear in contemporary audiences. That Duffett uses the witches in this way does not necessarily imply that the witches were not taken seriously in performances of *Macbeth*. Nonetheless, the fact that witchcraft could be used in such an obviously ridiculous manner provides support for the complaints of Glanvill and other believers in witchcraft that the subject was now regarded as laughable by a significant, if not necessarily a large, section of the population.

One play from the period which treats the subject of witchcraft seriously and at some length does so from a decidedly sceptical perspective. Henry Neville Payne's *The Fatal Jealousy* (1672) is, like Henry Porter's *The Villain* (1662), inspired by *Othello* (a play with interesting witchcraft elements of its own).[91] The Iago-like character, Jasper, has an aunt who practises as a witch, but she is a self-professed fraud and describes herself as preying on the credulity of the populace:

> The Vulgar People love to be deluded;
> And things the most unlikely they most dote on;
> A strange Disease in Cattle, Hogs or Pigs,
> Or any Accident in Cheese or Butter;
> Though't be but Natural, or a Sluts fault,
> Must strait be Witchcraft! Oh, the Witch was here!
> The Ears or Tail is burn'd, the Churn is burn'd;
> And this to hurt the Witch, when all the while
> They're likest Witches that believe such Cures.[92]

All of these observations are familiar from the arguments of Scot and others, and the last line repeats an argument made long before by George Gifford.[93] It seems likely, on the basis of this speech, that Payne had read some of the English sceptical writers.

---

90 Thomas Duffett, *Psyche Debauch'd* (London, 1678), p. 16.
91 On the witchcraft in *Othello* see Willis, pp. 164–65.
92 Henry Neville Payne, *The Fatal Jealousy* (London, 1673), II, p. 22. Subsequent references to this edition are given in parentheses.
93 Gifford, *Discourse*, sig. H3ʳ.

Scepticism in its more general, philosophical sense is also a major theme of the play.[94] Characters are repeatedly mistaken or deceived by their senses. In the blood-soaked denouement, these mistakes turn the play into a kind of gruesome farce: Eugenia is wrong about the man who kills her; she dies thinking it was Francisco. Gerardo dies believing, wrongly, that Francisco both murdered Eugenia and lied about it with his last words. Antonio first mistakes Eugenia for his wife and kills her, then mistakes Gerardo for Francisco and stabs his friend's corpse. Antonio, and later Francisco and Sebastian, hear other characters speaking but cannot make out the words. The point is made repeatedly: the evidence of the senses is not reliable; human knowledge and perception is limited and we cannot fully understand the world around us.

The play also represents human beings drawing the wrong conclusions from the evidence of their senses in order to undermine witchcraft belief specifically. Some of the characters obstinately cling to their mistaken interpretations despite being presented with evidence to the contrary. Jasper, having met his aunt and seen her familiar spirit – actually a young boy in disguise – is told at some length that all her magic is faked. Nevertheless, after the 'familiar' leaves, Jasper comments: 'I'm glad it's gone, for surely it was a Devil, / What ever you pretend' (II, p. 24). Antonio, despite the captain of the watch explaining to him that the witch is a trickster, later reverts to believing in her power. In contrast to the situation in *The Late Lancashire Witches*, it is the believers in witchcraft in Payne's play who obstinately resist the obvious conclusion.

As has been argued, one underlying function of belief in witchcraft was to guarantee the existence of the world of spirits. This vital question also seems to be addressed in *The Fatal Jealousy*, with less reassuring results. A range of spiritual creatures are 'seen' by characters in the play. Antonio and Jasper, among others, see the witch's familiar, who turns out to be a human boy. (In case the audience were in any doubt, the boy confesses all to the captain of the watch before the end of the play.) The nurse believes that she has seen Eugenia's ghost, which actually turns out to be her fellow servant, Flora. The case of the angel seen in a vision by Caelia, Antonio's virtuous wife, is a little more complicated. Upset when Antonio leaves the house with Jasper, and orders her to stay home, Caelia faints and in a dream or vision thinks she sees an angel leading her husband back. Gerardo's first reaction is that '[h]er

---

94 Hughes, p. 90.

fancy is disturb'd', but when Antonio suffers a nosebleed and, briefly, returns, Antonio and Eugenia take the apparent omen seriously. In the end, though, Antonio leaves, dismissing the idea that his nosebleed is any kind of portent.[95] If heaven is at work at this point in the play, however, it works indirectly, and its help is dependent on Antonio choosing to act on the hint, which he fails to do. Later in the play, when Gerardo calls on an angel for help, no aid is forthcoming.

The uncertainty pervading the play is not restricted to the events of the plot, or to the natural world. While the epilogue to the play claims that it contains 'no atheism', the text itself shows a great deal of concern with issues of faith and belief in the religious, as well as the epistemological, sense. Gerardo and Antonio debate free will and predestination in one scene, and later Gerardo, the most sympathetic of the male characters, speculates about the afterlife:

> Eternity, whose undiscover'd Countrey
> We Fools divide, before we come to see it;
> Making one part contain all happiness,
> The other misery, then unseen fight for't.
> Losing our certains for uncertainties;
> All Sects pretending to a Right of choyce;
> Yet none go willingly to take their part,
> For they all doubt what they pretend to know,
> And fear to mount, lest they should fall below:
> Be't as it will; my Actions shall be just,
> And for my future State I Heav'n will trust.
> (III, p. 34)

Payne was a Catholic and a Jacobite, arrested and imprisoned for his part in the Montgomery plot in 1689,[96] and Gerardo's criticism of 'sects' and the loss of certainty associated with difference of opinion in religion may reflect his beliefs.

While Gerardo's speech presupposes the existence of an afterlife, any possibility of direct knowledge of heaven, and the spiritual world more generally, is disavowed in the play. In renouncing ambitions to discover religious truth, and trusting instead to heaven,

---

95 Nosebleeds seem to have been regarded as bad omens; Adolph in *The Step-Mother* gets one and says: 'My nose bleeds, and these drops some hold to be / Ominous Effects, when they've a natural Cause' (III, p. 51). Adolph may be wrong to dismiss the significance of this portent, however, since he is stabbed by his mother soon afterwards.

96 ODNB, 'Henry Neville Payne'.

Gerardo adopts a fideistic attitude. He does not develop this into an argument in favour of accepting the authority of the Catholic Church, for obvious reasons, but such arguments were frequently advanced by leading figures in the French Counter-Reformation.[97] Gerardo's view appears alongside a clear denial of the reality of witchcraft, belief in which is based on a mistaken interpretation of empirical evidence, and this is no coincidence. Both God's realm and the devil's – the entire world of the supernatural – is unknown and unknowable for humans, and the supposed evidence of it on earth (witchcraft, and more broadly the communication of humans with spiritual beings such as demons) is either straightforward trickery or, as with Antonio's nosebleed, ambiguous at best. Philosophical scepticism and scepticism about witchcraft are inseparable within the play, and both are motivated by similar (religious) concerns.

Nonetheless, despite the play's rejection of witchcraft as a real phenomenon, it is again used as a kind of metaphor for the evil deeds of some of the characters, one of whom is depicted in ways reminiscent of the stereotypical witch. The nurse who arranged for Eugenia's rape is described by Eugenia as '[t]hou fatal Hagg, thou Mother of all mischief', by Gerardo as 'that old wrinkl'd Hag!', and by Jasper as a 'lying witch' (III, IV, V, pp. 37, 56, 71). The character of the nurse combines advanced age and an active sex life, which also accords well with the witch stereotype.[98] It was standard practice for stage witches to be played by male actors at the time,[99] and the nurse was played by James Nokes, who was famous for his 'comic transvestite' roles and was nicknamed 'Nurse Nokes' as a result.[100] Jasper's aunt, the fake witch, was played by a female actor, Mrs Norris. While the play discourages belief in actual witchcraft, the witch stereotype is used to emphasise the evil of some characters.

It has been argued that the Restoration debate on witchcraft was more openly concerned with the status of spirits than had previously been the case, and the content of plays would suggest that spirits

---

97 Popkin, p. 74.
98 While witches were not typically depicted as particularly lustful in Elizabethan and Jacobean pamphlet accounts, later witchcraft cases started to incorporate sexual elements into the narrative, a characteristic that became increasingly marked as the seventeenth century wore on; see Millar, 'Sleeping with Devils', pp. 207–31.
99 Plank, p. 398.
100 *ODNB*, 'James Nokes'.

became increasingly interesting to theatre audiences. The incidence in plays of the word 'spirits' and its variants increased in the Restoration, in similar proportion to the increasing incidence of references to witches. 'Spirits' and its variants appear in around a third of plays first performed in the 1580s and 1590s, which increases to a peak of three-quarters in the 1680s.[101] The plays themselves seem to support the contention that spirits were of greater interest – not merely in terms of their capacity to provide spectacular effect, but also on intellectual grounds. Several plays reflect an increasing concern about the nature of spirits.

Just as the role of the witches is expanded in Davenant's *Macbeth*, so the role of the spirits is expanded in his and Dryden's adaptation of *The Tempest* (1667). Act II is much altered, with Alonso and Antonio repentant from the start, and terrified by singing devils and personified sins who upbraid them with their crimes. Spirits are thus much more obviously involved in the action; in Shakespeare's version the men are magically deceived, but they remain unaware of Ariel's presence. The adaptation also introduces Milcha, a female spirit who appears to be Ariel's lover. In Thomas Shadwell's operatic *Tempest* (1674), closely based on the Davenant-Dryden version, several more spirits are introduced. After being presented with their sins (pride, fraud, rapine and murder) by two devils, Alonzo and Antonio are confronted by another devil, who bursts into song:

> Arise, arise! ye subterranean winds,
> More to disturb their guilty minds.
> And all ye filthy damps and vapours rise,
> Which use t' infect the Earth, and trouble all the Skies;
> Rise you, from whom devouring plagues have birth:
> You that i' th' vast and hollow womb of Earth,
> Engender Earthquakes, make whole Countreys shake,
> And stately Cities into Desarts turn;
> And you who feed the flames by which Earths entrals burn.
> Ye raging winds, whose rapid force can make
> All but the fix'd and solid Centre shake:
> Come drive these Wretches to that part o'th' Isle,
> Where Nature never yet did smile:
> Cause Fogs and Storms, Whirlwinds and Earthquakes there:
> There let 'em houl and languish in despair.
> Rise and obey the pow'rful Prince o'th' Air.[102]

---

101 Again, figures are based on searches in the *English Drama* database.
102 Thomas Shadwell, *The Tempest* (London, 1674), II.3, p. 30.

The stage direction immediately following this song also refers to dancing 'winds'. The concept of wind or air is so strongly identified with that of spirit in this song that the terms are treated as synonymous. Without actually using the word 'spirit', Shadwell's devil – a spirit himself – summons more spirits. The song provides a great deal of detail, not often present in earlier dramatic treatments, about the nature and activities of spiritual beings. In fact, these spirits – the 'subterranean winds' – are associated with all four of the elements – earth and air, of course, but also water ('damps and vapours') and fire ('the flames by which Earth's entrails burn'). This might suggest that they are tetrarchs – elemental spirits – rather than devils,[103] but it is their destructive power that is emphasised in the song. They are credited with a wide and frightening array of powers, and they are able to cause natural disasters such as plagues and earthquakes in the material world.

The four elements are certainly present in Shakespeare's *Tempest*. Ariel is described as an 'airy spirit', and is sometimes associated with fire; Caliban – although he is not a spirit – is associated with both earth and water. However, Shakespeare's *Tempest* does not really interrogate the nature of spirit: that spirits exist, and that they are airy and rapid, is merely taken for granted. The characteristics of spirits, and the nature of their operations in the material world, are dealt with much more explicitly and in much greater depth in the song above. This particular alteration to the story would not seem to be the result any particular enthusiasm for the existence of spirits on the part of the individual playwright, as Shadwell was, as Chapter 7 argues, in all probability a Hobbesian materialist, and a similar curiosity about spirit is also evident in Davenant's *Macbeth*. The nature of the changes made to Restoration adaptations of Shakespeare suggests a changing attitude towards, and growing interest in, spirits in theatregoing society as a whole.

The theatrical representations of witches seem to suggest widespread scepticism about the phenomenon among playwrights and theatregoers – a suggestion reinforced by the writings of many witchcraft theorists at this time, including those of the believers. But in both the theatre and the continuing witchcraft debate outside the theatre, witchcraft had important political resonance during the Restoration. Tyrants and rebels, especially in the early Restoration theatre, are tarred with the brush of the witch stereotype in plays

---

103 On tetrarchs see Lewis, pp. 134–35. Lewis suggests that Ariel is a tetrarch of air, or sylph.

like *The Step-Mother* and *The Fatal Jealousy*, even though the same plays disavow any kind of credulity about the reality of witchcraft either as magical power or as a pact with the devil. Many sceptical writers on witchcraft, such as Webster, also accepted the broad outline of the witch's character, as a person driven by an infernal desire for revenge:

> [T]he Devil is author and causer of that hatred, malice, revenge and envy, that is often abounding in those that are accounted Witches, which desire of revenge doth stimulate them to seek for all means by which they may accomplish their intended wickedness, and so they learn all the wicked and secret wayes of hurting, poysoning & killing.[104]

While the fake witches in the plays examined in this chapter are not possessed of magical powers, they are taken seriously as 'witches' in terms of their character and psychological motivation, as well as in the threat they present. The 'real' witches, meanwhile, are frequently used as little more than a source of bawdy humour, as well as providing an excuse to sing and dance.

Spirits seem to have become increasingly important in both the theatre and the witchcraft debate, with the question of the activities of spirits in the material world taking up an increasingly large part of the latter. In the theatre, new adaptations of older plays featuring witches and spirits point to an increased interest in the nature of these beings, as the role of the supernatural is both expanded and explained in the adaptations. However, this increased interest does not necessarily indicate a greater degree of belief in the spirit world. As I have argued, it is evident from the witchcraft debate and related writings that the increased discussion of spirits is associated with a greater diversity of opinion and an increase in challenges to conventional understandings of the subject – challenges which demanded the kind of clarification offered both in theoretical writings and in dramatic speeches and songs. The detailed descriptions of how spiritual beings interact with the physical world show that their activities were now expected to function within the physical world of cause and effect in a way that is, in principle, comprehensible to humans. This requirement for all of existence to operate within the boundaries of nature and human perception is a point of consensus between defenders of spirit and materialists, but one that inevitably worked to undermine the status of the spiritual realm as separate.

---

104 Webster, pp. 231–32. Webster follows Scot in this respect; see Scot, VI.1, p. 112.

7
The Lancashire Witches

By far the most surprising and controversial use of witchcraft as a dramatic symbol came towards the end of the Restoration in Thomas Shadwell's play *The Lancashire Witches* (1681). This play was staged at a time of political crisis, with Charles II's regime struggling to contain the so-called Popish plot and the increasingly rancorous debate about the succession to the throne which grew out of the plot. *The Lancashire Witches* is above all a political play – perhaps inevitably so, given its immediate context – and one whose use of witchcraft both extends and departs from the earlier Restoration plays discussed in Chapter 6.

Shadwell's play has not received much critical attention in the present day, largely because of its author's poor reputation following Dryden's attacks on him, but perhaps also because it has often been perceived to be unoriginal. *The Lancashire Witches* draws on previous witchcraft plays, including *The Late Lancashire Witches*, *The Witch of Edmonton*, and *The Masque of Queens*. The situation of the Shacklehead and Hartfort children resembles that in Lyly's *Mother Bombie*, in that the intelligent children of two prominent families are expected to marry two fools. But instead of leading to a marriage between two characters who had believed themselves to be siblings, as in *Mother Bombie*, the play concludes with the daughters marrying Doubty and Bellfort, young Yorkshire gentlemen who are worthy of them. The resort to a marriage outside of the local area, I argue, is also politically significant.

The character of Sir Edward Hartfort owes a great deal to previous witchcraft drama. Sir Edward is obviously derived from Generous in *The Late Lancashire Witches*; at one point the text of the play seems to acknowledge this explicitly, when Doubty tells Sir Edward, '[y]ou are Generous beyond expression Sir'.[1] Sir Edward, like Generous,

---

1 Shadwell, *The Lancashire Witches*, v.669. References to the play, given parenthetically hereafter, are to this edition.

is the old-fashioned, sensible, and hospitable country gentleman, a figure that became a stock character in Restoration drama. Sir Edward also aligns himself with Generous in his attitude towards witches, which echoes the earlier play when Sir Edward refers to 'Dreams, meer Dreams of Witches' (1.350; cf. *The Late Lancashire Witches* l. 286). Doubty, on the other hand, is not similar in character or function to Doughty in Heywood and Brome's play, apart from his name. The changed spelling of the name, however, does seem significant, hinting at the scepticism of the play towards witchcraft.

This use of scepticism, I argue, is closely tied to the play's politics. But while *The Lancashire Witches* raises serious doubts about the possibility of witchcraft, it ultimately employs this scepticism to encourage credulity about witch-hunting in another sense. It is a play which proudly displays the kind of outlook that is often thought of as distinctively modern – that is, a materialist outlook – and one that is intolerant of what it depicts as superstition. And yet, not coincidentally, it is at the same time a highly credulous play, in that it seeks to encourage belief in improbable claims about the world for ideological reasons. Indeed, the play refuses to entertain any doubt about some claims, and this refusal is expressed in a manner that is reminiscent of some of the more dogmatic witchcraft theorists. But before moving on to the politics of the play, this chapter begins with a discussion of its many sceptical elements, not least the attitude explicitly presented in the author's preface to the printed version of the play.

Scepticism in *The Lancashire Witches*

In his preface, Shadwell makes it clear that despite the content of the play, he does not believe in witchcraft:

> I am (as it is said of *Surly* in the *Alchymist*) somewhat costive of belief. The Evidences I have represented are natural, viz. slight, and frivolous, such as poor old Women were wont to be hang'd upon. For the Actions, if I had not represented them as those of real Witches, but had show'd the Ignorance, Fear, Melancholy, Malice, Confederacy, and imposture that contribute to the belief of Witchcraft, the people had wanted diversion, and there had been another clamor against it, it would have been call'd Atheistical.

Shadwell distinguishes between 'Evidences' and 'Actions', and makes it clear that while the play presents witches who are real within the fictional world of the play, this should not be taken to imply anything about the world beyond the play. Shadwell also outlines his reasons for making the witches appear real within the play. One issue is the vital question of entertaining the audience. The play, like Brome and Heywood's before it, makes use of the opportunities for spectacular visual effect. According to Richard Steele's mention of a revival of the play in 1711, 'the Actors have flown in the Air, and played such Pranks, and run such Hazards, that none but the Servants of the Fire-office, Tilers and Masons, could have been able to perform the like'.[2] The stage directions included in the printed version suggest that similar feats were also achieved in the first performances of the play.

Having established that he does not believe in witchcraft, Shadwell goes on to complicate this stance, writing that

> Witchcraft, being a Religion to the Devil (for so it is, the Witches being the Devil's Clergy, their Charms upon several occasions being so many offices of the Witches Liturgy to him,) and attended with as many Ceremonies as even the Popish Religion is, 'tis remarkable that the Church of the Devil (if I may catachrestically call it so) has continued almost the same, from their first Writers on this Subject to the last.

Coming immediately after Shadwell's denial of the reality of witchcraft, this passage is a little jarring. It is possible that Shadwell is using the word 'witchcraft' to mean 'the witchcraft that people have mistakenly believed in'. But if this is what Shadwell means, he chooses not to say so. Shadwell's manner of referring to witches in this passage seems to presuppose their existence and confirm their status as servants of the devil. It is at this point that Shadwell mentions the Catholic Church, which he compares to the 'religion' of witchcraft. The final reference to the 'Church of the Devil', as a result, has a touch of ambiguity about it: the phrase seems to refer to witchcraft, but it might also refer to Catholicism. Witchcraft may not be real, but a 'Religion of the Devil' certainly is.

While *The Late Lancashire Witches* is the source for many of the spectacular incidents in Shadwell's play – witches transforming themselves into cats, disappearing hares, and so on – there are significant differences in the way the magical elements are presented. *The Late Lancashire Witches* supports abstract belief in witchcraft while treating actual witchcraft accusations as matter for comedy.

---

2 Richard Steele, Review of *The Lancashire Witches*, *The Spectator* 141 (11 August 1711).

Shadwell's play also treats witchcraft as matter for comedy, and its plot also rests on the reality of the witches' magic. Paradoxically, however, the play simultaneously (and strenuously) denies the reality of witchcraft altogether. In other words, it establishes the *fictional* reality of the witches that appear on stage while at the same time making a clear case that witches do *not* exist in the real world, just as Shadwell argues in his preface. This is the most sceptical representation of witchcraft to be presented in the English theatre during the period in which witchcraft was a criminal offence.

The Late Lancashire Witches opens with a debate about the reasons for the disappearance of a hare, and a similar debate takes place in *The Lancashire Witches*. In the later play the discussion is much shorter:

> SIR JEFF. Now, Sir *Edward*, do you see, the Hare is vanish'd, and here is the Hag.
> SIR EDW. Yes, I see 'tis almost dark, the Hare is run from your tired Dogs, and here is a poor old Woman gathering of sticks.
> (1.386–89)

Shadwell merges a detail from *The Late Lancashire Witches* (the disappearance of the hare) with a detail from *The Witch of Edmonton* (the witch is first encountered gathering sticks). As in *The Late Lancashire Witches*, the sceptical argument – in this case, Sir Edward's – is wrong. The woman, named as Mother Demdike in the text, is indeed a witch, and later comments gleefully that she has 'fooled these fellows' (1.423). Nevertheless, the fact that Sir Jeffrey turns out to be right – discovered later on by the audience – pales into insignificance in the face of Sir Edward's superior credibility and argument in this earlier exchange. To use Shadwell's distinction, Sir Edward is wrong about the 'Action' but right about the 'Evidence'. In *The Late Lancashire Witches*, Arthur's witchcraft explanation was presented as satisfyingly complete comparasied to the vague and unlikely natural explanations offered by Bantam and Shakestone; but here it is Sir Jeffrey who clutches at straws, while Sir Edward's explanation of events is the reasonable and comprehensive one.

This pattern is repeated throughout the play: Sir Edward may be wrong, but he is a good deal more convincing than Sir Jeffrey. As Katherine Briggs points out, Sir Edward and the other sensible characters never change their minds about the existence of witchcraft, despite being proved wrong by the onstage action.[3] The closest any

---

3 Briggs, p. 105.

sensible character ever comes to acknowledging the existence of the witches is in the following passage:

BELL. 'Tis a little odd; but however, I shall not fly from my Belief, that every thing is done by Natural Causes, because I cannot presently assign those Causes.
SIR EDW. You are in the right, we know not the powers of matter.
DOUBT. When any thing unwonted happens, and we [do] not see the cause, we call it unnatural and miraculous.
PRIEST. By my Shoule you do talke like Heretick-Dogs, and Aathiests. (IV.460–66)

As in *The Late Lancashire Witches*, the sceptics in this play cling to their faith in a natural explanation in spite of empirical evidence to the contrary. In the earlier play, the irrational sceptics are contrasted with the reasonable and unbiased Arthur who believes, justifiably and correctly, in the reality of witchcraft. In *The Lancashire Witches*, however, the contrast is not with reasoned belief but with religious fanaticism. The Catholic priest, Tegue, wishes to see all who refuse to accept the authority of the Pope burned for heresy at Smithfield (III.326); he is prepared to die for his cause and gleefully discusses the possibility of being martyred and idolatrously 'worshipped' after his death (III.124–26). Sir Edward's popishly inclined chaplain, Smerk, also wishes to burn 'Hobbists and Atheists' at Smithfield (II.418–19).[4] Doubting the supernatural explanation, even in the absence of a satisfactory natural explanation, is no longer a weak position, as it was in *The Late Lancashire Witches*. Instead, it is the common-sense view accepted by all the reasonable characters in the play. Bellfort argues that entirely natural causes may simply be hidden, for now, from human knowledge. Sir Edward goes even further than this, assigning everything to 'the powers of matter' – that is, to the workings of an exclusively material universe of the kind described by Hobbes. Sir Edward suggests that any supernatural explanation relies on the existence of a non-material spirit world, and that such a world is not something he is prepared to believe in. Sir Edward is committed to a recognisably modern and materialistic understanding of the universe that precludes the existence of witches.[5] It is also one which – as Tegue recognises – might be understood to preclude the existence of God.

---

4 The last execution for heresy carried out at Smithfield took place in 1612, which indicates how extreme an opinion is attributed to Smerk in this passage.
5 For a discussion of the relevance of Hobbesian thought to Shadwell's works in general see Thomas B. Stroup, 'Shadwell's Use of Hobbes', *Studies in Philology* 35:3 (1938), 405–32. *The Lancashire Witches* is discussed on pp. 423–25.

The 'bad' characters Smerk and Tegue vehemently object to any such Hobbesian and materialist view, and they repeatedly use the term 'Hobbist' – common at the time – to refer to the opinions of their enemies. Despite their credulous belief in witchcraft and their paranoid suspicions of a Presbyterian plot, Tegue and Smerk are correct about this. The view expressed by Doubty in the passage above closely resembles that of Hobbes, expressed in *Leviathan*: 'they that see any strange, and unusuall ability, or defect in a mans mind; unlesse they see withal, from what cause it may probably proceed, can hardly think it naturall; and if not naturall, they must needs thinke it supernaturall'.[6] Such a belief is consistent with what can be inferred about Shadwell's own views. Shadwell left his edition of Hobbes's works to his son in his will – with a warning about Hobbes's authoritarian political views – and he was frequently accused by his political enemies of atheism, sometimes by way of dramatic caricatures.[7]

Shadwell claims in his preface that the play would have been attacked on the grounds that it supported atheism if it had denied the reality of witchcraft. This claim seems reasonable at first sight, given the long-standing association between scepticism about witchcraft and atheism. But there is something rather peculiar about Shadwell openly revealing his lack of belief and assertively attacking the 'Ignorance, Fear, Melancholy, Malice, Confederacy, and imposture' underlying witchcraft belief, if he genuinely wished to avoid causing controversy on these grounds. Furthermore, there is no shortage of accusations of atheism within the play itself. All of these accusations come from the contemptible characters, Smerk and Tegue. They do not seem to strike fear into the heart of Sir Edward, who in the opening scene tells Smerk that he 'scorn[s] the name of Atheist' (1.43). Shadwell's play courts accusations of atheism rather than avoiding them; throughout it, he sneers at those who use atheism as a rhetorical weapon.

Despite the reality of witchcraft, the foolish characters are frequently wrong to use it as an explanation. The play represents 'witchcraft' as imposture on several occasions, such as when the heroines disguise themselves as witches in order to drive Susan and Smerk away. Sometimes, as in earlier witchcraft plays, entirely natural problems are wrongly ascribed to witchcraft. Sir Jeffrey is mocked

---

6 Hobbes, 1.8, p. 144.
7 See Christopher J. Wheatley, *Without God or Reason* (Lewisburg: Bucknell University Press, 1993), p. 92 on Shadwell's will, and pp. 93–94 on D'Urfey's lampoon of him in *Sir Barnaby Whigg*.

particularly sharply when he attributes some personal difficulties to the actions of witches:

> SIR JEFF. I tell you, Sir *Edward*, I am sure she is a Witch, and between you and I, last night, when I would have been kind to my Wife, she bewitcht me, I found it so.
> SIR EDW. Those things will happen about five and fifty. (III.407–10)

Impotence magic was a well-known ability of witches, and this is another element of the play that seems to respond to *The Late Lancashire Witches*. In Heywood and Brome's play, the enchanted point is clearly identified as the cause of Lawrence's impotence. Shadwell's work, however, contains nothing to support Sir Jeffrey's attempt to blame his impotence on witchcraft. Sir Edward's response provides a much more plausible explanation, even within the context of a play in which witches are real.

Another factor which undermines the opinions of the believers in witchcraft within the play is their own testimony as to their methods. Sir Jeffrey, having caught a witch, explains how he will gather evidence against her:

> [N]ow you shall see my skill, wee'l search her, I warrant she has biggs or teats a handful long about her parts that shall be nameless; then wee'l have her watched eight and fourty hours, and prickt with Needles, to keep her from sleeping, and make her confess, Gad shee'l confess any thing in the world then; and if not, after all, wee'l tye her Thumbs and great Toes together and fling her into your great Pond. (I.397–403)

In claiming that he can make the alleged witch 'confess any thing in the world' Sir Jeffrey is made to reveal the cruelty, unfairness, and absurdity of his own methods. It is apparent that the supposed witch has little to lose by confessing; it is already too late for her. The portrayal of Sir Jeffrey in this passage counters one of the most powerful arguments in favour of the existence of witchcraft: the claim that witches freely confessed their crimes to disinterested interrogators.

In *The Late Lancashire Witches*, Generous is proved wrong about witchcraft when he sees the magic bridle removed from his wife, resulting in her transformation from a horse back into a woman. Shadwell's play has an equivalent scene, in which Clod has a magic bridle removed by Tom Shacklehead. But the 'transformation' is handled very differently:

> TOM SHA. What a Devils here! *Clod* tied by a Bridle and a Neighing! What a Pox ail'st thou? Const a tell?   [*Tom. Shac.* takes off the Bridle.]

> CLOD. Uds flesh, I am a Mon agen naw!
> Why, I was a Horse, a meer Tit, I had lost aw
> My speech, and could do naught but neigh;
> Flesh I am a Mon agen.
> TOM SHA. What a dickens is the fellee wood?
> (III.697–703)

In Heywood and Brome's play, Mistress Generous's transformation leads to a suspension of comedy and one of the few serious scenes in the play. The equivalent transformation in *The Lancashire Witches* is not treated very seriously. Clod apparently believes himself to have been transformed into a horse, but Tom Shacklehead – the only witness to Clod's transformation back into a human – does not see it that way, wondering instead if Clod is insane. The implication is that no actual magic has taken place; Clod has simply lived up to his name.

In a later scene featuring the same two characters, Tom Shacklehead, on entering, makes a comment without any relevance to the plot: 'Byr Lady 'tis meeghty strong Ale, Ay am well neegh drunken' (IV.476–77). He and Clod discuss the events depicted in the earlier scene, and Tom makes fun of Clod, who still insists he had been transformed into a horse. Shortly afterwards they encounter the witches, one of whom is shot by Tom, and Clod proceeds to bridle her and ride away on her back. This time, Tom – and the audience – have seen a transformation occur, but Tom has previously pointed out that he is drunk, and he does not seem to trust his own perceptions, commenting that 'I connot believe my Sences' (IV.502). Tom echoes an earlier comment by Sir Edward, who tells Sir Jeffrey: 'These are Prodigies you tell, they cannot be; your sences are deceived' (I.340–41). In the scene with Tom and Clod, the play carefully undermines its own Actions by compromising the Evidence.

Tom's comments echo a standard argument used by advocates of philosophical scepticism as well as by sceptics about witchcraft. The unreliability of the senses was one important aspect of the Pyrrhonian position that was so influential in the sixteenth and seventeenth centuries,[8] and it was also utilised by Scot and other sceptics in relation to witchcraft specifically. Discussing some of the more colourful aspects of witchcraft belief – the killing of children so that their corpses could be used to make potions – Scot comments that 'it is so horrible, unnaturall, unlikelie, and unpossible; that if I should behold such things with mine eies, I should rather thinke

---

8 Popkin, p. 53.

my selfe dreaming, dronken, or some waie deprived of my senses; than give credit to so horrible and filthie matters'.⁹ As has been remarked before, scepticism about witchcraft is not the result of a strictly empirical outlook. Instead, like witchcraft belief, it is a conviction which both precedes and guides the analysis of empirical evidence. Scot (and, in the play, Sir Edward and Tom Shacklehead) suggests the use of a sceptical argument about the reliability of sensory experience in order to maintain belief in the impossibility of witchcraft in the face of empirical evidence to the contrary.

Despite his own scepticism about witchcraft, Shadwell apparently considered it important to display his knowledge on the subject, and stressed in his preface that he based his witches on 'Authority'. Added to the printed text of the play were copious endnotes, justifying the inclusion of various pieces of witchcraft lore. At times this is done to justify the inclusion of material aimed at producing a laugh. When the witches summon their master – the devil – they have an unusual way of greeting him: 'Lo here our little Master's come. / Let each of us salute his Bum' (II.433–34). Shadwell's note to the second line explains:

> Kissing the Devils Buttocks is a part of the homage they pay the Devil, as *Bodin* says Doctor *Edlin* did, a *Sorbon* Doctor, who was burn'd for a Witch. *Scot* also quotes one *Danaeus*, whom I never read, for kissing the Devils Buttocks. About kissing the Devils Buttocks, see farther, Guaccius in the forequoted Chapter.

Shadwell's tone in the note quoted is remarkably similar to that of a present-day academic paper, although he is unusually honest in admitting that he has not read one of his sources. While various elements of the play itself undermine and mock belief in witchcraft, its scepticism would be impossible to discern from reading the notes alone. This may be a consequence of the fact that Shadwell's notes are for the most part copied from Jonson's *Masque of Queens*, but the neutral and learned tone also lends Shadwell's notes an air of intellectual authority.[10]

This intellectual authority is, of course, denied to the believers in witchcraft. Sir Jeffrey, arguing with Sir Edward about the existence of witches, attempts to show off his learning:

> SIR JEFF. No Witches? why I have hang'd above Fourscore. Read
> *Bodin, Remigius, Delrio, Nider, Institor, Sprenger,*

---

9 Scot, III.12 (p. 59).
10 Anthony Harris is one of several scholars who have pointed out the reliance on Jonson (p. 190).

>   *Godelman*, and *More*, and *Malleus Maleficarum*, a great
>   Author, that Writes sweetly about Witches, very sweetly.
> SIR EDW. *Malleus Maleficarum* a Writer, he has read nothing but
>   the titles I see.
>   (1.359–64)

Like Generous in *The Late Lancashire Witches*, Sir Edward may not believe in witches, but he does have an intellectually sophisticated understanding of witchcraft. His scepticism – like Shadwell's own – needs to be bolstered by the appearance of familiarity with, and understanding of, the theory of witchcraft, even though it is precisely that discourse that is being rejected and held up to ridicule.

Good and bad witchcraft

Plays from earlier in the Restoration, such as *The Step-Mother* and *The Fatal Jealousy*, used stereotypes connected with witchcraft to signify human, rather than supernatural, evil, and in particular the sort of evil which sought to upturn the social order, as the civil wars had done. A character such as Pontia in *The Step-Mother* – while not depicted as an actual witch – was associated with witchcraft in such a way as to make clear that her rebellion against the social, sexual, and political order was unnatural and impious. But the associations evoked by witchcraft in *The Lancashire Witches* are considerably more complex. The evil aspect of witchcraft remains; but it is complicated by more benign, even heroic, connotations.

Michael Alssid points out that the play associates the heroines with the witches in various ways.[11] The connection between Isabella and Theodosia and the witches is clearest when they disguise themselves 'with Vizors like Witches' in order to trick and scare away some of the foolish characters (v.120), but there are also subtler indications of this affinity. Isabella's vicious verbal attacks on her hapless fiancé Sir Timothy are particularly witch-like, given the close association between scolding and witchcraft in early modern England. Isabella also threatens to 'tear thy Eyes out' (II.332), shortly before another scene in which Mother Dickenson relates her exploits to the devil, which include the acquisition of 'Eye-balls with my nailes scoop'd out' (II.464), a detail which originates with Lucan's Erictho.

In fact, it is not only the heroines and Sir Timothy who are associated with the witches – the heroes are, too, although in a

---

11 Michael Alssid, *Thomas Shadwell* (New York: Twayne, 1967), p. 91.

more subtle manner. When Sir Timothy threatens to kick Belfort for holding hands with Isabella, he receives a peculiarly bloodthirsty response:

> BELL. If you do, you will be the fifteenth man I have run through the Body, Sir.
> SIR TIM. Hah! What does he say, through the body, oh.
> [...]
> BELL. Yes Sir, and my custom is (if it be a great affront, I kill them, for) I rip out their Hearts, dry 'em to powder, and make Snuff on 'em.
> SIR TIM. Oh Lord! Snuff!
> (III.191–98)

Belfort's threat is curiously reminiscent of some of a witch's activities, including the witches in Shadwell's play.

In a later scene, when the young men discuss their excitement at the prospect of marrying the heroines, the language they use to describe their emotions is equally striking:

> BELL. My Dear Friend, I am so transported with excess of Joy, it is become a Pain, I cannot bear it [...] My Bloud is Chill, and shivers when I think on't.
> DOUBT. One night with my Mistress would outweigh an Age of Slavery to come.
> BELL. Rather than be without a Nights enjoyment of mine, I would be hang'd next Morning.
> (IV.507–15)

While this kind of hyperbole about romantic love is not uncommon for the period, chilled blood, slavery, and hanging are not the most obvious images to use in expressing amorous yearning. The trade-offs that the young men envisage in this conversation suggest the kind of Faustian pact supposedly made by witches; the 'age of slavery to come', in particular, might refer to the eternal punishment in hell that follows a witch's bargain with the devil (as well as the years of marriage following the honeymoon).

The contemptible characters in the play are also associated with witchcraft, but in a very different way. Isabella insults Sir Timothy, calling him 'uglier than any Witch in *Lancashire*' (II.308), repeatedly castigating him for his physical unattractiveness in terms that are evocative of the stereotypical witch: 'thou hast a hollow Tooth would Cure the Mother beyond *Arsa fetida*, or burnt Feathers' (II.317–19). Fits of the mother – believed at the time to be a condition of the womb – had been proposed as a naturalistic explanation for cases of possession, most famously by Edward Jorden.[12] Sir Timothy's 'hollow tooth' is reminiscent of the variety of dental problems which were associated with witches,[13] and asafoetida or 'devil's turd' was recommended as a magical, as well as a medicinal, ingredient.[14] Isabella also mocks Sir Timothy for his 'shuffling' walk (III.238), another characteristic suggestive of the stereotypical Elizabethan witch.[15] Isabella's association of Sir Timothy with the threatening power of witchcraft is clearest when she says: 'I had rather be inoculated into a Tree, than to be made one Flesh with thee' (III.256–57). *The Tempest* was a popular play during the Restoration, and an operatic version had been produced by Shadwell himself in 1674, so the reference to the witch Sycorax's imprisonment of Ariel would have been obvious to most audience members.

The association with witchcraft is clearest in the case of the play's main comic villain, Tegue O'Devilly. Tegue's association with witchcraft harks back to a much older tradition within the witchcraft play genre. This is Tegue's cure for impotence:

> I will tell you now, Joy, I will cure you too. Taak one of de Tooths of a dead man, and bee, and burn it, and taak dee smoke into both your Noses, as you taak Snufh, and anoint your self vid dee Gaal of a Crow, taak Quicksilver, as dey do call it, and put upon a Quill, and plaash it under de shoft Pillow you do shit upon, den maake shome waater through de Ring of a Wedding, by St. *Patrick*, and I will shay shome *Ave Maarias* for dee, and dou wilt be sound agen: gra. (III.411–19)

As Shadwell's note points out, this recipe is taken from Scot, so it is unsurprising that Tegue's cure is ridiculous, not to mention disgusting.[16] The cure is also reminiscent of the kinds of remedies offered by witch characters in Tudor plays such as *Three Laws* and *Thersites*. As I have argued, these plays were designed to attack what was regarded as Catholic superstition by closely associating Catholic ritual with magic. While Tegue's remedies are similar to

---

12 Edward Jorden, *A Briefe Discouvrse of a Disease Called the Suffocation of the Mother* (London, 1603). See also Chapter 5.
13 John Gaule describes a typical witch as having a 'gobber tooth' (p. 5); Scot refers to witches as 'toothles' (I.6, p. 13).
14 Russell, pp. 90–91.
15 Samuel Harsnett writes that the witch of the popular imagination walks 'like a bow leaning on a shaft' (*A Declaration of Egregious Popish Impostures*, p. 136).
16 Scot, IV.8, p. 82.

those of the witches, his own 'magic' – Catholic ritual – is shown to be powerless against the supernatural. As in *Dr Faustus*, where the Pope and his friars' attempts to exorcise Faustus and Mephastophilis meet with ignominious failure, Tegue's attempts to exorcise evil spirits with holy water and relics in *The Lancashire Witches* are comically ineffective.

The play goes still further than this when the witches, in the form of cats, scratch Tegue's face. Scratching a witch's face was considered by many to be a way to remove the ill effects of her magic.[17] That Tegue's face is scratched can be taken to indicate that he, not Demdike, is the 'real' witch. As Anthony Harris points out, Tegue's link to witchcraft is perhaps strongest when he actually sleeps with a witch, after being tricked by her in a scene which may have been modelled on Marston's *Sophonisba*.[18] While Marston's play links witchcraft to tyranny (because the witch Erictho tricks the tyrant Syphax), Shadwell links witchcraft to Catholicism by putting a priest in Syphax's place.

That both sympathetic and unsympathetic characters are likened to the play's witches is an indication of the dual function that witchcraft performs in the play. In relation to the unsympathetic characters, witchcraft represents superstition and delusion, ugliness and stupidity – and also a particular kind of authority that is absolutely rejected: that of the Catholic Church. This double aspect of witchcraft is reminiscent of the ambivalence present in the most important English sceptical text: Scot's *Discoverie of Witchcraft*, which vacillates between treating witches as innocent – or even heroic – victims of mindless prejudice, and as fools or tricksters deserving of contempt. Alssid points out that the heroines, unlike Tegue, only practise their 'witchcraft' 'in the name of love and liberty'.[19] Nonetheless, at a time when the 1604 Act against witchcraft remained in force, the association of the sympathetic characters with witches does seem extraordinary. Moreover, the pursuit of liberty, in 1681, could have been understood to be a good deal less innocent than it now sounds. One important association of witchcraft that is of great relevance to the play is the idea of rebellion. As Stuart Clark points out, during the early modern period, '[i]t became usual to use the words "witch" and "witchcraft"

---

17 A recent discussion of 'scratching' witches is in Darr, pp. 173–84. While there were male witches, Tegue is the only example of a man having his face scratched that I have come across.
18 Harris, p. 191.
19 Alssid, p. 91.

(or "enchantment") when casting political opponents as disturbers of the established order, or when trying to deepen the seriousness of some perceived threat to the public peace'.[20] In *The Lancashire Witches*, the use of witchcraft as a metaphor with which to attack political opponents is turned on its head, as the play idealises some forms of rebellion against established authority. This aspect of the play is discussed in the following section.

The play and the plot

It has often been noted that the play was staged at a time of political unrest, but its political significance has not always been recognised. Ian Bostridge argues that Shadwell's play uses witchcraft as a 'useful distraction' from the political squabbles of the time, claiming that Shadwell 'hoped to use witchcraft as a non-contentious piece of theatrical entertainment'.[21] In similar vein, Arthur Scouten and Robert Hume argue that the play represented an attempt to avoid politics:

> The uproar attendant upon the Popish Plot and the Exclusion Crisis naturally bred a spate of political plays ... Shadwell turned to safer and more romantic play-types in *The Woman-Captain* (1679) and *The Lancashire Witches* (1681).[22]

These readings of the author's non-literary intentions would appear to be based entirely on Shadwell's preface to the play which voices a protest, common at the time, about the invasion of the stage by politics. But Shadwell's preface ought not to be taken at face value. Many of the claims he makes in it are strikingly at odds with the evidence of the play itself. The fact that the preface is misleading might be expected, given that it was written in defence of a play that was heavily censored in its stage version – precisely because it was far from 'safe' or 'non-contentious'. As Susan Owen points out, the play is highly political.[23]

---

20 Clark, *Thinking with Demons*, p. 558.
21 Bostridge, p. 91.
22 Arthur H. Scouten and Robert D. Hume, '"Restoration Comedy" and Its Audiences, 1660–1776', *The Yearbook of English Studies* 10 (1980), 45–69 (p. 53).
23 Susan J. Owen, *Restoration Theatre and Crisis* (Oxford: Clarendon Press, 1996), p. 185. In fact, even the preface is far from conciliatory in places, referring, for example, to 'Impudent Hot-headed Tantivy Fool[s]'. The word 'tantivy' was frequently applied to the emerging Tory grouping, who were said by their opponents to be 'riding tantivy [i.e. at a gallop] to Rome'.

One aspect of the play's controversial nature is its attitude to the Church. *The Lancashire Witches* is undoubtedly anti-Catholic, but it is also anti-clerical more generally. This anti-clerical element is often said to be the main reason why the play suffered stringent censorship in its stage version.[24] The printed version, owing to the temporary suspension of pre-print censorship after a divided parliament allowed the lapse of the Printing Act in 1679, restored all the censored lines, and italicised them in order to draw them to the readers' attention. Shadwell even altered Smerk's character, writing in the preface that 'I have now Ordained Smerk, who before was a young Student in Divinity'. This alteration, of course, can only have resulted in accentuating the implied criticism of the Anglican Church.[25]

The authority of the Anglican Church is controversially undermined and subordinated to the authority of the landed gentry in the play. But other kinds of authority are also undermined, most obviously by the fact that Sir Edward and Sir Jeffrey's daughters will not do what their parents want them to do. This is firmly established when Isabella and Theodosia discuss their parents' plans for the marriages:

> ISAB. Well, we are resolved never to Marry where we are designed, that's certain. For my part I am a free English woman, and will stand up for my Liberty, and Property of Choice.
> THEO. And Faith, Girl, I'le be a mutineer on thy side; I hate the imposition of a Husband, 'tis as bad as Popery.
> (1.272–76)

This rejection of parental authority is couched in terms redolent of political discourse: the ideal of Liberty is invoked, while the women describe themselves as 'mutineers', a significantly military and political metaphor. Furthermore, the personal situation of the heroines is once again linked to the combustible political issue of 'Popery', which they see as a kind of tyranny. The decision Isabella and Theodosia make in this scene is presented as an unambiguously good one in the play. The daughters find better husbands – Belfort

---

24 See, for example, Wheatley, p. 96.
25 The play was printed by John Starkey, a publisher with a 'reputation for printing factious texts', rather than Shadwell's regular publisher Henry Herringman: Judith Slagle, 'Dueling Prefaces, Pamphlets, and Prologues: Re-visioning the Political and Personal Wars of John Dryden and Thomas Shadwell', *Restoration and 18th Century Theatre Research* 21:1 (2006), 17–32 (p. 29).

and Doubty – for themselves than those their parents had arranged for them, and even Sir Edward accepts his new son-in-law's worth at the end of the play. Of course, challenging parental authority over the choice of a future spouse is not unusual in comedy at the time,[26] but the association of daughterly rebellion with political rebellion hints at the play's wider political commitments.

Several aspects of *The Lancashire Witches* reveal an engagement in contemporary constitutional debates which were closely linked to the major political crisis of the late 1670s and early 1680s. The so-called Succession Crisis reawakened fundamental questions about the relationship between the monarch and his people which threatened, once again, to destabilise the entire country. The play's political engagement tends to undermine the authority of the king over his subjects, a detail reflected in the political nature of the heroines' 'mutiny', since the authority of the king was frequently compared to that of a loving father. Most of the censored lines in the play are long sections of dialogue including Smerk, which show him in a particularly poor light, either presuming to demand that his master go through a form of confession or expressing sympathy with the Catholic Church. One exception, though, is a short speech of Sir Edward's. Having discussed the superiority of England to other nations (especially France) with Belfort and Doubty, Sir Edward concludes by declaring that

> *I am a true English-man, I love the Princes Rights and Peoples Liberties, and will defend 'em both with the last penny in my purse, and the last drop in my veins, and dare defy the witless Plots of Papists.* (III.47–50)

It might seem puzzling that this passage was censored for the stage, but although the statement might sound to modern ears like a declaration of loyalty to the king, in the context of the early 1680s it was nothing of the kind. As Owen points out, this is 'an explicitly Whiggish passage'.[27] The statement presumptuously places 'the Princes Rights' on a par with the 'Peoples Liberties', and these two ideals could easily be understood to be in conflict in 1681.

---

26 Jessica Munns, 'Theatrical Culture I: Politics and Theatre', in *The Cambridge Companion to English Literature, 1650–1740*, edited by Steven N. Zwicker (Cambridge: Cambridge University Press, 1998), pp. 82–103 (p. 91).
27 Owen, pp. 191–92. The attack on all things French might also be interpreted as hostile to the King, whose enthusiasm for French culture extended to the theatre (Maguire, pp. 54–55).

The question of the balance between liberty and authority was at the centre of the disturbances and debates connected to the Popish Plot and the Succession Crisis. The Popish plot was the name given to a supposed conspiracy to overthrow the government of England and restore the Church to the control of the Pope. Such a plot never existed in reality, but belief in and fear of it led to the execution of twenty-four English Catholics and the imprisonment of hundreds more. Fear of the plot also led to demands for an Exclusion Bill: a law preventing Charles II's brother James – who was known to be a Catholic – from becoming King. Apart from the testimony of a number of often quite shady witnesses,[28] no evidence of the existence of the plot was ever presented in court.[29] Nonetheless, widespread belief in the plot led to what has frequently and aptly been described as a witch-hunt.

The most important witness in the Popish Plot trials, Titus Oates, was at one stage reprimanded in Parliament for having expressed a sentiment very similar to that voiced by Sir Edward.[30] Oates's offending words were that '[t]he King holds his Crown by the same title I hold my liberty.' Even among his supporters in Parliament, this statement caused a great deal of consternation, especially when, after being reprimanded by the Speaker, Oates failed to give a satisfactory apology and added that 'it was my conscience, and it was truth; and though I may not say it here, I will say it elsewhere'. The immediate reaction to Oates's outburst, set down in parliamentary records, is illuminating:

> Mr Secretary Coventry. Pray consider what this House will come to, if persons be permitted to speak here at this rate.
> [...]
> Sir Robert Peyton. It will be very hurtful to give any discouragement to the King's Evidence. It has already gone all over the city.
> [...]
> Mr Secretary Coventry. This language is like a woman indicted for being a whore, and she says, 'she is as honest as any woman in the highest place.' This is very indecent.

---

28 Peter Hinds, *The Horrid Popish Plot: Roger L'Estrange and the Circulation of Political Discourse in Late Seventeenth-Century London* (Oxford: Oxford University Press, 2010) points to the example of 'Captain' William Bedloe, 'a thoroughly disreputable con-man and thief' (p. 47).
29 Some letters purporting to be to, and from, Jesuits were shown to the Privy Council, but were never used as evidence in court; see John Kenyon, *The Popish Plot* (London: Phoenix, 2000, first published in 1972), pp. 77–80.
30 Kenyon, p. 173.

Sir Robert Howard. I know not but your safety depends upon what Mr Oates has to say of the Plot, and I would not discourage him. Sir Thomas Lee. I am concerned to speak at this time. Could I sit still, I would. Though the words which fell from Mr Oates are very considerable, and though they were true, yet all truth is not to be said at all times. You can do no less than reprimand him for what he has said; yet, though he be great evidence, he is not to be privileged to say what he pleases. The Long Parliament, in the height of their discontents, &c. were very tender of any reflections upon the King, though Debates went high in the House. You can do no less than reprimand him.[31]

The responses by these MPs convey a sense of outrage at Oates's statement, which might be difficult for many twenty-first century readers to comprehend. Even his supporters seem exasperated by their star witness. Thomas Lee, who during these years formed part of the emerging Whig grouping, and who was a firm believer in the plot,[32] compares Oates's outburst (unfavourably) to the proceedings of the Long Parliament – the Parliament that actually waged war against King Charles I. Henry Coventry, by contrast, consistently opposed the Exclusion Bill, and would therefore come to be thought of as a Tory,[33] and he takes the opportunity to compare Oates to a prostitute, perhaps hinting that it is Oates who ought to be 'indicted'.[34] Oates's staunchest defenders only dared to argue that he ought not to be discouraged, urging the importance of dealing with the plot. This is true even of Sir Robert Peyton, a reckless man and a heavy drinker who was reputed to be a republican and an atheist, and was spied on by the government.[35] Interestingly, Peyton

---

31 Anchitell Grey (ed.), *Debates of the House of Commons*, vol. 7 (London, 1769), Tuesday, 25 March 1679, British History Online, www.britishhistory.ac.uk/greys-debates/vol7 (accessed 28 January 2014).
32 M. W. Helms and Leonard Naylor, 'Lee, Thomas I', www.historyofparliamentonline.org/volume/1660–1690/member/lee-thomas-i-1635-91 (accessed 28 January 2014).
33 Edward Rowlands, 'Coventry, Henry', www.historyofparliamentonline.org/volume/1660–1690/member/coventry-hon-henry-1618-86 (accessed 28 January 2014).
34 Such attitudes were being expressed, often cryptically, at a relatively early stage of the Popish Plot, for example in Richard Duke's bitingly sarcastic *Panegyrick upon Oates* (London, 1679), which includes the line 'Let Oates still hang before our eyes', as well as a pointed reference to the cropping of ears.
35 Eveline Cruickshanks, 'Peyton, Sir Robert', www.historyofparliamentonline.org/volume/1660–1690/member/peyton-sir-robert-1633-89 (accessed 28 January 2014).

also indicates that Oates's scandalous remarks were already well known outside parliament: 'It has already gone all over the city.' Shadwell's play expresses, in somewhat more guarded language, a very similar sentiment to that of Oates, implying that the 'Princes Rights' and the 'Peoples Liberties' are of equal importance. Even many Whigs who, like Sir Thomas Lee, seem to have agreed with the principle would have baulked at saying it. In Shadwell's play, Sir Edward is therefore located on the extreme 'Whig' end of the political spectrum in his attitude, or more exactly in his willingness to *express* his attitude, to royal authority.

The question of the succession to the throne is one which the play also appears to address, albeit in a more guarded manner. At the end of the play, Isabella marries Belfort and Theodosia marries Doubty. Sir Edward's son, Young Hartfort, the 'Clownish, Sordid Country Fool', is left without a bride. Sir Edward is at first distraught, and angry with Doubty, but after Young Hartfort expresses his relief and determination not to marry, Sir Edward uncharacteristically changes his mind, saying to his son: 'Eternal Blockhead! I will have other means to preserve my Name: Gentlemen, you are men of ample Fortunes and worthy Families – Sir, I wish you happiness with my Daughter, take her' (v.662–64). Sir Edward's change of heart is related to his realisation that there are other ways to ensure his estate can be passed on to the next generation: his daughter's marriage provides him with an alternative, and much more suitable, male heir from neighbouring Yorkshire.

The eventual solution to the problem of a Catholic monarch in a Protestant country was the so-called 'Glorious Revolution' of 1688, in which James II was replaced by William of Orange, a Protestant monarch who had many years previously married James's daughter Mary – also a Protestant, unlike her father. The idea that William of Orange might rule in place of James was being proposed as early as 1678.[36] Shadwell's play, in the line of Sir Edward's quoted above, seems to anticipate such a solution, suggesting that a son-in-law might be a better bet than the rightful male heir. The closing scene of the play displays a concern with issues of succession and inheritance that were both resonant and highly sensitive at the time of its performance.

As J. Douglas Canfield points out, there are limits to the play's anti-authoritarianism. Canfield focuses on the play's limited

---

36 Mark Knights, *Politics and Opinion in Crisis, 1678–1681* (Cambridge: Cambridge University Press, 1994), p. 34.

questioning of patriarchal authority,[37] but more pertinent from the perspective of this study is the play's unambiguous acceptance of royal and parliamentary authority on one specific question: the existence of the Popish Plot. For the favoured characters in the play, no amount of evidence can ever be sufficient to prove the reality of witchcraft; but no evidence at all is needed to prove the reality of the Popish Plot. The play supports scepticism regarding the existence of supernatural phenomena in general, and witchcraft in particular. It is therefore ironic, to say the least, that the play does not support scepticism about the great witch-hunt of its own time.[38]

The resemblances between the Popish Plot and the phenomenon of witchcraft are numerous and striking. As has been pointed out, legislation against witchcraft was reintroduced by the Elizabethan regime as a result of a Catholic plot. During the Popish Plot, as at the height of witchcraft persecution, people were convicted on extremely flimsy evidence, in many cases no more than the testimony of patently unreliable witnesses. Resistance to the Popish Plot frequently took the form of mockery, as did resistance to witchcraft belief, and this was understood by the supporters of the persecution to be dangerous to their cause.[39] The alleged use of poison was a recurring and sinister theme in both the Popish Plot and beliefs about witchcraft. Another curious point of similarity was the age and infirmity of many of the accused. As Kenyon points out, 'the five Catholic noblemen singled out by Titus Oates in 1678 as the leaders of armed insurrection were all old or ageing men'.[40] Another of the accused, Sir Thomas Gascoigne, 'did not seem the stuff of which assassins are made; he was eighty-five years old, deaf, half-blind and lame, and he had not been south of the river Trent for thirty

---

37 J. Douglas Canfield, 'Shifting Tropes of Ideology in English Serious Drama, Late Stuart to Early Georgian', in *Cultural Readings of Restoration and Eighteenth-Century English Theatre*, edited by J. Douglas Canfield and Deborah C. Payne (Athens, GA: University of Georgia Press, 1995), pp. 217–18.
38 This aspect of the play does not seem to have been discussed previously in any kind of detail. The closest thing to an extended discussion of the play's politics is in Don R. Kunz, *The Drama of Thomas Shadwell* (Salzburg: Institute for English Language and Literature, 1972). Kunz refers in passing to 'the rather obvious parallels being drawn between witchcraft and Popish plotting' (p. 254), but says little else about these 'parallels'.
39 Hinds, pp. 50, 53.
40 Kenyon, p. 36.

years'. Gascoigne at least was found not guilty, but Nicholas Postgate, an 80-year-old priest, was less fortunate and was hanged.[41]

A further similarity between the plot and the phenomenon of witchcraft was the sense that belief in the plot was a matter of piety, and that a failure to take it seriously as a threat implied religious and moral heterodoxy. It was, according to the recollections of the Tory judge Roger North, 'not safe for anyone to show scepticism. For upon the least occasion of the sort, What, replied they, don't you believe in the plot? (As if the Plot were turned into a creed).' North even claimed, in another tellingly religious analogy, that 'one might have denied Christ with more content than the Plot'.[42] This kind of zealotry meant that merely criticising the persecution could lead to accusations of involvement even for Anglicans, who could be smeared as 'Popishly inclined', as Smerk is in the play. Even those who had themselves carried out the prosecutions were not exempt: the Whigs turned against the Lord Chief Justice, William Scroggs, after he presided over the acquittal of Sir George Wakeman. Despite the many convictions and executions of supposed plotters which he had enthusiastically overseen, Scroggs was accused of complicity in the plot. Articles of impeachment read in the House of Commons accused him of seeking 'to introduce Popery, and Arbitrary and Tyrannical Government against Law'.[43] When this 'creed' lost its hold over the judiciary, as it did in Scroggs's case, it was not abandoned immediately but replaced by a distinction between the general and the particular. Just as Joseph Addison would later say that he could not doubt the existence of witchcraft in general, and could not believe in any particular instance of it, people suspected of involvement in the Popish Plot began to be acquitted by judges who made a distinction between the existence of a plot in general, which they claimed not to doubt, and the defendants in the particular case.[44]

What links the Popish Plot most clearly to witchcraft persecution as presented in authors like Bodin and James I is the unquestioning faith required by its advocates. The 'good' characters in *The*

---

41 Kenyon, pp. 225, 204.
42 Quoted in Kenyon, pp. 97–98, 111.
43 'Articles of Impeachment of Sir William Scroggs' (3 January 1681), repr. in Geoff Kemp (ed.), *Censorship and the Press, 1580–1720*, 4 vols (London: Pickering & Chatto, 2009), vol. 3, pp. 194–97 (p. 194). Employing a similar tactic, Bodin and James I accused the defenders of alleged witches (Scot and Weyer) of being witches themselves.
44 Kenyon, p. 201.

Lancashire Witches also demand absolute belief in the existence of the Popish Plot:

DOUBT. How now! Do not you believe a Popish plot?
SMERK. No, but a Presbyterian one I do.
BELL. This is great Impudence, after the King has affirm'd it in so many Proclamations, and three Parliaments have voted it, *Nemine Contradicente*.
SMERK. Parliaments, tell me of parliaments, with my Bible in my hand, I'le dispute with the whole House of Commons; Sir, I hate Parliaments, none but Phanaticks, Hobbists, and Atheists, believe the Plot.
(III.341–48)

Belfort makes no attempt to persuade Smerk of the existence of the Popish Plot by providing evidence of its existence. Instead, he points out the 'impudence' of doubt. Smerk is told that he is not *allowed* to doubt the plot. This surely cannot be a deliberate echo of the kinds of argument typical of witchcraft theorists, but the resemblance to, for example, Bodin is unmistakable. Bodin wrote that 'one must not doubt in any way ... one would be very impudent to try to deny that demons and evil spirits have carnal relations with women'.[45] Attacking the 'impudence' of those who doubt the existence of these secret crimes was one way of attempting to silence the opposition. The play refuses to acknowledge the legitimacy of questions about the reality of the plot.

The play makes strenuous efforts to present the political opponents of the emerging Whig faction as cruel and irrational at a time when the Whigs themselves were encouraging a climate of extreme animosity towards Catholics – behaviour that could itself be described in precisely these terms. In fact, the persecution of those supposedly involved in the Popish Plot *was* described as cruel and irrational, not least by playwrights on the other side of the emerging political divide. As Owen points out, in the epilogue to Whitaker's play *The Conspiracy* (1680), written by Edward Ravenscroft, 'those who gloat over the Popish Plot executions are accused of barbarism'.[46]

At first, opposition to the persecution of Popish plotters was tentative. While Ravenscroft may criticise 'gloating' over executions, he does not venture to suggest that the executions themselves should not have happened. Peter Hinds points out that Roger L'Estrange, the leading sceptic in relation to the plot, made heavy use of irony

---

45 Bodin, p. 41.
46 Owen, p. 188.

and humour in his attempts to undermine belief in the existence of the plot rather than explicitly denying its existence.[47] But after the initial excitement died down, the Popish Plot started to lose momentum. Historians of the plot such as John Kenyon and, more recently, John Gibney identify the turning point as the acquittal of Sir George Wakeman in July 1679.[48] By the time Shadwell's play came to be performed in 1681, the Popish Plot was very much in decline. In fact, by the summer of 1681, Stephen College, a Whig who was involved with some of those testifying against Catholics, was himself put on trial for high treason.[49]

Things also began to change in the literary representation of the plot. The most famous contribution to this controversy, Dryden's *Absalom and Achitophel*, admitted the reality of a plot, but added that the truth had been 'dash'd and brew'd with Lyes / To please the Fools, and puzzle all the Wise'.[50] Not long after the first performance of *The Lancashire Witches*, Thomas D'Urfey's *Sir Barnaby Whigg* (1681), a play that could be interpreted as a response to Shadwell's, was put on at the King's Theatre.[51] The prologue of D'Urfey's play directly challenges the reality of the plot:

> How long, alas! must our unhappy Stage
> Groan for the follies of this Plotting Age?
> When shall our doubts and anxious fears have end,
> That we may once more know a foe from friend?
> [...]
> Distraction rages now, and th' frantick Town,
> Plagu'd with Sham-plots, a very *Bedlam*'s grown.
> Like *Lunaticks* ye roar and range about;
> Frame Plots, then crack your brains to find 'em out;
> Like *Oliver*'s Porter, but not so devout.[52]

---

47 Hinds, pp. 269–70.
48 John Gibney, *Ireland and the Popish Plot* (London: Palgrave Macmillan, 2009), p. 117. Kenyon discusses the trial in detail; pp. 192–201.
49 Kenyon, p. 276.
50 John Dryden, *Absalom and Achitophel* (London, 1681), p. 5.
51 Hughes dates these plays to '?spring 1681' and '?summer 1681' respectively; pp. 230, 235.
52 Thomas D'Urfey, *Sir Barnaby Whigg* (London, 1681), sig. A4ʳ. Oliver Cromwell's porter, referred to occasionally in the literature of this period, was Daniel, an inmate of the Bethlehem mental hospital, who was said to be 7 feet 6 inches tall and to have been driven mad by an excess of religious fervour; see Sean Shesgreen, *The Criers and Hawkers of London: Engravings and Drawings by Marcellus Laroon* (Stanford: Stanford University Press, 1990), p. 218.

This is a very forthright statement: the plot is identified as a 'sham', and the people responsible for 'finding 'em out' are accused of actually inventing ('framing') these 'sham-plots' in the first place. In a typical Tory line of attack, the Whig party is linked to 'Oliver' (Cromwell), and neatly added to this is the insinuated accusation of atheism that Sir Edward, in *The Lancashire Witches*, claimed to 'scorn'. In contrast to the plaintive tone of previous dramatic comments from Tories on the plot, D'Urfey, by 1681, felt confident enough to be blunt about his scepticism. His prologue shows that doubts about the Popish Plot were being made public. Even Shadwell's play acknowledges this development by presenting the audience with characters who openly express their scepticism about the plot: Tegue and Smerk. Shadwell's play represents part of a wider Whig attempt to keep the Popish Plot alive.

The irony of the play's stance towards the plot is that it depends on the audience's prior belief in it. While Tegue and Smerk's sceptical doubts are shouted down in the play by the 'good' characters (that is, those characters whose principles are Whiggish), they are never really disproved. There is no direct evidence on stage of Tegue's involvement in any kind of plot; he makes frequent remarks about having been taught by the Jesuits, and expresses a readiness to take false oaths, but there is nothing on stage to suggest that he is actively plotting any crime, other than those crimes that, in 1681, were associated with the practice of his religion. At the end of the play, Tegue is arrested by a messenger:

MESS. I must beg your pardon Sir, I have a warrant against this *Kelly, Alias Tegue O Divelly* – he is accus'd for being in the Plot.
SIR EDW. My house is no refuge for Traytors Sir.
PRIEST. Aboo, boo, boo! by my shalvaation dere is no Plot, and I vill not go vid you. Dou art a damn'd Fanaatick, if dou dosht shay dere is a Plot. Dou art a Presbiterian Dogg.
MESS. No striving, come a long with me:
PRIEST. Phaat vill I do: I am Innocent as de Child dat is to be Born; and if they vill hang me, I vill be a shaint indeed. *My hanging Speech was made for me, long a go by de Jesuits, and I have it ready, and I vill live and dy by it, by my shoule.*
(v.686–96)

Sir Edward has not played any role in Tegue's arrest: he is therefore freed from any implication of cruelty or zealotry. Nonetheless, Sir Edward is extremely quick to conclude – solely on the basis of an accusation – that Tegue is guilty. Tegue himself never admits this, instead proclaiming his innocence. The censored lines at the end of his speech raise doubts about Tegue's innocence since they imply that the Jesuits have ordered him to maintain his innocence, even on the scaffold, despite his guilt. These lines, had they been permitted to be performed, would have been highly significant. All of the various people executed for taking part in the plot maintained their innocence to the end, despite the fact that they were offered incentives to confess.[53] As the executions mounted up, the continuing absence of even one confession presented a powerful argument against the reality of the plot – an argument which the play seeks to undermine in the censored lines.

In the preface to the play, Shadwell added further clarification as to Tegue's guilt. Here, he identifies the priest as 'Kelly (one of the Murderers of Sir Edmond-Bury Godfrey) which I make to be his feign'd Name, and Tegue O Divelly his true one'. Sir Edmund Godfrey, the magistrate who first took Titus Oates's deposition, was later found dead in circumstances that remain mysterious.[54] His death provided much of the impetus for the investigation of the Popish Plot. Some of Godfrey's supposed murderers were convicted on the testimony of Miles Prance, who became another witness to this part of the plot. Prance was a Catholic gold- and silversmith, who was arrested after neighbours had informed on him for making 'ill-considered remarks in favour of the Jesuits', and eventually testified that he was party to a plot to murder Godfrey. Involved in this plot were three of his acquaintances, who were eventually executed, but the ringleaders were said to be two Irish priests, Fathers Girald and Kelly, who escaped capture.[55]

Audience members who had followed the trials would have been able to identify Tegue as Father Kelly without the benefit of Shadwell's preface from his early exchange with Sir Edward, in which he reveals that '[t]hey do put the Name of *Kelly* upon me, Joy, but by my fait

---

53 Kenyon, pp. 206–07, describes evidence suggesting that the consistent denials and scaffold speeches of the people convicted – many of which were published – began to have an impact on public opinion.
54 Kenyon, pp. 88–89. Kenyon discusses a variety of theories which have been advanced, some of which are almost as outlandish as the plot itself, in an appendix; pp. 302–09.
55 Prance's story is told in detail in Alan Marshall, *The Strange Death of Edmund Godfrey: Plots and Politics in Restoration London* (Stroud: Sutton, 1999), pp. 124–30.

I am call'd by my own right Name, *Tegue O Divelly*' (III.109–10). Sir Edward has previously said of Tegue that 'he may be out of the damn'd Plot, if any Priest was? Sure they would never trust this Fool' (III.101–03). Sir Edward's fault, it seems, is that he is too kind-hearted and trusting: he is by the end of the play revealed to be wrong about Tegue, whose alias would probably have been familiar to most, if not all, of the play's original audience.

Tegue's declaration that he is 'Innocent as de Child dat is to be born' also has contemporary significance, as it closely resembles a phrase used in a pamphlet account of one of the men convicted for the murder of Edmund Godfrey. Samuel Smith, the Ordinary of Newgate prison, wrote that Robert Green 'lookt upon himself as Innocent as the Child Unborn'.[56] According to the pamphlet, however, there was no doubt in Smith's mind as to Green's guilt: rather, he thought that Green considered himself innocent because he had received a 'Popish absolution'. This is probably the sense in which Tegue's statement was intended to be understood by contemporary audience members. Despite his arrest at the end of the play, Tegue reappears in another of Shadwell's plays, *The Amorous Bigotte* (1690). In this play, Tegue, having escaped to Spain, confirms that he was 'deep in our brave Plott'.[57]

Nevertheless, within the onstage action, there is no clear evidence of Tegue's involvement in any plot, still less a murder. The audience is assumed to believe in his guilt before they have even arrived at the theatre. It would have been quite easy for Shadwell to provide more concrete evidence within the play – to demonstrate, unambiguously, that Tegue is guilty. Instead of appealing to evidence, however, the play relies on the authority of King and Parliament to establish the reality of the plot. Within the framework of a play that conspicuously rejects various forms of authority, this appeal seems eccentric. As noted, Shadwell distinguishes between 'Evidences' and 'Actions' in relation to the witches in his preface. The Evidence for witchcraft in the play is weak, even though the Actions are real; but in the case of the Popish Plot, there is little Evidence and no Action. The play seems unconcerned about whether Tegue's guilt can be proven or even if he is guilty at all; it demands his execution regardless.

---

56 Samuel Smith, *An Account of the Behaviour of the Fourteen Late Popish Malefactors, whil'st in Newgate* (London, 1679), p. 10. Marshall also refers to this pamphlet (p. 136).
57 Thomas Shadwell, *The Amorous Bigotte* (London, 1690), p. 3.

Shadwell's play appears at first sight to take a reasoned and sceptical attitude towards witchcraft. But on closer examination, it can be seen that the play relies not on evidence or reason but on faith: faith that there is always a natural explanation for the seemingly supernatural phenomenon of witchcraft, and faith in the existence of a Popish Plot. The former faith may be consistent with reason, but the latter is ultimately backed up by an appeal to authority and the threat implied by the accusation of 'impudence'. This appeal to authority – the authority of king (despite Charles's own scepticism towards the plot) and Parliament – is itself paradoxical, given the play's championing of 'the people's liberties' against the authority of Church and, implicitly, monarch.

The Lancashire Witches shows that scepticism about witchcraft need not be humane; it can be motivated by very different impulses. The play's unsubtle attack on witchcraft belief serves the more important purpose of attacking Catholicism and Shadwell's political opponents, the Tories. Casting the Tory, High Church, Catholic, and crypto-Catholic characters[58] as the hunters of witches neatly reverses the situation outside the theatre. Sir Edward's expressions of sympathy for the 'poor old woman' persecuted so cruelly by Sir Jeffrey and his followers establish the Whig characters as the humane ones – but it was the Whigs, outside the theatre, who were at this point engaging in the bloodthirsty persecution of Catholics, while Tories such as Roger L'Estrange attempted to cast doubt on the reality of the Plot in an attempt to end such persecution and resist the growing demands for the Exclusion Bill.

The doubts of the rational characters about witchcraft are used to establish them as, like Shadwell himself, 'somewhat costive of belief'. These doubts confirm their credibility and good judgement, reinforcing the audience's faith in their conclusions about the plot. Scepticism about witchcraft therefore supports belief in the existence of the plot. This feature of the play is very similar to the kind of rhetorical scepticism that can be found in other witchcraft plays, such as *The Witch of Edmonton*. The difference in this case is that the scepticism about witchcraft itself is apparently genuine; nevertheless, this scepticism is used to reinforce belief in a witch-hunt of a similar kind.

---

58 Sir Jeffrey can be identified as another character who is 'Popishly affected' by his use of the exclamation 'By'r Lady', and the clown character Clod also says 'by the Mass' and 'by'r Lady'.

The play identifies Catholics as the real witches, contrasting Tegue with the imagined witches of the title. Both priest and witches are arrested by the end of the play, but before this they exchange words:

> PRIEST.   Dost dou mutter? By my shoule I vill hang dee Joy; a plaague taak dee indeed.
> M. DICK. Thou art a Popish Priest, and I will hang thee.
> (v.196–98)

The witch has the last word in this argument, and contemporary audiences cannot have been unaware that Mother Dickenson's threat was, in the world outside the theatre, much more likely to be realised than Tegue's: during the Popish Plot, many more Catholics were executed than alleged witches. Heywood and Brome's seemingly credulous play tends not to support the persecution of witches, suggesting instead the dangers of Doughty's unrestrained credulity. In Shadwell's play, despite the expressions of sympathy for supposed witches, there is no mercy whatsoever for the 'real' witches. For Shadwell, just as for John Bale almost 150 years earlier, those real witches are not malevolent old women, but Catholics and their sympathisers.

Conclusion

The popularity of early modern English witchcraft as an object of historical study, both for academics and for general readers, is arguably out of proportion to the extent of the phenomenon. The early modern period saw a large number of executions for the crime, estimated at around 45,000 for the whole of Europe. However, these executions were spread out over a very long period – about 300 years – and were unevenly distributed geographically and temporally. Within this European context, England had relatively low levels of witchcraft persecution, and it appears to have had an unusually low execution rate as well.[1] Garthine Walker points out that women were much more likely to be charged with, for example, theft than with stereotypically 'female' crimes like witchcraft and infanticide, which were rarely prosecuted even during the Elizabethan peak.[2]

Of course, most people now will think that even one conviction for witchcraft would have been one too many. But in the context of a criminal justice system under which people could be executed for what would now be regarded as relatively minor thefts, the penalties for witchcraft (which typically only attracted a death sentence in cases of murder by witchcraft or repeat offences) were

---

1 Brian P. Levack, *The Witch-hunt in Early Modern Europe*, 4th edn (London: Routledge, 2016, first edn published in 1987), p. 21; Levack's estimates have been revised downwards since the first edition. Other recent surveys of witchcraft history provide very similar estimates: see, for example, Julian Goodare, *The European Witch-hunt* (London: Routledge, 2016), pp. 410–11; Hutton, p. 180. Some much higher estimates for the total number of executions in Europe – well into the millions – have been made, but lack any foundation in documentary evidence and tend to appear in polemical feminist texts. Diane Purkiss discusses such claims in a chapter aptly entitled 'A Holocaust of One's Own' (*The Witch in History*, pp. 7–29).
2 Garthine Walker, *Crime, Gender, and Social Order in Early Modern England* (Cambridge: Cambridge University Press, 2003), p. 4.

Conclusion

surprisingly lenient. The scarcity of prosecutions and the low rate of executions in England, notwithstanding the ferocious rhetoric of some demonologists, suggest not 'hysteria' or 'mania' – words still used too often to characterise witchcraft belief – but relative indifference, for most people, most of the time.

The underlying importance of witchcraft belief was that it provided a means of combating a broader scepticism that was perceived to threaten fundamental religious beliefs. The problem was that claims about the existence of witchcraft also tended to generate scepticism, necessitating a variety of strategies for counteracting it. I have used the term 'rhetorical scepticism' to describe many such strategies. One common version of rhetorical scepticism involves illustrating the process by which the author's own sceptical doubt has purportedly been overcome. Such a strategy is evident in a number of pamphlet accounts of witchcraft, and a dramatic analogue for it can also be detected in several early modern plays. Scepticism of this type, which establishes belief on firmer grounds, is evident not only in witchcraft belief but in a wide range of related questions in early modern thought. One particularly sophisticated version of it is exemplified by the Cartesian philosophical method.

Another version of rhetorical scepticism, used more by demonologists than by pamphlet writers, supported belief by ceding as much ground as possible to the claims of sceptics. The degree of consensus evident in the stated views of people who seem nonetheless to be at loggerheads is a notable feature of the early modern witchcraft debate. Where a sceptical argument posits melancholy as a cause of imagined witchcraft, a believer responds by accepting that witches suffer from melancholy, and adding that this is what drives them to make their bargain with the devil. Witches are tricksters who are only capable of 'juggling', a sceptic would say. The believer replies that it is precisely these juggling tricks that have been taught to the witches by the devil. Witches have no real magical power, argue the sceptics; the believers agree, and add that the devil inflicts supernatural harm himself, then tricks the witch into believing that she was responsible. The symptoms of bewitchment have natural causes, say the sceptics. The believers point out that the devil, following the instructions of a witch, is able to exacerbate the symptoms of natural disease. It is difficult to win an argument with somebody who keeps agreeing with you.

One of the simplest ways to attack witchcraft scepticism was to launch an irrelevant *ad hominem* attack, casting aspersions on the piety of the doubters. A more sophisticated version of this tactic involved representing scepticism as absurd, because it was so evidently contradicted by an abundance of evidence. If the sceptics were 'fools or madmen' who did not 'want to believe', as Bodin put it, then their scepticism was obviously comparable to the impious and irrational doubt of atheists. But this impious scepticism also implied foolish credulity: in allowing themselves to be blinded to the obvious truth, the sceptics had been taken in by the tricks of the devil, just as the ignorant village witch had been. Sceptics were thereby portrayed as both impiously sceptical and foolishly credulous, with the result that they came to seem witch-like themselves – and were sometimes even explicitly accused of witchcraft.

Another recurring theme in the fight against scepticism is the distinction made between particular and general instances. Any given example of witchcraft may be fraudulent, as a great many witchcraft theorists acknowledged, but this does not prove that all cases are fraudulent. The point is of course logically valid, even if one might suspect it to be made disingenuously in many cases, and it also neatly places the burden of proof on the sceptic. This allowed supporters of witchcraft belief to acknowledge the existence of fraudulent or otherwise unsatisfactory accusations of witchcraft: King James I, to take a prominent example, made much of his ability to distinguish between real and pretended cases of witchcraft and possession. However, the expression of both general belief and scepticism as to particular cases could also be used as a way of slowly backing away from beliefs which were no longer convincing but could not easily be abandoned, as happened with the judges who began to lose faith in the Popish Plot later in the seventeenth century. While scepticism as to a particularly unlikely case – such as that of the Lancashire witches of 1634 – was compatible with more general belief, establishing a distinction between general principles and particular instances could also be a way of gently dropping all the practical implications of belief that no longer appealed, without having to recant the belief and thereby provoke controversy.

The historical phenomenon of belief in witchcraft, or any confidently held belief now known to have been false, raises a number of wider epistemological questions with potentially sceptical answers which people in the present would do well to consider. A phenomenon like witchcraft illustrates the urgency of questions about how we arrive at our knowledge, whether we can be entirely confident in it, and whether we are aware of the kinds of unconscious and potentially inaccurate assumptions about causation which are concealed in everyday beliefs. It is tempting to brush such questions aside by comparing witchcraft belief in the seventeenth century with beliefs that are, in our own time, considered marginal in various ways. This is what the historian of witchcraft C. L. Ewen did in his own time, almost a century ago:

> It is customary for the present generation of critical writers to express amazement at the credulity and ignorance of the seventeenth century witch persecutors, yet considered impartially such gullibility and want of understanding have their counterpart in the twentieth century in the delusions of the spirit seekers, and their trusting belief in the genuineness and integrity of the numerous charlatans and tricksters, who provide them with psychic manifestations ... the extraordinary beliefs now held are the result of insufficient knowledge of such natural phenomena as telepathy, magnetism, hypnosis, and possibly other forces as yet unknown and unnamed, someday to be clearly explained by our scientists, and to be common knowledge of the man-in-the-street of the future.[3]

Ewen's belief in 'our scientists' and the ultimate triumph of rationalism reveals a faith in so-called Enlightenment values which are no longer fashionable, and which might strike readers today as naive. The idea that a basic grasp of, say, quantum mechanics is or ever could be 'common knowledge' certainly seems optimistic, and the assumption that higher levels of collective knowledge about the functioning of the world necessarily reduce the quantity of false beliefs in the general population is questionable. Furthermore, while he is clearly aware of the credulity of his contemporaries in respect of psychic phenomena, Ewen's apparent belief in the 'natural phenomenon' of telepathy suggests that the credulity of others is always easier to spot than one's own – a disconcerting thought for any author aiming for a degree of healthy scepticism.

Since even sceptical writers such as Ewen – or, for that matter, Reginald Scot – could not avoid adopting some beliefs that are now thought to be groundless, it has to be accepted that as individuals we are all, in practice, obliged to take much of our knowledge on trust. Some of this 'knowledge' is virtually certain to be wrong (determining exactly which parts are wrong is, of course, another matter). Despite living in an era in which people tend to regard their own widely shared beliefs about the world as grounded on evidence, as individuals we are as dependent on the received authority

---

3 Ewen, *Witch Hunting and Witch Trials*, p. 113.

of experts for our knowledge as ever. If anything, given the sheer volume of human knowledge – and pseudo-knowledge – in the present time, we may, as individuals, be more dependent on authority than ever; nobody could ever have the time and expertise to investigate every claim to truth independently. Montaigne's sceptical statement quoted in Chapter 1, which dates back more than 400 years and was not new then, remains true: as individuals, our knowledge of the world derives overwhelmingly from 'custom' rather than 'science'. This being the case, it seems to me that taking some of our beliefs on trust cannot be described as irrational. There is nothing irrational about accepting that other people know more about a given topic than one does oneself. From a strictly intellectual perspective, therefore, belief in witchcraft cannot be called irrational, given that so much of the knowledge that people absorbed, and upon which their understanding of the world was based – in particular, the belief in spirits as ubiquitous and deeply involved in the functioning of the physical world – supported it.

However, there is more to be said about the rationality (or otherwise) of believing in witchcraft. Joseph Glanvill produced a number of apparently compelling arguments in favour of witchcraft belief. He correctly pointed out a number of logical flaws in some typical sceptical arguments against witchcraft, and he often chided opponents for not keeping an open mind. This, it is sometimes said, is evidence of Glanvill's rationality and the defensibility of witchcraft belief within its early modern context. But it is not always rational to keep an open mind, especially if that open-mindedness is not evenly applied. Glanvill's 'open-minded' arguments are reminiscent of those of anti-Stratfordians, for whom no evidence of Shakespeare's authorship can ever be conclusive, while no alternative authorship theory can ever be too far-fetched. To apply an exacting standard of sceptical doubt to arguments one disagrees with while being disproportionately indulgent towards claims one happens to agree with, without examining the grounds for one's own beliefs, is surely not 'rational', though it may be widespread. But this is what Glanvill does, and in this sense his arguments, notwithstanding their logical consistency, are not rational but self-deluding, and this was as much the case when the arguments were written as it is now.

While the experience of daily life in early modern England was informed by different types of beliefs and assumptions, it was still a life governed, in reality, by the same physical laws as those in operation in our own time. Magical powers were not real, and the direct evidence for them must, therefore, have been flawed. In fact,

Conclusion

even supporters of witchcraft belief often conceded that the evidence put forward in cases of witchcraft *was* very often flawed. Witchcraft always produced some kind of scepticism in early modern people, including those early modern people who believed in witchcraft. It was accepted as an explanation because it worked, or could be made to work, intellectually, but also, and perhaps more importantly, because it performed various functions. By confronting their own incredulity, and defeating it, theologically inclined believers in witchcraft were able to reaffirm their religious faith – faith which was under increasing pressure from the huge uncertainties in religion arising from the Reformation. Witchcraft belief worked on a different level in the case of actual prosecutions. Inconvenient people who could not easily be got rid of in any other way – in England, at least, these people were almost always women – could be disposed of using the laws against witchcraft. The suspension of disbelief required by the fictions of witchcraft could be achieved by people motivated by fear, grief, or hatred.

It is important to recognise that such disbelief was, to some degree, always likely to be present. It was possible for early modern people to believe that women could feed the devil with their own blood in exchange for the power to harm their neighbours on the basis of the prevalent understanding of the world. But it cannot have been *very* easy. Every text on witchcraft that has been discussed in this study bears some trace of the difficulty of belief and the ubiquity of scepticism. Such scepticism could be overcome, but it was never overcome without some kind of ulterior motive. This is not to say that all accusations of witchcraft involved conscious fraud, although some cases did. But it is to say that any accusation of witchcraft, assertion of the existence of witchcraft, or instance of credit being granted to such claims, must have required some kind of effort to achieve the necessary suspension of disbelief in oneself and, when necessary, others.

Suspension of disbelief in relation to implausible and unfounded claims about historical reality continues to happen in our own time. Like the history of witchcraft, the history of witchcraft history can be disheartening, full of dubious scholarly activity and the kind of practices that Reginald Scot would have referred to as cozening. The prolific but unscrupulous scholar Montague Summers, who wrote on witchcraft in the 1920s, 1930s, and 1940s, made a name for himself by claiming to believe that witches really had been servants of the devil, to say nothing of vampires and werewolves. Margaret Murray studied the documentary evidence of the history of witchcraft and twisted it beyond recognition in her desire to find evidence for the 'Dianic cult' she wished to believe in.[4] Although it has now been comprehensively discredited as a historical explanation, Murray's thesis provided the founding myth for the creation of a new religion, Wicca, which it inspired in the mid-twentieth century. Murray's belief in a witch cult, though inaccurate, was so appealing to some that it ended up creating what might be described as a real (albeit harmless) witch cult. Later feminists developed Murray's narrative but emphasised the violent repression of the witches instead of the supposed religious aspects of witchcraft itself, exaggerating the numbers involved in the process and projecting a romanticised image of martyrdom on to the victims. Commenting on the largely fabricated claims made by some feminist writers on witchcraft, which are still circulating widely, Diane Purkiss writes that

> [t]his is, above all, a narrative of the Fall, of paradise lost. It is a story about how perfect our lives would be – how perfect we women would be, patient, kind, self-sufficient – if it were not for patriarchy and its violence. It is often linked with another lapsarian myth, the myth of an originary matriarchy, through the themes of mother-daughter learning and of matriarchal religions as sources of witchcraft. This witch-story explains the origins and nature of good and evil. It is a religious myth, and the religion it defines is radical feminism.[5]

It is ironic that writers who tend to identify patriarchal institutions such as the Church as responsible for witchcraft persecution have used the history of witchcraft to create 'a narrative of the Fall'. This is essentially what Walter Stephens claims Renaissance witchcraft theory itself was for: interpreting reality in ways that tended to support the religious beliefs (or control the undesirable scepticism towards those beliefs) of the author. Put to such use, witchcraft continues to be a means of self-delusion, a way of interpreting, or entirely reinventing, history in order to create a picture of reality that is more compliant with the ideological requirements of the present. In this sense, those authors identified by Purkiss who have used witchcraft to strengthen their own faith are not the intellectual opponents of the misogynistic demonologists, but their intellectual descendants.

---

4 Margaret Murray, *The Witch-cult in Western Europe* (Oxford: Oxford University Press, 1921).
5 Purkiss, *The Witch in History*, p. 8.

Conclusion

If the significance of witchcraft as a historical phenomenon has often been exaggerated, it may be because its appeal to the imagination was, and remains, powerful. Witchcraft belief appeals to a variety of people now for a variety of reasons. For many people, perhaps, the appeal is that witchcraft makes us feel good about ourselves; we can look back at the foolish people of the past and smile at their credulity. For others, in particular academic researchers, witchcraft appeals because it presents a challenge: we cannot easily comprehend the mentalities behind it. Unfortunately, attempts to account for witchcraft persecution have sometimes seemed to reveal as much about the imagination of the explainers as about the thing explained. Margaret Murray's pagan sect resembled the kind of fertility cult that was fashionable in the interwar period. In the 1960s, efforts were made to explain stories about witchcraft partly in terms of the ingestion of hallucinogenic drugs – a topic of special interest and concern in that era, but a hopelessly inadequate explanation for the phenomenon it sought to explain.[6] More recently, Wolfgang Behringer has suggested that the Little Ice Age, which led to poor harvests and starvation in many parts of Europe, might account for the persecution of witches, who were often believed to be responsible for extreme weather conditions.[7] Behringer's hypothesis is much more valuable than the others referred to, as it is based on historical evidence rather than supposition. Nevertheless, in invoking the effects of a changing climate, Behringer's view is very much an explanation of its time, and one which speaks to the concerns of the twenty-first century.

Witchcraft was imaginatively appealing to many early modern people as well, and many of them, too, may have found it appealing precisely because it was so difficult to account for. Witchcraft stories are often described as sensationalist, and they would not have been sensational if they had been easy to believe, although the surprising and exciting nature of such stories might make people *want* to believe them. Stories about witchcraft seem to have been at their least exciting early in the period covered by this book; up to around 1590, pamphlet accounts of witchcraft tend to be dry and

---

6 Michael Ostling, 'Babyfat and Belladonna: Witches' Ointment and the Contestation of Reality', *Magic, Ritual, and Witchcraft* 11:1 (2016), 30–72, provides a thorough account of, and response to, explanations of this type, which are occasionally still offered.

7 Wolfgang Behringer, *Witches and Witch-Hunts: A Global History* (Cambridge: Polity, 2004), pp. 87–89.

legalistic.[8] That this period also saw the main peak in prosecutions is perhaps no coincidence. If witchcraft was taken relatively seriously it may have been less entertaining, which suggests a partial explanation for the gap between Elizabethan understandings of 'real' witchcraft and the representation of witches in the drama of the time. The imaginative appeal of witchcraft in the early modern period, assuming that it can be measured in terms of the frequency with which it is mentioned in plays, seems to have grown in inverse relation to its real-world significance during the period covered in this study. Even in its Elizabethan heyday, however, scepticism towards witchcraft was considerable.

Perhaps partly as a result of this uncertainty about the phenomenon of witchcraft, witchcraft appeared in plays without being the subject of them for a large part of the early modern period, and was often used to raise more important concerns. The early Reformers used witchcraft as a symbol of Catholic superstition, Elizabethan dramatists portrayed varieties of witchcraft which were almost entirely divorced from the imagined everyday or demonological realities of it, and the Jacobean witchcraft drama was primarily concerned not with the activities of malevolent women but with high politics and the question of legitimate kingship. The issues of scepticism and belief, however, are central to some of these plays in that they depict the psychology of witches, and the clients duped by them, as characterised by both scepticism and credulity. Few plays from this period, however, examine belief in witchcraft itself. The main dramatic function of witchcraft is symbolic, meaning that the issue of belief itself need not be dealt with. At the same time, witchcraft is treated relatively seriously and scepticism about its reality remains submerged and is rarely, if ever, expressed or addressed.

Things changed as cases of witchcraft became less and less frequently prosecuted. Drama moved closer to the phenomenon of witchcraft in the perceived reality of early modern England, and further away from the witch stories of the ancient world, which were more likely to be perceived to be fictional. *The Witch of Edmonton* was the first witchcraft play to be based directly on a real case – an event which had by this time become a rarity. The historical case of Elizabeth Sawyer must have generated considerable scepticism and bemusement, judging by the tetchy and defensive pamphlet account of it written by Henry Goodcole. The play inspired

---

8 Gibson, *Reading Witchcraft*, pp. 107–08.

Conclusion

by the case represents (like Goodcole's account) an attempt to tread a line between outright scepticism and downright credulity, acknowledging the excesses of Sawyer's persecutors while affirming the reality of her crimes. The play builds scepticism into its plot and dialogue, but it does so in order to defeat a more thoroughgoing and threatening scepticism which remains unseen and offstage.

Together with *Macbeth*, *The Witch of Edmonton* is the most successful attempt to create a plausible picture of witchcraft. The plausibility of these two plays is partly a consequence of the marginality of the witches within them: making the witches less central circumvents the problems of witchcraft belief to some extent. In this way, both plays make the worlds they depict able to credibly support the existence of the witches. *Macbeth* does this by making its dramatic world so full of uncertainty that the existence of witches is unsurprising. *The Witch of Edmonton* takes the opposite approach; rather than making the everyday world as magical and full of uncertainty as the witches, it makes its witch as human, and mundane, as the rest of the community of Edmonton. Witchcraft becomes plausible because it is made ordinary – even, as Mother Sawyer puts it, 'universal'. It is not possible to know how audiences reacted to these depictions, but *The Witch of Edmonton* does at least as much as Goodcole's pamphlet to justify the execution of Elizabeth Sawyer, which had taken place earlier in the same year the play was first performed.

In the case of *The Late Lancashire Witches*, scepticism about witchcraft in general is emphatically denied by the play in what a contemporary audience member identified as its only serious scene. But combined with this apparent display of belief are highly sceptical undertones about the particular case which occasioned the play. Furthermore, the question of scepticism more generally – philosophical scepticism about the possibility of knowledge and the reliability of the senses – is among the concerns raised within the play. The play gestures towards anti-sceptical answers to these wider questions, but in addressing them at all it bears witness to their increasing influence in the 1630s. The close connection between philosophical scepticism and scepticism about witchcraft within the play also suggests that these phenomena are far from irrelevant to each other, even if the nature of the connection between them is not as straightforward as has sometimes been assumed.

Dramatic representations of witchcraft incorporate the mutually dependent themes of belief and scepticism in a variety of ways, often as a means of coping with the inherent implausibility of witchcraft. Scepticism and belief are just as important themes within dramatic works as they are within purportedly factual works on witchcraft, although they tend to make themselves known in subtler ways. *Dr Faustus* and *Macbeth* represent in their title characters the combination of credulity and scepticism which characterise both witch and witchcraft denier. *The Witch of Edmonton* provides an example of rhetorical scepticism in its questioning of the details of witchcraft beliefs and its mockery of the excessive credulity which threatens to undermine all belief. In using this sceptical technique, it is able to produce the most realistic and plausible village witch to be depicted on stage in the period. *The Late Lancashire Witches*, meanwhile, establishes a clear boundary between general belief and scepticism towards the particular instance in order to tread a delicate line between foolishness and impiety. The latter two tactics involve conceding an increasing amount of ground to the claims of sceptics, revealing an increasing degree of scepticism in the societies to which they are addressed.

Fiction of various kinds is clearly of great relevance to the phenomenon of witchcraft, and in this and previous studies the theatre has been found to display a kind of imaginative sympathy with witchcraft, since both are concerned with trickery and deceiving the senses. Partly as a result, previous studies of the theatre's role in witchcraft belief have often drawn conclusions that are optimistic and reassuring about the real-world impact of literature. Many scholars have regarded theatrical performance as inherently antagonistic towards belief in witchcraft, not least because of the obviously fictitious nature of theatrical representation. But witchcraft lore was frequently drawn from other sources which we would now describe as 'obviously' fictitious, such as Greek myth. While some authors had a view of such stories similar to that of most people in the present day, none could take this attitude for granted on the part of their readers or audiences. Many early modern writers had an interest in interpreting these myths as, for example, an approximation of the true Christian story. Moreover, even if the classical witches of the theatre were likely to be interpreted by their auditors as fictional, this need not rule out the possible existence of other, non-fictional witches.

Rather than undermining witchcraft belief, the Elizabethan theatre, at the historical moment in which persecution was at its peak, largely ignored it. Witches were repackaged as magicians or mythical characters, or even transformed into fairies, but belief in their existence was not questioned. Where 'real' witches did come into

Conclusion

the picture – which they did quite suddenly and without any obvious trigger – they were presented without much sympathy. Representations of witches such as Joan of Arc and Margery Jourdain were clearly possible to understand as historically accurate, and these representations are among the more hostile depictions of witches on stage. The earliest dramatic witch character to be based on recognisably demonological principles – Marlowe's Faustus – was quickly reabsorbed back into the discourse of witchcraft, providing Richard Bernard (and, as I have argued, possibly James I as well) with an example to be accounted for in demonological terms and further evidence demonstrating the existence of witchcraft. What is more, the play, performed again and again in various revivals and adaptations throughout the seventeenth century, played a significant role in disseminating understanding of demonology to those who could not – or did not – wish to read it for themselves. The theatre's role, in the case of this play at least, can hardly have been conducive to more widespread doubt about the existence of witches.

The accession of King James brought about an immediate change in dramatic writing on witchcraft. Playwrights in the Jacobean theatre recognised the new monarch's skilful exploitation of witchcraft belief for propagandistic ends and quickly followed suit, producing a number of plays which associated opposition to the King with witchcraft. Again, given the impetus for these representations of witchcraft, it is difficult to argue that the general tendency of such drama was sceptical, whatever the private beliefs of playwrights and audience members. It was not until the reign of Charles I that the theatre, together with the country as a whole, began to back away from witchcraft belief.

One striking circumstance in witchcraft drama is that the most sceptical plays – or, to put it another way, the plays that take witchcraft least seriously – tend to be those which are also politically radical. Political radicalism in the early modern English context tends to be almost synonymous with Protestant agitation. John Bale's *Three Laws* sets the tone for a sparse but long-lived tradition of explicitly or implicitly Protestant witchcraft plays. Bale's work of anti-papist propaganda depicts the Catholic faith and ritual of the time as barely distinguishable from witchcraft, exploiting a broader association of witchcraft and idolatry accepted by virtually all theologians at the time. The earlier Jacobean witch plays are neither radical nor sceptical in their support of the new monarch; but this pattern was brought to an abrupt end by the Overbury scandal and Thomas Middleton's play *The Witch*, Middleton's first venture into aligning himself with a clearly political brand of Calvinism which was beginning to emerge in the long build-up to the Civil War. *The Witch* sets a precedent for an even more radically antiauthoritarian play in the later Restoration, Shadwell's *The Lancashire Witches*. Witchcraft is largely a laughing matter in these plays, despite the fact that all three of them present serious polemical challenges to the established order of their respective times. The history of witchcraft in the theatre lends some support to those writers on witchcraft who associated disbelief in it with a threat to civil order as well as religion.

The fact that witchcraft is presented as absurd in these plays – although the reality of it is not actually denied before Shadwell's – also reveals a deeper Protestant scepticism towards witchcraft and other supernatural phenomena which finds its clearest expression in Reginald Scot's *Discoverie of Witchcraft*. Scepticism about the supernatural was a major intellectual strand of the Protestant Reformation, which could not help but raise uncomfortable questions about witchcraft, often in spite of the inclinations of those Protestants who were themselves hostile to witches. Of course, Protestant opinion on the matter of witchcraft specifically was not uniform; but the fact that both the greatest scepticism (Reginald Scot) and the strongest belief (Matthew Hopkins, William Perkins) tend to have been found among people who seem to have been reform-minded Protestants need not be regarded as coincidental, as the discussion of scepticism in Chapter 1 suggests. Both Shadwell's play and Bale's treat Catholic witchcraft as laughable but, at the same time, threatening. The seemingly contradictory status of witchcraft, especially in these highly polemical plays, is a consequence of the conflicting requirements of fear and contempt: Catholicism (and therefore witchcraft) must present a grave and supernatural threat and, at the same time, must be easily dismissed as mere superstition. Both scepticism and belief are required.

An earlier generation of historians tended to idealise scepticism about witchcraft, but scepticism about witchcraft need not be humane. George Gifford, a believer on the face of it, displayed far greater concern for the fate of his fellow humans than the hardline doubter Shadwell. When the theatre sets out to undermine or ridicule belief in witchcraft, as in Shadwell's *The Lancashire Witches*, the underlying motives for this scepticism are anything but enlightened. Shadwell's play sets itself up in opposition to witchcraft belief, and seemingly also to belief in any spiritual phenomena (perhaps even including the existence of God), but it is undoubtedly in favour of the

Conclusion

persecution of the group that had been symbolically depicted as witches, from Bale's time onwards: Catholics. The most recent example of a witch play that this study has examined, while it is the most sceptical, is also by far the most bloodthirsty, which speaks against the idea of the theatre in general as an agent of the 'liberating, tolerant doubt' which Stephen Greenblatt claims for Shakespeare.[9] It also speaks against any simplistic notion that human beings, simply by virtue of ceasing to believe in witches, might themselves have become more liberal or tolerant over the period. In its own way, Shadwell's play believes more fiercely in 'witches' and their persecution than any other play in this study.

Professions of scepticism towards and belief in early modern witchcraft discourse and theatre, regardless of the specific context in which they are expressed, always coexist. Within the psychology of the witch him- or herself, or the witches' clients, a mixture of scepticism and credulity can be found: both impious doubts as to the existence or mercy of God and foolish and impious faith in the power of the devil, which is of course entirely constrained by that of God. The plays themselves, too, tend to display both scepticism and credulity simultaneously. Some employ rhetorical scepticism in order to support a more credible and nuanced belief in witchcraft, and above all in the divinely controlled power of the devil. Conversely, the apparent scepticism of other plays towards witchcraft is often the result of what might seem to be unbridled credulity: the limitless power of Hecate in *The Witch* is part of what undermines any credibility she might otherwise have had as a witch. The plays that are sceptical about witchcraft also tend to be credulous in other respects – quite content to believe in almost any story about Sylvester II, Frances Carr, or Catholic plots against the state. Scepticism and credulity in connection with witchcraft are not fixed positions in a debate but argumentative tools within that debate: they are not diametrically opposed, but interdependent.

---

9 Greenblatt, p. 127.

Bibliography

Manuscript sources

London, British Library, MS Add. 62135
London, British Library, MS Harley 2302
London, British Library, MS Add. 25348

Plays

Axton, Marie (ed.), *Three Tudor Classical Interludes* (Cambridge: D. S. Brewer, 1982)
Bale, John, *The Complete Plays of John Bale*, edited by Peter Happé (Cambridge: Brewer, 1986)
Beaumont, Francis and John Fletcher, *The Knight of the Burning Pestle* (London: J. M. Dent, 1913)
Campion, Thomas, *The Description of a Maske: Presented in the Banqueting Roome at Whitehall, on Saint Stephens Night Last at the Mariage of the Right Honourable the Earle of Somerset: And the Right Noble the Lady Frances Howard* (London, 1614)
Corbin, Peter and Douglas Sedge (eds), *Three Jacobean Witchcraft Plays* (Manchester: Manchester University Press, 1986)
Davenant, William and William Shakespeare, *Macbeth* (London, 1674)
Dekker, Thomas, John Ford, and William Rowley, *The Witch of Edmonton*, edited by Peter Corbin and Douglas Sedge (Manchester: Manchester University Press, 1999)
Duffett, Thomas, *The Empress of Morocco* (London, 1674)
—— *Psyche Debauch'd* (London, 1678)
D'Urfey, Thomas, *Sir Barnaby Whigg* (London, 1681)
Greene, Robert, *Alphonsus King of Aragon* (Oxford: Malone Society, 1926)
—— *Friar Bacon and Friar Bungay* (London: Edward Arnold, 1964)
Heywood, Thomas, *The Wise Woman of Hogsdon* (London, 1638)
Heywood, Thomas and Richard Brome, *The Late Lancashire Witches*, edited by Laird Barber (New York: Garland, 1979)
—— *The Late Lancashire Witches*, Quarto Text, edited by Helen Ostovich, Richard Brome Online (www.hrionline.ac.uk/brome, 17 January 2010)

—— *The Witches of Lancashire* [i.e. *The Late Lancashire Witches*], edited by Gabriel Egan (London: Nick Hern, 2002)
Jonson, Ben, *The Complete Masques*, edited by Stephen Orgel (New Haven: Yale University Press, 1969)
Lyly, John, *Endymion*, edited by David Bevington (Manchester: Manchester University Press, 1996)
—— *Mother Bombie*, edited by Leah Scragg (Manchester: Manchester University Press, 2010)
—— *Sapho and Phao* (Oxford: Malone Society, 2002)
Marlowe, Christopher, *The Complete Works*, edited by Roma Gill (Oxford: Oxford University Press, 1990)
Marston, John, *Sophonisba*, edited by William Kemp (New York: Garland, 1979)
Middleton, Thomas, *The Witch*, edited by Elizabeth Schafer (London: A. & C. Black, 1994)
Munday, Anthony, *Fidele and Fortunio, the Two Italian Gentlemen* (London: Malone Society, 1910)
—— *John a Kent and John a Cumber*, edited by John Payne Collier (London, 1851)
Payne, Henry Neville, *The Fatal Jealousy* (London, 1673)
Peele, George, *The Old Wife's Tale*, edited by Charles Whitworth (London: A. & C. Black, 1996)
Rawlins, Thomas, *Tunbridge-Wells* (London, 1678)
Mr S., *Gammer Gurton's Needle*, edited by Charles Whitworth (London: A. & C. Black, 1997)
Shadwell, Thomas, *The Amorous Bigotte* (London, 1690)
—— *The Lancashire Witches*, edited by Judith Bailey Slagle (New York: Garland, 1991)
—— *The Tempest* (London, 1674)
Shakespeare, William, *King Henry VI Part 1*, edited by Edward Burns (London: Arden Shakespeare, 2000)
—— *King Henry VI Part 2*, edited by Ronald Knowles (London: Arden Shakespeare, 1999)
—— *Macbeth*, in *Comedies, Histories and Tragedies* (London, 1623)
—— *A Midsummer Night's Dream*, edited by Peter Holland (Oxford: Oxford University Press, 2008)
Stapylton, Robert, *The Step-Mother* (London, 1664)

Early modern printed works

A. M., *The Third Booke of Amadis de Gaule* (London, 1618)
Ady, Thomas, *A Candle in the Dark* (London, 1655)
Agrippa, Heinrich Cornelius, *Three Books of Occult Philosophy*, translated by J. F. (London, 1650)
—— *Of the Vanitie and Vncertaintie of Artes and Sciences*, translated by James Sandford (London, 1575)

Anon., *An Account of the Tryal and Examination of Joan Buts* (London, 1682)
Anon., *The Apprehension and Confession of Three Notorious Witches* (London, 1589)
Anon., *The Description of the Great Machines of the Descent of Orpheus into Hell* (London, 1661)
Anon., *A Detection of Damnable Driftes* (London, 1579)
Anon., *The Devill seen at St Albons* (London, 1648)
Anon., *The Divels Delusions* (London, 1649)
Anon., *The Examination of John Walsh* (London, 1566)
Anon., *Henry Cornelius Agrippa His Fourth Book of Occult Philosophy*, translated by Robert Turner (London, 1655)
Anon., *Lyfe of Saynt Edwarde Confessour and Kynge of Englande* (London, 1533)
Anon., *A Magical Vision, or a Perfect Discovery of the Fallacies of Witchcraft* (London, 1673)
Anon., *The Most Strange and Admirable Discoverie of the Three Witches of Warboys* (London, 1593)
Anon., *A Most True Discourse, Declaring the Life and Death of one Stubbe Peeter, being a Most Wicked Sorcerer* (London, 1590)
Anon., *A Pleasant Treatise of Witches* (London, 1673)
Anon., *A Rehearsall both Straung and True* (London, 1579)
Anon., *The Seuerall Notorious and Levvd Cousnages of Iohn West, and Alice West, Falsely Called the King and Queene of Fayries* (London, 1613)
Anon., *A Tryal of Witches Held at the Assizes at Bury St. Edmonds* (London, 1682)
Anon., *The Witches of Northamptonshire* (London, 1612)
Anon., *The Wonderfvll Discouerie of the Witch-crafts of Margaret and Philip Flower* (London, 1619)
Apuleius, Lucius, *The XI Bookes of the Golden Asse*, translated by William Adlington (London, 1566)
B., T., *Observations vpon Prince Rupert's White Dog, called Boy* (London, 1642)
Bernard, Richard, *A Gvide to Grand-Ivry Men* (London, 1627)
Browne, Thomas, *Pseudodoxia Epidemica* (London, 1646)
—— *Religio Medici* (London, 1643)
Casaubon, Meric, *Of Credulity and Incredulity in Things Divine & Spiritual* (London, 1670)
—— *A Treatise concerning Enthusiasme* (London, 1654)
Cooper, Thomas, *The Mystery of Witchcraft* (London, 1617)
Cotta, John, *The Triall of Witch-craft* (London, 1616)
Coxe, Francis, *A Short Treatise Declaringe the Detestable Wickednesse of Magicall Sciences* (London, 1561)
Daneau, Lambert, *A Dialogue of Witches* (London, 1575)
Davenport, John, *The Witches of Huntingdon* (London, 1646)
Dryden, John, *Absalom and Achitophel* (London, 1681)

Bibliography

Duke, Richard, *A Panegyrick upon Oates* (London, 1679)
Galis, Richard, *A Brief Treatise Containing the Most Strange and Horrible Cruelty of Elizabeth Stile alias Rockingham* (London, 1579)
Gaule, John, *Select Cases of Conscience Touching Witches and Witchcrafts* (London, 1646)
Gifford, George, *Dialogue concerning Witches and Witchcraftes* (London, 1593)
—— *A Discourse of the Subtill Practises of Deuilles by Witches and Sorcerers* (London, 1587)
Glanvill, Joseph and Henry More, *Saducismus Triumphatus* (London, 1688)
Goodcole, Henry, *The Wonderfull Discouerie of Elizabeth Sawyer, a Witch* (London, 1621)
Hall, John, *A Poesie in Forme of a Vision* (London, 1563)
Hammond, Henry, *Of Superstition* (Oxford, 1645)
Harsnett, Samuel, *Declaration of Egregious Popish Impostures* (London, 1603)
—— *Discovery of the Fraudulent Practises of Iohn Darrel* (London, 1599)
Hart, James, *Klinike, or the Diet of the Diseased* (London, 1633)
Heywood, Thomas, *Gynaikeion* (London, 1624)
—— *The Hierarchie of the Blessed Angels* (London, 1634)
Holinshed, Raphael, *The Third Volume of Chronicles* (London, 1587)
Holland, Henry, *A Treatise Against Witchcraft* (Cambridge, 1590)
Hopkins, Matthew, *The Discovery of Witches* (London, 1647)
Howard, Henry, *A Defensatiue against the Poyson of Supposed Prophecies* (London, 1620)
Hyperius, Andreas, *Two Common Places Taken out of Andreas Hyperius, a Learned Diuine* (London, 1581)
James I, *Daemonologie* (Edinburgh, 1597)
Jorden, Edward, *A Briefe Discouvrse of a Disaease Called the Suffocation of the Mother* (London, 1603)
Paracelsus, *Of the Supreme Mysteries of Nature*, translated by Robert Turner (London, 1655)
Perkins, William, *A Direction for the Government of the Tongue According to God's Word* (Cambridge, 1603)
—— *A Discourse of the Damned Art of Witchcraft So Farre Forth as It Is Reuealed in the Scriptures* (Cambridge, 1610)
Roberts, Alexander, *A Treatise of Witchcraft* (London, 1616)
Scot, Reginald, *The Discoverie of Witchcraft* (London, 1584)
Selden, John, *Table Talk* (London, 1689)
Smith, Samuel, *An Account of the Behaviour of the Fourteen Late Popish Malefactors, whil'st in Newgate* (London, 1679)
Stearne, John, *A Confirmation and Discovery of Witchcraft* (London, 1648)
W. W., *A True and Just Recorde, of the Information, Examination and Confession of all the Witches, taken at S. Oses in the countie of Essex* (London, 1582)

Wagstaffe, John, *The Question of Witchcraft Debated* (London, 1671)
Webster, John, *The Displaying of Supposed Witchcraft* (London, 1677)

Secondary sources

Addison, Joseph, *The Spectator* 117 (14 July 1711)
Alford, Stephen, *The Watchers: A Secret History of the Reign of Elizabeth I* (London: Penguin, 2013)
Allen, Marguerite De Huszar, *The Faust Legend: Popular Formula and Modern Novel* (New York: Lang, 1985)
Almond, Philip, *England's First Demonologist* (London: I. B. Tauris, 2011)
Alssid, Michael, *Thomas Shadwell* (New York: Twayne, 1967)
Anglo, Sidney, 'Reginald Scot's *Discoverie of Witchcraft*: Scepticism and Sadduceeism' in *The Damned Art*, edited by Sidney Anglo (London: Routledge & Kegan Paul, 1977)
Anon., 'Letchery did consult with witcherye', *Early Stuart Libels*, www.earlystuartlibels.net/htdocs/essex_nullity_section/F2.html
Apuleius, *Apologia*, translated by H. E. Butler (Oxford: Clarendon Press, 1909)
Arber, Edward (ed.), *A Transcript of the Registers of the Company of Stationers of London*, 5 vols (London: privately printed, 1875)
Arikha, Noga, *Passions and Tempers* (New York: HarperCollins, 2007)
Asprem, Egil, *The Problem of Disenchantment* (Leiden: Brill, 2014)
Atkinson, David, 'Moral Knowledge and the Double Action in *The Witch of Edmonton*', *Studies in English Literature, 1500–1900* 25:2 (Spring 1985), 419–37
St Augustine, *The City of God*, translated by John Healey, edited by R. V. G. Tasker, 2 vols (London: Dent, 1945)
—— *Confessions*, translated by E. B. Pusey (London: J. M. Dent, 1962)
Barry, Jonathan, *Witchcraft and Demonology in South-West England, 1640–1789* (Basingstoke: Palgrave Macmillan, 2012)
Bawcutt, N. W., 'Was Thomas Middleton a Puritan Dramatist?' *Modern Language Review* 94:4 (1999), 925–40
Behringer, Wolfgang, *Witches and Witch-Hunts: A Global History* (Cambridge: Polity, 2004)
Bellany, Alastair, *The Politics of Court Scandal in Early Modern England: News Culture and the Overbury Affair, 1603–1660* (Cambridge: Cambridge University Press, 2002)
Berger, Thomas L., William C. Bradford, and Sidney L. Sondergard, *An Index of Characters in Early Modern English Drama: Printed Plays, 1500–1660* (Cambridge: Cambridge University Press, 1998)
Berry, Herbert, *Shakespeare's Playhouses* (New York: AMS, 1987)
Bloom, Harold, *William Shakespeare's Macbeth* (New York: Infobase, 2010)
Bodin, Jean, *On the Demon-Mania of Witches*, translated by Randy A. Scott (Toronto: Centre for Reformation and Renaissance Studies, 1995)

Boehrer, Bruce, 'Gammer Gurton's Cat of Sorrows', *English Literary Renaissance* 39:2 (March 2009), 267-89
Bonavita, Helen Vella, 'Maids, Wives and Widows: Multiple Meaning and Marriage in *The Witch of Edmonton*', *Parergon* 23:2 (2006), 73-95
Booth, Roy, 'Witchcraft, Flight and the Early Modern English Stage', *Early Modern Literary Studies* 13.1 (May 2007) https://extra.shu.ac.uk/emls/13-1/bootwitc.htm
Bostridge, Ian, *Witchcraft and its Transformations, c.1650-c.1750* (Oxford: Oxford University Press, 1997)
Botica, Allan, 'Audience, Playhouse and Play in Restoration Theatre, 1660-1710' (unpublished doctoral thesis, Oxford University, Worcester College, 1986)
Braden, Gordon, 'An Overview', *The Oxford History of Literary Translation in English*, edited by Gordon Braden, Robert Cummings and Stuart Gillespie, vol. 2 (Oxford: Oxford University Press, 2010)
Bradley, A. C., *Shakespearean Tragedy* (Basingstoke: Macmillan, 1992, first published 1904)
Briggs, Katherine M., *Pale Hecate's Team* (London: Routledge & Kegan Paul, 1962)
Brodwin, Leonora, 'The Domestic Tragedy of Frank Thorney in *The Witch of Edmonton*', *Studies in English Literature, 1500-1900* 7:2 (Spring 1967), 311-28
Burke, Peter, *The Renaissance Sense of the Past* (London: Edward Arnold, 1969)
Burkert, Walter, *Greek Religion*, translated by John Raffan (Cambridge, MA: Harvard University Press, 1985, first published 1977 as *Griechische Religion*)
Burrow, John, *A History of Histories* (London: Penguin, 2009)
Burton, Robert, *The Anatomy of Melancholy* (London: J. M. Dent, 1972)
Bushnell, Rebecca W., *Tragedies of Tyrants* (Ithaca: Cornell University Press, 1990)
Calvin, Jean. *Institutes of the Christian Religion*, edited by John T. McNeil, translated by Ford Lewis Battles (Philadelphia: Westminster Press, 1960)
Canfield, J. Douglas, 'Shifting Tropes of Ideology in English Serious Drama, Late Stuart to Early Georgian', in *Cultural Readings of Restoration and Eighteenth-Century English Theatre*, edited by J. Douglas Canfield and Deborah C. Payne (Athens, GA: University of Georgia Press, 1995)
Carlton, Charles, *Archbishop William Laud* (London: Routledge & Kegan Paul, 1987)
Carver, Robert H. F., *The Protean Ass: The Metamorphoses of Apuleius from Antiquity to the Renaissance* (Oxford: Oxford University Press, 2007)
Clark, Arthur M., *Thomas Heywood* (Oxford: Blackwell, 1931)
Clark, Sandra, 'The Critical Backstory', in *Macbeth: A Critical Reader*, edited by John Drakakis and Dale Townshend (London: Bloomsbury, 2013)

Clark, Stuart, 'King James's *Daemonologie*: Witchcraft and Kingship', in *The Damned Art: Essays in the Literature of Witchcraft*, edited by Sydney Anglo (London: Routledge & Kegan Paul, 1985)
—— *Thinking with Demons* (Oxford: Oxford University Press, 1997)
—— *Vanities of the Eye* (Oxford: Oxford University Press, 2007)
Cohn, Norman, *Europe's Inner Demons* (London: Heinemann, 1975)
Comensoli, Viviana, *Household Business* (Toronto: University of Toronto Press, 1996)
Cottingham, John, *Descartes* (Oxford: Blackwell, 1986)
Cox, John, *The Devil and the Sacred in English Drama, 1350–1642* (Cambridge: Cambridge University Press, 2000)
Crocker, Robert, *Henry More* (Dordrecht: Kluwer, 2003)
Cruickshanks, Eveline, 'Peyton, Sir Robert', www.historyofparliamentonline.org/volume/1660-1690/member/peyton-sir-robert-1633-89
Curry, W. C., *Shakespeare's Philosophical Patterns* (Baton Rouge: Louisiana State University Press, 1937)
Darby, Trudi L., 'The Obsession with Spain', in *Thomas Middleton in Context*, edited by Suzanne Gossett (Cambridge: Cambridge University Press, 2011)
Darr, Orna Alyagon, *Marks of an Absolute Witch* (Farnham: Ashgate, 2011)
Davies, Julie A., 'Poisonous Vapours: Joseph Glanvill's Science of Witchcraft', *Intellectual History Review* 22:2 (2012), 163–79
Davies, R. Trevor, *Four Centuries of Witch Beliefs* (London: Methuen, 1947)
Davies, S. F., 'The Reception of Reginald Scot's Discovery of Witchcraft: Witchcraft, Magic, and Radical Religion', *Journal of the History of Ideas* 74:3 (July 2013), 381–401
Deats, Sara Munson, '*Doctor Faustus*: From Chapbook to Tragedy', *Essays in Literature* 3 (1976), 3–16
Descartes, René, *Meditations on First Philosophy*, translated by John Cottingham (Cambridge: Cambridge University Press, 1986)
Devine, Michael, 'Treasonous Catholic Magic and the 1563 Witchcraft Legislation: The English State's Response to Catholic Conjuring in the Early Years of Elizabeth I's Reign', in *Supernatural and Secular Power in Early Modern England*, edited by Marcus Harmes and Victoria Bladen (Farnham: Ashgate, 2015)
Dolan, Frances, *Dangerous Familiars* (Ithaca: Cornell University Press, 1994)
Duffy, Eamon, *The Stripping of the Altars* (New Haven: Yale University Press, 1992)
Durousseau, Clifford Hubert, 'Yah: A Name of God', *Jewish Bible Quarterly* 42 (2014), 21–26
Eagleton, Terry, *Myths of Power: A Marxist Study of the Brontës* (Basingstoke: Palgrave Macmillan, 2005, first published 1975)
Elmer, Peter, 'Towards a Politics of Witchcraft in Early Modern England', in *Languages of Witchcraft*, edited by Stuart Clark (Basingstoke: Macmillan, 2001)

—— *Witchcraft, Witch-Hunting, and Politics in Early Modern England* (Oxford: Oxford University Press, 2016)
Engle, Lars, 'Marlowe and the Self', in *Christopher Marlowe in Context*, edited by Emily C. Bartels and Emma Smith (Cambridge: Cambridge University Press, 2013)
Ewen, C. L., *Witch Hunting and Witch Trials* (London: Kegan Paul, 1929)
—— *Witchcraft and Demonianism* (London: Muller, 1933)
Fairfax, Edward, 'A Discourse of Witchcraft', in *Miscellanies of the Philobiblon Society* (London, 1859)
Fanger, Claire, *Rewriting Magic* (Pennsylvania: Pennsylvania State University Press, 2015)
Fielding, Henry, *Tom Jones* (Oxford: Oxford University Press, 2008)
Findlay, Alison, *Illegitimate Power* (Manchester: Manchester University Press, 1994)
Flint, Valerie, *The Rise of Magic in Early Medieval Europe* (Oxford: Clarendon Press, 1991)
—— *Witchcraft and Magic in Europe: Ancient Greece and Rome* (London: Athlone Press, 1999)
Floyd-Wilson, Mary, 'English Epicures and Scottish Witches', *Shakespeare Quarterly* 57:2 (Summer 2006), 131–61
Fox, Cora, *Ovid and the Politics of Emotion in Elizabethan England* (Basingstoke: Palgrave Macmillan, 2009)
Friesen, Ryan Curtis, *Supernatural Fiction in Early Modern Drama and Culture* (Brighton: Sussex Academic, 2010)
Gadamer, Hans-Georg, *Truth and Method*, translated by Joel Weinsheimer and Donald G. Marshall (New York: Continuum, 1998, first published 1960 as *Wahrheit und Methode*)
Gaisser, Julia Haig, *The Fortunes of Apuleius and the Golden Ass: A Study in Transmission and Reception* (Princeton: Princeton University Press, 2008)
Gardiner, S. R., 'On Certain Letters of Diego Sarmiento de Acuna, Count of Gondomar', *Archaeologia* 41 (1867), 151–86
Garrett, Julia M., 'Dramatizing Deviance: Sociological Theory and *The Witch of Edmonton*', *Criticism* 49:3 (Summer 2007), 327–75
Gaskill, Malcolm, 'Witchcraft in Early Modern Kent: Stereotypes and the Background to Accusations', in *New Perspectives on Witchcraft, Magic, and Demonology* edited by Brian Levack (New York: Routledge, 2001)
Gibney, John, *Ireland and the Popish Plot* (London: Palgrave Macmillan, 2009)
Gibson, Marion, 'Applying the Act of 1604: Witches in Essex, Northamptonshire and Lancashire before and after 1604', in *Witchcraft and the Act of 1604*, edited by John Newton and Jo Bath (Leiden: Brill, 2008)
—— *Possession, Puritanism and Print: Darrell, Harsnett, Shakespeare and the Elizabethan Exorcism Controversy* (London: Pickering & Chatto, 2006)
—— *Reading Witchcraft* (London: Routledge, 1999)

—— 'Understanding Witchcraft? Accusers' Stories in Print in Early Modern England', in *Languages of Witchcraft*, edited by Stuart Clark (Basingstoke: Macmillan, 2001)

Goddard, Harold, *The Meaning of Shakespeare* (Chicago: University of Chicago Press, 1951)

Goodare, Julian, *The European Witch Hunt* (London: Routledge, 2016)

Green, Richard Firth, *Elf Queens and Holy Friars* (Philadelphia: University of Pennsylvania Press, 2016)

Greenblatt, Stephen, 'Shakespeare Bewitched', in *New Historical Literary Study*, edited by Jeffrey N. Cox and Larry J. Reynolds (Princeton: Princeton University Press, 1993)

Grey, Anchitell (ed.), *Debates of the House of Commons*, vol. 7 (London, 1769), British History Online www.british-history.ac.uk/greys-debates/vol7

Hamlin, William M., 'Casting Doubt in Marlowe's *Doctor Faustus*', *Studies in English Literature, 1500–1900* 41:2 (Spring 2001), 257–75

Happé, Peter, *English Drama before Shakespeare* (London: Longman, 1999)

Harris, Anthony, *Night's Black Agents* (Manchester: Manchester University Press, 1980)

Heinemann, Margot, *Puritanism and Theatre: Thomas Middleton and Opposition Drama under the Early Stuarts* (Cambridge: Cambridge University Press, 1980)

Helms, M. W. and Leonard Naylor, 'Lee, Thomas I', www.historyofparliamentonline.org/volume/1660–1690/member/lee-thomas-i-1635-91

Henry, John, 'The Matter of Souls: Medical Theory and Theology in Seventeenth-Century England', in *The Medical Revolution of the Seventeenth Century*, edited by Roger K. French and Andrew Wear (Cambridge: Cambridge University Press, 1989)

Herrington, H. W., 'Witchcraft and Magic in the Elizabethan Drama', *The Journal of American Folklore* (1919), 447–85

Hinds, Peter, *The Horrid Popish Plot: Roger L'Estrange and the Circulation of Political Discourse in Late Seventeenth-Century London* (Oxford: Oxford University Press, 2010)

Hirsch, Brett D., 'Three Wax Images, Two Italian Gentlemen, and One English Queen', in *Magical Transformations on the Early Modern English Stage*, edited by Lisa Hopkins and Helen Ostovich (Farnham: Ashgate, 2014)

—— 'Werewolves and Severed Hands: Webster's *The Duchess of Malfi* and Heywood and Brome's *The Witches of Lancashire*', *Notes and Queries* 53:1 (March 2006), 92–94

Hirschfeld, Heather, *Joint Enterprises: Collaborative Drama and the Institutionalization of the English Renaissance Theatre* (Amherst: University of Massachusetts Press, 2004)

Hobbes, Thomas, *Leviathan* (London: Penguin, 1968)

Holbrook, Peter, 'Jacobean Masques and the Jacobean Peace', in *The Politics of the Stuart Court Masque*, edited by David Bevington and Peter Holbrook (Cambridge: Cambridge University Press, 1998)

Hopkins, Lisa, *The Female Hero in English Renaissance Tragedy* (Basingstoke: Palgrave Macmillan, 2002)
Howell, T. B. (ed.), *A Complete Collection of State Trials*, vol. 2 (London, 1816)
Hughes, Derek, *English Drama 1660–1700* (Oxford: Oxford University Press, 1996)
Hunter, G. K., *John Lyly: The Humanist as Courtier* (London: Routledge & Kegan Paul, 1962)
Hutton, Ronald, *The Witch* (New Haven: Yale University Press, 2017)
Institoris, Heinrich and Jakob Sprenger, *The Hammer of Witches*, translated by Christopher S. Mackay (Cambridge: Cambridge University Press, 2009)
Jobe, Thomas Harmon, 'The Devil in Restoration Science: The Glanvill-Webster Witchcraft Debate', *Isis* 72:3 (September 1981), 343–56
Johnstone, Nathan, *The Devil and Demonism in Early Modern England* (Cambridge: Cambridge University Press, 2006)
Jones, John Henry (ed.), *The English Faust Book* (Cambridge: Cambridge University Press, 1994)
Jones, Norman, 'Defining Superstitions: Treasonous Catholics and the Act against Witchcraft of 1563', in *State, Sovereigns and Society in Early Modern England*, edited by Charles Carlton (New York: St Martin's Press, 1998)
Jones-Davies, M. T. and Ton Hoenselaars, 'Masque of Cupids', in *The Collected Works of Thomas Middleton*, edited by Gary Taylor and John Lavagnino (Oxford: Oxford University Press, 2010)
Josephson-Storm, Jason A., *The Myth of Disenchantment* (Chicago: University of Chicago Press, 2017)
Kapitaniak, Pierre, 'Reginald Scot and the Circles of Power: Witchcraft, Anti-Catholicism and Faction Politics', in *Supernatural and Secular Power in Early Modern England*, edited by Marcus Harmes and Victoria Bladen (Farnham: Ashgate, 2015).
Kemp, Geoff (ed.), *Censorship and the Press, 1580–1720*, vol. 3 (London: Pickering & Chatto, 2009)
Kenyon, John, *The Popish Plot* (London: Phoenix, 2000)
Kernan, Alvin, *Shakespeare: The King's Playwright* (New Haven: Yale University Press, 1995)
Kesson, Andy, *John Lyly and Early Modern Authorship* (Manchester: Manchester University Press, 2014)
Kezar, Dennis, '*The Witch of Edmonton* and the Guilt of Possession', in *Solon and Thespis: Law and Theater in the English Renaissance*, edited by Dennis Kezar (Notre Dame: University of Notre Dame Press, 2007)
Kittredge, George Lyman, *Witchcraft in Old and New England* (Cambridge, MA: Harvard University Press, 1929)
Knights, Mark, *Politics and Opinion in Crisis, 1678–1681* (Cambridge: Cambridge University Press, 1994)

Kolb, Laura, 'Playing with Demons: Interrogating the Supernatural in Jacobean Drama', *Forum for Modern Language Studies* 43:4 (2007), 337–50

Kunz, Don R., *The Drama of Thomas Shadwell* (Salzburg: Institute for English Language and Literature, 1972)

Lancashire, Anne, '*The Witch*: Stage Flop or Political Mistake?' in *'Accompaninge the Players': Essays Celebrating Thomas Middleton, 1580–1980*, edited by Kenneth Friedenreich (New York: AMS Press, 1983)

Levack, Brian P., 'The Decline and End of Witchcraft Prosecutions', in *The Oxford Handbook of Witchcraft in Early Modern Europe and Colonial America*, edited by Brian P. Levack (Oxford, Oxford University Press: 2013)

—— *The Witch-hunt in Early Modern Europe*, 4th edn (London: Routledge, 2015, 1st edn published 1987)

Levin, Richard, 'My Magic Can Lick Your Magic', *Medieval & Renaissance Drama in England* 22 (2009), 201–28

Lewalski, Barbara K., *Writing Women in Jacobean England* (Cambridge, MA: Harvard University Press, 1993)

Lewis, C. S., *The Discarded Image* (Cambridge: Cambridge University Press, 1964)

Lewis, Matthew, *The Monk* (London: Bibliolis, 2010)

Lucan, *Pharsalia*, translated by Jane Joyce Wilson (Ithaca: Cornell University Press, 1993)

Lucretius, *On the Nature of Things*, translated by W. H. D. Rouse, rev. Martin F. Smith (Cambridge, MA: Harvard University Press, 1992)

Lucy, Margaret, *Shakespeare and the Supernatural* (Liverpool: Shakespeare Press, 1906)

Lund, Roger D., *Ridicule, Religion and the Politics of Wit in Augustan England* (Farnham: Ashgate, 2012)

MacCulloch, Diarmaid, *A History of Christianity* (London: Penguin, 2010)

—— *Tudor Church Militant* (London: Penguin, 1999)

Macfarlane, Alan, 'A Tudor Anthropologist: George Gifford's *Discourse* and *Dialogue*', in *The Damned Art*, edited by Sidney Anglo (London: Routledge & Kegan Paul, 1977)

—— *Witchcraft in Tudor and Stuart England* (London: Routledge & Kegan Paul, 1970)

Maguire, Nancy, *Regicide and Restoration* (Cambridge: Cambridge University Press, 1992)

Malay, Jessica L., 'Performing the Apocalypse: Sibylline Prophecy and Elizabeth I', in *Representations of Elizabeth I in Early Modern Culture*, edited by Alessandra Petrina and Laura Tosi (Basingstoke: Palgrave Macmillan, 2011)

Manninen, Alisa, '"The Charm's Wound Up": Supernatural Ritual in *Macbeth*', in *Magical Transformations on the Early Modern English Stage*, edited by Lisa Hopkins and Helen Ostovich (Farnham: Ashgate, 2014)

Marshall, Alan, *The Strange Death of Edmund Godfrey: Plots and Politics in Restoration London* (Stroud: Sutton, 1999)
McDonald, Michael (ed.), *Witchcraft and Hysteria in Elizabethan London: Edward Jorden and the Mary Glover Case* (London: Routledge, 1991)
McFarland, Ronald, '"The Hag is Astride": Witches in Seventeenth-Century Literature', *The Journal of Popular Culture* 11:1 (1977), 88–97
McKerrow, R. B. (ed.), *Works of Thomas Nashe*, vol. 1 (London: A. H. Bullen, 1904)
McMillin, Scott and Sally-Beth MacLean, in *The Queen's Men and Their Plays* (Cambridge: Cambridge University Press, 1998)
McLuskie, Kathleen, 'Politics and Aesthetic Pleasure in 1630s Theater', in *Localizing Caroline Drama: Politics and Economics of the Early Modern English Stage, 1625–1642*, edited by Adam Zucker and Alan B. Farmer (New York: Palgrave Macmillan, 2006)
—— *Renaissance Dramatists* (Hemel Hempstead: Harvester Wheatsheaf, 1989)
Meskill, Lynn Sermin, 'Exorcising the Gorgon of Terror: Jonson's *Masque of Queenes*', *ELH* 72:1 (2005), 181–207
Millar, Charlotte-Rose, 'Sleeping with Devils: The Sexual Witch in Seventeenth-Century England', in *Supernatural and Secular Power in Early Modern England*, edited by Marcus Harmes and Victoria Bladen (Farnham: Ashgate, 2015)
de Montaigne, Michel, *Essays*, translated by John Florio (London: Folio, 2006)
Mora, George (ed.), *Witches, Doctors and Devils in the Renaissance* (Binghampton: Medieval & Renaissance Texts and Studies, 1991)
Mulready, Cyrus, *Romance on the Early Modern Stage: English Expansion before and after Shakespeare* (Basingstoke: Palgrave Macmillan, 2013)
Munns, Jessica, 'Theatrical Culture I: Politics and Theatre', in *The Cambridge Companion to English Literature, 1650–1740*, edited by Steven N. Zwicker (Cambridge: Cambridge University Press, 1998)
Murphy, Kathryn, 'The Physician's Religion and *salus populi*: The Manuscript Circulation and Print Publication of *Religio Medici*', *Studies in Philology* 111:4 (2014), 845–74
Murray, Margaret, *The Witch-cult in Western Europe* (Oxford: Oxford University Press, 1921)
Nelson, Alan H., *Monstrous Adversary: The Life of Edward de Vere, 17th Earl of Oxford* (Liverpool: Liverpool University Press, 2003)
Nelson, William, *Fact or Fiction: The Dilemma of the Renaissance Storyteller* (Cambridge, MA: Harvard University Press, 1973)
Neufeld, Christine M., 'Lyly's Chimerical Vision: Witchcraft in *Endymion*', *Forum for Modern Language Studies* 43:4 (October 2007), 351–69
Nicol, David, 'Interrogating the devil: Social and Demonic Pressure in *The Witch of Edmonton*', *Comparative Drama* 38:4 (Winter 2004–5), 425–45

Normand, Lawrence, 'Witches, King James, and *The Masque of Queens*', in *Representing Women in Renaissance England*, edited by Claude J. Summers and Ted-Larry Pebworth (Columbia: University of Missouri Press, 1997)
Normand, Lawrence and Gareth Roberts, *Witchcraft in Early Modern Scotland* (Exeter: University of Exeter Press, 2000)
North, John A., *Roman Religion* (Oxford: Oxford University Press, 2000)
Notestein, Wallace, *A History of Witchcraft in England from 1558 to 1718* (Washington: American Historical Society, 1911)
O'Connor, Marion, Introduction to *The Witch*, in *The Collected Works of Thomas Middleton*, edited by Gary Taylor and John Lavagnino (Oxford: Oxford University Press, 2010)
Oldridge, Darren, *The Devil in Tudor and Stuart England* (Stroud: The History Press, 2010, first published 2000)
Orgel, Stephen, 'Jonson and the Amazons', in *Soliciting Interpretation*, edited by Elizabeth D. Harvey and Katharine Eisaman Maus (Chicago: University of Chicago Press, 1990)
Ostling, Michael, 'Babyfat and Belladonna: Witches' Ointment and the Contestation of Reality', *Magic, Ritual, and Witchcraft* 11:1 (2016), 30–72
Ovid, *Metamorphoses*, translated by David Raeburn (London: Penguin, 2004)
Owen, Susan J., *Restoration Theatre and Crisis* (Oxford: Clarendon Press, 1996)
Parry, Glyn, *The Arch-Conjuror of England: John Dee and Magic at the Courts of Renaissance Europe* (New Haven: Yale University Press, 2011)
Parsons, Coleman O. (ed.), *Saducismus Triumphatus* (Gainesville: Scholars' Facsimiles & Reprints, 1966)
Paul, Henry N., *The Royal Play of Macbeth* (New York: Macmillan, 1950)
Plank, Stephen, '"And Now about the Cauldron Sing": Music and the Supernatural on the Restoration Stage', *Early Music* 18:3 (August 1990), 392–407
Popkin, Richard, *The History of Scepticism*, 3rd edn (Oxford: Oxford University Press, 2003, 1st edn published 1960)
Portrait of Queen Elizabeth I (1533–1603) with a Hidden Serpent', www.npg.org.uk/assets/files/pdf/displays/concealedandrevealed/panel1.pdf
Price, Curtis, *Henry Purcell and the London Stage* (Cambridge: Cambridge University Press, 1984)
Purkiss, Diane, *At the Bottom of the Garden* (New York: New York University Press, 2001)
—— *The Witch in History* (London: Routledge, 1996)
Riggs, David, *The World of Christopher Marlowe* (London: Faber & Faber, 2004)
Roberts, Gareth, 'The Descendants of Circe: Witches and Renaissance Fictions', in *Witchcraft in Early Modern Europe: Studies in Culture and Belief*, edited by Jonathan Barry, Marianne Hester, and Gareth Roberts (Cambridge: Cambridge University Press, 1996)

—— 'Marlowe and the Metaphysics of Magicians', in *Constructing Christopher Marlowe*, edited by James Alan Downie and J. T. Parnell (Cambridge: Cambridge University Press, 2000)

Rosen, Barbara, *Witchcraft in England 1558–1618* (Amherst: University of Massachusetts Press, 1969)

Rowlands, Edward, 'Coventry, Henry', www.historyofparliamentonline.org/volume/1660–1690/member/coventry-hon-henry-1618–86

Rozemond, Marleen, *Descartes' Dualism* (Cambridge, MA: Harvard University Press, 1998)

Russell, Jeffrey Burton, *Lucifer: The Devil in the Middle Ages* (Ithaca: Cornell University Press, 1984)

Sackville-West, Edward, 'The Significance of *The Witch of Edmonton*', *Criterion* 17:66 (1937), 23–32

Schwarz, Kathryn, 'Amazon Reflections in the Jacobean Queen's Masque', *Studies in English Literature* 35:2 (1995), 293–319

Scouten, Arthur H. and Robert D. Hume, '"Restoration Comedy" and Its Audiences, 1660–1776', *The Yearbook of English Studies* 10 (1980), 45–69

Shapiro, Barbara J., *Probability and Certainty in Seventeenth Century England* (Princeton: Princeton University Press, 1983)

Sharpe, James, *The Bewitching of Anne Gunter* (London: Profile, 1999)

—— 'In Search of the English Sabbat: Popular Conceptions of Witches' Meetings in Early Modern England', *Journal of Early Modern Studies* 2 (2013), 161–83

—— *Instruments of Darkness: Witchcraft in England, 1550–1750* (London: Hamish Hamilton, 1996)

—— *Witchcraft in Early Modern England* (Harlow: Pearson, 2001)

Shaw, Catherine, *Richard Brome* (Boston: G. K. Hall, 1980)

Shesgreen, Sean, *The Criers and Hawkers of London: Engravings and Drawings by Marcellus Laroon* (Stanford: Stanford University Press, 1990)

Sidney, Philip, *An Apology for Poetry* (Manchester: Manchester University Press, 2002)

Slagle, Judith, 'Dueling Prefaces, Pamphlets, and Prologues: Re-visioning the Political and Personal Wars of John Dryden and Thomas Shadwell', *Restoration and 18th Century Theatre Research* 21:1 (2006), 17–32

Sluhovsky, Moshe, *Believe Not Every Spirit* (Chicago: University of Chicago Press, 2007)

Smialkowska, Monika, '"Out of the authority of ancient and late writers": Ben Jonson's Use of Textual Sources in *The Masque of Queens*', *English Literary Renaissance* 32:2 (2002), 268–86

Smith, David Chan, *Sir Edward Coke and the Reformation of the Laws* (Cambridge: Cambridge University Press, 2014)

Smith, Nigel, 'The Charge of Atheism and the Language of Radical Speculation, 1640–1660', in *Atheism from the Reformation to the Enlightenment*,

edited by Michael Hunter and David Wootton (Oxford: Oxford University Press, 1992)
Sokol, B. J. and Mary Sokol, *Shakespeare, Law and Marriage* (Cambridge: Cambridge University Press, 2003)
Somerset, Anne, *Unnatural Murder: Poison at the Court Of James I* (London: Orion, 1998)
Starnes, D. T., 'Shakespeare and Apuleius', *PMLA* 60:4 (December 1945), 1021–50
Steele, Richard, Review of *The Lancashire Witches*, *The Spectator* 141 (11 August 1711)
Steggle, Matthew, *Richard Brome: Place and Politics on the Caroline Stage* (Manchester: Manchester University Press, 2004)
Stephens, Walter, *Demon Lovers* (Chicago: University of Chicago Press, 2002)
—— 'The Sceptical Tradition', in *The Oxford Handbook of Witchcraft in Early Modern Europe and Colonial America*, edited by Brian Levack (Oxford: Oxford University Press, 2013)
Stoyle, Mark, *The Black Legend of Prince Rupert's Dog* (Exeter: University of Exeter Press, 2011)
Stratton, Kimberly B. and Dayna S. Kalleres, *Daughters of Hecate: Women and Magic in the Ancient World* (New York: Oxford University Press, 2014)
Stroup, Thomas B., 'Shadwell's Use of Hobbes', *Studies in Philology* 35:3 (1938), 405–32
Taylor, Gary, 'Empirical Middleton: *Macbeth*, Adaptation and Microauthorship', *Shakespeare Quarterly* 65:3 (2014), 239–72
Taylor, Gary and John Lavagnino (eds), *Thomas Middleton: The Collected Works* (Oxford: Oxford University Press, 2007)
Thomas, Keith, *Religion and the Decline of Magic* (Harmondsworth: Penguin Books, 1991, first published 1971)
Thompson, Janet A., *Wives, Widows, Witches and Bitches: Women in Seventeenth Century Devon* (New York: Peter Lang, 1993)
Thormählen, Marianne, *Rochester: The Poems in Context* (Cambridge: Cambridge University Press, 1993)
Thornton, Tim, *Prophecy, Politics and the People in Early Modern England* (Woodbridge: Boydell Press, 2006)
Truitt, E. R., 'Celestial Divination and Arabic Science in Twelfth-Century England: The History of Gerbert of Aurillac's Talking Head', *Journal of the History of Ideas* 73:2 (April 2012), 201–22
Vickers, Brian, 'Disintegrated', *Times Literary Supplement* (28 May 2010), 14–15
Walker, D. P., 'The Cessation of Miracles', in *Hermeticism and the Renaissance*, edited by Ingrid Merkel and Allen G. Debus (Washington: Folger Books, 1988)
Walker, Garthine, *Crime, Gender, and Social Order in Early Modern England* (Cambridge: Cambridge University Press, 2003)
Warner, Marina, 'Old Hags', in *London: City of Disappearances*, edited by Iain Sinclair (London: Hamish Hamilton, 2006)

Bibliography

Watt, Jeffrey R., 'Calvin's Geneva Confronts Magic and Witchcraft: The Evidence from the Consistory', *Journal of Early Modern History* 17 (2013), 215–44

West, Robert Hunter, 'The Impatient Magic of Dr. Faustus', *English Literary Renaissance* 4 (1974), 218–40

—— *The Invisible World; a Study of Pneumatology in Elizabethan Drama* (Athens: University of Georgia Press, 1939)

Wheatley, Christopher J., *Without God or Reason* (Lewisburg: Bucknell University Press, 1993)

White, Paul Whitfield, *Theatre and Reformation: Protestantism, Patronage and Playing in Tudor England* (Cambridge: Cambridge University Press, 1992)

Wickham, Glynne, Herbert Berry, and William Ingram, *English Professional Theatre, 1530–1660* (Cambridge: Cambridge University Press, 2000)

Wilby, Emma, 'The Witch's Familiar and the Fairy in Early Modern England and Scotland', *Folklore* 111 (2000), 283–305

Wills, Garry, *Witches and Jesuits: Shakespeare's Macbeth* (New York: Oxford University Press, 1995)

Wootton, David, 'Reginald Scot/Abraham Fleming/The Family of Love', in *Languages of Witchcraft*, edited by Stuart Clark (Basingstoke: Macmillan, 2001)

Wright, Thomas (ed.), *Narratives of Sorcery and Magic*, vol. 2 (London, 1851)

Wrightson, Keith, *English Society 1580–1680* (London: Hutchinson, 1982)

Yearling, Rebecca, 'John Marston, Stoic?: *Sophonisba* and the Early Modern Stoic Ideal', *Ben Jonson Journal* 18:1 (2011), 85–100

Index

Note: Page references followed by 'n' indicate a footnote on that page.

Abbot, George 162, 163, 169n
   see also Essex divorce; Overbury scandal
Acheron 96–97
Addison, Joseph 209, 226, 242, 243, 298
Adlington, William 90, 94–97
   see also Apuleius, *The Golden Asse*
Ady, Thomas 20–21, 33
Aesop 29, 30
Agrippa, Heinrich Cornelius 71–73, 93, 112, 117, 118, 122, 123
Albertus Magnus 72n
Alford, Stephen 61
Alighieri, Dante 32n
Almond, Philip 23n, 28n, 85n
Alssid, Michael 287, 290
Amadis de Gaule 29
Anderson, Edmund 227–28
Anglo, Sidney 20, 23
animals, transformation into 3, 23, 32, 34, 92–94, 222–23, 237, 241, 284–85
Anne of Denmark 138, 140, 155, 156n, 158
Apollo *see* Phoebus
Apuleius 3, 59, 71, 90, 97, 248, 249, 254
   The Golden Asse 59, 84n, 89–98, 101
Aquinas, Thomas 11, 13, 214n, 247, 249–51, 255n
Arikha, Noga 195n, 246n, 250n
Aristotle 10, 50, 252, 253
Arnold, Margaret 35–36
Arundel, Charles 87
Asprem, Egil 259n
astronomy/astrology 16–17n, 62, 71, 73, 120

atheism 126, 145, 207, 230, 256, 261, 273, 283, 301
Atkinson, David 192–93
Augustine, St 16–17n, 29, 32n, 41, 85, 93–95, 97n, 248

Babington plot 87
Bacon, Roger 72n
   see also Greene, Robert, *Friar Bacon and Friar Bungay*
Bale, John 47, 305
   Three Laws 48–51, 289, 317
Barber, Laird 224n, 225n
Barry, Jonathan 1n
Bates, William 257n
Bawcutt, N. W. 173n
Baxter, Richard 257
Behringer, Wolfgang 313
Bellany, Alastair 165, 166n, 167
Bernard, Richard 17, 96n, 120, 134n, 244n, 317
Berry, Herbert 221n, 223, 234n, 242–43
Bible, the 18n, 20, 25, 65, 67, 69n, 71, 118, 123
blood pact 65, 105, 106, 119, 124, 125, 250, 269, 311
Bloom, Harold 149n
Bodin, Jean 11, 21–23, 27, 32n, 40–43, 48, 125, 189, 190n, 209, 217, 220, 229n, 231, 260, 286, 298–99, 308
Boehrer, Bruce 52
Boguet, Henri 223n
Bolingbroke, Roger 109
Bonavita, Helen Vella 204n
Boniface VIII, Pope 119
Booth, Roy 263n

Index

Bostridge, Ian 211n, 244n, 246, 253–54, 256, 258, 259, 291
Bothwell, Stewart Francis, Earl of 139–40
Botica, Allan 261n
Braden, Gordon 90n
Bradley, A. C. 143, 147, 149n
Breuer, Heidi 7
Briggs, Katherine 6, 59n, 74n, 81n, 103, 217, 221n, 281
Brodwin, Leonora 183n, 192
Brome, Richard *see The Late Lancashire Witches*
Browne, Thomas 226
  Pseudodoxia Epidemica 69n, 145, 149
  Religio Medici 213–16
Burke, Peter 19n
Burkert, Walter 96n
Burns, Edward 108n
Burr, George Lincoln 26
Burrow, John 28n
Burton, Robert 32n, 92n, 194–95
Bushnell, Rebecca W. 131n
Buts, Joan 236n, 237

Calvin, Jean 26, 27, 48n, 56–57
Calvinism 69, 70n, 122, 174, 188–91, 318
Campion, Thomas
  Masque of Squires 161
Canfield, J. Douglas 296–97
Canon *Episcopi* 11, 67
Cariden, Joan 4n
Carlton, Charles 211
Carr, Frances *see* Howard, Frances
Carr, Robert 161, 164–67, 174
  see also Frances, Howard; Essex divorce; Overbury scandal
Carver, Robert H. F. 90, 98n, 102
Casaubon, Meric 13, 14, 18, 22, 31, 256
Catholicism
  associated with witchcraft 46–52, 54–56, 121, 188, 289–90, 317–19
  hostility towards 158, 166, 171, 174, 280, 299, 304
  plots associated with Catholics 60–61, 87, 166, 273
  see also Babington plot; Popish plot

Cecil, Robert 63
Ceres 94–97
Charles I of England 267, 317
Charles II of England 260–61, 263, 267, 304
Charleton, Walter 257n
charms, magical 47, 49–50, 137, 188–89, 221
Cicero 10, 29
Circe 3, 67, 84n, 93, 217
Ciruelo, Pedro 228n
Clark, Arthur M. 217n
Clark, Sandra 137
Clark, Stuart 11n, 13n, 15, 23n, 49, 52n, 70n, 82n, 128, 132, 147, 149n, 244n, 246, 290–91
Cobham, Eleanor 109
Cohn, Norman 119, 189n
Coke, Edward 165–68, 180
College, Stephen 300
Collier, John Payne 114n
Comensoli, Viviana 184n, 192n, 200–1, 206n
Cooper, Thomas 16n, 168–72, 176, 200
coral 68, 69n
Cotta, John 11, 31n, 167–68, 229n
Cottingham, John 252
Coventry, Henry 294–95
Cox, John 192n
Coxe, Francis 65, 106
Coxe, John 60
Crocker, Robert 246n
Cromwell, Oliver 267, 300n
Cullender, Rose 35
cunning men/women 63, 86, 164, 198, 219
Cunny, Joan 106n
Curry, W. C. 143, 144

Daneau, Lambert 66, 67, 88n
Darby, Trudi L. 174n
Darr, Orna Alyagon 21n, 22n, 290n
Darrel, John 56, 210, 235
  see also Harsnett, Samuel
Davenant, William 263
  Macbeth 141, 267–270
  The Tempest 275
Davenport, John 199
Davies, Julie A. 251n
Davies, R. Trevor 210, 211, 223

Davies, Simon F. 28n
Deats, Sara Munson 118n
Dee, John 63, 67, 128
Dekker, Thomas *see The Witch of Edmonton*
demonic possession 34–36, 130, 187n, 210, 212n, 216, 227, 234–35
Descartes, René 13, 33, 246, 252, 253, 255
despair 117, 121–23, 126, 147, 186–87
devil, the
  bargains with 50, 96–97, 102, 105, 106n, 118n, 124, 170, 196–97, 204, 240–41, 288, 307
    see also blood pact; familiar spirits
  kissing buttocks of 52, 286
  and pagan gods 31, 96–97, 146
    see also Phoebus
  physical manifestation of 42, 53, 196, 221n
  Protestant views of 57, 193–94
  sexual intercourse with 91n, 239, 274n
Devine, Michael 60n
Diomedes 93
Dipsas *see* Lyly, John, *Endymion*
disenchantment 258–59
Dolan, Frances 5n, 7–8, 183, 192n
Dryden, John
  Absalom and Achitophel 300
  Notes and Observations on The Empress of Morocco 270
  The Tempest 275
Duffett, Thomas
  The Empress of Morocco 263, 270
  Psyche Debauch'd 271
Duffy, Eamon 47
Duke, Richard 295n
Duncan, Gillis 154
Duny, Amy 35
D'Urfey, Thomas
  Sir Barnaby Whigg 283n, 300–1
Durousseau, Clifford Hubert 118n

Eagleton, Terry 65n
Edward the Confessor 150

effascination 212
Egypt, biblical magicians of 67, 111n
Elizabeth I of England 63, 79, 87
  representations of 85, 88, 95n
Elmer, Peter 15, 16n, 56n, 87n, 130n, 211
empiricism 20, 21, 23, 226–31, 285–86
Endor, Witch of 82, 134, 136n, 146, 147
Engle, Lars 122n, 125
'enthusiasm' 256–57
Erictho 82, 84n, 133–37, 287, 290
  see also Lucan; Marston, John, *Sophonisba*
Eriugena, John Scottus 10
Essex divorce 160–64, 173
Eurydice 64
Ewen, C. L. 76n, 103, 130, 223n, 224n, 309
Ewstace, Elizabeth 52

Fairfax, Edward 34–36, 43
fairies 98–102, 144, 145
familiar spirits 7, 64, 99, 105, 106, 119, 128, 240, 250–51, 266, 272
Fanger, Claire 72n
fiction
  concept of 2–5, 28–32, 37–39, 92–95, 217
  fairies understood as fictional 98, 103
  ghosts understood as fictional 150n
  witchcraft understood as fictional 58–60, 89, 103, 127, 141, 159, 266, 279–81, 314, 316
Fielding, Henry 262
Findlay, Alison 222
Fleay, Frederick 143
flight, witches' *see* transvection
Flint, Valerie 66n, 71n, 79n
Floyd-Wilson, Mary 143n
Ford, John *see The Witch of Edmonton*
Fox, Cora 30
Fraunces, Elizabeth 106n
Friesen, Ryan Curtis 8, 117, 141n

Gadamer, Hans-Georg 19
Gaisser, Julia Haig 90n, 94n

Index

Galis, Richard 53
Gammer Gurton's Needle 51–55
Gardiner, S. R. 165n
Garrett, Julia 187n
Gascoigne, Thomas 297–98
Gaule, John 185, 198n, 207n, 257n, 289n
gender and witchcraft 58, 59, 61, 63–71, 73, 74, 306, 312
Gibney, John 300
Gibson, Marion 3, 4, 43n, 60, 108n, 128, 210n, 212n, 236n, 314n
Gifford, George 16–18, 67n, 69, 96n, 106, 119n, 189–91, 197, 198, 202, 271, 318
Glanvill, Joseph 21, 144, 245–47, 250–58, 260–62, 268, 269, 271, 310
 see also More, Henry
gleaning 185, 281
Glover, Mary 227–28
God, names of 117–18
Goddard, Harold 143
Godfrey, Edmund 302, 303
Gondomar, Diego Sarmiento de Acuña, count of 165, 174
Goodare, Julian 306n
Goodcole, Henry 36–39, 183, 186n, 188, 190–91, 200, 222, 314, 315
Green, Richard Firth 98n, 99n
Green, Robert 303
Greenblatt, Stephen 5n, 8, 152, 319
Greene, Robert 59, 89
 A Looking Glass for London and England 118
 Alphonsus King of Aragon 50, 81–83, 103, 133
 Friar Bacon and Friar Bungay 3, 50, 110–15, 118, 120
 James IV 101
 Menaphon 90
Greyme, Richard 139
Grindal, Edmund 61
Gunter, Anne and Brian 187n

Hale, Matthew 3
Hall, John 62
hallucinogens 313
Hamlin, William M. 121
Hammond, Henry 126
Happé, Peter 47

Harris, Anthony 6, 7, 38, 59n, 132n, 134, 135n, 139n, 141n, 221n, 235n, 263, 267, 286n, 290
Harsnett, Samuel 56, 185n, 210n, 234n, 289n
Hart, James 212–13, 216
Harvey, John 87–88
Hatton, Christopher 88
Haworth, Samuel 257n
Hecate (goddess) 95–96, 113, 176–77, 267
 see also Macbeth, Shakespeare, William; *The Witch*, Middleton, Thomas
Heinemann, Margot 46, 173, 176
Henry, John 246n
heresy 2, 11, 110, 189n, 282
Herrington, H. W. 74, 75
Heywood, Thomas
 Gynaikeion 217–20, 222, 223
 The Hierarchie of the Blessed Angels 217, 219, 220, 222, 242
 The Wise Woman of Hogsdon 74, 85, 182, 219
 see also The Late Lancashire Witches
Hinds, Peter 294n, 297n, 299–300
Hirsch, Brett D. 3n, 78n, 79, 217n, 223n
Hirschfeld, Heather 221n, 225, 226, 233
Hobbes, Thomas 246, 249, 251–55, 257, 261
Holbrook, Peter 155n
Holinshed, Raphael 104, 109
Holland, Henry 26n, 91n, 112n, 189n, 214n
Hopkins, Lisa 5n, 184
Hopkins, Matthew 15n, 21, 81, 243, 318
Horace 31n, 79
Howard, Frances 160, 161, 164–67, 170, 173n, 174n, 176, 177, 180
 see also Essex divorce; Overbury scandal
Howard, Henry 63–65, 68, 87, 97n, 103, 106, 111
Hughes, Derek 263n, 300n
Hunter, G. K. 84, 85, 89n
Huszar Allen, Marguerite de 119n

Hutton, Ronald 79n, 84n, 99n, 214n, 306n
Hyperius, Andreas 66, 67, 70, 85, 88n, 93
hysteria *see* mother, suffocation of the (disease)

idolatry 19, 48, 49, 135, 317
image magic 49, 79, 109
impotence magic 161–64, 169, 173, 220, 237, 284, 289
ingredients, magical 49, 62, 73, 78, 84, 154, 289
Institoris, Heinrich *see Malleus Maleficarum*
Isidore of Seville 66n, 71n
Isis *see* Ceres

James VI of Scotland and I of England 36, 39, 74, 106, 128, 130–32, 137–40, 152, 154, 159, 161, 162, 165, 167, 168, 169, 171, 175, 180, 308
   Daemonologie 18, 21, 26, 39–41, 69n, 70–71, 99, 112, 119, 120, 130, 131, 136n, 144, 145, 147, 162, 168, 214, 215, 220, 245
Joan of Arc 65, 110, 317
   see also Shakespeare, *1 Henry VI*
Jobe, Thomas Harmon 245n, 246–47, 258
John of Morigny 72n
Johnson, Margaret 221, 224, 239, 240
Johnstone, Nathan 57n, 146n, 193n, 194, 196, 199, 205n
Jones, John Henry 110n, 115n
Jones, Norman 61
Jonson, Ben
   The Masque of Queens 131, 155–60, 175, 180–81, 278, 286
Jorden, Edward 227–28, 289
Josephson-Storm, Jason A. 259n
Jourdain, Margery 109
Julian of Norwich 57

Kapitaniak, Pierre 56n
Kenyon, John 294n, 297–98, 300, 302n
Kernan, Alvin 138, 139n
Kesson, Andy 89n

Kezar, Dennis 203
Killigrew, Thomas 263
Kittredge, George Lyman 3, 130, 215n, 223n
Knights, Mark 296n
Kolb, Laura 39, 142n
Kunz, Don R. 297n

Lancashire, Anne 172, 173
The Late Lancashire Witches 3, 6, 92, 124n, 134, 154, 182, 198, 209–43, 267, 272, 278–82, 284, 287, 315, 316
Laud, William 210–11
laws against witchcraft 2, 17, 55, 61, 62, 87, 128, 311
Le Loyer, Pierre 229
Lee, Thomas 295–96
L'Estrange, Roger 299, 304
Levack, Brian P. 236n, 258, 306n
Levin, Richard 111
Lewalski, Barbara K. 155n, 156n
Lewis, C. S. 248, 251, 276n
Lewis, Matthew
   The Monk 56
Lucan 3, 69n, 83n, 91n
   see also Erictho
Lucretius 259
Lucy, Margaret 141n
Lund, Roger D. 261n
Lyly, John 59, 89
   Endymion 81n, 83, 84, 87, 90n, 103, 127, 134n
   Mother Bombie 85–87, 89, 127, 278
   Sapho and Phao 84, 85, 90

MacCulloch, Diarmaid 2n, 55n
Macfarlane, Alan 16n, 81n, 103, 130
McFarland, Ronald 187n
Mackenzie, George 257n
McLuskie, Kathleen 184n, 192n, 224, 240n
McMillin, Scott 110n
Maguire, Nancy 263n, 265n, 267n, 293n
Mahomet 82–83
Maitland, John 139
Malay, Jessica 88
Malleus Maleficarum 2, 3, 20, 22–25, 32n, 93, 97, 162n, 189, 222, 223n, 244, 249, 252

Index

maleficium 1, 87, 128, 139, 198, 220n, 244
maleficium versus hanc see impotence magic
Manlove, Timothy 257n
Manninen, Alisa 143n
marks, witch's 21, 196, 284
Marlowe, Christopher 110n
  Dr Faustus 60, 96, 97, 102, 110–11, 115–27, 144, 149, 182, 197, 317
Marshall, Alan 302n, 303n
Marston, John
  Sophonisba 83n, 132–37, 148n, 154, 181, 290
materialism 251–59
Medea 84n, 91n
  see also Greene, Robert, *Alphonsus, King of Aragon*
Medusa *see* Munday, Anthony, *Fedele and Fortunio*
melancholy 32, 45, 186, 213, 230, 279, 307
menstrual blood 73
Meroe 84n, 90n, 91
Meskill, Lynn Sermin 159n
Middleton, Thomas
  A Game at Chess 174
  Masque of Cupids 161
  The Two Gates of Salvation 174
  The Witch 96, 132, 172–81, 270, 317
Millar, Charlotte-Rose 91n, 274n
miracles 13–14, 55–56, 67, 121, 214, 256
mockery of witchcraft belief 23–27, 38, 50, 163, 190, 259–61, 297
Monck, George 265
Montaigne, Michel de 14n, 15, 229, 310
More, Henry 245–47, 252–58
  see also Glanvill, Joseph
More, Thomas 28, 30
Morrison, Richard 46–47
mother, suffocation of the (disease) 216, 227, 288–89
Mother Deuell 106n
Mother Joan 63–64
Mother Margaret 106n
Mother Redcap 76n
Mother Smith 106n
Mulready, Cyrus 77n

Munday, Anthony
  Fedele and Fortunio 59, 60, 77–81, 103, 134
  John a Kent and John a Cumber 110, 114–16
Munns, Jessica 293n
Murphy, Kathryn 213n
Murray, Margaret 311–13
mythology 31, 59, 82, 94n, 96, 142, 217, 312
  see also Apuleius, *The Golden Asse*; Ceres; Circe; Diomedes; Erictho; Eurydice; Hecate; Meroe; Medea; Odysseus; Pamphile; Panthia; Phoebus; Priapus; sibyls; Venus

Nashe, Thomas 26n, 250
natural magic 68–69, 214
Nebuchadnezzar 94
  see also animals, transformation into
necromancy 62, 70–71, 82, 95, 135–36
  see also Endor, Witch of
Nelson, Alan H. 28n, 87n
Nelson, William 22n, 29, 94n
Neufeld, Christine M. 83n
Newes from Scotland 39, 153–54
Nicol, David 186, 188n, 195, 198, 201
Nokes, James 274
Normand, Lawrence 138n, 139n, 140, 155n
North Berwick witches 138–39
  see also Newes from Scotland
North, John A. 90n
North, Roger 298
nosebleeds 273n
Notestein, Wallace 15n, 26, 245, 255

Oates, Titus 294–97
oaths *see* swearing
Ockham, William of 10
O'Connor, Marion 176–77
Odysseus 93
  see also Circe
Oldridge, Darren 57n, 193n, 221n
Orgel, Stephen 155n, 157
Origen 112
Ostling, Michael 313n
Overbury scandal 165–68, 173, 175, 177, 178, 180, 317

Overton, Richard 256–57n
Ovid 3, 30, 31, 90n, 91n, 92, 93, 159, 180
Owen, Susan J. 291, 293, 299

Pamphile 92–93
pamphlet accounts of witchcraft 3–4, 33–39, 43–45, 60, 91, 98, 106n, 119, 153–54, 187n, 199, 210, 212n, 215–16, 219, 236–37
Panthia 91
Paracelsus 72, 73, 97n
Parry, Glyn 56n, 63, 67n, 128n
Parsons, Coleman O. 260n
Paul, Henry N. 137, 138, 143, 148n, 149n
Payne, Henry Neville
  The Fatal Jealousy 271–74
Peele, George
  The Old Wife's Tale 84n, 90n
Peeter, Stubbe 33–34
Perkins, William 16, 53n, 70, 86, 96n, 106, 170n, 172, 189, 190n, 198, 220
Peter Martyr 257n
Peyton, Robert 294–95
Phoebus 83, 84, 136
Pico della Mirandola, Gianfrancesco 11, 39n
Plank, Stephen 264–65, 274n
pneumata 195, 250–51, 269
Popish Plot 294–305
Popkin, Richard 10, 11n, 12, 19, 122, 229n, 254n, 274n, 285n
Porter, Henry
  The Villain 271
Postgate, Nicholas 298
Prance, Miles 302
pregnancy, grounds for clemency 108n
Priapus 79n
Price, Curtis 265
prophecy 71, 82–89, 105, 109, 114, 145, 146, 266
Pseudo-Dionysius 10, 249
Psyche 101
  see also Duffett, Thomas, *Psyche Debauch'd*; Shadwell, Thomas, *Psyche*
puritans 16, 46, 173, 210, 223
Purkiss, Diane 5n, 7, 67, 68n, 74n, 75, 83n, 98n, 99n, 101n, 132n, 143, 144, 153, 154, 187, 306n, 312

Ravenscroft, Edward 299
Rawlins, Thomas
  Tunbridge-Wells 264
Reformation, the 12, 46–48, 55–57, 311, 318
remora fish 69
rhetorical scepticism 33–39, 154–55, 184, 232–33, 304, 307–8, 316
Riggs, David 122n
Roberts, Alexander 70n, 134n, 167–68, 170n
Roberts, Gareth 4, 91n, 93, 118, 119, 217n
Robinson, Edmund 221, 222, 234
Robson, Donald 139
Rochester, John Wilmot, earl of 261
romance plays 77
Rosen, Barbara 60
Rowley, William *see The Witch of Edmonton*
Rozemond, Marleen 251n, 253n
Russell, Jeffrey Burton 10n, 11n, 32n, 52n, 57n, 83n, 112n, 138n, 139n, 140, 193n, 197, 198n, 289n

Sackville-West, Edward 192–93
Sadducees 26n
Saducismus Triumphatus see More, Henry and Glanvill, Joseph
Samuel, Alice and Agnes *see* Warboys, witches of
Sampson, Agnes 139
Sawyer, Elizabeth (historical person) 36–39
  see also The Witch of Edmonton
Schafer, Elizabeth 173n, 174n
Schwarz, Kathryn 158
Scot, Reginald 15, 17–20, 23–28, 30–32, 42–46, 48, 49, 53, 56, 62, 67–69, 79n, 85, 98, 100, 124, 152, 185–86, 193, 207, 214, 229–30, 245n, 257, 277n, 285, 286, 289, 290, 318
Scouten, Arthur H. 291
Scragg, Leah 87n
scratching witches 290
Scroggs, William 298
Selden, John 17n, 19n
Settle, Elkanah
  The Empress of Morocco 270
Sextus Empiricus 10, 11, 121

Index

Shadwell, Thomas
  The Lancashire Witches 6, 27, 166, 278–305, 318, 319
  Psyche 264, 271
  The Tempest 275, 276
Shakespeare, William 74–75, 310
  1 Henry VI 104–9
  2 Henry VI 109
  Macbeth 8, 58, 73–75, 78, 97, 100, 109, 131, 137–56, 172, 178, 181, 182, 267–71, 275, 276, 315, 316
  A Midsummer Night's Dream 59, 89, 91, 97–103, 134
  Othello 271
  The Tempest 128–29, 275–76
Shapiro, Barbara J. 246, 258
Sharpe, James 36n, 61n, 63n, 108n, 130n, 153n, 187n, 211, 215n, 216, 227n, 236n, 243n
Shaw, Catherine 240
Shesgreen, Sean 300n
Sidney, Philip 29, 30
Slagle, Judith 292n
Sluhovsky, Moshe 228n
Smialkowska, Monika 157, 158n, 159
Smith, David Chan 167n
Smith, Nigel 256n
Smith, Samuel 303
Socrates 64
Socrates (character in *The Golden Asse*) 91
Sokol, B. J. and Mary 173n
Somerset, Anne 164n, 165n, 168n, 174n, 180n
songs 153–54, 265, 266, 269–70, 275–76
soul, the
  animals, of 126, 253
  doctrine of equal souls 65n
  immortality of 26n, 257
  nature of 246, 248, 250, 252, 253
  possibility of selling 124, 241
  see also blood pact; devil, the; familiar spirits
Spenser, Edmund 84n
Sprenger, Jakob *see Malleus Maleficarum*
spirit, transformation into 102
Stapylton, Robert
  The Step-Mother 265–67
Starkey, John 292n
Starnes, D. T. 98n

Stearne, John 3n
  see also Hopkins, Matthew
Steele, Richard 280
Steggle, Matthew 240n
Stephens, Walter 3, 11–12, 20n, 21, 39n, 40, 41n, 67n, 93, 97n, 237, 249n, 251n, 255n, 257n, 258, 312
Stoyle, Mark 259n
Stratton, Kimberly B. 84n
Stroup, Thomas B. 282n
Succession Crisis 293–96
  see also Popish Plot
suffumigations 73
Summers, Montague 311
superstition 55, 56, 126, 140, 189, 191, 279, 289, 290, 314
sibyls 71, 85, 88
swearing 38, 52–54, 199–200, 205, 301
swimming test 21
Sylvester II, Pope 50, 120n

tantivy 291n
Taylor, Gary 146n
tetrarchs 276
thatch, burning (as test for witchcraft) 190–91
Thersites 50
Thomas, Keith 47, 55n, 112n, 186, 235n, 236n
Thompson, Janet A. 216n
Thormählen, Marianne 261n
Thornton, Tim 88n
Tomkyns, Nathaniel 221, 239, 240, 242–43
transvection 93, 263n
trials of witches 3, 16, 21, 35–37, 52, 108, 130, 139–40, 167, 215–16, 227–28, 236
Trithemius, Johannes 72n
Truitt, E. R. 50n
A Tryal of Witches 215
Turner, Anne 167

Valla, Lorenzo 19n
van der Delft, François 55
Venus 79, 82, 85, 271
Vere, Edward de 87
Vergil, Polydore 20
Vickers, Brian 146n

Wadsworth, Thomas 257n
Wagstaffe, John 254n

Wakeman, George 298, 300
Walker, D. P. 55n
Walker, Garthine 306
Walsh, John 99
Walsingham, Francis 61
Warboys, witches of 108n, 187n, 218–19
Warner, Marina 76n
Watt, Jeffrey R. 57n
Weber, Max 259
Webster, John 223n, 230, 234, 245–47, 249n, 254, 277
West, John and Alice 98
West, Robert H. 69, 116n, 230
Weyer, Johannes 15, 18, 41, 44, 85n, 186, 207, 251n, 298n
Wheatley, Christopher J. 283n, 292n
White, Paul Whitfield 46
Wicca 312
Wilby, Emma 99n
William of Orange 296
Willis, Deborah 7, 143n, 271n
Willis, Thomas 246
Wills, Garry 75
wise men/women *see* cunning men/women
The Witch of Edmonton 36, 85, 124n, 154, 181, 182–208, 220–22, 224, 232, 240, 243, 278, 281, 304, 314–16
The Witches of Northamptonshire 189n
The Wonderfvll Discouerie of the Witch-crafts of Margaret and Philip Flower 43–45
Wootton, David 23n
Wrightson, Keith 185
Wyatt, George 26

Yearling, Rebecca 136